FIX YOUR OWN MAC

Upgrading and Troubleshooting

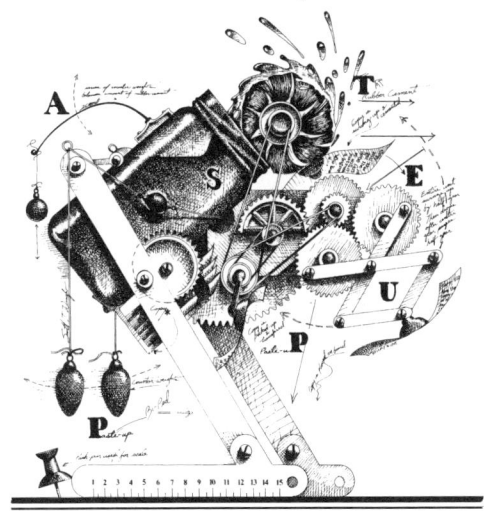

JAN L. HARRINGTON

A Subsidiary of
Henry Holt and Co., Inc.

Copyright ©1993 MIS:Press
a subsidiary of Henry Holt & Company, Inc.
115 West 18th Street
New York, NY 10011

All rights reserved. Reproduction or use of editorial or pictorial content in any manner is prohibited without express permission. No patent liability is assumed with respect to the use of the information contained herein. While every precaution has been taken in the preparation of this book, the publisher assumes no responsibility for errors or omissions. Neither is any liability assumed for damages resulting from the use of the information contained herein.

Throughout this book, trademarked names are used. Rather than put a trademark symbol after every occurrence of a trademarked name, we used the names in an editorial fashion only, and to the benefit of the trademark owner, with no intention of infringement of the trademark. Where such designations appear in this book, they have been printed with initial caps.

First Edition—1993

ISBN 1-55828-299-8

Printed in the United States of America.

10 9 8 7 6 5 4 3 2 1

MIS:Press books are available at special discounts for bulk purchases for sales promotions, premiums, fund-raising, or educational use. Special editions or book excerpts can also be created to specification.

For details contact: Special Sales Director
MIS:Press
a subsidiary of Henry Holt and Company, Inc.
115 West 18th Street
New York, New York 10011

Development Editor: Cary Sullivan
Production Editor: Joanne Kelman
Copyeditor: Ron Harris
Associate Production Editor: Stephanie Doyle

Contents

Preface   xiii

   What You Need to Know Before You Begin 4
   Acknowledgments 5

Chapter 1: A First Look at Computer Hardware   *1*

   The CPU 1
   Math Coprocessors 3
   Main Memory 3
   Measuring Memory (and Other Things) 4
   External Storage 6
   Input Devices and Output Devices 7
   Connecting the Parts 7
   A Tour Around a Motherboard 10
   The Major Circuits on a Motherboard 10
      Parameter RAM 10
      Versatile Interface Adapter 10
      Serial Communications Controller 12
      Floppy Disk Controller 12
      Other Circuits 12

Chapter 2: The Macintosh Product Line   *13*

   Compact Macintoshes 13
      Macintosh Plus 13
      Macintosh SE 14
      Macintosh SE/30 14
   Macintosh Classic, Classic II, and Performa 200 15

Macintosh Color Classic	17
Entry-Level Modular Macintoshes	18
Macintosh LC	18
Macintosh LC II and Performa 400, 405, and 430	18
Macintosh LC III and Performa 450	19
Mid-range Modular Macintoshes	20
Macintosh II and IIx	20
Macintosh IIcx	21
Macintosh IIci	21
Macintosh IIsi	23
Macintosh IIvi, IIvx, and Performa 600	23
High-End Modular Macintoshes	25
Macintosh IIfx	25
Macintosh Centris 610 and 650 and 660av	26
Macintosh Quadras	29
The Workgroup Servers	31
Portable/Laptop Macintoshes	32
The Macintosh Portable	32
Powerbooks	34
Hybrid Machines: The PowerBook Duos	38

Chapter 3: A First Look at Upgrading — 41

Types of Upgrades	41
Making the Choice to Upgrade	43
Upgrading 68000 Macs	45
Upgrading 68030 Macs	55
Upgrading 68040 Macs	63
Upgrades for all NuBus Macs	64
New Homes for Old Macs	64
Hardware Upgrade Basics	66
Anatomy of an Expansion Board	66
Case-Opening Hints	67
Getting Inside a Compact Macintosh	67

Getting Inside the LC Line 70
Getting Inside Other Modular Macintoshes 70
Getting Inside a Portable 72
Getting Inside a PowerBook 73
Installing an Expansion Board 73

Chapter 4: Troubleshooting Techniques — 77

Crash Protection 77
Hardware Versus Software Problems 78
    Viruses 78
    INIT Conflicts 80
    Application Software Versus the Operating System 82
    Application Software Versus the 68040 83
Basic Hardware Diagnostic Techniques 84
    Component Swapping 84
    Diagnostic Software 86
    Diagnostics with Snooper 87
    Diagnostics with Peace of Mind 90
    MacTest Pro 91
Diagnostics When the Machine Won't Boot 93
    What to Do When Your Startup Hard Disk Is Corrupted 93
    What to Do When INIT Conflicts Prevent Booting 96
    What It Means When You See the Sad Mac 96
    Snooper's NuBus Board 99
The Apple TechStep 101

Chapter 5: Adding Memory — 103

How Much Memory Do I Need? 103
Hardware and Software Limits to RAM Expansion 104
    Memory and the System Bus 104
Understanding SIMMs 108
    Types of SIMMs 108

Fix Your Own Mac: *Upgrading and Troubleshooting*

SIMM Banks	109
SIMM Speeds	109
Anatomy of a SIMM Slot	110
Where to Get SIMMs	110
General SIMM Installation Procedure	111
RAM and the 68000 Compact Macs	113
Mac Plus RAM Configurations	113
Macintosh SE RAM Configurations	114
Installing RAM in the Macintosh Plus and SE	115
Macintosh Classic RAM Configurations	116
Installing SIMMs in a Classic	117
RAM and Macintoshes with Two 30-Pin SIMM Slots	118
RAM Configurations for Macs with Two 30-Pin SIMM Slots	118
Installing SIMMS in the LC, LC II, Performa 400, Performa 405, and Performa 430	119
Installing SIMMs in a Classic II/Performa 200	119
Installing SIMMs in the Color Classic	120
RAM and Macintoshes with Four 30-Pin SIMM Slots	120
RAM Configurations for the Macintosh IIsi	121
Installing RAM in the Macintosh IIsi	121
RAM Configurations for the Macintosh IIvx, IIvi, and Performa 600	121
Installing RAM in the IIvx, IIvi, and Performa 600	122
RAM Configurations for the Quadra 700	122
Installing RAM in the Quadra 700	122
RAM and Macintoshes with Eight 30-Pin SIMM Slots	124
Installing RAM in the SE/30	124
Macintosh II RAM Considerations	126
Macintosh IIx RAM Considerations	127
Mac IIfx RAM Considerations	127
Installing RAM in the Macintosh II, IIx, and IIfx	128
Installing RAM in the IIcx and IIci	129
RAM and the 16-Slot Quadras	129
RAM Configurations for the Quadra 900 and 950	129

Installing RAM in the Quadra 900 and 950 131
RAM and Macintoshes with 72-Pin SIMM Slots 131
    RAM Configurations for the Macintosh LC III
        and Performa 450 131
    RAM Configurations for the Centris 610 and 660av 131
    RAM Configurations for the Centris 650, Quadra 800,
        and Quadra 840av 133
    Installing SIMMs in Macintoshes with 72-Pin SIMM Slots 134
RAM and the Portables and PowerBooks 134
    RAM Configurations for the Macintosh Portables 135
    Installing RAM in the Macintosh Portable 136
    RAM Configurations for the PowerBook 100, 140, 145, and 170 136
    RAM Configurations for the PowerBook 160, 165c, 180, 180c 137
    RAM Configurations for the PowerBook Duos 138
    Installing PowerBook RAM 138

Chapter 6: *CPU Accelerators* **141**

CPU Structure and Program Execution 142
    Choosing an Accelerator 146
        Type of Microprocessor 146
        Microprocessor Speed 147
        FPU 147
        Effect on SIMM Requirements 147
        Video Adapter Circuitry 148
        Type of Installation 148
        Installation Procedures 149
        Upgradability 149
        Compatibility 150
        Warranty and Support Policies 150
    Where to Get an Accelerator 151
    Accelerator Survey 151
        Accelerators for 68000 Compact Macs 152
        Accelerators for 68020 Macs 157

Fix Your Own Mac: Upgrading and Troubleshooting

    Accelerators for 68030 Macs 160
    PowerBook Accelerators 171

Chapter 7: Caches, PMMUs, and Math Coprocessors (FPUs)   173

Caches 173
    Write-Through Versus Write-Back Caches 174
    Cache Availability 175
Paged Memory Management Units 176
Math Coprocessors 178
    Storing Floating-Point Numbers 179
    Deciding When an FPU Is Necessary 181
    FPU Availability 181
    Types of FPUs 181

Chapter 8: Logic Boards   183

What You Get with a New Logic Board 183
Available Logic Board Upgrades 184
Logic Board Upgrade Installation Issues 186
Troubleshooting Logic Board Problems 186
    Cold Solder Problems 187
    Bus and Slot Problems 188
    Problems with On-Board Video 189

Chapter 9: Power Supplies and Power Protection   191

Internal Power Supplies 191
    Standard Macintosh Power Supplies 192
    Power Requirements of Internal Devices 192
    Troubleshooting Power Supply Problems 192
    Macintosh Plus Power Supply Problems 194
ADB Chains and Power Requirements 194
Electric Power Problems 196

Chapter 10: Disk Storage 201

An Introduction to Disk Storage 201
    Read/Write Heads 202
    Physical Disk Organization 203
    Disk Rotation Speeds 204
    Data Encoding and Disk Compatibility 205
    Disk Formatting 206
    Interleaving 207
    Logical Disk Organization 208
Floppy Drive Upgrades 211
    Adding a Second Internal Floppy Drive 212
    Upgrading to a SuperDrive 212
Diagnosing Floppy Drive Problems 213
    Misalignment 213
    Dirt 214
Hard Disk Upgrades 215
    Adding More Mass Storage 215
Diagnosing Hard Drive Problems 220
    Problems with Disk Contents 220
    Media Damage 221
    Other Drive Problems 223
    Disk Diagnostic and Repair Software 223
Problems with the SCSI Bus 230
    Physical Position in the Chain 231
    Total Length of Cabling 231
    SCSI IDs 231
    SCSI Termination 232
SCSI Accelerators and SCSI-2 235

Chapter 11: Video 237

Monitor Technology 237
    Describing Monitors 237
    CRT Displays 239

    Monochrome and Grayscale CRTs 239
    LCD Displays 243
Representing Colors and Shades of Gray 245
Adding Video RAM 247
    Video RAM for the Color Classic 247
    Video RAM for the LC, LC II, and Performa 400, 405, and 430 247
    Video RAM for the LC III and Performa 450 247
    Video RAM for the IIvi, IIvx, and Performa 600 247
    Video RAM for the Centris 610 248
    Video RAM and the Centris 660av 248
    Video RAM for the Centris 650 and Quadra 800 248
    Video RAM for the Quadra 700 248
    Video RAM for the Quadra 900 and 950 249
    Video RAM for the Quadra 840av 249
Video Accelerators 249

Appendix A: Upgrading Older Macs   253

Dealing with a Macintosh 128K or 512K 253
Dealing with a Macintosh 512Ke 254
    Macintosh 512Ke Accelerators 255
    Hard Disks for the Macintosh 512Ke 255
    Floppy Drives for the Macintosh 512Ke 256
    External Monitors for the Macintosh 512Ke 257
    The 512Ke Power Supply 257

Appendix B: Product/Vendor List   259

Software 259
Hardware Upgrades 260
    CPU Accelerators 260
    Cache Cards 261
    Expansion Chassis 261
    FPUs and PMMUs 262

Power Supplies	262
SIMMs and Video RAM	262
SCSI Accelerators	263
Video Accelerators	264
SCSI FLoppy Drives	264
Slot Expanders	264
Miscellaneous	264
Sales, Repairs, and Parts	265
Used Hardware Brokers	265
Used Macintosh Purchasers/Resellers	265
Macintosh Parts	265
Repairs	266

Glossary **267**

Photo Credits **281**

Index **283**

PREFACE

Like many Macintosh owners, you may have discovered that no more than six months after you purchased your computer, Apple Computer introduced some new models, making your pride and joy seem a lot less like the state-of-the-art technology it was when you bought it. It's an incontrovertible fact that microcomputer technology advances at a blinding pace. In the case of Macintoshes, that means new products approximately every six months.

There are three things you can do. (Crying a lot doesn't count.) First, you can continue to use your computer just as it is. (Doing nothing is always an alternative, regardless of what type of decision you are trying to make.) The drawback to this solution is that over time the computer becomes so outdated that it can't run current software. The second solution is to buy a newer model. If your current machine is relatively old, then this a viable option. However, for most people, buying a new computer every six months isn't financially realistic, even though all the goodies on the new models probably tempt you very much. The third option is to upgrade your computer so that it keeps up with the changing technology.

In this book you will find in-depth coverage of the many options for upgrading a Macintosh. In some cases, you can take a six-year-old computer and upgrade it so that it is the functional equivalent of a current model for less than one-third the cost of buying the new machine. (That's what I've done with my Mac II, which I intend to keep for some time to come, or at least until the PowerPC leaves it far in the dust.) In other cases, you can upgrade an older Mac so that it can run the most recent version of the operating system, albeit a bit more slowly than current machines.

Along with descriptions of types of upgrades, you'll find explanations of many of the hardware concepts that make it easier to decide on the right upgrade for your computer. For example, you'll learn why RAM upgrades are rated at different speeds and what those speeds mean to your particular Mac. You'll also learn

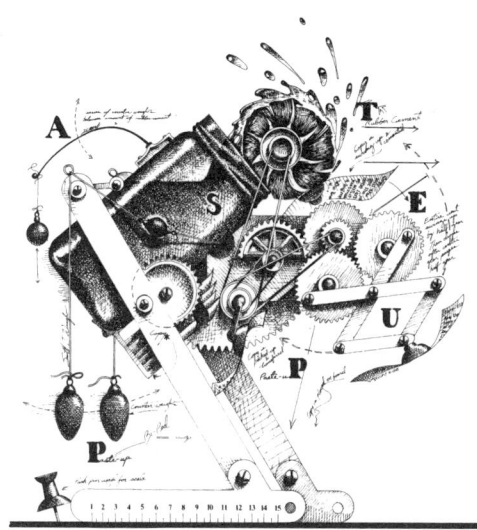

about computer buses and how they affect the amount and type of RAM your computer can use, how caches work, how disk drives store and access data, how the Macintosh represents color video, and why video RAM is important. You'll also find details about how the CPU runs programs and why one CPU is faster than another.

Most people can install some upgrades themselves. Whenever such an installation is more or less the same for all Macintosh models (for example, installing RAM upgrades), you will find complete instructions in this book. By the same token, you will also learn about which upgrades should probably be left to an authorized Macintosh service technician.

Even if an upgrade is theoretically user-installable, you may not feel comfortable fooling around inside your Macintosh. (Those with compact Macintoshes, such as one of the Classics, are the most likely Mac owners to feel this way.) If that's the case, give in to your feelings. Don't try to do anything that makes you nervous or afraid. A poorly installed upgrade can damage your computer. It makes a lot more sense to pay a service technician $30 to $50 to install some main memory, for example, than to run the risk of damaging the computer's main circuit board (the *motherboard* or *logic board*). The typical way to repair such damage is to replace the entire motherboard at a cost of nearly $400.

 By the way: Some people can repair parts of circuit boards. However, they are few and far between. If you can find one, you must remove the board from your Macintosh and somehow get it to the technician (you may have to ship it somewhere). Your machine is therefore unusable until the repair is complete. Most repair shops, including authorized Apple service technicians, simply swap a damaged circuit board for a working circuit board and charge you for the entire board. Then they send your damaged board back to the manufacturer (in many cases, Apple Computer), where the board is repaired and made ready to install as a replacement in somebody else's Macintosh. (Sorry if board swapping seems a bit cheesy, but that's the way it's done.)

Regardless of whether you use your Macintosh unmodified, replace it frequently with a new model, or upgrade it, your computer may not always work perfectly. (Yes, even the easy-to-use Macintosh can break down.) And there's nothing scarier than being faced with a

Preface

Macintosh that won't work. What do you do? Where do you start?

> **By the way:** If screaming, yelling, or beating your head against the wall makes you feel better, by all means do so. Unfortunately, such actions don't do much for the computer. By the same token, try to resist throwing the computer across the room; it's definitely bad for the machinery.

There aren't many parts you can actually repair yourself inside a Mac, but you can save yourself a great deal of time and effort if you can troubleshoot problems. Once you've isolated the offending component, you can reinstall it, replace it, send it back to the manufacturer for repair, or head straight for your local "computer doctor" (an alias for the nearest Apple authorized service technician), whichever is appropriate under the circumstances (see Figure P.1).

This book will help you diagnose hardware problems. The first step in the process is to distinguish hardware problems from software problems, which isn't always easy. Therefore this book looks at identifying common software problems such as virus contamination and INIT conflicts. Once you've ruled out software problems, you can turn to analyzing your hardware. In this book you'll read about hardware diagnostic software as well as some simple techniques for isolating the specific component responsible for the problem. You'll also find some guidelines as to how you might go about getting the component repaired. (Sometimes it makes sense to replace a component rather than repair it.)

Along with upgrade and troubleshooting, this book contains a lot of information about how computer hardware works. To get you started, Chapter 1 presents some computer hardware fundamentals. The purpose is to give you a basic understanding of the major hardware components of a computer and how they interact. In addition, you'll learn about the major circuits found on the Macintosh motherboard. These circuits are tested by diagnostic software and can occasionally be the source of hardware problems.

> **By the way:** You will find discussions of diagnostic and utility software throughout this book. Please keep in mind that these are truly descriptions of software and not reviews. Although I've tried to pick the most capable and/or widely used products in each category, a mention in this book doesn't constitute an endorsement of a product; it's up to you

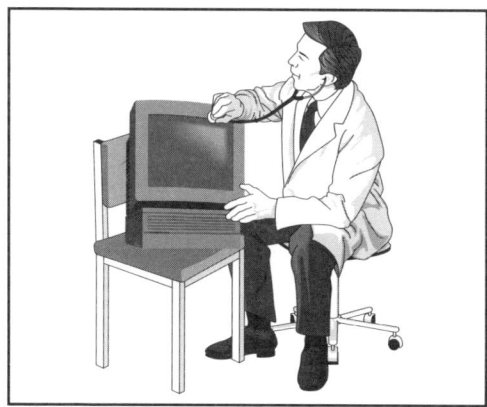

Figure P.1 *The computer doctor*

to decide which product best suits your needs. To help, where available I've included references to product reviews that have appeared in Macintosh magazines and newspapers.

Chapter 2 looks at the models in the Macintosh product line (in particular, their standard configurations). This will help you understand where your machine stands in terms of current technology, something that's very important when it comes to deciding how much (or even if) you should upgrade.

Chapter 3 introduces upgrading. It covers the types of upgrades that are available and helps you decide whether or not an upgrade really makes sense. If you decide not to upgrade, you'll find suggestions about what to do with an old machine. Chapter 4 introduces troubleshooting. In it you'll learn how to distinguish hardware problems from software problems as well as some general troubleshooting techniques. Chapter 4 also looks at a variety of diagnostic software and hardware.

The rest of the book focuses on each of the major Macintosh hardware components: main memory, CPUs, caches, math coprocessors (FPUs), logic boards, power supplies, disk drives, and video.

In Chapters 5 through 11 you'll find upgrade options, main memory installation instructions, and techniques for diagnosing specific hardware problems.

In most cases, the body of the book relates to Macintosh models from the Plus on. It's an unfortunate fact that upgrade options for older models are extremely limited. The single-sided to double-sided floppy drive upgrade for the 128K and 512K Macintosh is no longer available. Without that upgrade (and the new ROMs that go with it), there is very little you can do. However, if you have a 512Ke (a 512K Macintosh that has been upgraded with a double-sided floppy drive), you can upgrade it to a Macintosh Plus. Upgrade options for older Macintoshes are covered in Appendix A.

What You Need to Know Before You Begin

This book assumes very little hardware knowledge beyond the ability to identify major hardware components such as a monitor, hard disk, and floppy disk. However, you should be comfortable with using the Macintosh operating system and with a variety of application software (for example, a word processor, spreadsheet, or graphics program).

Preface

ACKNOWLEDGMENTS

A lot of people helped make this book a reality. (Although it would be fruitless to try to keep this even as short as a speech at a TV, music, or movie award ceremony, I'll try to be brief.) I'd like to thank all the following wonderful folks:

The people at MIS Press who were with the book from start to finish:

- Steve Berkowitz, publisher
- Cary Sullivan, the editor who shepherded this project through
- Erika Putre, editorial assistant
- Joanne Kelman, who did the wonderful design and layout

For providing hardware and software goodies:

- John Love, Apple Computer, who arranged the loan of the TechStep and MacTest Pro
- Rebecca Smith of MicroMat Computer Systems, who supplied MacEKG
- Sarah Kavanagh of McLean Public Relations, who represents MAXA Corp. and supplied Snooper and the Snooper NuBus Board
- Joshua Rosen and Herb Jacobs at Polybus for Peace of Mind
- The folks at Teknosys for Help!
- Sean Gorman at Stratos for the SIMM extractors
- Judith Frey at Casady and Greene for Conflict Catcher
- The folks at FWB for HDTookKit
- The folks at Symantec for Norton Utilities

For providing the photos that appear in the book:

- Gary Dailey, Gary Dutton, and David Mathven of DayStar Digital (most of the "hands-on" photos are from their excellent installation manuals)
- Charles Kronauer of FOCUS Enhancements
- Tad Shelby at PLI
- Jennifer Nielson at Pinnacle Micro
- Paul McGraw at APS

And last, but certainly not least, I owe deep thanks to Carole McClendon, my agent, who put me in touch with the good folks at MIS Press. (Actors seem to think it's goofy to thank their agents when they win an award, but it certainly doesn't seem that way to a writer!)

J.L.H.

A First Look at Computer Hardware

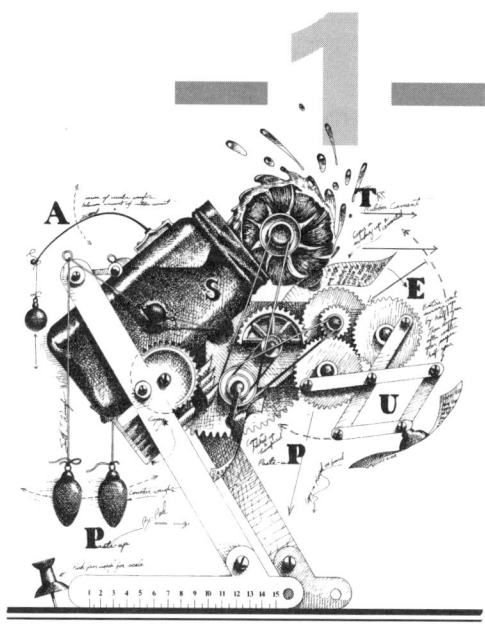

To make good decisions about upgrading your Mac and to be able to perform some basic system diagnostics, you need to know something about the hardware components of your computer. In some cases, you also need to know something about how software interacts with the hardware. This chapter therefore discusses hardware and software components and how they work together to make your computer work.

A Macintosh has five types of hardware components. As you can see from Figure 1.1, at least two of those components—the CPU and main memory—are contained within the system unit. The system unit is the box in which your Macintosh is housed. (If you have a compact Macintosh, such as a Classic, then your system unit also contains a monitor.)

The CPU

The *central processing unit* (CPU) is often called the brain of a computer. Regardless of whether you think a computer can have a brain, the CPU is where a computer runs programs. All data manipulation is performed by the CPU. In most Macintoshes, the CPU is also in charge of input and output operations.

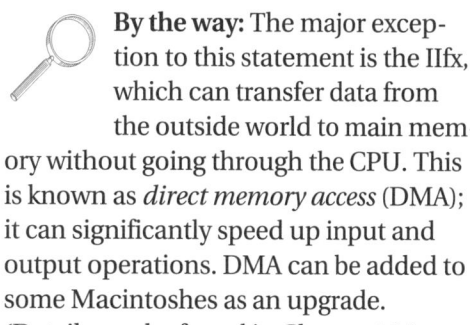 **By the way:** The major exception to this statement is the IIfx, which can transfer data from the outside world to main memory without going through the CPU. This is known as *direct memory access* (DMA); it can significantly speed up input and output operations. DMA can be added to some Macintoshes as an upgrade. (Details can be found in Chapter 10.)

The CPUs used in Macintoshes are made by the Motorola Corp. They have numbers like 68000, 68020, 68030, and 68040. Each CPU is a tiny microchip about 0.25 inch square. It is placed in a *package* that is approximately 1.5 inches square. Most Motorola packages have a black border and gold interior, just like the 68020 in Figure 1.2. The CPU connects to the motherboard through the many fine pins that extend downward from the bottom of the package. The pins may

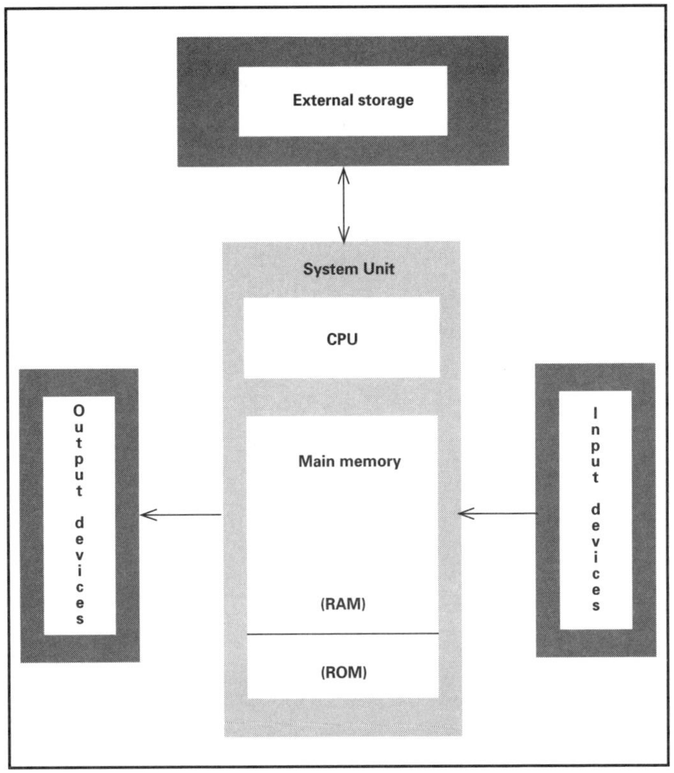

Figure 1.1 The major hardware components of a Macintosh

plug into a socket or may be soldered to the motherboard.

In general, the higher the model number of the CPU, the more powerful the CPU and the faster it runs. However, even CPUs with the same model number don't run at the same speed. The 68030, for example, might run at 16, 25, 33, 40, or 50 *megahertz* (Mhz). (One megahertz is a million clock cycles per second.) These numbers refer to the speed of the CPU's internal clock (this clock has nothing to do with the clock that keeps track of the date and time), which pulses (or *cycles*) at a regular interval. In general, the faster the CPU's internal clock, the faster the CPU executes programs. However, comparing a 50Mhz 68030 with a 33Mhz 68040 can be a bit tricky. You'll find more about the various CPUs and how they rate against one another in Chapter 6.

Inside, a CPU has three major parts (see Figure 1.3). *Registers* are small, temporary storage areas. They are used, for example, to hold data the CPU needs to manipulate as it runs a program. The *arithmetic logic unit* (ALU) performs arithmetic and logical operations on data. The *control unit* contains the CPU's clock as well as circuitry to decode the program instructions that are telling the CPU what to do. The control unit also directs the actions of the rest of computer. For example, it sends signals to main memory telling main memory to write a piece of data to a specific location. (More details about the internals of the CPU can be found in Chapter 6.)

Every CPU has an instruction set, that is made up of the specific things a CPU knows how to do. Instructions include such actions as performing arithmetic on two quantities, moving data from one location to another, or comparing two quantities and taking an action based on the result of that comparison.

Macintosh CPUs are what is known as *complex instruction set computing* (CISC) microprocessors. This means that procedures for performing the actions requested by every instruction in the CPU's instruction set are actually wired into the CPU's hardware. Some of the next generation of Apple computers, however, will feature *reduced instruction set computing* (RISC) microprocessors.

Chapter 1: A First Look at Computer Hardware

RISC microprocessors have very few built-in instructions. Instead, RISC microprocessors emulate most of the instructions in their instruction set with software. These microprocessors are generally faster than CISC microprocessors. Therefore, their performance doesn't suffer from using software to perform many basic actions.

Math Coprocessors

A Macintosh may include a special processor designed to speed up some arithmetic operations. Known as a *math coprocessor* or *floating-point unit* (FPU), this type of processor handles operations on floating-point numbers (numbers with digits to the right of the decimal point, such as 2.19482 or $10.3845921 \times 10^{15}$). Some Macintoshes come with the FPU built in; in others it can be added as an option. A few Macintoshes cannot accept an FPU.

Main Memory

The system unit also contains main memory. Main memory is divided into two parts—*random access memory* (RAM) and *read-only memory* (ROM). RAM is temporary storage that is used when the computer is turned on. Although its contents can be modified, whatever is stored in RAM is lost when the computer is turned off. Macintoshes tend to be gluttons when it comes to RAM—the more the merrier, so to speak. For that reason, adding RAM to a Macintosh is the most common type of upgrade. To add RAM, you install one or more *single in-line memory modules* (SIMMs). A SIMM is a small circuit board that contains RAM circuitry.

Many Macintosh models also have some special-purpose RAM to handle the display on the computer's monitor or monitors. Macintosh video displays are *bit-mapped*. That means that the color of each dot on a monitor's screen is represented individually in memory. The more colors or shades of gray the monitor uses and the larger the monitor, the more memory it takes to represent the screen image. (You'll learn more about exactly how much memory it takes in Chapter 11.) To avoid using large chunks of RAM for color and grayscale displays, many Macs use *video RAM* (VRAM) to store screen bit-maps.

ROM is permanent storage; it keeps its contents when the computer is turned off. On the other hand, the contents of ROM can't be changed by a computer program. For most microcomputers, ROM contains just enough of the operating system to start up the computer

Figure 1.2 A 68020 microprocessor

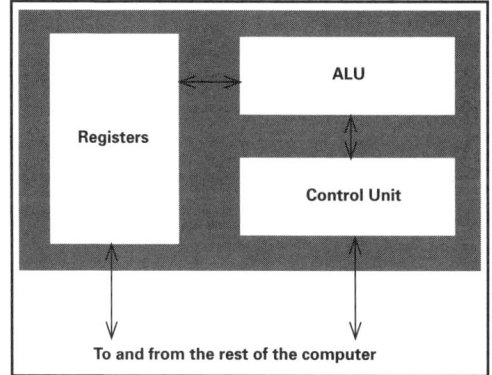

Figure 1.3 The major component of a CPU

when it is first turned on. The Macintosh ROM, however, is a storehouse of literally hundreds of programs used by both the operating system and application programs to do things such as create the Macintosh user interface (windows, menus, dialog boxes, and so on), print documents, create graphics, manipulate text characteristics, handle lists of things, and interact with an AppleTalk network. Without its ROM, a Macintosh simply isn't a Macintosh.

By the way: The complexity of the Macintosh ROM is largely the reason that there is only one Macintosh clone on the market. (The company that developed the clone used "clean room" techniques, developing a functionally equivalent Macintosh ROM using only publicly available documentation. The computer uses a graphic user interface whose look and feel is different from the Macintosh user interface.) Computers such as the Amiga, which provide Macintosh emulation, cannot work unless a Macintosh ROM is installed. Such ROMs are usually harvested from Macs that have gone to computer heaven and are therefore usually not state-of-the-art.

Each new generation of Macintoshes does contain ROM that is different to some extent from older models. However, although it is common to add RAM to a Macintosh, a ROM upgrade is unusual. In most cases, you won't upgrade the ROM unless it is absolutely required. For example, if you want to add a SuperDrive (high-density floppy drive) to a Macintosh II, you must also upgrade the ROM so that the Mac II can use the new disk drive.

MEASURING MEMORY (AND OTHER THINGS)

To measure main memory (and to store numbers and characters), a computer uses the *binary* numbering system. Binary, or base 2, uses only the digits 0 and 1. Because the circuits in today's computers carry either a high voltage or a low voltage, the voltage of a circuit is a convenient way to represent a binary digit (a *bit*).

Counting in binary is similar to counting in base 10, the decimal system we use every day. However, whereas in base 10 each place in a number represents a power of 10, in binary each place represents a power of 2. As an example, look at the binary number in Figure 1.4. This number is an *integer*, a whole number with no fractional portion to the right of the *binary point* (the binary equivalent of the decimal point). Notice that the right-most digit (the *least significant digit*) represents 2^0, or 1. (Any number raised to the 0 power is the number itself.) Each digit to the left represents 2 raised to the next highest power. Because bits are always numbered beginning with 0, the left-most bit (the *most significant digit*) will always have the place value 2^{n-1}, where *n* is the number of bits in the number.

To convert a binary number to its value in base 10, add the base 10 place values for each binary place that has a 1 in it. In Figure 1.4, the conversion becomes:

4 + 8 + 64 + 128 = 204

Some powers of 2 useful to Macintosh users can be found in Table 1.1.

Like most computers, the Macintosh doesn't access each bit individually; instead it works with groups of bits. The smallest grouping is a *byte* (8 bits). A byte, which can store values in the range 0 through 255, is used to measure main memory.

By the way: There is an easy way to figure out the decimal equivalent of the maximum number that can be stored in any number of bits: Take the place value of the next highest power of 2 and subtract 1. For example, keeping in mind that the least significant bit is always 2^0, the left-most bit in a byte has the place value 2^7. Therefore the maximum value that can be stored in a byte is $2^8 - 1$, or 256 − 1 (255).

Because computer storage is typically measured in thousands, million, and trillions of bytes, computer people use the terms *kilobyte* (abbreviated *K*) to mean roughly 1,000 bytes, *megabyte* (abbreviated *M*, *Mb*, *meg*, or *Mbyte*) to mean roughly 1 million bytes, and *gigabyte* (abbreviated *Gb* or *G*) to mean roughly 1 trillion bytes. Today's Macintoshes have at least 4Mb of RAM. As you will discover in Chapter 6, 4Mb is really the minimum for useful work under System 7, but more RAM is certainly better.

By the way: Technically, a kilobyte is 2^{10}, or 1,024, bytes; a megabyte is 2^{20}, or 1,048,576, bytes; and a gigabyte is 2^{30}, or 1,073,741,824, bytes.

The bytes of storage in main memory are numbered, beginning with zero. This gives each byte a unique *address*. Computer programs can then access main memory by specifying the address from which they want to read something or the address at which they wish to write something.

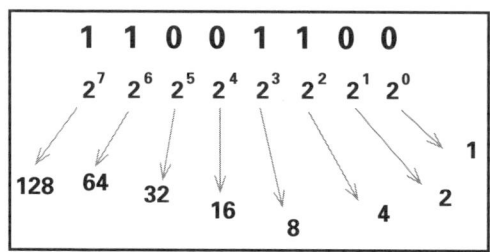

Figure 1.4 A binary number

Table 1.1 Powers of two

n	2n
0	1
1	2
2	4
3	8
4	16
5	32
6	64
7	128
8	256
9	512
10	1,024
11	2,048
12	4,096
13	8, 192
14	16, 384
15	32,768
16	65,536
20	1,048,576
30	1,073,741,824
31	2, 147,483,648
32	4,294,967,296

> **By the way:** If you can program in a high-level language like BASIC, Pascal, or C, then you might be interested to know that a program variable is nothing more than a label on a storage location in main memory. Variables mean that the programmer doesn't have to be concerned with actual addresses; the compiler or interpreter that translates the program to machine language takes care of assigning a unique main memory address to each variable.

In addition to bytes, computers work with a grouping of bits known as a *word*. A word is the number of bits that the computer typically handles as a unit. Although the size of a byte doesn't vary from one type of computer to another, the size of a word does. The Macintosh has a 32-bit word. As you will see in Chapter 6, although all Macintoshes can operate on 32-bit quantities within their CPUs, not all can transfer a word at a time between the computer's components. This has a major impact on the computer's processing speed.

The Macintosh stores integers in either 16- or 32-bit groupings. [Storing floating-point numbers (numbers with digits to the right of the decimal point) is discussed in Chapter 7.] A 16-bit integer can store values in the range ±32,767.

Notice that this is the maximum value that can be stored in 15, rather than 16, bits. This is because the most significant bit isn't part of the value of the number but is used instead to indicate whether the number is positive or negative. By the same token, a 32-bit integer stores ±2,147,483,647. If you need values greater or smaller than what can fit in a 32-bit integer, then you must use a floating-point number.

To store characters, the Macintosh uses a coding scheme called the *American Standard Code for Information Interchange* (ASCII). Each unique 8-bit pattern represents one letter, number, or special character. In fact, it is often easy to visualize how much a given amount of memory can hold by recognizing that a byte equals one character.

EXTERNAL STORAGE

The main memory in the system unit isn't really suitable for long-term storage. ROM can't be changed by a program, and the contents of RAM are lost whenever the computer is turned off. The storage capacity of RAM is also rather limited. Computers therefore have external storage devices that are permanent and spacious. External storage includes things like floppy disk drives, hard disk drives, tape drives, and optical disk drives.

Like main memory, external storage space is measured in bytes. The original Macintosh floppy disks held only 400K; the Macintosh Plus introduced an 800K floppy drive. The 800K drive was replaced by the SuperDrive, which holds 1.4Mb.

The first Macintosh hard disk held 20Mb. Today, microcomputer hard disks can hold as much as 2.1G. The only thing you can say for certain about hard disk storage capacities is that they continue to rise at the same time that the cost per megabyte goes down. When compared byte for byte, disk storage is considerably cheaper than RAM. (To find out more about types of disk storage and how the Macintosh stores and retrieves data from disks, see Chapter 10.)

Input Devices and Output Devices

In addition to storing information, a computer needs a way to get information from the outside world. *Input devices* are a type of hardware that takes external information and translates it into a form the computer can understand. Every Macintosh has at least two input devices: the mouse and the keyboard. You may also decide to add other input devices, such as trackballs, graphics tables, optical scanners, and video cameras.

An *output device* is the exact opposite of an input device. It's a piece of hardware that takes information inside the computer and presents it to the outside world in a way a human can understand. The two most common output devices are monitors and printers. Macintosh monitors can be *monochrome* (black and white), *grayscale* (shades of gray), or color. (More information about Macintosh monitor technology can be found in Chapter 11.) A Macintosh can also send information to plotters, film recorders (for making slides), and videocassette recorders.

Connecting the Parts

A computer has to have some way to connect its parts to one another. The electronic pathway that provides that type of connection is called a *bus* (see Figure 1.5). To transfer something from one part of the computer to another, the hardware component sending the information places it on the bus. The component to which the information is sent retrieves it from the bus. (If you like, data and addresses ride the bus from one part of the computer to another.)

Only one message can be on the bus at time. The CPU therefore uses its internal clock to synchronize access to the bus; a component can only place some-

Fix Your Own Mac: Upgrading and Troubleshooting

thing on the bus when the CPU's clock pulses and no other message is already on the bus. (The CPU also has a way of dealing with the problem that arises when two components attempt to access the bus at exactly the same time.) The faster the clock, the more often messages can be placed on the bus. That's why a higher clock speed generally means a faster computer.

As you can see in Figure 1.6, the system unit contains one main bus that connects all the components (the system bus). The CPU and main memory are connected directly. RAM upgrades are plugged into special SIMM slots. A slot is an opening into the bus, designed to make it easy to add new components. The CPU, the system bus, and main memory (including the SIMM slots) are collected onto a single circuit board (the motherboard or logic board) that lays across the very bottom of the Macintosh.

The remaining components do not plug directly into the bus. Instead an adapter circuit provides an interface for external storage, input, and output devices. Some adapter circuits are part of the motherboard. For example, every Macintosh has circuits to connect a keyboard and a mouse and to connect such devices as printers, disk drives, and modems. The adapter circuit is connected to the bus; the external device connects to the adapter circuit via a port.

The electrical characteristics of the bus vary somewhat from one Macintosh model to another. Expansion boards made for one Macintosh therefore may not work in another. However, many Macintoshes, especially the Macintosh II, Centris, and Quadra lines, have one or more NuBus slots. NuBus is a bus standard. If your Mac has NuBus slots, then you can use most NuBus cards in your computer. The other type of slot found in Macintoshes is a processor direct slot (PDS). Because this type of slot gives direct access to the CPU, its electrical characteristics vary, depending on the type of CPU found in the computer. In other words, a 68020 processor direct slot is different from a 68030 processor direct slot, which in turn is different from a 68040 processor direct slot. An expansion board must be made specifically for the type of processor direct slot found in a given Macintosh for it to work in that computer.

Every Macintosh has at least one *Apple Desktop Bus* (ADB) port. The ADB port is used to connect input devices such as a keyboard, mouse, or graphics tablet. Every Mac also has at least one *Small Computer Systems Interface* (SCSI) port for connecting disk drives, tape drives,

Figure 1.5 Riding the bus, with station stops at RAM, the CPU, and all I/O ports

Chapter 1: A First Look at Computer Hardware

scanners, and some printers. The SCSI port handles parallel transmissions—data travel one *word* at a time.

A Macintosh also has a port for connecting the computer to an AppleTalk network (commonly also used to connect a printer) and a port for connecting a modem. These are *serial* ports that transfer 1 bit at a time. They adhere to the RS-422 standard. The other standard ports vary from one Macintosh to another; you will learn more about which model of Macintosh has which ports in Chapter 2.

By the way: The other major standard for serial ports is RS-232C. Apple chose RS-422 because it felt this design was less susceptible to noise and signal degradation over long distances.

In addition to the adapter circuits provided on the motherboard, most Macintoshes have one or more slots into which adapter circuits can be plugged. These are either NuBus slots or processor direct slots. The adapter circuits and ports for connecting components are placed on *expansion boards*, which are circuit boards designed to be inserted directly into a slot. You will be introduced to a variety of expansion boards throughout this book.

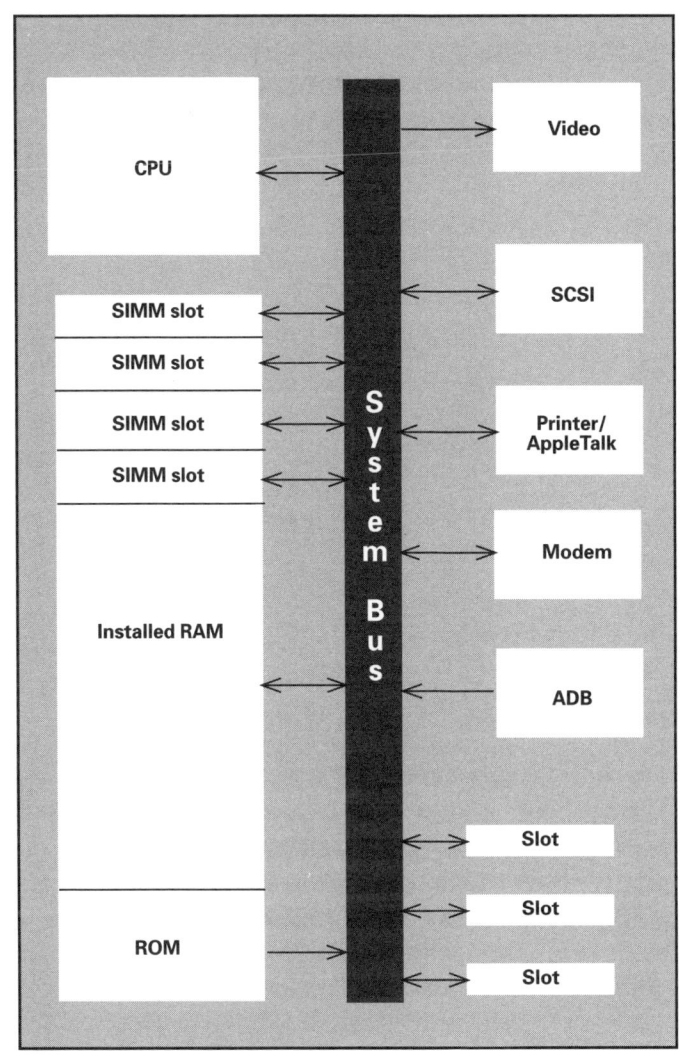

▶ *Figure 1.6* Connecting the parts of a computer with a system bus

A Tour Around a Motherboard

In Figure 1.7 you can see the motherboard from a Macintosh IIci. The ports that connect to built-in adapter circuits appear along the right edge. From the bottom up they are the following: external floppy disk connector, SCSI port, monitor port, printer port, modem port, stereo audio jack, and two ADB ports.

At the center top of the motherboard are three NuBus slots. Below them is a single processor direct slot. Along the center left edge (directly left of the processor direct slot) are eight SIMM slots. The bottom four have SIMMs plugged in; the top four are empty. The ROMs are directly below the SIMM slots.

There are four ROM chips along the left edge of the motherboard. The CPU is centered between the left and right edges of the motherboard, even with the second ROM. (It is marked with an *M*, for *Motorola*, which appears upside down in the photo.) Next to it are connectors for an internal hard disk and internal floppy disk drive. The FPU is just above and to the right of the PDS.

The Major Circuits on a Motherboard

There are a number of major circuits on a Macintosh logic board. Although you aren't aware of them for most day-to-day computing, both the hardware diagnostics that the Macintosh performs when you power up the computer and hardware diagnostic software can identify problems with the individual circuits. You will find it easier to understand what diagnostic software is telling you if you understand the major functions of these circuits.

Parameter RAM

Parameter RAM, or PRAM, is a real-time clock chip that keeps track of system configuration parameters, such as the current date and time, serial port configuration, and the start-up drive. PRAM is like any other type of RAM—it must continually receive power to retain its contents. PRAM is therefore maintained by the Macintosh's battery. (One signal that the battery needs replacing is that your Mac starts to forget the date and time!)

Versatile Interface Adapter

The *Versatile Interface Adapter* (VIA) handles many of the Macintosh's input and output operations. In early Macs (the Plus and earlier models), the VIA acts as the interface between the motherboard and the keyboard, mouse, and real-time clock. In addition, it provides *control signals* (signals that indicate the action a component should take, such as read or write) for the floppy disk drives, monitor, speaker, and serial ports.

The VIA was modified slightly with the introduction of the SE, providing generalized support for ADB devices and some SCSI control signals as well as the real-time clock. In the Macintosh Portable and PowerBook 100, it also has a major role as the interface with the Power Manager circuit (the circuit that attempts to minimize power use and thus prolong battery life).

The SE/30 and some members of the Macintosh II family have two VIAs (VIA1 and VIA2). VIA1 performs the functions found in the VIAs of earlier Macs with only one VIA. VIA2 adds support for expansion cards and the Apple Sound Chip. Other Macs (including the IIfx, IIci, IIvx, IIvi, Quadra 900, Quadra 950, Performa 600, PowerBook 160, PowerBook 165c, and PowerBook 180) have a physical VIA1 chip but use another circuit to emulate VIA2 functions.

In general, the fewer circuits used in a computer, the cheaper the computer is to produce. The computer is also less likely to have hardware problems. Apple is therefore always trying to reduce the number of chips on a motherboard. As a result, more recent Macintoshes have their VIA functions combined in a single

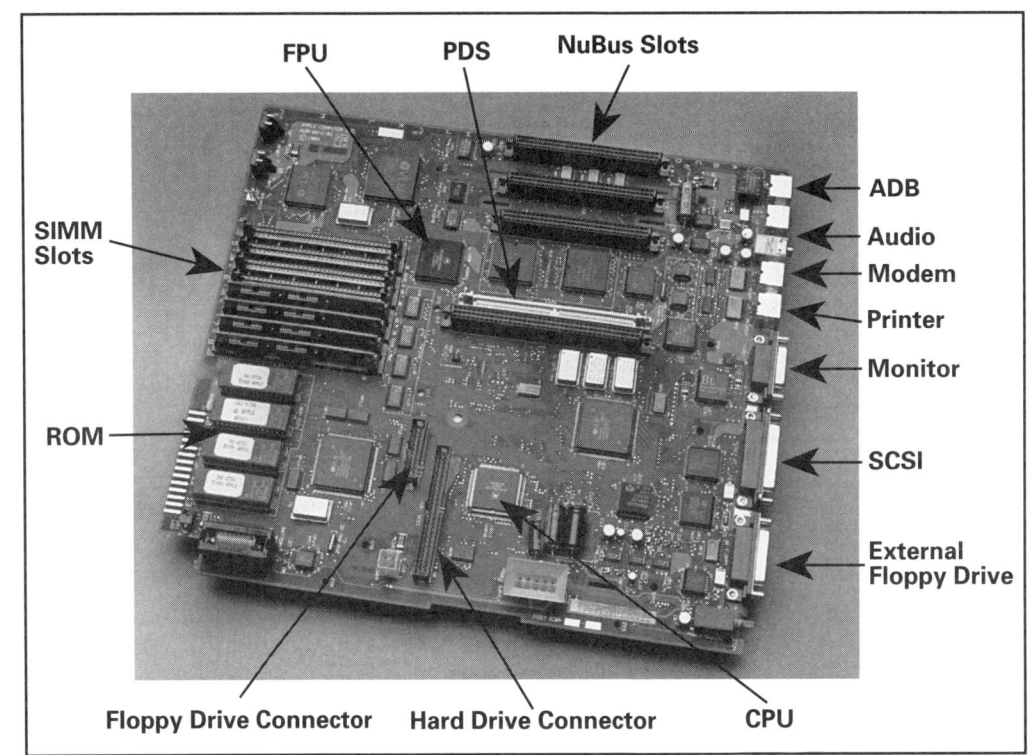

Figure 1.7 The Macintosh IIci motherboard

chip along with other circuits. For example, the LC and LC II include a V8 *gate array*. This chip, custom designed for the Macintosh, merges the functions of several circuits into one. Included in the V8 gate array are VIA1 and VIA2 functions as well as circuitry for decoding main memory addresses and handling sound input and output. With the LC III, the V8 gate array has been replaced by a chip called Sonora, which contains a VIA1, emulation of a VIA2, and support for sound input and output.

The Color Classic's VIA functions are part of the Spice circuit. Spice not only takes care of VIA functions, but also handles interaction with the monitor and front-panel pushbuttons. The Quadra 800, Centris 610, and Centris 650 have their VIA1 and VIA2 functions performed by the IOSB chip.

Serial Communications Controller

The *Serial Communication Controller* (SCC) takes care of the Mac's two serial ports and participates in floppy disk reads and writes. It also translates between parallel (one word at a time) and serial (1 bit at a time) transmissions. This is used, for example, to route signals from the SCSI port, which uses parallel transmission, to one of the serial ports, perhaps transmitting the contents of a file on a hard disk to another computer through a modem and the telephone lines.

Floppy Disk Controller

Steve Wozniak, one of the original developers of the Apple Computer, was instrumental in the development of the Macintosh floppy disk controller. The chip therefore bears his name: the *Integrated Wozniak Machine* (IWM). In conjunction with VIA1 and the SCC, it takes care of floppy disk operations in Macs through the Macintosh II. Later Macintoshes have either a *Super Woz Integrated Machine* (SWIM) or SWIM2 chip. A SWIM is required to support the SuperDrive. It is also nearly twice as fast as the IWM.

Other Circuits

In addition to the circuits about which you have just read, hardware diagnostic software tests all or some of the following circuits:

- SCSI: The SCSI circuit handles internal SCSI devices and all operations through the Macintosh's SCSI port.

- ASC (Apple Sound Chip): The ASC produces sound through the Macintosh's internal speaker.

- *Memory management unit* (MMU) or *paged memory management unit* (PMMU): On stock 68020 Macs, the MMU aids in memory access. To use virtual memory, the MMU in a 68020 Mac is replaced with a PMMU. The PMMU is integrated into the 68030 and 68040. (The 68000 Macs do not contain an MMU or a PMMU.)

The Macintosh Product Line

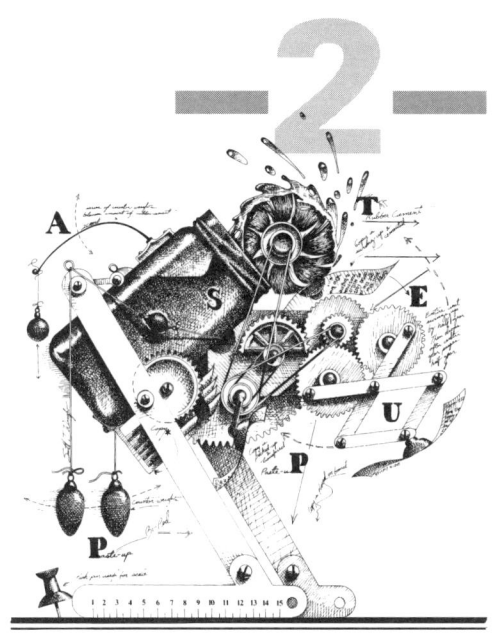

As you read this, it will have been ten years since the introduction of the first Macintosh. That first computer had one 400K floppy disk drive, 128K RAM, and no expansion slot. A second floppy drive wasn't available for several months; a hard drive didn't appear until nearly a year later. Who would have thought, in those early days, that the Macintosh product line would have become so diverse?

If you wanted a Macintosh in 1984, you had one choice. Today you have many. The rest of this chapter will introduce you to the Macintosh product line from the Macintosh Plus onward. It will help you understand where your computer fits into the product line and give you a point of reference when you make the upgrade-or-replace decision.

> **By the way:** It you get confused by the plethora of models and specifications, don't worry—you're not alone. With Apple Computer adhering to its goal of announcing new computers every six months, the variety of models and their configurations is staggering.

Compact Macintoshes

Compact Macintoshes (sometimes called "toaster Macs" because of their shape and the way a floppy disk is ejected out the front) have a monitor built into the system unit. Until the release of the Color Classic in early 1993, all compact Macintoshes shared the same 9-inch monochrome monitor.

Macintosh Plus

The Macintosh Plus debuted in January 1986. It was the first Macintosh to have many of the features included in today's Macintoshes, such as a SCSI port and SIMM slots. (Its characteristics are summarized in Table 2.1.) Although the Macintosh Plus included some hardware breakthroughs, its major contribution to the future of the Macintosh actually had very little to do specifically with those hardware innovations. The first laser printer (the Apple LaserWriter) was released at the same time as the Macintosh Plus. Coupled with Aldus PageMaker, the first software for doing desktop publishing, the power of the Macintosh Plus and

Fix Your Own Mac: Upgrading and Troubleshooting

> **Table 2.1** The Macintosh Plus
>
> | | |
> |---|---|
> | **Status:** | Discontinued |
> | **Microprocessor:** | 68000 running at 7.83Mhz |
> | **Math coprocessor:** | None available |
> | **Main memory:** | |
> | RAM: | 1Mb (expandable to 4Mb) |
> | ROM: | 128K |
> | **Floppy disk drive:** | 800K (double-sided) |
> | **Hard disk drive:** | Internal hard disk drive not available* |
> | **Expansion slots:** | None |
> | **Keyboard:** | Included |
> | **Mouse:** | Included |
> | **Built-in monitor:** | 9-inch monochrome |
> | **Ports:** | |
> | | Printer/AppleTalk Network |
> | | Modem |
> | | SCSI |
> | | Mouse (nine-pin connector) |
> | | Audio (for connecting a single external speaker) |
> | | External floppy disk drive |
>
> *Although the Mac Plus was not designed to accept internal hard disks, some third-party manufacturers did provide them.

the laser printer combined to make it possible, for the first time, to produce typeset-quality materials on the desktop. The Macintosh Plus, LaserWriter, and PageMaker effectively created the entire field of desktop publishing.

Macintosh SE

The Macintosh SE debuted in March 1987 as the replacement for the Macintosh Plus (see Figure 2.1). Its design included ADB ports, internal hard drives, and an expansion slot. (All these features had debuted earlier with the Macintosh II, the first modular Mac.) The major difference between the SE and today's compact Macintoshes is that of storage capacity and speed. Initially, SEs were shipped with 800K floppy drives. However, later models included the SuperDrive. The SE's features can be found in Table 2.2.

Macintosh SE/30

The SE/30, whose features can be found in Table 2.3, was the first high-performance Macintosh. Although only marketed from January 1989 through late 1990, it remains a popular computer with many users because of its speed.

> **Table 2.2** The Macintosh SE
>
> | | |
> |---|---|
> | **Status:** | Discontinued |
> | **Microprocessor:** | 68000 running at 7.83Mhz |
> | **Math coprocessor:** | None available |
> | **Main memory:** | |
> | RAM: | 1 or 2Mb (expandable to 4Mb) |
> | ROM: | 256K |
> | **Floppy disk drive:** | 800K (double-sided) in early models, 1.4Mb in later models |
> | **Hard disk drive:** | 20 or 40Mb |
> | **Drive configurations:** | |
> | | Two floppy disk drives |
> | | One floppy disk drive and one hard disk |
> | **Expansion slots:** | One SE bus expansion slot |
> | **Keyboard options:** | Any ADB keyboard |
> | **Mouse:** | Included |
> | **Built-in monitor:** | 9-inch monochrome |
> | **Ports:** | |
> | | Printer/AppleTalk Network |
> | | Modem |
> | | SCSI |
> | | ADB |
> | | Audio (for connecting a single external speaker) |
> | | External floppy disk drive |

Chapter 2: The Macintosh Product Line

Table 2.3 The Macintosh SE/30

Status:	Discontinued
Microprocessor:	68030 running at 15.667Mhz
Math coprocessor:	68882 FPU included
Main memory:	
RAM:	1 or 4Mb (expandable to 128Mb)
ROM:	256K
Floppy disk drive:	1.4Mb
Hard disk drive:	40 or 80Mb
Drive configurations:	One floppy disk drive One floppy disk drive and one hard disk
Expansion slots:	One 030 Direct slot
Keyboard options:	Any ADB keyboard
Mouse:	Included
Built-in monitor:	9-inch monochrome
Ports:	Printer/AppleTalk Network Modem SCSI ADB Audio (for connecting a single external speaker) External floppy disk drive

Figure 2.1 The Macintosh SE with a standard keyboard

MACINTOSH CLASSIC, CLASSIC II, AND PERFORMA 200

The emergence of the Classic, Classic II, and Performa 200 marked a new strategy in the Macintosh line. Trying to compete with low-cost IBM and IBM-clone computers, Apple dramatically lowered the suggested retail price on its computers and altered the way in which they were marketed. Some Macintoshes—in particular, the Performa series—were designed to be sold through mass market retailers such as Sears rather than through computer stores.

Fix Your Own Mac: Upgrading and Troubleshooting

▶ **Table 2.4** *The Macintosh Classic*

Status:	Discontinued
Microprocessor:	68000 running at 7.8336Mhz
Math coprocessor:	None available
Main memory:	
RAM:	1 or 2Mb (expandable to 4Mb)
ROM:	512K
Floppy disk drive:	1.4Mb
Hard disk drive:	40Mb
Drive configurations:	One floppy disk drive
	One floppy disk drive and one hard disk
Expansion slots:	None
Keyboard:	Standard included
Mouse:	Included
Built-in monitor:	9-inch monochrome
Ports:	
	Printer/AppleTalk network
	Modem
	SCSI
	ADB
	Audio (for connecting a single external speaker)
	External floppy disk drive

The hardware of the Classic II and that of the Performa 200 are identical. They differ in where they can be purchased (the Classic II through computer dealers, the Performa 200 through a mass market retailer), the software shipped with the machine (the Performa includes application software), and the type of support provided by the warranty (the Performa provides better support). In general, Macintoshes in the Performa series cost a bit more than their computer dealer twins.

The original Classic (see Table 2.4) was a replacement for the SE. Released in October 1990, it had a rounded rather than a straight front. The Classic has two drawbacks. First, it has no expansion slot. Second, its 68000 microprocessor is very slow when compared to the CPUs in other current Macintoshes.

The Classic II and Performa 200 (see Table 2.5), which appeared in October 1991, are designed to provide a compact Macintosh with more speed than the Classic. Although still lacking an expansion slot, the Classic II/Performa 200 includes a microphone for audio input as well as support for more RAM than the Classic.

▶ **Table 2.5** *The Macintosh Classic II and Macintosh Performa 200*

Status:	Available
Microprocessor:	68030 running at 16Mhz
Math coprocessor:	None available
Main memory:	
RAM:	2 or 4Mb* (expandable to 10Mb)
ROM:	512K
Floppy disk drive:	1.4Mb
Hard disk drive:	40 or 80Mb
Drive configurations:	One floppy disk drive and one hard disk
Expansion slots:	None
Keyboard:	Standard included
Mouse:	Included
Built-in monitor:	9-inch monochrome
Ports:	
	Printer/AppleTalk network
	Modem
	SCSI
	ADB
	Audio (for connecting a single external speaker)
	Microphone
	External floppy disk drive

*The Performa 200 is available only in the 4Mb RAM configuration.

Chapter 2: The Macintosh Product Line

MACINTOSH COLOR CLASSIC

The Color Classic, shown in Figure 2.2 with an extended keyboard, is the first compact Macintosh to support color. The Color Classic, which made its debut in February 1993, has a 10-inch monitor with a Sony Trinitron picture tube, making it look a bit like a one-story building with a false front. There is every indication that Color Classic will soon become the only Classic. Its features can be found in Table 2.6.

Table 2.5   The Macintosh Color Classic

Status:	Available
Microprocessor:	68030 running at 16Mhz
Math coprocessor:	Optional
Main memory:	
RAM:	4Mb (expandable to 10Mb)
ROM:	512K
Floppy disk drive:	1.4Mb
Hard disk drive:	40, 80, or 160Mb
Drive configurations:	One floppy disk drive and one hard disk
Expansion slots:	One 030 Processor direct slot
Keyboard:	Standard included
Mouse:	Included
Built-in monitor:	9-inch monochrome
Ports:	Printer/AppleTalk network Modem SCSI ADB Audio (for connecting a single external speaker) Microphone External floppy disk drive

Figure 2.2   The Macintosh Color Classic

Entry-Level Modular Macintoshes

A modular Macintosh has no built-in monitor. Instead it uses a separate monitor. The adapter circuit for monitor support may be on the motherboard, or you may need to add an expansion board (often called a video card) containing adapter circuits and video RAM.

The low end of the modular Macintosh line is represented by the Macintosh LC, LC II, and LC III, all of which look identical from the outside (see Figure 2.3). The Performa 400 is the mass market version of the LC II. Although technically a low-end machine, the LC III is faster than some of the older models in the mid-range Macintosh II line. It has all but replaced the LC and LC II.

Macintosh LC

The LC (released October 1990) was the first low-priced modular Macintosh. Like its successors, it is small and light and has some video circuits on its motherboard. It also includes a microphone for recording sound. The feature list can be found in Table 2.7.

Macintosh LC II and Performa 400, 405, and 430

As you can see from Table 2.8, the LC II (released March 1992) and the Performa 400, 405, and 430 are similar to the LC. However, they have a 68030 rather than a 68020 microprocessor. As a result, these Macintoshes can use virtual mem-

Figure 2.3 The Macintosh LC III

ory to extend physically installed RAM up to the machine's limit of 10Mb.

> **By the way:** The 68020 microprocessor is missing a piece of hardware—a PMMU (paged memory management unit), required for virtual memory. Although a PMMU can be added to the Macintosh II (the only other Macintosh to use the 68020), the LC has no socket for one. The 68030, however, has a built-in PMMU. For more details see Chapter 7.

MACINTOSH LC III AND PERFORMA 450

The LC III and Performa 450, although of limited expandability because of their single expansion slot, are powerful, fast Macintoshes for users who want a reasonably priced modular computer. Notice in Table 2.9 that their 68030 microprocessor runs at 25Mhz. As you will see shortly, this is faster than some of the models in the Macintosh II line. The LC III/Performa 450 also has a socket for an FPU so that a math coprocessor can be added without taking up the single expansion slot.

Table 2.7 The Macintosh LC

Status:	Discontinued
Microprocessor:	68020 running at 16Mhz
Math coprocessor:	Optional (takes up expansion slot)
Main memory:	
RAM:	2Mb (expandable to 10Mb)
ROM:	512K
Floppy disk drive:	1.4Mb
Hard disk drive:	40Mb
Drive configurations:	One floppy disk drive and one hard disk
Expansion slots:	One 020 processor direct slot
Keyboard options:	Any ADB keyboard
Mouse:	Included
Built-in video support:	Up to 14-inch color monitor (256K video RAM; can be upgraded to 512K for larger monitors and/or more colors)
Ports:	Printer/AppleTalk network Modem SCSI ADB Audio (for connecting a single external speaker) Microphone External floppy disk drive

Table 2.8 The Macintosh LC II and Performa 400, 405, and 430

Status:	Available
Microprocessor:	68030 running at 16Mhz
Math coprocessor:	Optional (takes up expansion slot)
Main memory:	
RAM:	4Mb (expandable to 10Mb)
ROM:	512K
Floppy disk drive:	1.4Mb
Hard disk drive:	40, 80, or 120Mb*
Drive configurations:	One floppy disk drive and one hard disk
Expansion slots:	One 030 processor direct slot
Keyboard options:	Any ADB keyboard
Mouse:	Included
Built-in video support:	40Mb configuration: up to 14-inch color monitor (256K video RAM expandable to 512K) 80Mb configuration: up to 16-inch color monitor (512K video RAM)
Ports:	Printer/AppleTalk network Modem SCSI ADB Audio (for connecting a single external speaker) Microphone External floppy disk drive

*The LC II is available with a 40 or 80Mb hard disk. The Performa 400 and 405 are available only in the 80Mb hard disk configuration. The Performa 430 comes with the 120Mb hard disk.

Mid-range Modular Macintoshes

The story of modular Macintoshes actually began with the Macintosh II line. When the Macintosh II debuted in 1987, it represented the high end of the Macintosh line. It provided enhanced performance and ease of expandability. However, the rapid rate at which microcomputer technology has advanced has meant that a Macintosh II is now in the middle of the Macintosh line.

Macintosh II and IIx

The release of the Macintosh II in March 1987 was greeted with a great deal of excitement. It was the first color Macintosh and was literally twice as fast as the SE. However, Apple's claims that it could run all existing Macintosh software were a bit exaggerated.

Although Apple had been warning software developers for some time that they shouldn't assume that the Macintosh screen was a fixed size, many apparently had done so. For example, when MacPaint (the black-and-white drawing program shipped with early Macintoshes) was run on the Macintosh II, the screen image was compressed vertically until it was about 1 inch high. Then the screen image was repeated four times down the monitor in evenly spaced bands. Display problems of that type sent users frantically to the telephone, hoping that software upgrades were available. In most cases, developers had upgraded or were in the process of upgrading their software. Nonetheless, the experience of going from the 9-inch screen on the compact Macintosh to the color screen on the Macintosh II was very much like going from System 6 to System 7 when it came to software compatibility.

At first glance, the Macintosh II (see Table 2.10) seems to be less powerful than the LC III. Keep in mind, however, that it can be upgraded with a SuperDrive and can use more than 8Mb of main memory. It also has six NuBus expansion slots, which is one reason that users tend to keep their Macintosh IIs and upgrade them. Although all Macintosh II configurations shipped with only one floppy drive, the box is big enough to install a second floppy drive without taking up space allocated for an internal hard disk. Presumably this is the reason that the Macintosh II has no connector for an external floppy disk drive.

Table 2.9 The Macintosh LC III

Microprocessor:	68030 running at 25Mhz
Math coprocessor:	Optional (FPU plugs into socket; does not take up expansion slot)
Main memory:	
RAM:	4 or 8Mb (expandable to 36Mb)
ROM:	512K
Floppy disk drive:	1.4Mb
Hard disk drive:	40, 80, 120, or 160Mb*
Drive configurations:	One floppy disk drive and one hard disk
Expansion slots:	One 030 processor direct slot
Keyboard options:	Standard keyboard included
Mouse:	ADB Mouse II included
Built-in video support:	Up to 16-inch color monitor (512K video RAM in all configurations, upgradable to 768K)
Ports:	Printer/AppleTalk network Modem SCSI ADB Audio (for connecting a single external speaker) Microphone External floppy disk drive

*The 120Mb hard disk is available only with the Performa 450.

Chapter 2: The Macintosh Product Line

The Macintosh IIx (see Table 2.11) was released in September 1968 as an incremental upgrade to the Macintosh II line. It provided a SuperDrive as well as a 68030 microprocessor. It also has room for a second internal floppy disk drive and no connector for an external floppy disk drive.

Macintosh IIcx

The Macintosh IIcx (*c* for *compact*) was the first three-slot Macintosh. Appearing in March 1989, it had most of the features of the IIx in a smaller, less expensive box (see Table 2.12). Because the smaller box doesn't have room for a second floppy disk drive, the IIcx included a connector for an external floppy disk drive.

Macintosh IIci

The Macintosh IIci (see Figure 2.4) is the successor to the IIcx. It made its debut in September 1989 and is the fastest of the three-slot Macintoshes and has therefore been used as an all-purpose machine for developing software and for business and home productivity. Nonetheless, speed tests indicate that the LC III is just as fast. However, when comparing the IIci against the LC III, consider more than just speed. The IIci (see Table 2.13), for example, has more slots and can accept more RAM.

Table 2.10 The Macintosh II

Status:	Discontinued
Microprocessor:	68020 running at 15.7Mhz
Math coprocessor:	Included
Main memory:	
RAM:	1 or 4Mb (expandable to 8Mb without additional hardware or software; expandable to 68Mb with original ROMs and Mode32 software; expandable to 128Mb with upgraded ROMs and Mode32 software)
ROM:	256K
Floppy disk drive:	800K (can be upgraded to 1.4Mb)
Hard disk drive:	40Mb
Drive configurations:	One floppy disk drive One floppy disk drive and one hard disk
Expansion slots:	Six NuBus slots
Keyboard options:	Any ADB keyboard
Mouse:	Included
Built-in video support:	None (must use NuBus video card)
Ports:	Printer/AppleTalk network Modem SCSI ADB Audio (for connecting a single external speaker)

Table 2.11 The Macintosh IIx

Microprocessor:	68030 running at 15.667Mhz
Math coprocessor:	Included
Main memory:	
RAM:	1 or 4Mb (expandable to 8Mb without additional software or hardware; expandable to 128Mb with the addition of Mode32 software)
ROM:	256K
Floppy disk drive:	1.4Mb
Hard disk drive:	40, 80, or 160Mb
Drive configurations:	One floppy disk drive One floppy disk drive and one hard disk
Expansion slots:	Six NuBus slots
Keyboard options:	Any ADB keyboard
Mouse:	Included
Built-in video support:	None (must use video card)
Ports:	Printer/AppleTalk network Modem SCSI ADB Audio (for connecting a single external speaker)

Fix Your Own Mac: Upgrading and Troubleshooting

Figure 2.4 The Macintosh IIci

Table 2.12 The Macintosh IIcx

Status:	Discontinued
Microprocessor:	68030 running at 15.667Mhz
Math coprocessor:	Included
Main memory:	
RAM:	1 or 4Mb (expandable to 8Mb without additional software; expandable to 128Mb with the addition of Mode32 software)
ROM:	256K
Floppy disk drive:	1.4Mb
Hard disk drive:	40 or 80Mb
Drive configurations:	
	One floppy disk drive
	One floppy disk drive and one hard disk
Expansion slots:	Three NuBus slots
Keyboard options:	Any ADB keyboard
Mouse:	Included
Built-in video support:	None (must use video card)
Ports:	
	Printer/AppleTalk network
	Modem
	SCSI
	ADB
	Audio (for connecting a single external speaker)
	External floppy drive

Chapter 2: The Macintosh Product Line

Macintosh IIsi

The IIsi (see Table 2.14) was released at the same time as the LC (October 1990), designed to be the lowest-priced Macintosh II. It has one expansion slot and built-in video support.

Macintosh IIvi, IIvx, and Performa 600

The IIvi, IIvx, and Performa 600 were designed to be multimedia machines. The IIvi (see Table 2.15) was the first Macintosh to include a configuration with a CD-ROM player. The IIvx (see Figure 2.5) and its mass market sibling, the Performa 600, are higher-performance Macintoshes with features similar to those first found in the IIvi (see Table 2.16). Released in October 1992, the IIvx is the only member of the Macintosh II line still being manufactured.

Notice that the CD-ROM configurations for all three machines include more video RAM than any previous Macintosh, providing support on the motherboard for thousands of colors.

▶ **Table 2.13** *The Macintosh IIci*

Status:	Discontinued
Microprocessor:	68030 running at 25Mhz
Math coprocessor:	Included
Main memory:	
RAM:	1 or 4Mb (expandable to 128Mb)
ROM:	512K
Floppy disk drive:	1.4Mb
Hard disk drive:	40 or 80Mb
Drive configurations:	
	One floppy disk drive
	One floppy disk drive and one hard disk
Expansion slots:	Three NuBus slots
Keyboard options:	Any ADB keyboard
Mouse:	Included
Built-in video support:	Supports up to 14-inch color monitor (512K video RAM)
Ports:	
	Printer/AppleTalk network
	Modem
	SCSI
	ADB
	Audio (for connecting a single speaker)

▶ **Table 2.14** *The Macintosh IIsi*

Status:	Discontinued
Microprocessor:	68030 running at 20MHz
Math coprocessor:	Included
Main memory:	
RAM:	2 or 5Mb (expandable to 65Mb)
ROM:	512K
Floppy disk drive:	1.4Mb
Hard disk drive:	40 or 80Mb
Drive configurations:	One floppy disk drive and one hard disk
Expansion slots:	One 030 processor direct slot (can be transformed into a NuBus slot by adding an adapter)
Keyboard options:	Any ADB keyboard
Mouse:	Included
Built-in video support:	Supports up to 14-inch color monitor (256K video RAM)
Ports:	
	Printer/AppleTalk network
	Modem
	SCSI
	ADB
	Stereo audio (for connecting external speakers)
	External floppy drive

Fix Your Own Mac: Upgrading and Troubleshooting

Figure 2.5 The Macintosh IIvx

Table 2.15 The Macintosh IIvi	
Status:	Discontinued
Microprocessor:	68030 running at 16MHz
Math coprocessor:	Optional
Main memory:	
RAM:	4Mb (expandable to 68Mb)
ROM:	512K
Floppy disk drive:	1.4Mb
Hard disk drive:	40 or 80Mb
Drive configurations:	One floppy disk drive and one hard disk One floppy disk drive, one hard disk, and one CD-ROM drive
Expansion slots:	Three NuBus slots One 030 processor direct slot
Keyboard options:	Any ADB keyboard
Mouse:	Included
Built-in video support:	Up to 256 colors on a 14-inch color monitor (512K video RAM in configurations without CD-ROM) Up to 32,000 colors on a 14-inch color monitor (1Mb video RAM in configuration with CD-ROM)
Ports:	Printer/AppleTalk network Modem SCSI ADB Audio (for connecting a single speaker) External floppy drive

Chapter 2: The Macintosh Product Line

> **Table 2.16** The Macintosh IIvx and Performa 600

Status:	Available
Microprocessor:	68030 running at 33MHz
Math coprocessor:	Included*
Main memory:	
RAM:	4 or 5Mb† (expandable to 68Mb)
ROM:	512K
Floppy disk drive:	1.4Mb
Hard disk drive:	80Mb or 230Mb‡
Drive configurations:	One floppy disk drive and one hard disk
	One floppy disk drive, one hard disk drive, one CD-ROM drive§
Expansion slots:	Three NuBus slots
	One 030 processor direct slot
Keyboard options:	Any ADB keyboard
Mouse:	Included
Built-in video support:	Up to 256 colors on a 14-inch color monitor (512K video RAM in configurations without CD-ROM)
	Up to 32,000 colors on a 14-inch color monitor (1Mb video RAM in configuration with CD-ROM)
Ports:	Printer/AppleTalk network
	Modem
	SCSI
	ADB
	Audio (for connecting a single speaker)
	External floppy drive

> **Table 2.16** Continued
>
> *The math coprocessor is optional with the Performa 600.
>
> †Configurations without CD-ROM have 4Mb RAM; configurations with CD-ROM have 5Mb RAM.
>
> ‡Some Performa 600s are available with hard drives up to 400Mb.
>
> §The IIvx CD-ROM configuration is available only with an 80Mb hard drive.

HIGH-END MODULAR MACINTOSHES

At the high end of the Macintosh line are machines with high clock speeds and other enhancements to make them fast performers. Such machines can be used as network servers or database servers. They also have enough power for processor-intensive tasks such as three-dimensional image rendering.

Macintosh IIfx

Until the emergence of the Quadras, the IIfx (see Table 2.17)—appearing in March 1990—was the fastest Macintosh. Although it was placed in the same six-slot box as the II and IIx, it contained several features not found in other Macintoshes to this date. In particular, it is one of only three Macintoshes ever to include a coprocessor for

Table 2.17 The Macintosh IIfx	
Status:	Discontinued
Microprocessor:	68030 running at 40MHz
Math coprocessor:	Included
Main memory:	
RAM:	4Mb (expandable to 128Mb)
ROM:	512K
Floppy disk drive:	1.4Mb
Hard disk drive:	80 or 160Mb
Drive configurations:	
	One floppy drive
	One floppy disk drive and one hard disk
Expansion slots:	
	Six NuBus slots
	One 030 processor direct slot
Keyboard options:	Any ADB keyboard
Mouse:	Included
Built-in video support:	None (video card required)
Ports:	
	Printer/AppleTalk network
	Modem
	SCSI
	ADB
	Audio (for connecting single speaker)

direct memory access (DMA). DMA allows input and output operations to occur directly between main memory and I/O devices, without the intervention of the CPU. Because the CPU doesn't have to take time to handle I/O, the overall performance of the computer is better.

The IIfx has another peculiarity not found in other Macintoshes—it uses its own type of SCSI termination. This causes problems with SCSI devices that are internally terminated. If the internal termination can't be removed (as in some older devices) and the IIfx-specific termination added externally, the hardware isn't compatible with the IIfx.

Macintosh Centris 610, 650 and 660av

The Centris line debuted in February 1993. Like the top-of-the line Quadras, the Centris 610, 660av, and 650 use the 68040 microprocessor. The 68040 has an internal architecture similar to that of the 68030 but contains some enhancements that give it extra speed. There are two versions of the 68040, one with an internal FPU, the other without.

The Centris 610 (see Table 2.18) is the entry-level 68040 computer (if any 68040 machine can ever be considered entry level). Two options that make it attractive for multimedia and network are the optional internal CD-ROM drive and Ethernet support.

Chapter 2: The Macintosh Product Line

The Centris 660av (announced August 1993) lives in a Centris 610 case. However, it contains special circuitry for multimedia processing. These circuits include video capture in NTSC (American) and PAL (European) formats and a digital signal processor (DSP) for voice recognition and speech synthesis. In addition, The Centris 660av provides direct memory access to speed I/O as well as a new type of serial port (a GeoPort).

By the way: The Centris 660av and the Quadra 840av are the first Macintoshes equipped to handle Apple's speaker-independent voice recognition technology. Called PlainTalk, speaker-independent voice recognition lets a Macintosh recognize spoken words and phrases from a variety of speakers without previously training the computer to recognize each voice.

The Centris 650 (see Figure 2.6) is an enhanced version of the 610 (see Table 2.19). It provides a faster microprocessor, supports an integrated FPU, and can accept more RAM. The availability of an internal CD-ROM player makes it yet another Macintosh designed for ease of use in multimedia applications. Notice that it is also more expandable than the 610, providing three NuBus slots in addition to the single processor direct slot found in the 610.

Table 2.18 The Macintosh Centris 610

Status:	Available
Microprocessor:	68040 running at 20MHz*
Math coprocessor:	Not available
Main memory:	
RAM:	4 or 8Mb (expandable to 68Mb)
ROM:	512K
Floppy disk drive:	1.4Mb
Hard disk drive:	80, 230, or 500Mb
Drive configurations:	
	One floppy disk drive and one hard disk
	One floppy disk drive, one hard disk, and one CD-ROM drive
Expansion slots:	One 040 processor direct slot (can be transformed into a NuBus slot by adding an adapter)
Keyboard options:	Any ADB keyboard
Mouse:	Included
Built-in video support:	Supports up to 16-inch color monitor (512K video RAM)
Ports:	
	Printer/AppleTalk network
	Ethernet (optional)
	Modem
	SCSI
	ADB
	Audio (for connecting a single speaker)

*The Centris 610 actually has a 68LC040, a version of the 68040 that cannot accept a math coprocessor.

Fix Your Own Mac: Upgrading and Troubleshooting

Figure 2.6 The Macintosh Centris 650

Table 2.19 The Macintosh Centris 650	
Status:	Available
Microprocessor:	68040 running at 25MHz*
Math coprocessor:	Optional†
Main memory:	
RAM:	4 or 8Mb (expandable to 132Mb)
ROM:	512K
Floppy disk drive:	1.4Mb
Hard disk drive:	80, 230, or 500Mb
Drive configurations:	
	One floppy disk drive and one hard disk
	One floppy disk drive, one hard disk, and one CD-ROM drive
Expansion slots:	
	Three NuBus slots
	One 040 processor direct slot
Keyboard options:	Any ADB keyboard
Mouse:	Included
Built-in video support:	
	Up to 256 colors on 14-inch color monitor (512K video RAM in configurations without CD-ROM) Up to 32,000 colors on 14-inch color monitor (1Mb video RAM in configurations with CD-ROM)
Ports:	
	Printer/AppleTalk network Ethernet (optional) Modem SCSI ADB Audio (for connecting a single speaker) Stereo mini headphone jack

> **Table 2.19** Continued

*The low-end configuration of the Centris 650 (4Mb RAM, 512K video RAM, 80Mb hard disk) has a 68LC040.

†An FPU is optional in the sense that if you purchase the low-end configuration with a 68LC040, an FPU isn't available. If you purchase either of the other configurations, then the Centris 650 has a standard 68040, which included an integrated FPU.Macintosh Quadra 700, 800, 900, and 950.

MACINTOSH QUADRAS

Until the release of the Power PCs some time in 1984, Quadras (the 700, 800, 840av, 900, and 950) represent the top of the Macintosh line. They are intended both for desktop use by individuals and for use as network and database servers. The Quadras were, for example, the first Macintoshes to offer built-in Ethernet support.

The Quadra 700 (see Table 2.20) was released in October 1991. Its major market was individual users who wanted fast performance on the desktop. Along with the Quadra 700, Apple released the Quadra 900 (see Table 2.21), a computer designed for network use.

The Quadra 950 (see Table 2.22) replaced the Quadra 900 in the Macintosh product line in May 1992. It includes a faster CPU but fewer SIMM slots (eight as opposed to 12 in the 900). Because of its speed and large internal hard disk capacity (230 or 400Mb), it is well suited for use as a network or database server or high-end graphics workstation.

> **Table 2.20** The Macintosh Quadra 700

Status:	Discontinued
Microprocessor:	68040 running at 25MHz
Math coprocessor:	Included
Main memory:	
RAM:	4Mb (expandable to 68Mb)
ROM:	512K
Floppy disk drive:	1.4Mb
Hard disk drive:	80 or 160Mb
Drive configurations:	
	One floppy disk drive
	One floppy disk drive and one hard disk
Expansion slots:	
	Two NuBus slots
	One 040 processor direct slot
Keyboard options:	Any ADB keyboard
Mouse:	Included
Built-in video support:	Supports up to 21-inch color monitor (512K video RAM upgradable to 2Mb)
Ports:	Printer/AppleTalk network Modem SCSI ADB Audio (for connecting a single speaker) Microphone

> **Table 2.21** The Macintosh Quadra 900

Status:	Discontinued
Microprocessor:	68040 running at 25MHz
Math coprocessor:	Included
Main memory:	
RAM:	4Mb (expandable to 256Mb)
ROM:	512K
Floppy disk drive:	1.4Mb
Hard disk drive:	160Mb
Drive configurations:	
	One floppy disk drive
	One floppy disk drive and one hard disk
Expansion slots:	
	Five NuBus slots
	One 040 processor direct slot
Keyboard options:	Any ADB keyboard
Mouse	Included
Built-in video support:	Supports up to 21-inch color monitor (512K video RAM upgradable to 2Mb)
Ports:	Printer/AppleTalk network Modem SCSI ADB Audio (for connecting a single speaker) Microphone

Fix Your Own Mac: Upgrading and Troubleshooting

▶ *Table 2.22* The Macintosh Quadra 950

Status:	Discontinued
Microprocessor:	68040 running at 33MHz
Math coprocessor:	Included
Main memory:	
RAM:	8Mb (expandable to 256Mb)
ROM:	512K
Floppy disk drive:	1.4Mb
Hard disk drive:	230 or 400Mb
Drive configurations:	
	One floppy disk drive
	One floppy disk drive and one hard disk
Expansion slots:	
	Five NuBus slots
	One 040 processor direct slot
Keyboard options:	Any ADB keyboard
Mouse:	Included
Built-in video support:	Supports up to 21-inch color monitor (1Mb video RAM upgradable to 2Mb)
Ports:	
	Printer/AppleTalk network
	Ethernet
	Modem
	SCSI
	ADB
	Audio (one port that delivers both stereo channels)
	Microphone

▶ *Figure 2.7* The Macintosh Quadra 800

The Quadra 800 (see Figure 2.7) is a recent addition to the Quadra line (February 1993). It more or less replaces the Quadra 700, although it is more powerful and flexible. Notice in Table 2.23 that it has a 33MHz CPU (as opposed to the 25MHz CPU in the 700) and that it has room in its case to install an internal CD-ROM player.

Chapter 2: The Macintosh Product Line

Table 2.23 The Macintosh Quadra 800

Status:	Available
Microprocessor:	68040 running at 33MHz
Math coprocessor:	Included
Main memory:	
RAM:	8Mb (expandable to 136Mb)
ROM:	512K
Floppy disk drive:	1.4Mb
Hard disk drive:	230* or 500Mb
Drive configurations:	One floppy disk drive One floppy disk drive and one hard disk
Expansion slots:	Three NuBus slots One 040 processor direct slot
Keyboard options:	Any ADB keyboard
Mouse:	Included
Built-in video support:	Up to 256 colors on a 16-inch color monitor (512K video RAM in configurations without a CD-ROM player) Up to 32,000 colors on a 16-inch color monitor or 256 colors on a 21-inch monitor (1Mb video RAM in configuration with a CD-ROM player)
Ports:	Printer/AppleTalk network Ethernet Modem SCSI ADB Audio (one port that delivers both stereo channels) Microphone

*The configuration with a CD-ROM player is available only with a 230Mb hard drive.

The Quadra 840av (announced August 1993) is built on the Quadra 800. Intended for heavy-duty multimedia use, it has a 40MHz rather than a 33MHZ 68040 and special circuits that enhance multimedia performance. Its video RAM can also be expanded to a full 2Mb. The Quadra 840av's special circuits include video capture circuitry for NTSC (American) and PAL (European) video and a digital signal processor chip for speaker-independent voice recognition and speech synthesis. (These are the same circuits found in the Centris 660av.) Like the Centris 660av, the Quadra 840av also includes DMA circuitry to speed I/O.

The Workgroup Servers

For some time business users have wanted Macintoshes specially tailored for use as network servers. Such machines don't necessarily need all the features that make a Macintosh intended for a single user easy and convenient to use. Apple has therefore reconfigured the Centris 610, Quadra 800, and Quadra 950 for network use. Collectively, these machines are known as the *Workgroup Servers*. (Apple is quick point out that *Macintosh* isn't part of the name of these computers.)

In terms of hardware configurations, the Workgroup Servers are little different from their parent machines. However, all three come bundled with A/UX (Apple's version of the UNIX operating system) and AppleShare share software, so that they can function as file and print servers right out of the box.

Portable/Laptop Macintoshes

For several years, Macintosh users watched with envy as their friends and coworkers who were using MS-DOS had access to smaller and smaller computers. A Macintosh user had to find a case for a 30-pound compact Macintosh, put it on a luggage cart, and lug. Airplane travel with such an arrangement was a formidable challenge. Even in a soft-sided case, a compact Mac is too big to fit under most airplane seats, too heavy to place in an overhead bin, and so bulky that it's difficult to convince flight attendants to place it in the bottom of a closet.

Prior to the release of the Macintosh Portable, a few vendors tried to satisfy Macintosh users' portable hunger by providing non-Apple portables that used Macintosh ROMs. (Initially, the purchaser had to obtain his/her own ROMs.) Such Macintosh compatibles," however, couldn't provide state-of-the-art performance or capabilities; they typically used ROMs from the previous generation of Macintoshes. (The success of the PowerBooks has driven the "compatible" makers out of the Macintosh portable business.) What Macintosh users really wanted was a real portable Macintosh.

The Macintosh Portable

The first portable Macintosh, simply called the Macintosh Portable (see Figure 2.8), was greeted with enormous enthusiasm. (There were actually two versions of the Macintosh Portable. The first had no light behind its display screen; the second had a back-lit display and 2Mb or 4Mb rather than 1Mb of RAM.) With the battery in place, it weighed about 17 pounds. Although it was considerably heavier than most portable computers, it was a real Macintosh (see Table 2.24), approximately comparable in speed and power to an SE.

The Portable included a separate power management processor designed to extend the computer's battery life. It turned off the hard drive (made it stop spinning) after a set period of inactivity. It could also send the computer to "sleep," sending just enough power to RAM to retain its contents.

Chapter 2: The Macintosh Product Line

Table 2.24 The Macintosh Portable

Status:	Discontinued
Microprocessor:	68000 running at 16MHz
Math coprocessor:	Not available
Rated battery life:	6 to 12 hours
Main memory:	
RAM:	1, 2, or 4Mb (expandable to 9Mb without backlit screen, 8Mb with backlit screen)
ROM:	256K
Floppy disk drive:	1.4Mb
Hard disk drive:	40Mb
Drive configurations:	
	One floppy disk drive
	One floppy disk drive and one hard disk
Expansion slots:	
	One modem slot
	One processor direct slot
Keyboard options:	Any ADB keyboard
Mouse:	
	Trackball built into unit
	External mouse included
Built-in display:	Monochrome active-matrix LCD
Ports:	
	Printer/AppleTalk network
	External floppy drive
	Modem
	SCSI
	ADB
	Audio (one port that delivers both stereo channels)
	Video (to connect video adapter for external monitors)

Figure 2.8 The Macintosh Portable

Fix Your Own Mac: *Upgrading and Troubleshooting*

Figure 2.9 *A Macintosh PowerBook*

Powerbooks

The biggest problem with the Macintosh Portable was that it was simply too heavy. (Try carrying 17 pounds of computer over your shoulder for very long!) In fact, the number of portable Macintoshes sold didn't become significant until Apple released the first PowerBook models. True laptop computers, the PowerBooks weigh between 5 and 10 pounds. There have been seven PowerBooks, spanning a wide range of microprocessors and display screen technology. (The PowerBook Duos, hybrid desktop and laptop machines, are discussed in the following sections.) At first glance, they appear very similar (see Figure 2.9).

The initial set of PowerBooks included three models, the 100, the 140, and the 170. Although inexpensive, the 100 (see Table 2.25) had several drawbacks. First, it had no internal floppy disk drive; it had to be connected to another Macintosh via its SCSI port to transfer files from either the other Macintoshes floppy drive or hard disk. Second, even though its supertwist LCD screen was backlit, it was not as clear as an active-matrix LCD. In addition, the 100's 68000 microprocessor was too slow for many users' needs.

Chapter 2: *The Macintosh Product Line*

▶ **Table 2.25** *The Macintosh PowerBook 100*

Status:	Discontinued
Microprocessor:	68000 running at 16MHz
Math coprocessor:	Not available
Modem:	Optional
Rated battery life:	2 to 4 hours
Main memory:	
RAM:	2 (expandable to 8Mb)
ROM:	256K
Floppy disk drive:	1.4Mb
Hard disk drive:	20Mb
Drive configurations:	One hard disk (no internal floppy disk drive)
Expansion slots:	None
Keyboard option:	Built into unit
Mouse:	Trackball built into unit
Built-in display:	Backlit monochrome supertwist LCD
Ports:	
	Printer/AppleTalk network/Modem
	External floppy drive
	SCSI
	ADB
	Audio (one port that delivers both stereo channels)

Apple expected the mid-range PowerBook (the 140, described in Table 2.26) to be its bestseller. The 140 had an internal hard floppy disk drive and a faster CPU than the 68000. However, it was still handicapped by the supertwist screen. As it turned out, it was the high-end PowerBook (the 170, described in Table 2.27) that was the most popular. Apple, caught by surprise, was unable to keep up with the demand. It seemed that Macintosh users wanted as much power as they could get into their briefcases! The 170 included an even faster microprocessor and an active-matrix display in place of the 100 and 140's supertwist screens.

▶ **Table 2.26** *The Macintosh PowerBook 140*

Status:	Discontinued
Microprocessor:	68030 running at 16MHz
Math coprocessor:	Optional
Modem:	Optional
Rated battery life:	2 to 3 hours
Main memory:	
RAM:	2 or 4Mb (expandable to 8Mb)
ROM:	256K
Floppy disk drive:	1.4Mb
Hard disk drive:	20 or 40Mb
Drive configuration:	One floppy disk drive and one hard disk
Expansion slots:	None
Keyboard option:	Built into unit
Mouse:	Trackball built into unit
Built-in display:	Backlit monochrome supertwist LCD
Ports:	
	Printer/AppleTalk network
	Modem
	SCSI
	ADB
	Audio (one port that delivers both stereo channels)
	Microphone

The second generation of PowerBooks (the 145, 160, and 180) replaced the original three models. The 145 and the lower-cost 145B (see Table 2.28) provide performance and features similar to the 170 but at the price of the 100. The 160 (see Table 2.29) is appealing to many users because it provides larger hard disks and a grayscale rather than a monochrome screen. The high end of the second-generation PowerBooks is the 180 (see Table 2.30). It has the fastest CPU of all the PowerBooks, comes with a grayscale active-matrix screen, and has a large hard disk.

By the way: Once the 100 was discontinued, the remaining stock was liquidated by mass market discount houses for under $800. That was the only time in the 100's history that it was in great demand!

Table 2.27 The Macintosh PowerBook 170

Status:	Discontinued
Microprocessor:	68030 running at 25MHz
Math coprocessor:	Included
Modem:	Included
Rated battery life:	2 to 3 hours
Main memory:	
RAM:	4Mb (expandable to 8Mb)
ROM:	256K
Floppy disk drive:	1.4Mb
Hard disk drive:	40Mb
Drive configuration:	One floppy disk drive and one hard disk
Expansion slots:	None
Keyboard option:	Built into unit
Mouse:	Trackball built into unit
Built-in display:	Backlit monochrome active-matrix LCD
Ports:	Printer/AppleTalk network Modem SCSI ADB Audio (one port that delivers both stereo channels) Microphone

Table 2.28 The Macintosh PowerBook 145 and 145B

Status:	Discontinued
Microprocessor:	68030 running at 25MHz
Math coprocessor:	Included
Modem:	Included
Rated battery life:	2 to 3 hours
Main memory:	
RAM:	4Mb (expandable to 8Mb)
ROM:	256K
Floppy disk drive:	1.4Mb
Hard disk drive:	40Mb or 80 Mb
Drive configuration:	One floppy disk drive and one hard disk
Expansion slots:	None
Keyboard option:	Built into unit
Mouse:	Trackball built into unit
Built-in display:	Backlit monochrome supertwist LCD
Ports:	Printer/AppleTalk network Modem SCSI ADB Audio (one port that delivers both stereo channels) Microphone

Chapter 2: The Macintosh Product Line

Although many users like the PowerBook 180's grayscale screen, others have been clamoring for a color PowerBook. The PowerBook 165c debuted in early 1993 with a passive-matrix color LCD screen. As you can see in Table 2.31, the 165c is essentially a 180 with a color screen. There are two drawbacks to the 165c's color screen. First, because it is a passive- rather than an active-matrix screen, images aren't as bright as they are on the 180's grayscale screen. Second, the color screen requires more power than a grayscale or monochrome screen, significantly reducing the computer's battery life. Although the 165c's battery is rated at 1.5 to 2 hours, some reviewers have only been able to make it last about an hour.

Table 2.29 The Macintosh PowerBook 160

Status:	Available
Microprocessor:	68030 running at 25MHz
Math coprocessor:	Optional
Modem:	Optional
Rated battery life:	2.5 to 3 hours
Main memory:	
RAM:	4Mb (expandable to 14Mb)
ROM:	256K
Floppy disk drive:	1.4Mb
Hard disk drive:	40, 80, or 120Mb
Drive configuration:	One floppy disk drive and one hard disk
Expansion slots:	None
Keyboard option:	Built into unit
Mouse:	Trackball built into unit
Built-in display:	Backlit grayscale super-twist LCD
Ports:	
	Printer/AppleTalk network
	Modem
	SCSI
	ADB
	Audio (one port that delivers both stereo channels)
	Microphone
	External video

Table 2.30 The Macintosh PowerBook 180

Status:	Available
Microprocessor:	68030 running at 33MHz
Math coprocessor:	Included
Modem:	Optional
Rated battery life:	2.5 to 3 hours
Main memory:	
RAM:	4Mb (expandable to 14Mb)
ROM:	256K
Floppy disk drive:	1.4Mb
Hard disk drive:	80 or 120Mb
Drive configuration:	One floppy disk drive and one hard disk
Expansion slots:	None
Keyboard option:	Built into unit
Mouse:	Trackball built into unit
Built-in display:	Backlit grayscale active-matrix LCD
Ports:	
	Printer/AppleTalk network
	Modem
	SCSI
	ADB
	Audio (one port that delivers both stereo channels)
	Microphone
	External video (to drive external monitor or projection panel)

> **Table 2.31** The Macintosh PowerBook 165c

Status:	Available
Microprocessor:	68030 running at 33MHz
Math coprocessor:	Included
Modem:	Optional
Rated battery life:	1.5 to 2 hours
Main memory:	
RAM:	4Mb (expandable to 14Mb)
ROM:	256K
Floppy disk drive:	1.4Mb
Hard disk drive:	80 or 160Mb
Drive configuration:	One floppy disk drive and one hard disk
Expansion slots:	None
Keyboard option:	Built into unit
Mouse:	Trackball built into unit
Built-in display:	Backlit color passive-matrix LCD
Ports:	Printer/AppleTalk network Modem SCSI ADB Audio (one port that delivers both stereo channels) Microphone External video (to drive external monitor or projection panel)

As much as PowerBook purchasers wanted a color laptop, the 165c's passive-matrix screen did not seem to satisfy. Many people wanted to wait for the brighter, sharper screen of an active-matrix LCD. That machine, the PowerBook 180c, appeared in June 1993. It is virtually the same as a 180 but with the color screen. Its major drawback is that the active-matrix LCD draws large amounts of power. Without an external battery pack, the 180c cannot run much more than an hour without a recharge.

Hybrid Machines: The PowerBook Duos

Some users want the portability of a PowerBook but the power and expandability of a desktop machine. The PowerBook Duos are one answer to that need. Each Duo model is a PowerBook that can be docked" into a desktop unit (the Duo Dock or Duo MiniDock) that provides room for an internal hard disk, support for external monitors (including 512K video RAM that can be expanded to 1Mb), NuBus expansion slots, and connectors such as an SCSI port typically found on desktop Macintoshes.

There are two PowerBooks designed for docking: the Duo 210 and Duo 230. Notice that although the Duo 210 (see Table 2.32) can accept more RAM than any other PowerBook, it has no internal floppy disk drive. To gain access to a floppy disk, it must be connected to a Dock or to an external floppy disk drive specially designed for a PowerBook Duo. The Duo 230 (see Table 2.33) is an enhanced version of the Duo 210. It provides a slightly faster CPU and a grayscale screen.

Chapter 2: The Macintosh Product Line

▶ **Table 2.32** *The Macintosh PowerBook Duo 210*

Status:	Available
Microprocessor:	68030 running at 25MHz
Math coprocessor:	Optional
Internal modem:	None available
Rated battery life:	2 to 4.5 hours
Main memory:	
RAM:	4Mb (expandable to 24Mb)
ROM:	256K
Floppy disk drive:	None
Hard disk drive:	80Mb
Drive configuration:	One hard disk
Expansion slots:	None
Keyboard option:	Built into unit
Mouse:	Trackball built into unit
Built-in display:	Backlit monochrome supertwist LCD
Ports:	Printer/AppleTalk network Modem PDS connector (used to connect the PowerBook to a Dock)

▶ **Table 2.33** *The PowerBook Duo 230*

Status:	Available
Microprocessor:	68030 running at 33MHz
Math coprocessor:	Optional
Modem:	None available
Rated battery life:	2 to 4.5 hours
Main memory:	
RAM:	4Mb (expandable to 24Mb)
ROM:	256K
Floppy disk drive:	None
Hard disk drive:	80 or 120Mb
Drive configuration:	One hard disk
Expansion slots:	None
Keyboard option:	Built into unit
Mouse:	Trackball built into unit
Built-in display:	Backlit grayscale active-matrix LCD
Ports:	Printer/AppleTalk network Modem PDS connector (used to connect the PowerBook to a Dock)

A First Look at Upgrading

Deciding whether to use your Macintosh just as it is, to upgrade, or to purchase a new computer isn't always an easy decision (see Figure 3.1). You need to take into consideration not only the cost of upgrading or replacing but also the amount of increased computing capacity received from the upgraded or new machine. As you will see, some inexpensive upgrades can bring as much increased computing capacity as something more expensive.

This chapter looks at the types of upgrades available for a Macintosh as well as their relative costs and benefits. It also looks at ways for deciding when and whether to upgrade and what you can do if you decide *not* to upgrade. In addition, the final sections of this chapter provide instructions for opening a Macintosh to install an upgrade.

Types of Upgrades

There are eight types of upgrades that you might choose to add to your Macintosh:

- **RAM:** The most common type of Macintosh upgrade is adding RAM. RAM upgrades are among the most inexpensive upgrades and yet can provide a significant increase in computing capacity. With added RAM you can run more programs concurrently (assuming you are using System 7 or MultiFinder under System 6), run larger programs, and handle larger document files. You might also decide to set aside extra RAM as a RAM disk, speeding disk access while you are working. Almost every Macintosh could use a RAM upgrade. Under System 7, the 4Mb of RAM standard with most of today's Mac models is just not enough. RAM upgrades are covered in depth in Chapter 5.

- **CPU:** A CPU upgrade (usually achieved by adding an *accelerator board*) replaces the computer's CPU with a faster microprocessor. (It's like giving your Macintosh a brain transplant.) CPU upgrades are rela-

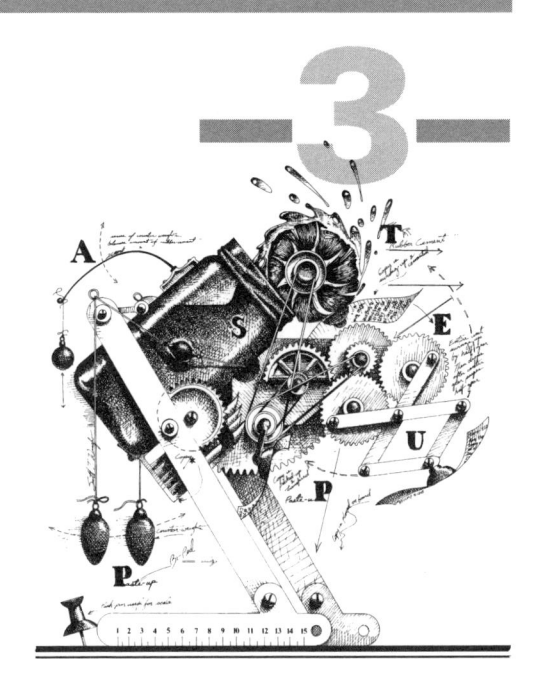

Figure 3.1 Upgrading your Mac—avoiding obsolescence

tively expensive but can provide significantly faster performance. CPU upgrades are covered in Chapter 6.

- **Instruction cache:** An *instruction cache* is a small amount of fast RAM used to speed program execution. Instruction caches are relatively expensive. However, like CPU upgrades, they can help achieve faster overall performance. You can find more about caches in Chapter 7.

- **Math coprocessor (FPU):** A math coprocessor is an inexpensive upgrade that can speed up operations involving floating-point numbers. If you don't do a lot of number crunching, then adding an FPU won't have much effect on system performance. Details on FPUs appear in Chapter 7.

- **Pages memory management unit (PMMU):** To use virtual memory a Macintosh needs a PMMU. A 68000 Mac cannot accept one; PMMU circuitry is built into the 68030 and 68040. However, one can be added as an upgrade to a 68020 Mac. You can find more about virtual memory and PMMUs in Chapter 7.

- **Logic board:** If giving your Macintosh a new CPU is like giving it a brain transplant, then replacing your Mac's logic board is like an entire body transplant. A logic board upgrade means that you replace your Mac's motherboard with the motherboard of a newer model, effectively turning your computer into the newer model. A logic board upgrade is just about the most expensive type of system unit upgrade. However, it is considerably less expensive than buying a new computer. Logic board upgrades are discussed in Chapter 8.

- **Power supply:** Many components, including main memory, internal disk drives, and expansion boards, get their power from the Macintosh's internal power supply. Some Macintoshes don't have enough power to drive the computer when expansions slots begin to fill up. If you have one of those Macintoshes, a larger power supply may be necessary if you are going to add multiple upgrades. You can find details about power supplies in Chapter 9.

- **Disk drives:** Disk drive upgrades fall into several categories. First, you can add an external hard disk. Second, you can exchange your internal hard disk for a larger one. Third, some Macintoshes with 800K floppy disk drives can be upgraded to a

SuperDrive; you might also want to add a second floppy drive. Most disk drive upgrades bring added external storage for a reasonable price, but only small performance gains. However, Macintoshes with NuBus slots can accept expansion boards containing SCSI accelerators. A SCSI accelerator can provide both faster disk access and a second SCSI controller, letting you have 14 rather than seven SCSI devices. Disk drives designed specifically to work with these accelerators provide significantly faster disk access. However, such expansion board/disk drive combinations tend to be expensive.

Upgrading disk storage is discussed in depth in Chapter 10.

- **Video:** To be brutally honest, unless you are working with color graphics (for print or multimedia), photo retouching, or desktop publishing, you don't really *need* anything other than a black-and-white monitor. However, there's no question that color makes everything from game playing to word processing a lot easier and more fun. For Macintoshes that have video support on the motherboard, you can increase the number of colors or shades of gray and the size of the monitor your Mac can handle by adding video RAM. If your Mac doesn't have video support on the motherboard, you can increase the number of colors or shades of gray and the size of the monitor you can use by changing an expansion board. Macs with multiple expansion slots also support more than one monitor.

Video upgrades are also available for Macintoshes that don't have expansion slots. In other words, you can add an external monitor to a Mac such as a Plus or Classic. Installing this type of upgrade is more difficult than simply adding an expansion board to a Macintosh with slots. It sometimes involves cutting a hole in the case and plugging at least one chip into the motherboard.

Video upgrades are covered in Chapter 11.

MAKING THE CHOICE TO UPGRADE

Deciding when to upgrade and exactly what upgrades to purchase is both an art and a science. For many people, the *when* to upgrade turns into *now* when it suddenly seems that the computer that was once perfect has become a source of frustration. The source of that frustration might be hardware related: You don't have enough memory to run the applications you need; it takes too long to do something; you've run out of disk space; disk access takes too long; your screen takes too long to update; you don't have enough colors or shades of gray on the monitor to create the graphics you need. The impetus to upgrade can also be triggered because you can't run the latest version of the Macintosh operating system or can't take advantage of some of its features. You may even simply decide that your Macintosh is getting too out of date and that unless you upgrade soon, it'll be so out of date you'll run into problems.

There are two philosophies about when to upgrade, both of which have validity. Some people believe that you shouldn't upgrade until you actually have a need to do so. This conservative strategy means that you don't spend money until you really have to. Over time, upgrades for a given model also tend to become cheaper. The major drawback is that if you wait too long to upgrade, the upgrade may no longer be available. For example, it's now too late to get the 800K disk drive/ROM upgrade that turns a Mac 512K into a 512Ke. Your Mac also becomes increasingly out of date, unable to handle current software demands.

By the way: To be totally accurate, the 800K/ROM upgrade is no longer available from Apple. However, if you're persistent, you may be able to find a dealer in used Macintoshes and Macintosh parts who has one to sell you. More about upgrading older Macs can be found in Appendix A; a list of used Macintosh dealers can be found in Appendix B.

The second upgrade strategy is to upgrade as soon as a new model makes your Macintosh obsolete or a new technology becomes available. The big advantage to doing this is that your computer is always up to date. There are, however, a couple of drawbacks. First, like any type of electronics, upgrades cost more when they are first brought to market. Second, there may be software incompatibilities with some upgrades. For example, when the 68040 first appeared (in the Quadras and on accelerator boards), a lot of existing Macintosh software wouldn't run. People who wanted to upgrade their CPUs were wise to wait until software manufacturers had upgraded their products to run on the new microprocessor.

Given that you've reached the point where you want to upgrade, which upgrades you can add depends on your Macintosh. By the same token, whether you should upgrade depends on a combination of your current Macintosh model, your computing needs, and the cost of upgrading versus the cost of purchasing a new computer.

Upgrading 68000 Macs

Given the technology of today's Macintoshes, a Macintosh with a 68000 microprocessor is at a significant disadvantage. It can address only 16Mb of memory (only 8 of which are available to the user), virtual memory isn't available, and it's dreadfully slow. It also can't use a math coprocessor or a color or grayscale monitor. Although most current software will run on a 68000, the performance of many programs is unacceptably slow. Any 68000 Mac is therefore a prime candidate for upgrading or replacing.

Options for the Mac Plus

Once the computer of choice for desktop publishing, the Mac Plus has fallen far behind current technology. Although it can still be a useful computer, its standard configuration of 1Mb RAM is far too small to run most of today's application software. At best, you can run System 6 without MultiFinder and one moderate-sized application.

If you want to run System 7 or use MultiFinder with System 6, you must add some RAM. Adding RAM is a relatively cheap upgrade and buys you more computing capacity for your money than any other upgrade. To bring the Mac Plus to its maximum 4Mb RAM costs around $125. (You must remove the existing 256K SIMMs and replace them with 1Mb SIMMs.) If you intend to keep your Mac Plus, then adding RAM is the least you should do.

However, deciding whether you should add more than RAM to a Plus is not easy. To give a Plus the approximate functionality of a Classic II requires the components in Table 3.1. Notice that the upgrades include replacing the power supply. The power supplies in older compact Macs (the Plus and earlier models) are notorious for being the source of many problems. If you are going to load your Plus with upgrades other than RAM, then it is almost certain that the power supply will be strained and eventually fail. It is often wiser to replace it at the same time you upgrade the machine. In addition, the Mac Plus has no internal fan, and upgrade boards generate more heat than the Plus can dissipate. You'll therefore need to add a fan of some type. Also keep in mind that regardless of what you add to a Mac Plus, it still has the Mac Plus ROMs. These ROMs, for example, don't contain the routines to support color monitors.

By the way: The cost figures in the tables throughout this chapter were current at the time this book went to press. A price of $800 was used whenever a CPU accelerator was included in a total, representing a fast 68030 CPU with an FPU. Nonetheless, keep in mind that electronics costs generally go down over time (both computers and upgrades). The major exception is SIMM prices. The cost of SIMMs is very volatile. Since the introduction of the Macintosh, 1Mb SIMMs have cost as much as $400 and as little as $25. At the time this book went to press, SIMM prices were rising, but there is no way to predict which way prices will have moved when you are reading this.

As you can see, the total cost of the suggested upgrades is more than the cost of purchasing either a Classic II (without external monitor) or an LC III (with an external monitor). (Table 3.1 doesn't even include the cost of adding more than 4Mb RAM to an accelerator board!) You can bring down the cost of upgrading somewhat by purchasing a combination upgrade board. For example, the

Table 3.1 Upgrade Options for the Macintosh Plus

Type of Upgrade	Benefits	Drawbacks	Cost
RAM	More/larger programs in memory. Can use System 7	Limit of 4Mb still isn't enough for comfortable System 7 use	$125
CPU accelerator	Increased performance Allows use of math coprocessor Allows use of virtual memory Allows installation of more than 4Mb RAM		$300–$2,000
Video	Lets you use a larger monitor	May require cutting a hole in the case Can't display color	$750[†]
Power supply	Avoids problems that occur with older Plus power supplies Supports added components		$200
External SuperDrive	Reads/writes 1.44Mb disks	Slow	$400
Fan	Keeps components cool		$40
Total (without monitor)			**$1,565**
Total (with monitor)			**$2,315**

*This price includes a math coprocessor (FPU).
†This price includes a full-page monochrome monitor.

ImagePro board (produced by Systech, distributed by Peripheral Outlet) contains a 68030 accelerator (16MHz, 25MHz, 33MHz, or 50MHz) and adapter circuitry for an external monitor. The board sells for around $900. Add a full-page display for around $400 and your total upgrade cost is down to $2,025 (with external monitor). Nonetheless, this is still more than replacing the computer with a Color Classic or an LC III with a color monitor.

Should you upgrade a Mac Plus (beyond adding RAM)? The answer is, "It depends." If you are going to use the computer for light word processing, spreadsheet use, or telecommunications, then it can continue to serve you as is for some time. It makes an excellent computer for students going to college or clerical workers who do little more than word processing. The most you should need to do to keep a Plus going is replace the battery and the power supply. A Mac Plus can also be used on an AppleTalk network as an e-mail or fax server, where speed isn't critical.

By the way: You know it's time to replace the battery when the Mac begins to forget the date and time.

On the other hand, graphics and desktop publishing require lots of memory and large monitors (often color monitors). Data management and financial analysis require a fast CPU and often an FPU. If those are types of applications for which you use your Mac, then upgrading a Plus probably doesn't make sense. Your money will be better spent purchasing a replacement machine.

Options for the SE

An unmodified Macintosh SE is in relatively the same shape as a Mac Plus. It can accept only 4Mb of RAM, has a slow CPU, can't accept an FPU or use virtual memory, and doesn't support color. Nonetheless, an SE is easier to upgrade than a Plus. It has a processor direct slot that can accept an accelerator board, a board for an external monitor, or a network board. It also has a more robust power supply.

If you plan to keep your SE, you should at least add enough RAM to bring it to the maximum of 4Mb. However, as you can see in Table 3.2, bringing an SE to Classic II functionality is close to the cost of a Classic II if you already have an internal SuperDrive; if you don't, the upgrade costs more. With or without the internal SuperDrive, upgrading an SE to use an external monitor generally costs more than replacing it with an LC III and a color monitor.

Should you upgrade? It depends on how you intend to use the computer. Assuming the computer has the maximum 4Mb

RAM, an unmodified SE makes an excellent computer for a student or for light clerical work. Like an unmodified Plus, it can also be used on an AppleTalk network as an e-mail or fax server. If you install an Ethernet board (less than $200) in the SE's processor direct slot, it can also function on an Ethernet network.

On the other hand, for uses that require higher-end processing or color support (data management, financial analysis, graphics, desktop publishing, and so on), upgrading probably doesn't make economic sense. Just adding an accelerator still leaves a computer with a 9-inch monitor that can't support color. By the time you add an external monitor, total upgrade costs are beyond those of purchasing a new computer.

Options for the Mac Classic

The Mac Classic shares the drawbacks of the Plus and SE (for example, limited RAM capacity and a slow CPU) but comes with one major advantage:

Table 3.2 Upgrade Options for the Macintosh SE

Type of Upgrade	Benefits	Drawbacks	Cost
RAM	More/larger programs in memory Can use System 7	Limit of 4Mb still isn't enough for comfortable System 7 use	$125
CPU accelerator*	Increased performance Allows use of math coprocessor Allows use of virtual memory Allows installation of more than 4Mb RAM		$300–$2,000
Video	Lets you use a larger monitor	Can't display color	$750
Internal SuperDrive†	Reads/writes 1.44Mb disks		$385
Total (without SuperDrive upgrade/without monitor)			**$925**
Total (with SuperDrive upgrade/without monitor)			**$1,310**
Total (without SuperDrive upgrade/with monitor)			**$1,675**
Total (with SuperDrive upgrade/with monitor)			**$2,060**

*The logic board upgrade (SE to SE/30) is no longer available. If you want to upgrade an SE's CPU, you must now purchase a third-party accelerator.

†The early SEs were shipped with 800K floppy drives. After the introduction of the SE/30, SEs were also shipped with the SuperDrive. If you have one of these later SEs, then you don't need this upgrade.

Because it is a recent computer, a logic board upgrade is available. On the other hand, because it has no expansion slots, it is as difficult to upgrade as the Plus.

As with the Plus and SE, any Classic that you intend to keep should be upgraded to the maximum 4Mb RAM. Unfortunately, 4Mb is really too little RAM to run System 7 comfortably. Therefore if you want to use your Classic for high-end applications (for example, color/grayscale graphics, financial analysis, data management, or desktop publishing), you should consider a CPU upgrade. Many third-party accelerator boards are available. The logic board upgrade, which turns the Classic into a Classic II, is also available and is generally cheaper than a CPU accelerator. However, the Classic II is limited to 10Mb RAM, whereas many accelerators can accept more. In addition, the Classic II's 68030 runs at only 16MHz; CPU accelerators are available at 25MHz and 33MHz.

If you need a larger monitor, you can add a video board to the Classic. Keep in mind, however, that because the Classic has no expansion slots, adding that board may mean cutting a hole in the case or

Table 3.3 *Upgrade Options for the Macintosh Classic*

Type of Upgrade	Benefits	Drawbacks	Cost
RAM	More/larger programs in memory Can use System 7	Limit of 4Mb still isn't enough for comfortable System 7 use	$125
CPU accelerator	Increased performance Allows use of math coprocessor Allows use of virtual memory Allows installation of more than 4Mb RAM		$300–$2,000
Logic board	Turns Classic into Classic II	Includes only 2Mb RAM Limit of 10Mb RAM	$630
Video	Lets you use a larger monitor	Can't display color	$750
Total (with CPU accelerator/without monitor)			**$925**
Total (with logic board replacement/without monitor)			**$580**
Total (with CPU accelerator/with monitor)			**$1,675**
Total (with logic board replacement/with monitor)			**$1,505**

purchasing a new case. In addition, as Table 3.3 reveals, upgrading a Classic to a Classic II plus adding an external monitor (monochrome only) costs more than a Color Classic and approaches the price of an LC III with a color monitor.

Options for the Mac Portable

When the Mac Portable debuted, hordes of Macintosh users starved for a portable Mac cheered. The cheering lasted about as long as it took to find out how heavy the Portable got when it was carried for more than 10 minutes. The Portable, especially the model with the backlit screen, is nonetheless as usable as an unmodified Mac Classic. Unfortunately, it isn't as upgradable.

The Portable can actually use up to 9Mb of RAM, but upgrades above 4Mb are only available from third-party vendors. To make matters worse, Portable RAM is very expensive (see Table 3.4). Beyond RAM, the Portable can accept an internal modem but not much else. If you have a Portable and find it useful, go ahead and stay with it. However, bringing the RAM to more than 4Mb costs more than replacing the Portable with a low-end PowerBook.

Possibly the best upgrade you can give your Portable is a luggage cart ($25 to $50). Putting it on wheels will relieve your shoulder muscles and make you much more tolerant of the Portable's shortcomings while you're saving your pennies for a PowerBook.

Options for the PowerBook 100

When it was a "current" model, the PowerBook 100 didn't sell very well. Once it was discontinued and Apple sold off its remaining inventory at fire sale prices, people suddenly discovered that it wasn't such a bad computer after all, even if it didn't have a built-in floppy drive. If you happen to own one, there are several things you can do to make it more usable.

As with any other Mac, you should add some RAM. PowerBook memory is relatively affordable, although more expen-

Table 3.4 Upgrade Options for the Macintosh Portable

Type of Upgrade	Benefits	Drawbacks	Cost
RAM	More/larger programs in memory	Very expensive	(9Mb) $1,500
Internal modem	Easy telecommunications	Can't be transferred to any other Mac	$360
Total			**$1,750**

sive than that for other Macs (see Table 3.5). In addition, you may want the external floppy disk drive. If you don't want to spend the $200 on the external floppy drive, you'll need the SCSI adapter that lets the 100 appear like an external hard disk to another Mac. Without either the external floppy drive or the SCSI adapter, you'll have no way to get files onto the 100's hard disk or to back up files you've created. In addition, if you find the trackball difficult to use, you can purchase a mouse.

Upgrading 68020 Macs

Only two Macintoshes—the II and the LC—used the 68020 microprocessor. The 68020 is significantly faster than the 68000, can use a math coprocessor, and with the addition of a PMMU (paged memory management unit) can use virtual memory. Nonetheless, the 68020 is much slower than the 68030 and 68040. In general, the II and LC run too slowly for many of today's high-end application programs.

Options for the Macintosh LC

The LC is a useful but handicapped machine. It has the relatively slow 68020 microprocessor, is limited to 10Mb of RAM, has no socket for a PMMU (preventing it from using virtual memory), is underpowered, and has only one expansion slot. (The reason for the 10Mb RAM limit is discussed in Chapter 5.)

▶ *Table 3.5 Upgrade Options for the PowerBook 100*

Type of Upgrade	Benefits	Drawbacks	Cost
RAM	More/larger programs in memory		$150 (4Mb)
			$200 (6Mb)
SCSI disk adapter	Lets PowerBook 100 be used as an external hard disk by any SCSI-equipped Mac		$40
External SuperDrive	Provides floppy disk access without needing to connect the PowerBook to another Mac		$200
Mouse	Provides an alternative to the built-in trackball		$80
Total (4Mb RAM)			**$470**
Total (6Mb RAM)			**$520**

If you plan to keep your LC, you should at least add enough RAM to bring it to the maximum 10Mb. Beyond that, you should consider carefully whether it makes sense to use it as it is, upgrade it, or replace it with an LC III. (Keep in mind that if you replace the computer, you can use the monitor you are already using with the LC.) An unmodified LC (assuming that it has the maximum 10Mb RAM) is a useful, albeit slow, computer. Although it can't take advantage of virtual memory, it can run System 7 comfortably and has no problems with most of today's application programs. However, you may find that some software runs too slowly for the computer to be practical for high-end graphics, financial analysis, desktop publishing, or database work.

If you decide to upgrade, you can add an FPU for faster arithmetic operations, a CPU accelerator, video RAM (if you don't already have the maximum 512K), and a larger power supply. You may also want to add an expansion chassis, which provides a second power supply, room for another hard drive, and multiple processor direct slots. Nonetheless, the cost, including an expansion chassis, is more than the cost of the LC III; excluding the expansion chassis, it is similar to the cost of the LC III (see Table 3.6).

An alternative to adding a CPU accelerator is to replace the LC's motherboard with an LC III motherboard. This logic board upgrade provides the faster CPU (a 68030 with an integrated PMMU), virtual memory support, access to more than 10Mb RAM, and a socket for an FPU. Having a socket for an FPU means that you don't have to take up the single processor direct slot with an FPU on a card, as you do with the standard LC. Installing the logic board upgrade and an expansion chassis is about the cost of purchasing an LC III. The only drawback to the logic board upgrade is that it uses different SIMMs from the LC; you won't be able to transfer any SIMMs from the LC motherboard to the LC III motherboard. Nonetheless, if you decide to forgo the expansion chassis, you can still get away for less than the cost of a new machine.

By the way: A logic board upgrade to bring an LC to an LC II is also available. But given the increased performance of the LC III and the fact that the LC II logic board upgrade costs more than the LC III logic board upgrade, going to an LC II doesn't make much sense.

Table 3.6 Upgrade Options for the Macintosh LC

Type of Upgrade	Benefits	Drawbacks	Cost
RAM	More/larger programs in memory		(to maximum 10Mb) $270
FPU	Speeds up math operations		$80
CPU	Increased performance Allows use of math coprocessor Allows use of virtual memory		$300–$2,000
Logic board	Turns computer into LC III		$600
Video RAM	More colors/shades of gray		$80
Power supply	Power for expansion boards		$200
Expansion chassis	More slots and therefore more upgrade options		$350+
Total (with CPU accelerator/without expansion chassis)			**$1,200**
Total (with logic board upgrade/without expansion chassis)			**$1,030**
Total (with CPU accelerator/with expansion chassis)			**$1,580**
Total (with logic board upgrade/with expansion chassis)			**$1,380**

Options for the Macintosh II

The Macintosh II, the first modular Mac, is one of the most upgradable Macs. Its box has six slots and room for both a hard disk and two floppy drives. It also has a very robust power supply. With some judicious upgrading, a Mac II can be made to perform as well as or better than a Quadra 700 for less than $2,000. If you need a lot of expansion capability, then an upgraded Mac II may be a better choice than some of the newer members of the Macintosh line.

By the way: There is still a good market for Mac IIs. For example, a Mac II with a 50MHz 68030 accelerator, FPU, 8Mb RAM, and 80Mb hard disk sells for around $2,800.

If you have a Mac II, you should probably keep it. To bring it up to date, there are two essential upgrades. The first is the internal SuperDrive/ROM upgrade. This upgrade not only adds the 1.44Mb floppy drive, but includes new ROMs that let the Mac II access more than 20Mb RAM (up to 128Mb, assuming you fill all eight SIMM slots with 16Mb SIMMS). The second essential upgrade is a CPU accelerator. You can get a 50MHz 68030 with an FPU for as little as $800; 68040 accelerators will run more but can bring even better performance. Assuming you already have enough RAM, then the floppy drive and CPU upgrades run about $1,185 (see Table 3.7), far less than the cost of any of the current high-performance Macintoshes.

Because the Mac II has plenty of slots, you might consider adding a second monitor or exchanging your current video card for one that can handle more colors or shades of gray.

An alternative to adding the CPU accelerator is to exchange the Mac II motherboard for a IIfx motherboard. The IIfx provides a 40MHz 68030 and direct memory access capabilities; an FPU is included. There are, however, some drawbacks to the IIfx. First, it requires special SIMMs. You won't be able to transfer your Mac II SIMMs to the IIfx

Table 3.7 Upgrade Options for the Macintosh II

Type of Upgrade	Benefits	Drawbacks	Cost
RAM	More/larger programs in memory	Limited to 20Mb without SuperDrive upgrade	$750
PMMU*	Allows use of virtual memory		$100
CPU	Increased performance		$300–$2,000
Logic board	Turns computer into IIfx	Requires special SIMMs Requires special SCSI termination	$1,799
Internal SuperDrive	Reads/writes 1.44Mb disks		$385
ROM	Allows access to >20Mb RAM		
Video	Larger work surface More colors/shades of gray		$1,200–$3,000
Total (with CPU accelerator)			**$1,665**
Total (with logic board upgrade)			**$3,415**

*Required to let 68020 use virtual memory. Not necessarily required if a CPU accelerator (68030 or 68040) or logic board upgrade is added to the machine.

logic board; you'll have to purchase new ones. Second, the IIfx uses a type of SCSI termination not found in any other Mac. At the very least, you will need to replace all your SCSI terminators; if you have any devices with internal termination, you must remove the termination and add a special IIfx external terminator. If the internal termination can't be removed from a SCSI device, then you can't use it with the IIfx. Finally, the IIfx logic board upgrade is extremely expensive, costing far more than upgrading the machine with a SuperDrive/ROM upgrade and a CPU accelerator.

Upgrading 68030 Macs

Many of the 68030 Macs provide good performance and have excellent upgrade potential. In most cases, it makes sense to keep your older 68030 Mac and upgrade it. Nonetheless, the performance of 68030 Macs varies a great deal. As you may remember from Chapter 1, the speed of the 68030 used in Macintosh models varies from 16MHz to 40MHz (accelerator boards are available with 50MHz 68030s). If your '030 isn't peppy enough, you may decide to add an accelerator board (perhaps a 68040), along with an FPU, an instruction cache card, and a larger monitor.

Options for the Macintosh SE/30

The SE/30 is a relatively fast machine (much faster than the Classic II that theoretically replaced it in the Macintosh product line). Although it can accept any

Table 3.8 Upgrade Options for the Macintosh SE/30

Type of Upgrade	Benefits	Drawbacks	Cost
RAM	More/larger programs in memory		(to 8Mb) $256
			(to 16Mb) $472
			(to 32Mb) $896
			(to 128Mb) $3,832
CPU	Increased performance		$300–$2,000
Video	Larger monitor		$800–$3,000
	Color video		
Expansion chassis	Adds NuBus slots		$1,295
Sample total (32Mb RAM/no expansion chassis)			**$2,469**

number of CPU accelerators, you may find that its unmodified performance is quite acceptable. In that case, consider adding lots of RAM and an external monitor. The costs, for example, for 32Mb RAM and external monitor and card run less than $2,000 (see Table 3.8). Unlike other compact Macs except the Color Classic, the SE/30 does support color when a color video board and color monitor are attached. If you need additional expansion capabilities, an expansion chassis—although rather expensive—is available to add four to eight NuBus slots.

Options for the Classic II and Performa 200

Despite having a 68030 CPU, the Classic II and Performa 200 aren't exceptionally speedy machines (Their performance is slower than that of the SE/30.) They also don't have any expansion slots, making upgrading them as difficult as upgrading a Plus or Classic. The Classic II and Performa 200's 68030 microprocessor nonetheless gives the computers better performance than the Plus or Classic and lets them accept an FPU.

At the very least, you should add enough memory to bring your Classic II or Performa 200 to the maximum of 10Mb. Two 4Mb SIMMs plus an FPU to speed arithmetic operations cost under $400 (see Table 3.9), giving the computer its maximum performance potential without major surgery.

The Classic II and Performa 200 have limited upgrade potential. There are no CPU accelerators are available. If you can find an expansion board with video circuitry, it will be difficult to install and won't support color/grayscale images. If your Classic II or Performa doesn't provide fast enough performance or if you need better video support, seriously consider replacing the computer with an LCIII.

Options for the Macintosh LC II, Performa 400, Performa 405, and Performa 430

Unmodified, the LC II, Performa 400, Performa 405, and Performa 430 are good computers for student, in-home, and clerical work. However, they support only 10Mb of RAM and don't execute programs fast enough for high-end graphics, financial analysis, or database processing. If the computer's perfor-

Chapter 3: A First Look at Upgrading

Table 3.9 Upgrade Options for the Macintosh Classic II and Performa 200

Type of Upgrade	Benefits	Drawbacks	Cost
RAM	More/larger programs in memory Can use System 7	Limit of 10Mb	$270
FPU	Speeds up arithmetic operations		$125
Video	Allows use of larger monitor	May require cutting a hole in the case	$800–$2,000
Total (to 10Mb RAM and FPU)			**$395**

mance meets your needs, you should at least bring the RAM to the maximum 10Mb. You may also want to add more video RAM and an FPU. These upgrades, which cost just over $400 (see Table 3.10), coax the maximum performance out of an LC II/Performa 4XX without installing a new CPU.

If your LC II, Performa 400, Performa 405, or Performa 430 doesn't have enough horsepower for your applications, you have two options: You can add a third-party accelerator board or you can replace the logic board with an LC III logic board. The LC III logic board upgrade is relatively affordable and comes

Table 3.10 Upgrade Options for the Macintosh LC II, Performa 400, Performa 405, and Performa 430

Type of Upgrade	Benefits	Drawbacks	Cost
RAM	More/larger programs in memory	Limit of 10Mb	$270
Video RAM	More colors/shades of gray		(256K) $17
FPU	Speeds up arithmetic operations		$125
CPU accelerator	Increased performance Allows installation of more than 4Mb RAM		$300–$2,000
Logic board	Turns the computer into an LC III		$600
Total (RAM, video RAM, FPU)			**$412**

with 4Mb of RAM; it can accept up to 36Mb. However, it uses different SIMMs from the LC II; you will therefore be unable to transfer any existing SIMMs to the new motherboard. Nonetheless, it is still cheaper than purchasing an LC III.

A third-party CPU accelerator, although somewhat more expensive than the logic board upgrade, avoids the logic board upgrade's problem: You can reuse your existing SIMMs. High-end accelerators also can provide faster performance than the CPU on the LC III logic board.

Options for the Color Classic, LC III, and Performa 450

Because the Color Classic, LC III, and Performa 450 are relatively recent Macintoshes, there is little upgrading that can (or needs to) be done. Nonetheless, you will probably want to bring the Color Classic to its maximum RAM of 10Mb; install at least 10Mb RAM in an LC III or Performa 450 as well (they accept up to 36Mb). In addition, you may want to add an FPU to either machine to speed arithmetic operations and video RAM to the LC III so that you can support more colors or shades of gray on a larger monitor.

Options for the Macintosh IIx

The IIx, essentially a Mac II with a 68030, is a "keeper." Like the Mac II, it has six NuBus slots and room in its box for two floppy drives and a hard disk. It also already has a SuperDrive; unmodified, it can handle 128Mb RAM. Assuming that you decide to keep your IIx, there are two major upgrade paths.

The first upgrade path involves adding individual components. You can add a CPU accelerator (a 50MHz 68030 with FPU runs about $800; a 33MHz 68040 runs about $1,500). Even if you don't add an accelerator, you should add as much RAM as you can afford; Mac software is RAM greedy, with what appears to be no end to its appetite for more space.

Table 3.11 Upgrade Options for the Color Classic, LC III, and Performa 450

Type of Upgrade	Benefits	Drawbacks	Cost
RAM	More/larger programs in memory		($229/8Mb SIMM)
			($499/16Mb SIMM)
Video RAM	More colors/shades of gray		($17/256K)
FPU	Speeds up arithmetic operations		$79

Because the IIx has so many slots, you might also consider adding a second monitor or a new video board to support more colors or shades of gray.

The second upgrade path includes the IIfx logic board replacement. The benefit to the upgrade is that it produces a computer that performs better than any other 68030 Macintosh and as well as some of the 68040s. However, the drawbacks to doing so are similar to those for installing the new logic board in a Mac II. First, the upgrade is expensive. If you purchase it from Apple, be prepared to spend more than $2,000; some third-party vendors may have it for less (see Table 3.12). Nonetheless, it is still more expensive than many CPU accelerators. In addition, if you turn your IIx into a IIfx, you must deal with the IIfx's unusual SCSI termination (used in the IIfx and nowhere else) and must replace all your RAM. (The IIfx requires a type of RAM not used in any other Mac.)

Options for the Macintosh IIfx

The IIfx is an unusual Macintosh, with features not found in any other machine. Its 40MHz 68030 microprocessor and direct memory access capabilities make it the fastest of the six-slot Macs. The only upgrade you are likely to need to add to a IIfx is RAM. However, if you want to push the machine to its maximum, consider adding a 68040 CPU accelerator (see Table 3.13).

Options for the Macintosh IIcx and IIci

The IIcx and IIci are essentially miniature versions of the IIx. They have three

Table 3.12 Upgrade Options for the Macintosh IIx

Type of Upgrade	Benefits	Drawbacks	Cost
RAM	More/larger programs in memory		(to 128Mb) $4,000
CPU	Increased performance		$300–$2,000
Logic board	Turns computer into IIfx	Requires special SIMMs Requires special SCSI termination	$1,799*
Video	Larger work surface More colors/shades of gray		$1,200–$3,000

*This price reflects Apple's price for the logic board replacement. However, third-party vendors, such as Shreve Systems, sell the IIfx logic board for under $1,000.

Table 3.13 *Upgrade Options for the Macintosh IIfx*

Type of Upgrade	Benefits	Drawbacks	Cost
RAM	More/larger programs in memory		(to 128Mb) $4,000
CPU	Increased performance		$1,500–$2,000

NuBus slots and 68030 microprocessors. Both continue to be useful computers, although slower than today's 68040 machines. If three slots provide enough expandability for your needs, then it makes sense to keep your IIcx or IIci.

Just like any Mac, the first upgrade you want to install is RAM. Both machines can take up to 128Mb; add as much RAM as you can afford (see Table 3.14). You can coax the maximum performance out of your IIcx or IIci by adding an instruction cache. If you want even faster performance, then you need to consider doing something about the CPU.

There are two ways to upgrade a IIcx's or IIci's CPU. The first is to install a CPU accelerator. Many CPU accelerators install directly onto the motherboard, without taking up a NuBus slot. There is, however, one caution with regard to the IIcx: In some early models the CPU is soldered to the IIcx motherboard; unlike IIcxs with socketed CPUs, the soldered CPU can't be easily removed to install the accelerator, nor is there a socket into which the accelerator can be installed. In that case, you may have to send the motherboard to the manufacturer of the accelerator board to have the soldered CPU replaced with a socketed CPU.

Table 3.14 *Upgrade Options for the Macintosh IIcx and IIci*

Type of Upgrade	Benefits	Drawbacks	Cost
RAM	More/larger programs in memory		(to 128Mb) $4,000
CPU accelerator	Increased performance		$300–$2,000
Instruction cache	Increased performance		$319
Quadra 700 logic board	Turns IIcx or IIci into Quadra 700		$1,999

Alternatively, the IIcx and IIci logic boards can be upgraded with a Quadra 700 motherboard. As you can see from Table 3.14, the logic board upgrade is rather expensive. The logic board upgrade includes only 4Mb of RAM (you won't be able to transfer existing RAM), two NuBus slots, and one '040 processor direct slot. In general, a 50MHz 68030 accelerator with an instruction cache brings performance equal to the Quadra 700 at less than half the cost.

Options for the IIsi

The IIsi is a moderate-speed Macintosh. Because it has only one slot, its upgradability is limited. As with any other Mac, you will probably want to add as much RAM as you can afford (up to the maximum 65Mb, 1Mb of which is soldered on the motherboard). Beyond that, there are several things you can do to increase the IIsi's performance and upgrade flexibility.

The IIsi has one expansion slot. Before you can install a card in that slot, you must add a slot adapter. A "slot adapter" prepares the slot to accept one '030 processor direct board (see Table 3.15); a "NuBus adapter" prepares the slot to accept a NuBus board. Apple's version of either adapter also includes an FPU.

The IIsi can accept an FPU, CPU accelerator, and/or instruction cache to increase performance. Keep in mind, however, that any of these upgrades can take up the IIsi's single expansion slot. When shopping for an expansion board, you may want to look for one that has room

Table 3.15 Upgrade Options for the Macintosh IIsi

Type of Upgrade	Benefits	Drawbacks	Cost
RAM	More/larger programs in memory		(to 65Mb) $500
FPU	Faster arithmetic operations	May take up single slot	$125
CPU accelerator	Increased performance		$300–$2,000
Slot adapter	Lets computer use one '030 processor direct card Includes FPU		$199
NuBus adapter	Lets computer use one NuBus card		$199
Instruction cache	Increased performance		$139

on the board for all the upgrades you want to add. For example, the DayStar PowerCache's IIsi adapter has not only a connector for the new CPU, but a socket for an FPU and a cache card as well.

As an alternative, you can increase the IIsi's expandability by installing a slot adapter that contains two expansion slots. Such slot doublers let you install two expansion boards rather than just one. However, two expansion boards may place an unacceptable drain on the IIsi's power supply. (See Chapter 9 for details.)

Options for the IIvx and Performa 600

The IIvx and Performa 600, with their three NuBus slots and one processor direct slot, are as upgradable as the IIci and IIcx. Their 33MHz 68030 CPU is relatively speedy. Unless you have a need for high-end multimedia work, you probably will want to leave your IIvx/Performa 600 as is.

To get the most out of your IIvx/Performa 600, add as much RAM as you can afford (see Table 3.16). Then if the 33MHz 68030 CPU isn't fast enough for your needs, consider a CPU accelerator or a logic board upgrade. A 68040 CPU accelerator costs a bit less than a logic board upgrade ($1,500 versus $1,600). However, the Centris 650 logic board upgrade does include 8Mb of RAM (you won't be able to transfer existing RAM), 512K video RAM, an FPU, and Ethernet support. This is one instance where the logic board upgrade can be more economical than adding a stand-alone accelerator, especially if you haven't already invested in a lot of RAM.

Options for 68030 PowerBooks

You can add two types of upgrades to a 68030 PowerBook: more RAM and an in-

Table 3.16 Upgrade Options for the Macintosh IIvx and Performance 600

Type of Upgrade	Benefits	Drawbacks	Cost
RAM	More/larger programs in memory		(to 68Mb) $500
CPU accelerator	Increased performance		$300–$2,000
Centris 650 logic board	Turns computer into Centris 650		$1,600

Chapter 3: A First Look at Upgrading

ternal modem. Assuming you are running System 7, you should bring your PowerBook to its maximum RAM capacity. In addition, you might choose to add just a data modem or a combined fax/data modem.

CPU accelerators with FPUs are also available for the PowerBook 140 and 160. Stand-alone FPUs are available for the PowerBook 145 and 160.

Upgrading 68040 Macs

The 68040 Macs are currently the top of the Macintosh line. That means that upgrade options are somewhat limited. (This isn't necessarily a bad situation; it's just that most of the 68040 machines haven't yet been superseded by new technology and therefore don't need significant upgrading.)

In most cases, you will want to add more RAM to your 68040 Mac (see Table 3.18). You may also want to add some video RAM to support more colors/shades of gray, and/or a larger monitor. In addition, you can eke out a bit more performance by adding an instruction cache. Beyond that (unless you have a Centris 610, Quadra 800, or Quadra 900), just sit back and enjoy having a top-of-the-line computer.

If you have a Quadra 900, you can turn it into a 950 with a logic board upgrade. The major benefit of doing so is a 33MHz 68040 rather than 25MHz 68040 found in the 900. There is one drawback to the upgrade: The logic board upgrade is rather expensive.

▶ **Table 3.17** Upgrade Options for 68030 PowerBooks

Type of Upgrade	Benefits	Drawbacks	Cost
RAM	More/larger programs in memory		($200/4Mb SIMM)
			($225/6Mb SIMM)
			($375/8Mb SIMM)
CPU accelerator	Increased performance		$400–$450
FPU	Increased performance		$350
Fax/data modem			$200

You can also upgrade a Centris 610 to a Centris 660av and a Quadra 800 to a Quadra 840av. These logic board upgrades, although expensive, can give your computer the video and speech capabilities of the newer multimedia models.

Upgrades for all NuBus Macs

In addition to the upgrades that are machine-specific, some upgrades can be added to any Macintosh with NuBus slots. These include the following:

- **SCSI accelerator cards:** SCSI accelerators, many of which are based on the new SCSI-2 standard, provide faster disk I/O, especially when connected to a SCSI-2 hard disk. SCSI-accelerators can also provide a second SCSI chain.

- **Network interface cards:** Although every Macintosh since the Plus has AppleTalk networking built in, many Macintoshes need to be connected to other types of networks. In particular, you may install a board to connect your Mac to an Ethernet or Token-Ring network.

By the way: Ethernet is built in to some of the 68040 Macintoshes. It can also be added to non-NuBus Macs through either a SCSI device or a processor direct board.

NEW HOMES FOR OLD MACS

Okay, you've decided that it doesn't make sense to upgrade your Mac; you're going to shell out for a new one. What in the world do you do with the old machine? There are actually several reasonable options:

- Sell it. There is a lively market for used computers. You can advertise in a local newspaper or on an information

Table 3.18 Upgrade Options for 68040 Macs

Type of Upgrade	Benefits	Drawbacks	Cost
RAM	More/larger programs in memory		($30/Mb)
Video RAM	More colors/shades of gray		($30/256K)
Quadra 950 logic board	Turns 900 into 950		$1,899
Centris NuBus adapter	Lets Centris use longer NuBus cards		$99
Instruction cache	Increased performance		$250

service such as America Online or Compuserve. You can also list the computer with an agency that specializes in matching buyers and sellers of used computer equipment (for example, the Boston Computer Exchange). When you use an agency, you pay a commission to the agency based on the selling price of the computer. There are also a number of businesses that specialize in buying and selling used Macintoshes. (See Appendix B for a list of some of them.) When you contact one of these vendors, you can be almost certain of a sale. However, the selling price will generally be less than what you would receive by selling it through an information service, newspaper, or agency.

Although it might seem inviting to turn an old Mac into cash, you need to be realistic when you consider the possibility. Older Macs, such as Pluses and SEs, aren't worth more than a few hundred dollars on the open market. In that case, it may make more sense to give the machine away and take a tax deduction.

- Use it for something where speed and/or lots of RAM aren't essential. For example, a business might choose to use an older Mac as an electronic mail server on a network or pass it on to an employee who doesn't need state-of-the-art computing power. A family might give an older Mac to a student to take to college or to a young child who's just learning to compute.

- Give it away. If you donate a computer to a nonprofit organization, you can take a tax deduction for the fair market value of the computer. Some organizations will welcome older computers. However, be aware that many don't want hardware without software, training, and technical support. (You really can't blame them; without software, training, and technical support, a "free" computer can be a very expensive liability.)

- Keep it as a spare. You may want to keep your old Mac as a spare or backup machine. If your new Mac needs to go in for repair, you will at least have a computer that can do some work for you. The old Mac can also be a source of spare parts.

- Get creative. If an older Mac is unusable, too expensive to repair or upgrade, and in such bad shape you can't sell or donate it to anyone, then you have to get creative. You can always throw it out (not creative, but certainly practical) or use it for a doorstop (especially suitable for 30-

pound compact Macs), or even turn it into a fishbowl.

Hardware Upgrade Basics

Although you can add many kinds of expansion boards to your Macintosh, the way in which you install one is pretty much the same, regardless of the type of board. (SIMMs are installed somewhat differently from expansion boards. The details can be found in Chapter 5.) To install an expansion board, you need to open the Mac's case.

Anatomy of an Expansion Board

Expansion boards vary a great deal in size, but they have basically the same architecture. The board in Figure 3.2 is a typical NuBus board. At the right edge of the board is a metal plate. If the expansion board provides a port (for example, a video board), then the port is attached to this plate. When the board is installed in the computer, the plate completely covers the hole in the Macintosh's case, preventing dust from entering the computer and at the same time providing a connection between the adapter circuit on the board and the outside world.

At the bottom of the expansion board is a connector that plugs into a slot on the Macintosh's motherboard. Inside the connector are wires (sometimes called *pins*) that make the actual connection. When installing the board, these wires must line up with the holes in the slot.

What appears on the body of the board depends on the type of board. In most cases, you will have one or more ROMs containing programs that operate the board. Such chips are often installed in plug-in sockets rather than being soldered to the board so that they can be replaced

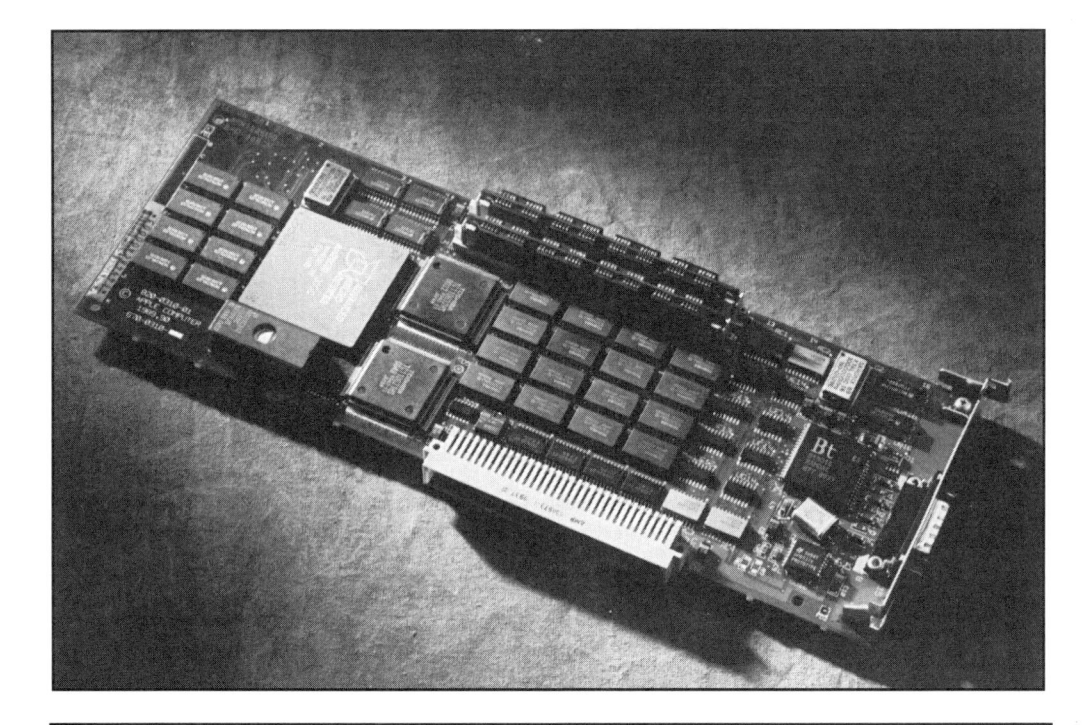

Figure 3.2 *A NuBus expansion board*

easily. Expansion boards may also contain RAM (in particular, video boards).

Some NuBus boards are *bus master* boards. A bus master board can take control of the system bus, transferring data directly from the board to RAM, without the intervention of the CPU; the CPU can be running a program while the data transfer is occurring. Bus mastering is particularly useful for I/O boards such as SCSI accelerators.

Case-Opening Hints

To perform any sort of upgrade to the system unit, you will need to open your Macintosh's case. The procedures for doing so vary from one type of Macintosh to another. Nonetheless, there are a few things you should keep in mind whenever you are performing surgery on your computer.

First, remember that the electronics inside a Macintosh can be disrupted by static electricity. For example, a static discharge could damage what's stored on a hard drive or what's stored in ROM. Whenever you plan to crack a Macintosh case, you should make sure you aren't carrying a static charge. Some upgrade vendors supply a grounding bracelet with their products, but there is some question as to how effective such bracelets are. To be perfectly safe, work on a wood or tile floor. If you must work on carpeting, stand on plastic such as a rug protector that is used to keep a chair from damaging a carpet. In all cases, ground yourself by touching something metal before touching the Macintosh case. If you are carrying a static charge, touching metal will discharge the electricity.

Second, before you begin, make sure you have enough room to work. Opening a compact Mac (other than a Color Classic) takes an area about 3 feet wide by 2 feet deep. Since you will need to lay the Macintosh on its face (the monitor side), make sure that the work table is either very smooth or covered with a lint-free cloth. (Flour sack dish towels work well.) Opening modular Macintoshes takes enough space for the Macintosh, its monitor (assuming you had the monitor sitting on top), and the lid. If the type of upgrade you're performing requires removing disk drives, you'll also need a dust and lint-free place to set them. Regardless of the type of Macintosh, you'll need a safe place for any screws you will remove (somewhere the cats and kids can't get them).

Getting Inside a Compact Macintosh

Opening a compact Macintosh, with the exception of the Color Classic, is more

Fix Your Own Mac: Upgrading and Troubleshooting

difficult than opening any other type of Macintosh. This difficulty is both practical and technical. The practical issue is that if your machine is under warranty, opening the case voids that warranty. If your Macintosh is less than one year old and you want to retain warranty protection, it may pay to let an authorized Apple service technician install any upgrades (Figure 3.3).

Opening Compact Macintoshes Other Than the Color Classic

Assuming that your Macintosh isn't under warranty or that you don't mind voiding the warranty, then opening a compact Mac case is still a challenge. First, you need a *torx* screwdriver like that in Figure 3.4. You can purchase one from many Macintosh retailers or from any mail-order outlet that sells upgrades for compact Macs; the cost is around $20. Second, you need a *case spreader* to separate the back and sides of the case from the rest of the computer. Case spreaders come in all sorts of shapes and sizes. In Figure 3.4, for example, a case spreader is found at the end of the screwdriver. However, depending on the type of torx screwdriver you purchase, you may need a separate case spreader.

With torx screwdriver and case spreader in hand, you are ready to crack the case:

1. Remove the programmer's switch (the combination reset and interrupt buttons) if it has been installed.

2. Remove all cords and cables, including the power cord, serial cables, SCSI cable, and ADB cables.

3. Use the torx screwdriver to remove the screws that hold the case together. There are four screws in most compact Mac cases. As you can see in Figure 3.5, two are located inside the handle; the other two are just above the ports at either side of the case.

The Macintosh Plus also has a fifth screw, located inside the cover to the battery case. To access that final screw, you must remove the battery cover and the battery. Keep in mind

▶ **Figure 3.3** A service technician to the rescue

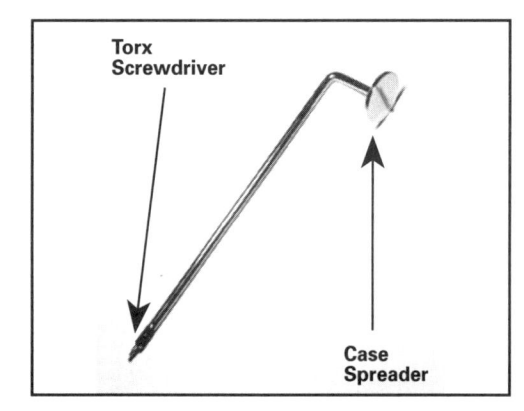

▶ **Figure 3.4** A torx screwdriver

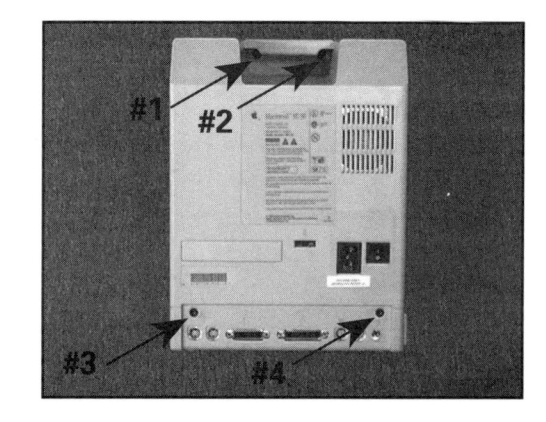

▶ **Figure 3.5** The location of screws in a Compact Macintosh case

Chapter 3: A First Look at Upgrading

that removing the battery removes power from the PRAM. If the battery is out for more than a few minutes, you will need to reset the date and time and, if necessary, your start-up drive once you get the computer put back together.

4. Use the case spreader to separate the back of the case from the front, as in Figure 3.6.

5. Place the Macintosh face down on the table. Gently remove the back from the computer. Note that if your computer is a Classic, you'll need to press down on the metal connectors at the base of the case (Figure 3.7). You will see something like Figure 3.8. The motherboard isn't visible; it lies along the very bottom of the computer.

WARNING The yoke of the CRT inside a compact Macintosh can carry a high voltage. Be very careful that you don't touch it.

6. Set the Macintosh upright once more. At this point you are ready to work.

Opening the Color Classic

The Color Classic is the first compact Macintosh that gives you access to the computer's motherboard without requiring you to take the case apart. It has a small access door at the back of the case. To open a Color Classic,

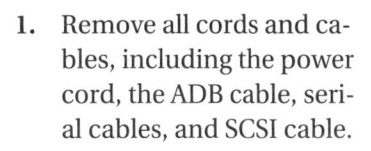

1. Remove all cords and cables, including the power cord, the ADB cable, serial cables, and SCSI cable.

2. Remove the two screws at the base of the back of the computer (see Figure 3.9).

3. Press the two latches at the top of the access panel (Figure 3.10).

4. Pull the access door down and away from the computer. You now have access to the motherboard.

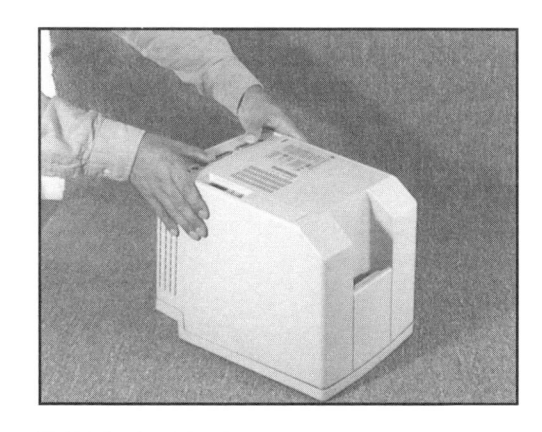

Figure 3.6 Opening a compact Macintosh

Figure 3.7 Opening a Macintosh Classic case

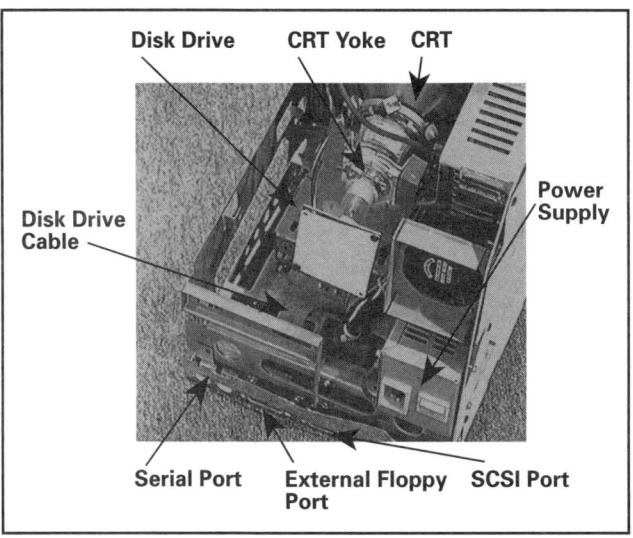

Figure 3.8 Inside a compact Macintosh

Fix Your Own Mac: Upgrading and Troubleshooting

Figure 3.9 Opening a Color Classic

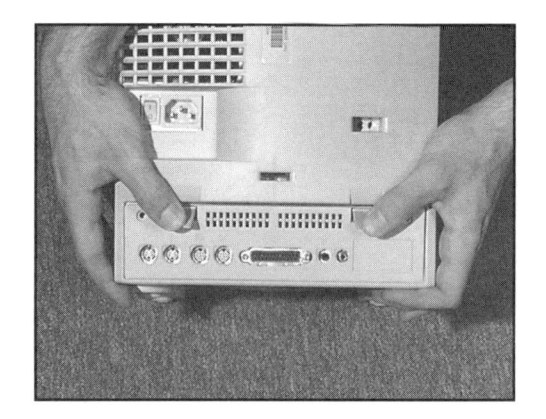

Figure 3.10 Pressing the latches on the Color Classic's upgrade panel

Getting Inside the LC Line

Compared to opening a compact Macintosh case, opening a modular Mac is easy. To get inside any Macintosh in the LC line (the LC, LC II, LC III, Performa 400, Performa 405, Performa 430, and Performa 450), make sure you have enough space to work. Then you should

1. Remove all cords and cables, including power cord, serial cables, ADB cables, and SCSI cable.

2. Turn the computer so that the back is facing you. If there is a screw in the middle of the lid, remove it.

3. Locate the two latches at either edge of the top of the lid (Figure 3.11).

4. Lift the latches, pulling the lid of the computer up and toward you (Figure 3.12). With the cover off, you'll see something like Figure 3.13.

Getting Inside Other Modular Macintoshes

To open any other modular Macs, make sure you have enough space to work. Then

1. Remove all cords and cables, including the power cord, serial cables, ADB cables, and SCSI cable.

2. If your Mac has a *tower case* (a case that stands on its end on the floor)—the Quadra 800, 900, and 950—lay the machine on its side on a table so that the side that can be removed in essence becomes the top of the machine.

Figure 3.11 The latches on the lid of an LC

Figure 3.12 Pulling latches to open the lid of an LC

Chapter 3: A First Look at Upgrading

3. Check to see if there is a screw in the center back of the case's lid (see Figure 3.14). If there is, remove it.

4. If your Mac has latches at the side of the lid (e.g., the IIx in Figure 3.15), press the latches in. If your Macintosh has latches on the top of the lid (e.g., the IIci in Figure 3.16), pull the latches toward you.

5. Holding the latches in, pull the top of the case up and toward you (see Figure 3.17).

The view inside your computer, of course, depends on what type of Macintosh it is. A six-slot Macintosh (see Figure 3.18) has more room inside either the LC or other Mac IIs (for example, the IIsi in Figure 3.19). All the desktop modular Macs have room for at least one floppy disk drive (the six-slot Macs have room for two) and one hard disk drive. Note that in Figure 3.18 the SIMMs aren't visible because they are underneath the disk drive platform.

Figure 3.14 Location of the screw in the back of a modular Macintosh

Figure 3.13 Inside an LC

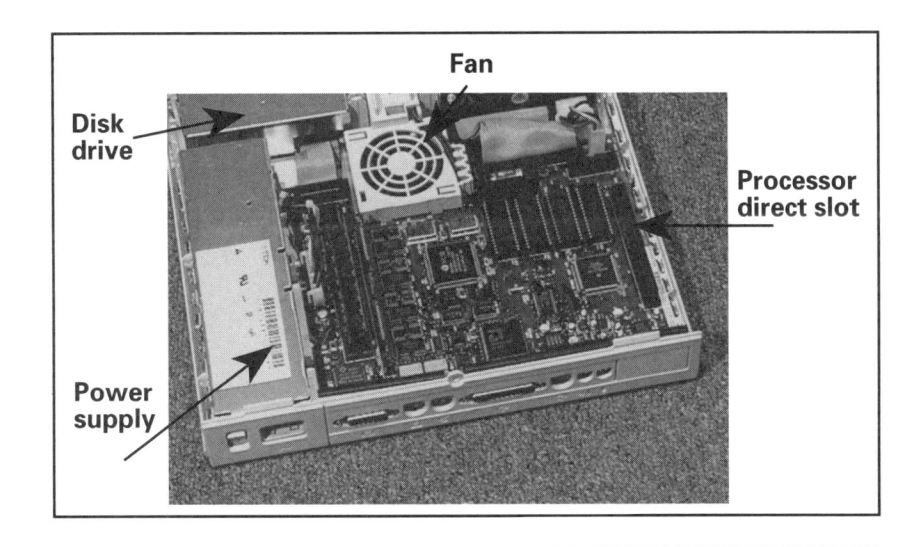

Figure 3.15 Pressing latches on the back of a modular Mac

Fix Your Own Mac: Upgrading and Troubleshooting

Figure 3.16 Pulling latches on the top of a modular Mac

The inside of the Quadra 700 looks very similar to that of a six-slot Macintosh. However, it is just a bit smaller. If you look at Figure 3.20 you can see that there is only room for one floppy drive and that there are only three slots (two NuBus and one PDS). You can't see the SIMM slots because they are underneath the disk drive platform.

The Quadra 900 in Figure 3.21, for example, is turned on its side, as it would be after you had removed the side. At this point, the motherboard is on the bottom (when turned upright, it sits along one side). The SIMM slots are visible at the top right of the picture.

Getting Inside a Portable

The Macintosh Portable's expansion slots are accessible without any tools. To open a Portable:

1. Remove all cords and cables, including the power cord, ADB cable, serial cable, and/or SCSI cable.

2. Press and hold the two buttons at the edges of the top back of the cover (see Figure 3.22).

3. With the buttons depressed, lift the cover up and off the computer. When the computer is open, you will see something like Figure 3.23.

Figure 3.17 Removing the lid of a desktop Mac

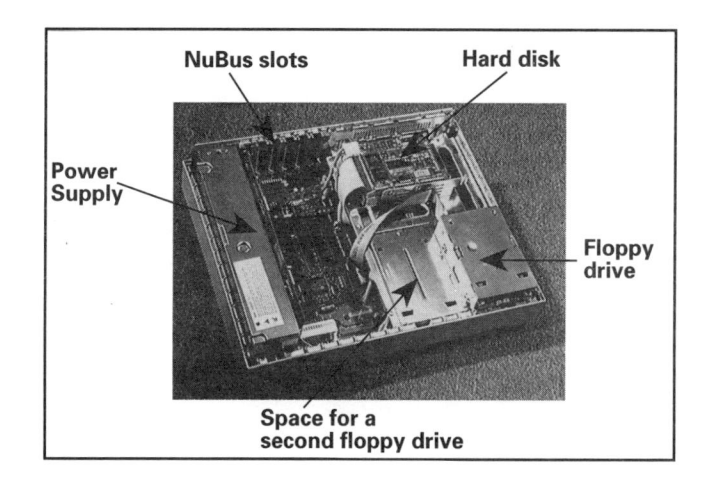

Figure 3.18 Inside a six-slot Macintosh

Chapter 3: A First Look at Upgrading

Getting Inside a PowerBook

As with the older compact Macs, getting inside a PowerBook requires a torx screwdriver. To open a PowerBook,

1. Remove all cords and cables, including a power cord, ADB cable, serial cable, or SCSI cable.

2. Use a #10 torx screwdriver to remove all screws on the bottom of the PowerBook and a #9 torx screwdriver to remove the one located beneath the port cover (see Figure 3.22).

3. Lift the top of the PowerBook off the base, exposing the logic board. Carefully unplug the ribbon cable that connects the top and the base.

With the PowerBook taken apart, you'll see something like Figure 3.23.

Installing an Expansion Board

Once you have opened your Macintosh's case and exposed the expansion slot into which you are going to install a board, the actual installation is straightforward:

1. Place the expansion board directly above the slot, lining up the left and right edges.

2. Press the board gently into the slot. It should seat itself into the slot with little resistance. If the board doesn't go in easily, don't force it. Any resistance probably means that the pins in the board aren't lined up correctly with the holes in the slot. If you continue to press, you may bend the pins. Instead, raise the board, realign it with the slot, and try again.

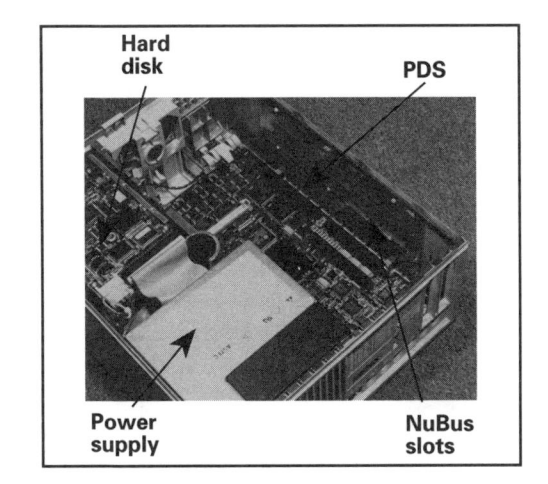

▶ *Figure 3.20* Inside a Quadra 700

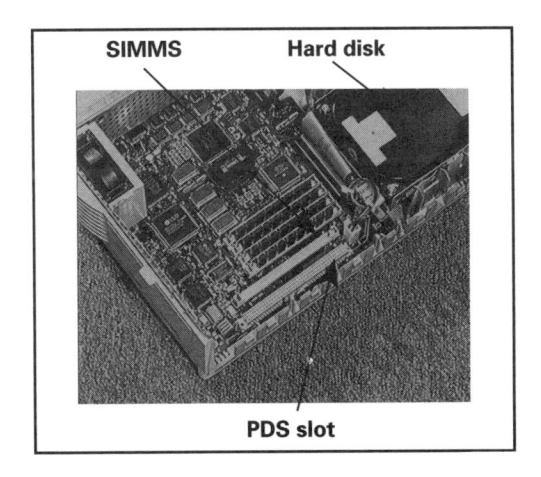

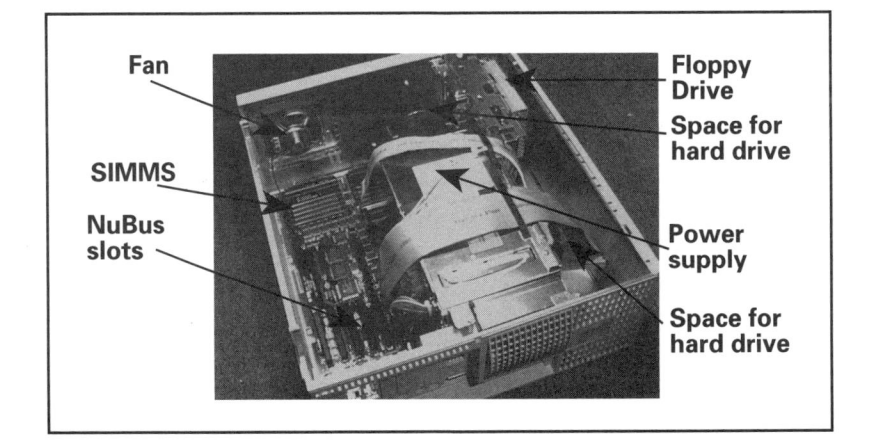

▶ *Figure 3.19* Inside a Macintosh IIsi

▶ *Figure 3.21* Inside the Quadra 900

Fix Your Own Mac: Upgrading and Troubleshooting

3. Plug in the power cord and turn on the computer. If you hear normal startup sounds, turn off the computer. Connect the monitor and the mouse and restart. Assuming the computer boots normally, shut it down, and turn off the power. Reconnect everything and restart. You can then install any software the board may need and test the operation of the board.

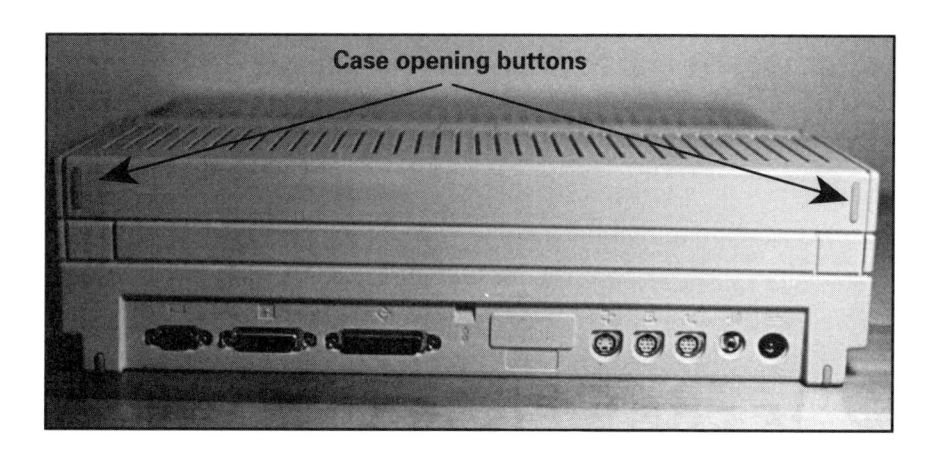

Figure 3.22 Location of case-opening buttons on the Macintosh Portable

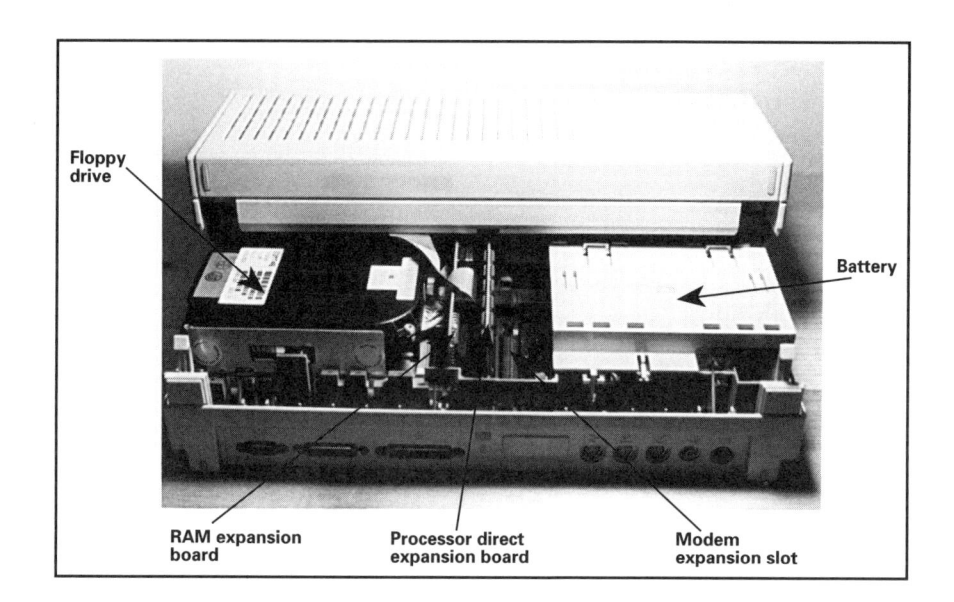

Figure 3.23 Inside the Macintosh Portable

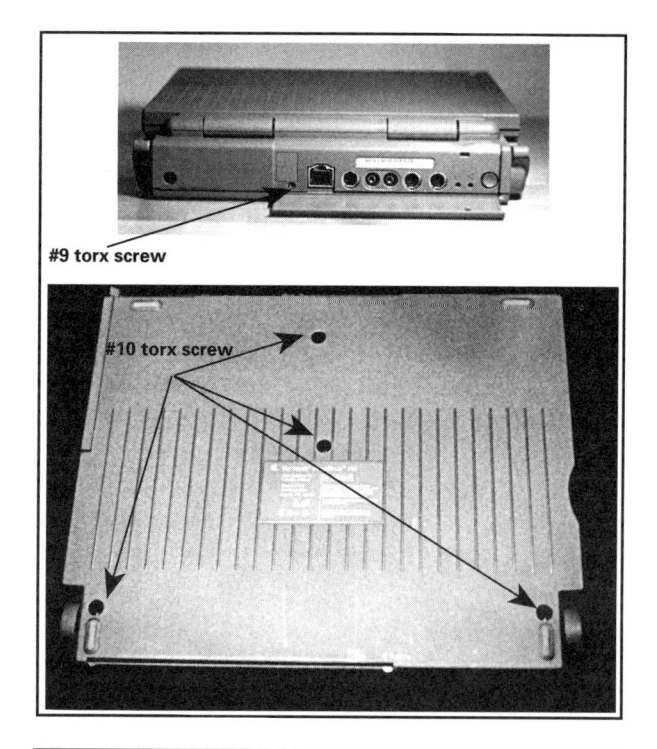

Figure 3.24 Location of screws in a PowerBook

Chapter 3: A First Look at Upgrading

If the Mac doesn't start normally at any point, turn off the power and disconnect all cables and cords. Remove the expansion board, plug it in again, and repeat the testing process.

If the board still doesn't function properly after two or three attempts to install it, you should suspect a problem with the board itself. At this point, contact the dealer, mail-order firm, or manufacturer from whom your purchased the board for help.

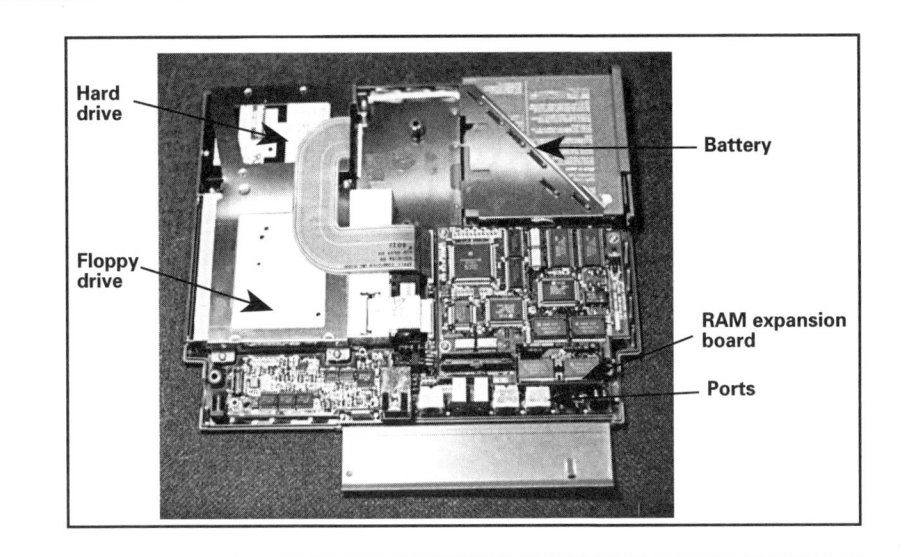

Figure 3.25 *Inside a PowerBook*

Troubleshooting Techniques —4—

Most of the time, a Macintosh works without a hitch. When it doesn't, you may feel helpless and frustrated (see Figure 4.1). Knowing some basic troubleshooting procedures can help you locate the source of the problem and give you some clues about how to get things fixed. This chapter therefore introduces some general strategies for figuring out just what might be behind your Mac's strange behavior. (Additional specific diagnostic tricks and techniques appear throughout the book.) But first, this chapter looks at one way to minimize data loss when a problem occurs.

Crash Protection

When your Macintosh crashes or hangs, most of the time there's nothing you can do but restart. Not only do you lose work in progress for the program that crashed or hung, but you also lose any unsaved changes to documents from other applications that are running at the same time. There is a utility—Crash Barrier from Casady & Greene—that can at least give you the chance to save changes to documents other than those involved in the crash or hang. In some cases, it can also get the problem program limping again so that you can save your work before you restart the Mac and begin your troubleshooting.

By the way: There is an old joke that goes something like this: A patient walks into a doctor's office and raises his right arm straight up. "It hurts when I do this," he tells the doctor. The doctor shrugs wisely and says, "Well, then, don't do that." There is a direct analogy between that joke and problems with a computer. If certain actions make a program crash or hang, don't keep repeating the actions, hoping the problem will go away. It almost never does. Instead, use some of the troubleshooting techniques presented in this chapter to try to figure out what's causing the problem.

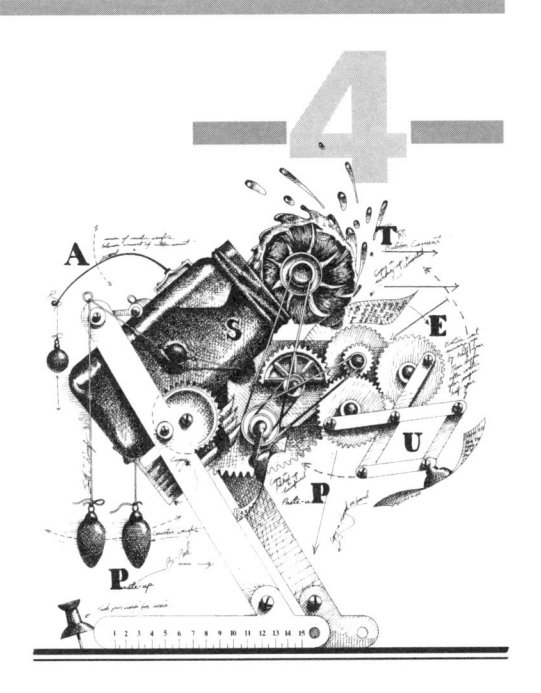

Crash Barrier installs as an INIT. You can invoke it from the keyboard (particularly useful if a program hangs); it also appears automatically instead of the dreaded bomb box whenever an application crashes. In Beginner Mode, Crash Barrier gives you three possible actions (see Figure 4.2). Fix tries to repair the crashed application, at least long enough for you to save your work. Even if Fix doesn't work, you can always Quit to the Finder so you can then return to other applications and at least save everything else in progress.

The Expert mode dialog box (see Figure 4.3) provides a wider range of options. The availability of several options, however, depends on the application you are trying to recover. For example, the Resume option is available only if an application has been written to resume after a system error. (Unfortunately, very few are.)

HARDWARE VERSUS SOFTWARE PROBLEMS

A problem with your Mac can be caused by hardware or software. Therefore the first thing you should do when your Mac is acting up is to try to determine whether you have a hardware or a software problem. There are three major causes of software problems: viruses, INIT conflicts, and conflicts between application software and the operating system.

Viruses

A virus is a malicious piece of software designed, at the very least, to interrupt normal data processing, and, at the worst, to destroy data. Although some people joke about viruses and find them fanciful and clever (see Figure 4.4), there is nothing funny about a virus. Virus infestations are costly, both in terms of the time it takes to diagnose and fix the problem and in terms of lost data.

If your Macintosh is crashing, hanging, or files are mysteriously disappearing or being altered, then you should consider the possibility of a virus. Viruses spread by attaching themselves to other pieces of software. Whenever an infected piece

Figure 4.1 Hardware problems—fear, frustration, and panic

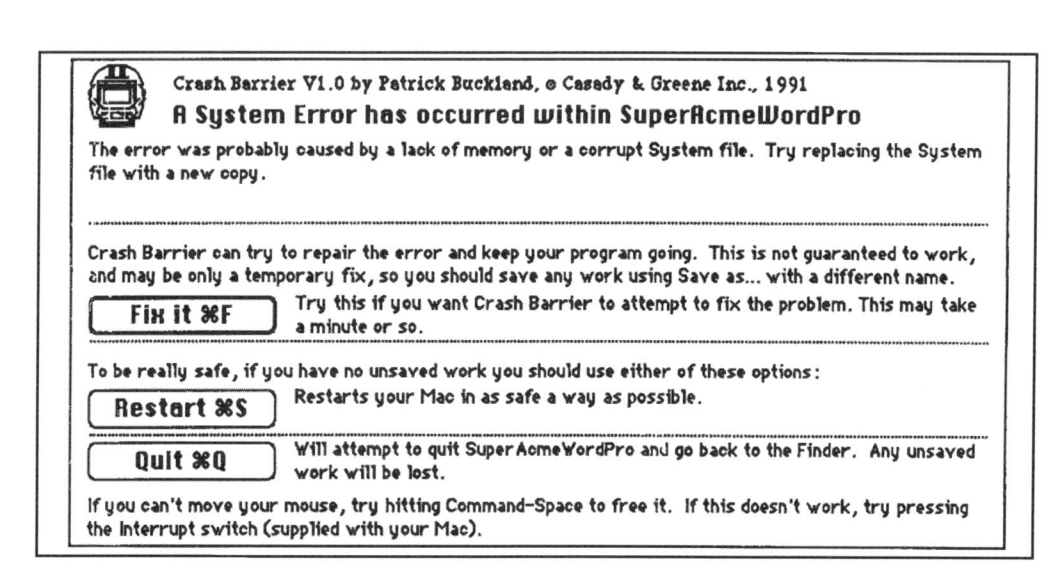

Figure 4.2 Crash Barrier options in Beginner Mode

of software is copied (either from disk to disk or over telecommunications lines), the virus goes along too. A virus is therefore a distinct possibility if you download software from an information service or obtain public-domain/shareware software from a user group. Although information services and user groups make an effort to ensure that software is virus-free, they aren't infallible. On rare occasions, viruses have also been known to creep into commercial software.

By the way: Viruses are the favorite cause of trouble for some hardware technical support people. If you call tech support with a hardware problem that isn't a problem with which they're familiar, they may insist you have a virus. You can save yourself a lot of frustration (and often telephone charges) if you rule out the possibility of a virus before calling tech support.

When you suspect a virus, the first thing to do is run virus detection software such as Disinfectant (see Figure 4.5), Virex, or SAM (Symantec Anti-Virus). Such software scans a disk, looking for known viruses. When the software recognizes a virus, it attempts to remove it from the disk, without damaging existing files.

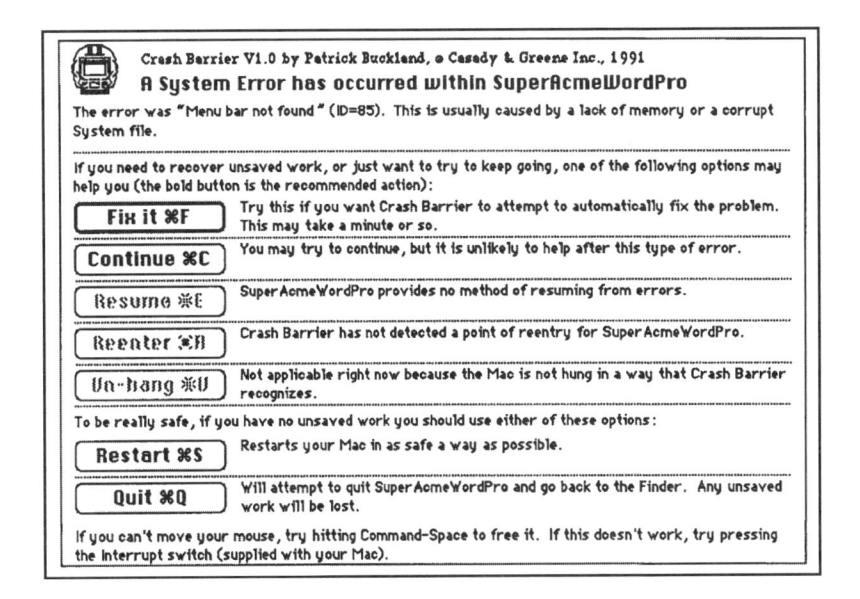

Figure 4.3 Crash Barrier options in Expert Mode

Figure 4.4 Computer viruses—disruptive and destructive

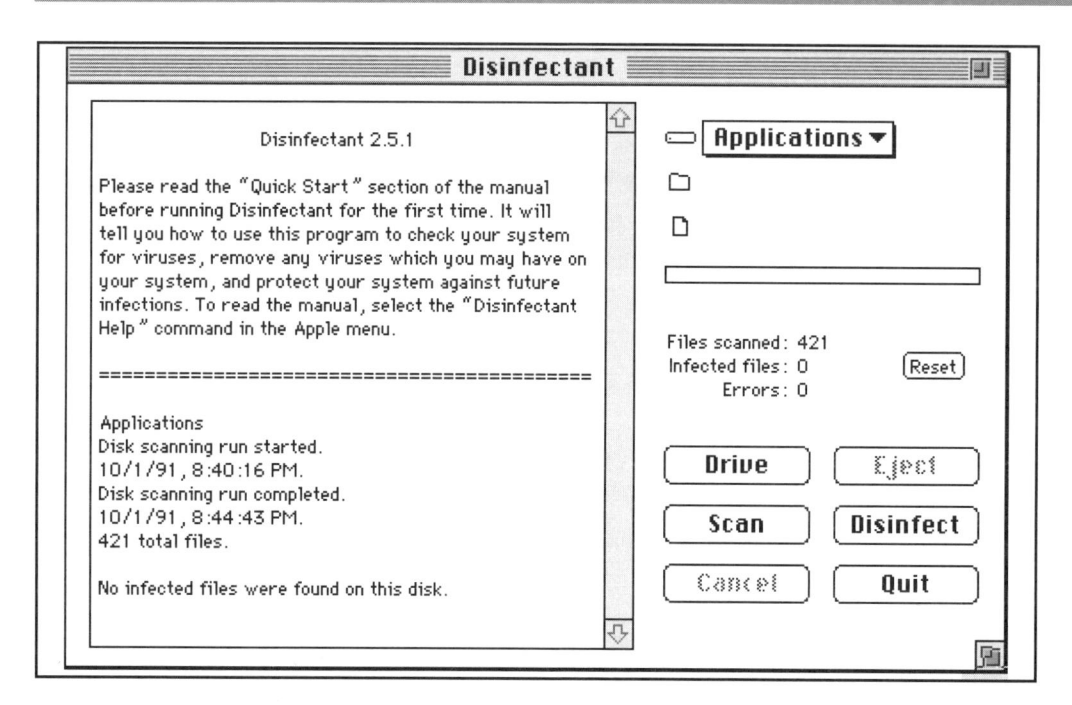

Fix Your Own Mac: Upgrading and Troubleshooting

Figure 4.5 Checking a disk for a virus infection

Unfortunately, no virus detection software can catch all viruses. Virus detection software can only identify viruses that the software developers have programmed into their detection software. Although virus detection software is updated regularly, there is a continual escalation of virus wars. As soon as virus detection software can handle a new virus, someone creates yet another one.

Even if your virus detection software doesn't find any viruses, there are some signs that a virus might be present:

- File sizes that are different from what they were before you installed new software. This typically occurs with viruses that attach themselves to operating system files. Of course, to be able to verify file sizes, you must have good, recent backup copies of your disks.

- File modification dates that are different from what they were before you installed new software. When a virus invades a file on a disk, it changes the modification date. As with file size changes, you must have good, recent backup copies of your disks against which you can compare current files.

INIT Conflicts

Given the complexity of today's Macintosh operating environment, it's not surprising that the source of many software problems is conflicts between INITs, those little programs that load during the system boot process and hang around in main memory as long as the computer is turned on. There are several symptoms of an INIT conflict:

- The system won't boot; instead, the computer hangs during the boot process.

- The system crashes when you try to open a control panel.

Chapter 4: Troubleshooting Techniques

- An application program doesn't run properly. Such problems might include, for example, a multimedia program in which the sound and video aren't in sync.

There are two basic strategies for identifying INIT conflicts. The first doesn't require any special software, but it can be tedious. The process is as follows:

1. Remove all INITs from your System folder. You needn't delete them from the disk: simply place them outside the System folder.

2. Reboot the Mac and retry whatever action caused the problem to appear. If all goes well, then you've verified that the problem was caused by an INIT conflict.

3. Replace one INIT in the System folder.

4. Repeat steps 2 and 3 until the problem recurs. The last INIT you replaced is the cause of the problem. If you put all INITs back and the problem is still there, then it isn't caused by an INIT conflict.

By the way: INIT conflicts are another favorite scapegoat of both hardware and software technical support people. To save yourself frustration, time, and the cost of a long phone call, be sure to eliminate the possibility of INIT conflicts before calling tech support.

You can make the process of moving all those INITs into and out of the System folder a bit easier by using some INIT management software. For example, the Start-up Manager (see Figure 4.6), available as part of the NOW Utilities package, lets you indicate which INITs

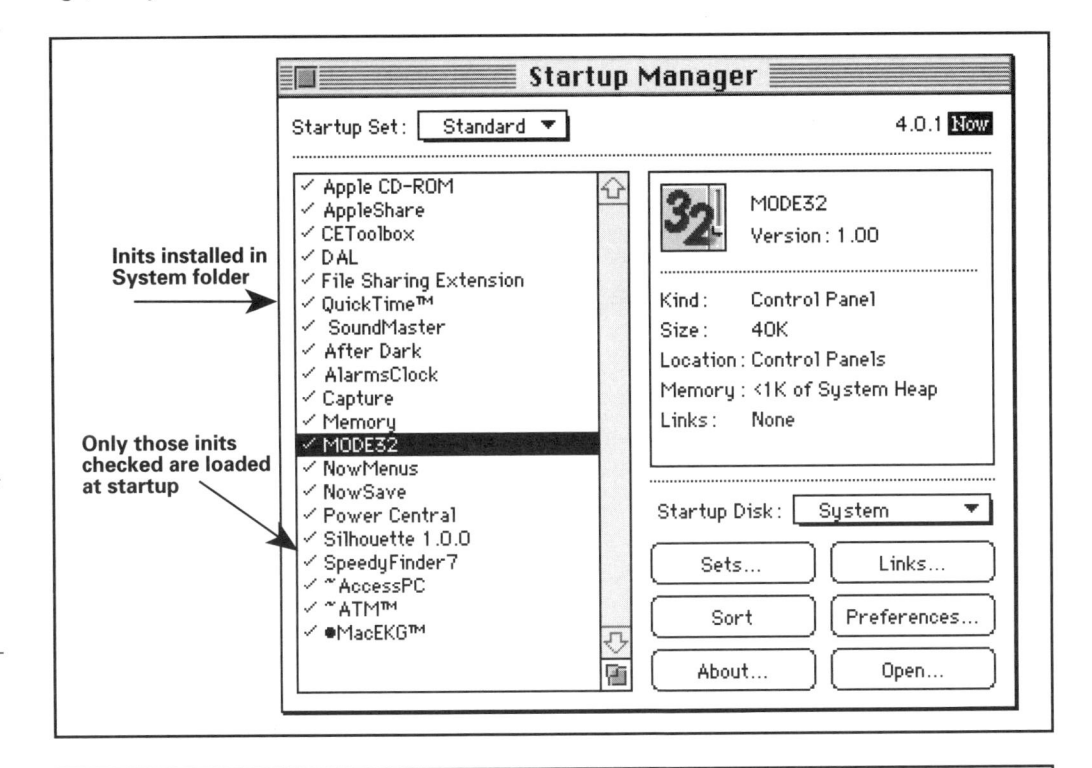

Figure 4.6 Using the Start-up Manager to simplify looking for INIT conflicts

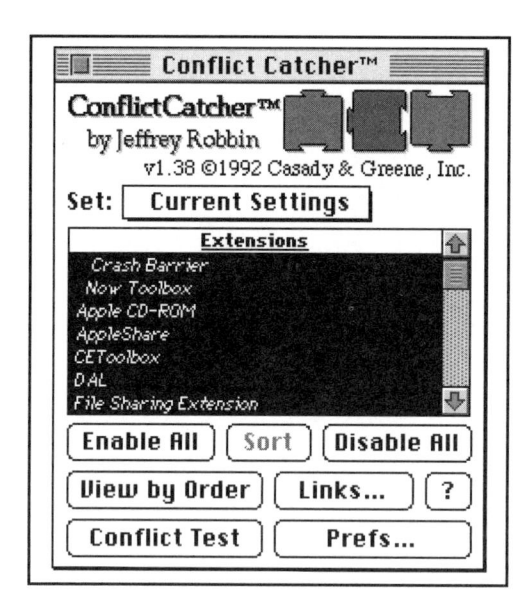

Figure 4.7 *Using Conflict Catcher to identify a problem INIT*

shouldn't be loaded without physically removing any from the System folder.

Conflict Catcher (see Figure 4.7), from Casady & Greene, can further automate the process. Conflict Catcher automatically disables INITs by moving them to separate folders within the System folder. Once you indicate which INITs *must* be loaded (those without which your system can't boot), it deactivates half your INITs and you reboot the computer. If the problem recurs, then the offending INIT is in the INITs that are still active. In that case, Conflict Catcher deactivates half the currently active INITs. However, if the problem didn't recur, then Conflict Catcher turns to the INITs that were inactive during the previous test. It keeps cutting the number of INITs in half until the one causing the conflict is identified. This process of looking at half and then half again is a very effective search technique and can significantly cut down on the amount of time it takes to identify which INIT is responsible for a conflict.

> **By the way:** Programmers may recognize Conflict Catcher's technique as a binary search.

The second strategy for identifying INIT conflicts is to use software diagnostic software. For example, Help! works against a knowledge base of known conflicts. As you can see in Figure 4.8, Help! identified some potential INIT conflicts. Notice that the information includes potential solutions and, wherever possible, phone numbers and contact persons for software vendors. For software like Help! to remain useful, its knowledge base of software conflicts must be updated regularly. Help!'s manufacturer (Teknosys) therefore sells an update subscription for about $75 per year.

Application Software Versus the Operating System

Another source of software problems is a conflict between application software and the version of the Macintosh operating system you're running. For example, a lot of application software originally wasn't compatible with System 7. Even today some application software packages that haven't been upgraded recently can run under System 7, but not with 32-bit addressing in effect.

The biggest hint that you've got 32-bit dirty software is repeated bombs with a "bus error." (You'll learn exactly what causes this error in Chapter 5.) Assuming you are working in 32-bit mode, then the easiest way to verify that a bus error is indeed caused by 32-bit dirty software is to

1. Turn off 32-bit addressing.

2. Reboot in 24-bit mode.

3. Do whatever it was you were doing when the bus error occurred. If the system doesn't bomb, then the software is 32-bit dirty. If the system does bomb again, then there may be a bug in the software. (Remember to rule out INIT conflicts before calling tech support!)

The only reasonable solution to 32-bit dirty software is an upgrade from the manufacturer. (You can always run the software in 24-bit mode, but switching between 24-bit and 32-bit modes requires rebooting the computer and is therefore rather inconvenient.) If the manufacturer doesn't want to make the effort to do an upgrade, then you should seriously consider moving to another program of the same type.

Application Software Versus the 68040

When the Macintosh Quadras first appeared, a number of software packages had trouble running on the 68040. If you have a Macintosh with a 68040 CPU and are using software that hasn't been updated since late 1991, then the problem may be that the software isn't compatible with the microprocessor. The reason for the problem lies in the way in which the 68040 manages its internal caches.

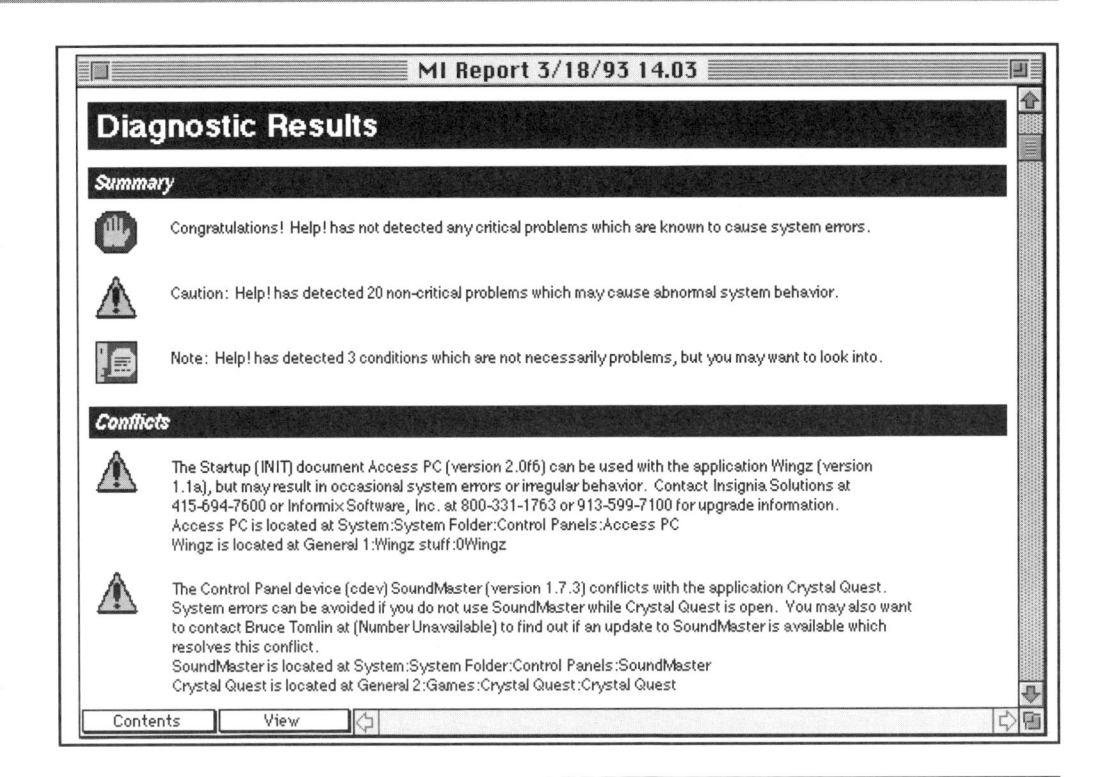

Figure 4.8 Using Help! diagnostic software to identify INIT conflicts

(Details on this problem can be found in Chapter 7.)

If you are experiencing problems with a 68040 Mac and older software, the easiest way to deal with the problem is to contact the software manufacturer. In most cases, technical service personnel will be aware of any 68040 incompatibilities and will have already produced an updated version of the product that fixes the problem.

For a time, Apple did provide a control panel device that turned off the 68040's internal caches. However, even if you can find a copy of this control panel, using it isn't a good solution to the problem. Turning off the CPU's caches severely impairs its performance, negating the benefits of the 68040 for which you paid more in the first place. The only reasonable solution is a software upgrade.

Basic Hardware Diagnostic Techniques

The goal of hardware diagnostics for those of us who aren't trained service technicians is to isolate the component that is the source of the problem. Although you may not be able to fix the problem yourself, you can at least approach a service technician with a good idea of what is wrong, saving yourself both time and money.

There are two general techniques for identifying which part of your Macintosh is having trouble. The first involves swapping components until you isolate exactly which part of the system is at fault. The second uses diagnostic software that tests components and circuits.

Component Swapping

The idea behind component swapping is to eliminate, one by one, parts of the system as the cause of a hardware problem. For example, assume that you have powered up your Mac but your monitor has no picture (the screen is dark). First, you verify that the monitor is plugged in and turned on. Beyond those obvious sources of the problem, there are five other possible culprits: the power cord, the video circuitry, the slot containing the video board (assuming the video circuitry is on an expansion board), the monitor cable, or the monitor itself. To isolate the problem, you would do the following:

1. Make sure the monitor is turned off. Replace the power cord and turn the monitor on again. If the monitor still doesn't come on, then the problem isn't with the power cord.

2. Turn off the power to the monitor and the computer. Replace the cable between the video circuitry and the monitor. Turn on the monitor and computer. If the monitor still has no picture, the problem isn't with the monitor cable.

3. Turn off the power to the monitor and the computer. If your video circuitry is on an expansion board and you have more than one slot of the same type, move the expansion board to another slot. Turn on the monitor and computer. If the monitor still has no pic-

ture, the problem isn't with the slot in which the board was placed. (If you want to be doubly sure, try the board in yet another slot.)

4. Locate a friend or colleague with a Macintosh that can use your monitor. Attach your monitor to the second Macintosh. If the monitor doesn't work, then the problem is with the monitor. If it does work, then it is likely that the problem is with the video circuitry.

5. If your video circuitry is on an expansion board, you can perform a final test by installing the board in a second Macintosh. If the board doesn't work in the second Mac, then it is almost certainly the cause of the problem.

When the problem is a cable, you can simply replace it. However, if the problem is with the video circuitry or the monitor, then it's time to get outside help. If your video circuitry is the problem and is on the logic board, you'll need a service technician. If your video circuitry is the problem but it's on an expansion board, you'll probably need to contact the manufacturer of the board. The same holds true for problems with a monitor: If it's an Apple monitor, contact a service technician; if it's a third-party monitor, contact the manufacturer.

The trick to this process is having components that you know are in good working condition for swapping. Although most people can't afford to keep a second Mac around just for troubleshooting, you should always have extra cables. Most components use the same type of power cord. (The major exception is monitors that plug into the system unit.) There are only four types of SCSI cables. Monitor cables are often specific to the monitor, but a second cable is affordable. Also consider keeping extra network cables (handy, for example, for figuring out whether you've got a printer problem or a network problem). By having extra cables on hand, you can do some preliminary component swapping before you have to go hunting for a second Mac.

Where can you get a second Mac if you don't work in an office that has lots of Macs or have a friend or family member with a Mac that can use the component you want to test? If all else fails, you can take the component to an authorized Apple service center. Most have enough machines on hand to test your hardware. Authorized Apple service centers also have diagnostic tools that, although available to the general public, are too expensive for most individual purchasers. (One such tool, the TechStep, is discussed later in this chapter.) Service

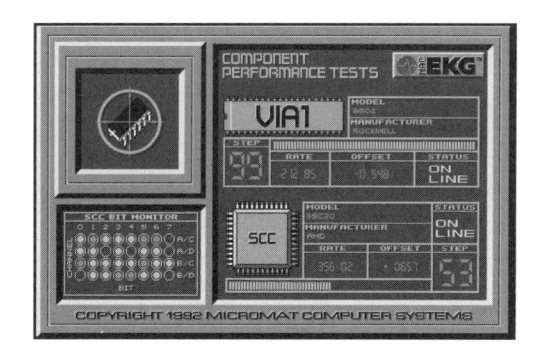

Fix Your Own Mac: Upgrading and Troubleshooting

Figure 4.9 MacEKG component tests

Figure 4.10 MacEKG's performance histogram

technicians are often able to do testing that you can't. Unfortunately, they probably won't do it for free.

Diagnostic Software

Diagnostic software performs tests on your hardware, reporting on the performance of many components, including some of the circuits on the logic board. There are three major third-party software diagnostic products (MacEKG, Snooper, and Peace of Mind). In addition, Apple has its own suite of diagnostic software utilities called MacTestPro.

> **By the way:** A comparative review of MacEKG, Snooper, and Peace of Mind can be found in the June 21, 1993 issue of *MacWEEK*.

Diagnostics with MacEKG

MacEKG is a system monitoring tool. It has two basic uses. First, it can be used on a one-time basis to test individual system components. For example, in Figure 4.9 MacEKG is testing the SCC. However, MacEKG is used to its best advantage as a system monitor that is run at least once each time your Macintosh is booted. The software computes its "MicroMat Performance Rating" (MPR) as a composite of all performance measures and graphs them over time (see Figure 4.10). Running MacEKG regularly therefore not only can identify acute problems with individual components, but detects gradual system degradation.

In addition, MacEKG can help diagnose those pesky intermittent problems. Its ReActivator feature automatically reboots the Mac, runs MacEKG, and reboots again. By setting ReActivator to cycle 13 or more times (for example, Figure 4.11), you can simulate a couple of weeks of system start-ups. ReActivator is also good for testing a machine before and after an upgrade or repair is performed.

MacEKG performs the following hardware tests:

- Logic (tests CPU and FPU operation)
- Components (tests of major circuits on the motherboard)
- VIA1
- VIA2
- SCC
- SCSI
- PRAM
- ASC
- RAM
- Media (tests of SCSI devices attached to built-in SCSI ports;

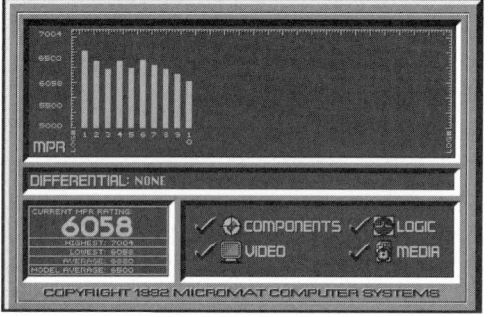

Chapter 4: Troubleshooting Techniques

MacEKG cannot access most SCSI-2 cards)

- Video (tests of the startup monitor; MacEKG cannot check other monitors)

If any MacEKG test detects a problem, the program displays a warning. For example, in Figure 4.12, MacEKG has detected a problem with the VIA1 chip. MacEKG also issues a warning if the MPR drops below a threshold level in any of the four major test areas.

MacEKG installs like an INIT. However, its behavior is different from most INITs. When configured to run at system startup, MacEKG loads last, after all INITs have been loaded but before the Finder is loaded. It therefore has access to more RAM than it does if run at any other time. After finishing its work, MacEKG removes most of its code from memory.

MacEKG stores the result of its tests in its logs. The logs can be viewed on-line from the MacEKG control panel or exported to text files for printing. Log data are retained for the 25 most recent runs, making it easy to go back and see patterns in system performance.

Diagnostics with Snooper

Snooper is a diagnostics program that not only tests Macintosh hardware components, but provides benchmarks that compare the performance of your Mac against other models in the Macintosh line. Unlike MacEKG, Snooper is a stand-alone application program. It works with any Macintosh from the Mac Plus onward.

Snooper runs four groups of tests. The logic tests (see Figure 4.13) test the following components:

- RAM
- PRAM
- Real-time clock
- SCSI
- Serial ports (AppleTalk must be turned off and any connectors in the printer and modem ports must be replaced with the LoopBack Plugs supplied with the Snooper package.)
- CPU
- ADB
- FPU
- Video RAM (if present)
- CPU accelerator (if present)
- SCSI expansion board (if present)

The disk tests (see Figure 4.14) perform several measures on any attached hard drive:

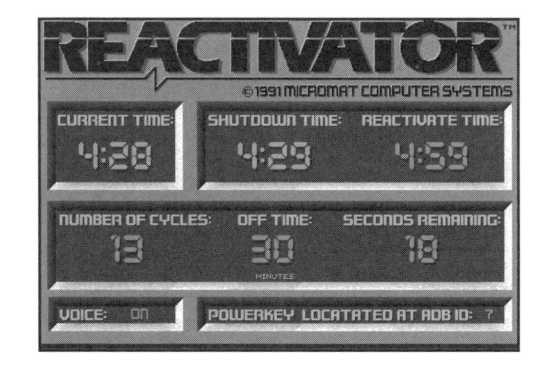

Figure 4.11 Using MacEKG's ReActivator function to repeatedly reboot and test a Mac

Figure 4.12 A MacEKG warning

87

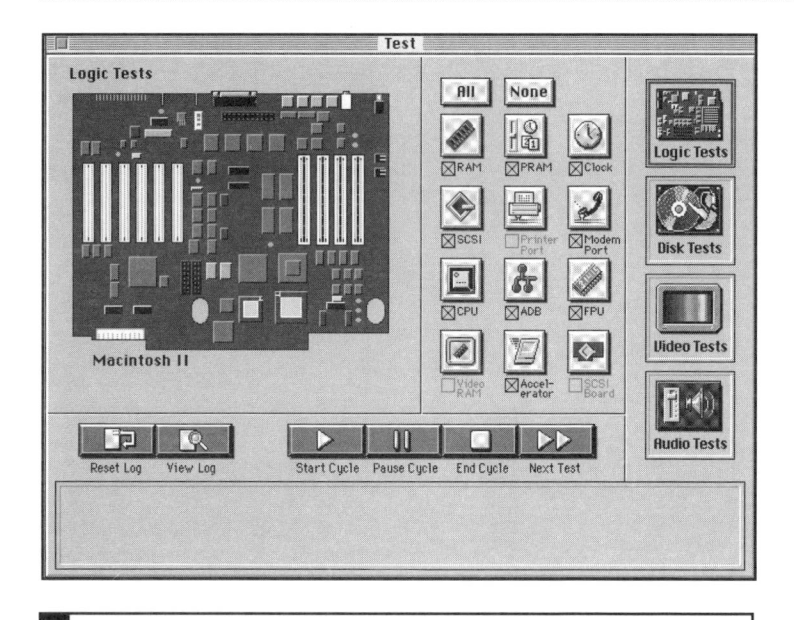

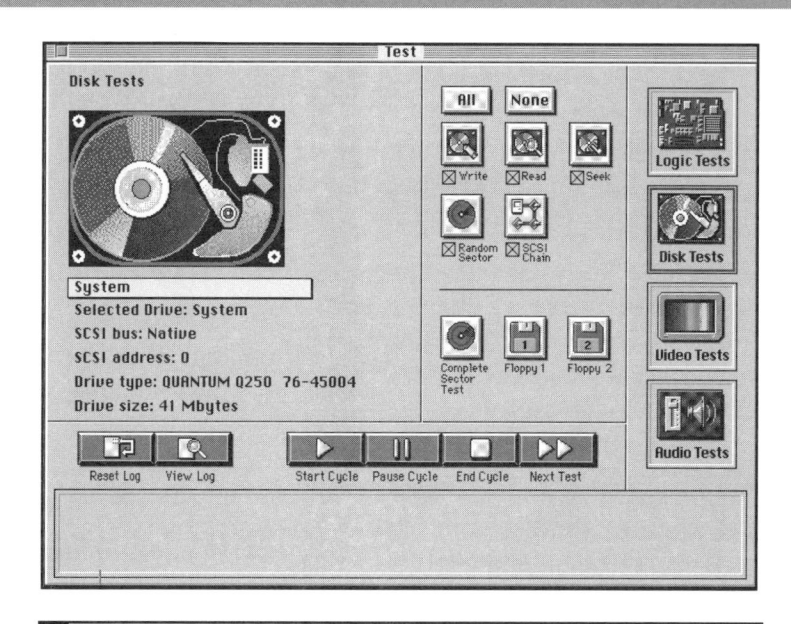

Fix Your Own Mac: Upgrading and Troubleshooting

Figure 4.13 *Using Snooper to conduct logic tests*

Figure 4.14 *Using Snooper to test SCSI disk drives*

- Write (Writes and verifies a 4K file.)
- Read (Reads and verifies a 4K file.)
- Seek (*Seek time* is the average time it takes to move a disk drive's read/write heads from one cylinder to another. A disk *cylinder* represents a cross-section of a disk made up of the same track through all disk surfaces. It's like taking a stack of pancakes and then using a circular cookie cutter to cut out a circle with a circumference but no contents from the stack. In this analogy, the circumference of the circle is as wide as a single track.)
- Random sector (Randomly checks disk sectors.)
- SCSI chain (Verifies all disks in the SCSI bus.)

In addition, the drive tests can perform a complete sector test to test every sector on the selected drive. Regardless of the size of the drive, this type of test takes a long time. However, if you are having disk read or write problems, this is one way to find out if the problems are caused by bad sectors on the disk. Finally, if you have a floppy disk inserted into a floppy drive, Snooper can test the performance of that drive.

Chapter 4: Troubleshooting Techniques

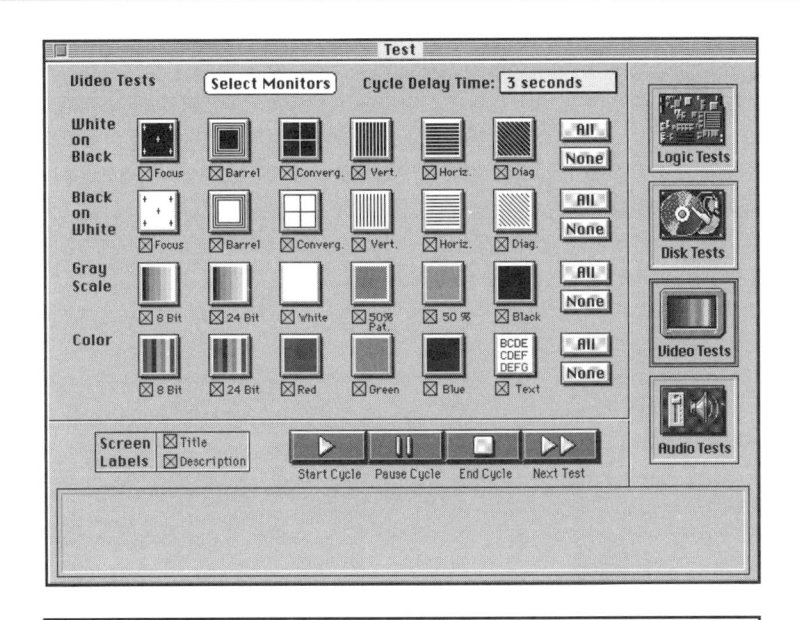

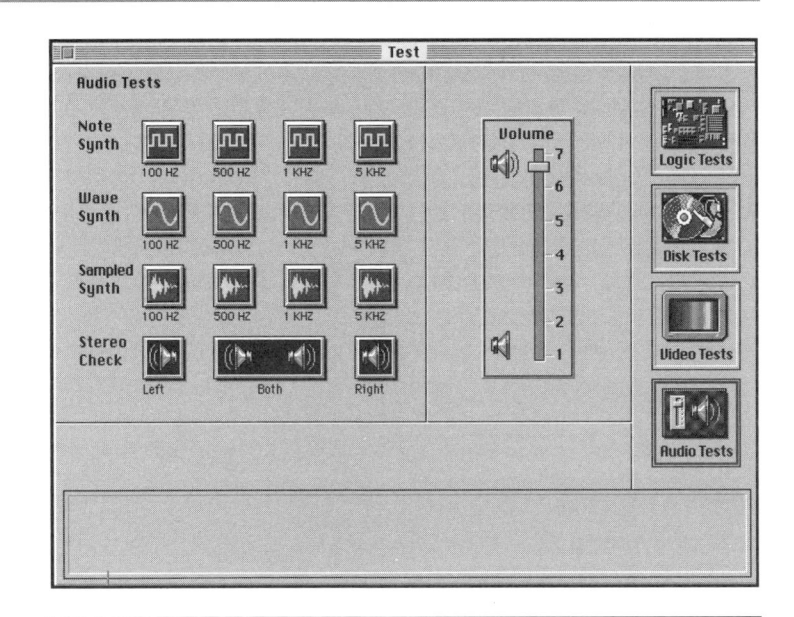

Figure 4.15 Snooper's video tests

Figure 4.16 Using Snooper to check system audio

The video tests (see Figure 4.15) let you evaluate all installed monitors. The tests display a series of patterns on your monitor(s) and let you know what you should be seeing and the kind of problems that a pattern can identify. These tests therefore aren't automatic. You must look at the screen as the patterns are being displayed so that you can recognize when a pattern isn't displayed as it should be.

The final group of tests evaluates the Macintosh's audio capabilities (see Figure 4.16). These tests generate sounds through the Macintosh's speakers and check the stereo capabilities of specific Macintosh models. In addition, they test sound input for those Macs that have built-in microphone capabilities.

When working interactively, Snooper signals a failed test with a system beep and a message at the bottom of the screen. However, Snooper's reports store the result of all component tests. Reports can be viewed on the screen or printed. All report data are kept until you specifically clear the reports, making it possible to check system performance over a period of time.

Fix Your Own Mac: *Upgrading and Troubleshooting*

Diagnostics with Peace of Mind

Peace of Mind provides a wide range of hardware tests, including some that require user assistance. It has two user interfaces. The first (the "Normal" interface in Figure 4.17) consists of a series of buttons, each of which initiates a group of tests ("Quick Tests"). If a type of hardware passes its tests, the word *Passed* appears under the type of hardware's icon; otherwise, the word *Failed* appears and details are written to a report. The report can be viewed on the screen or printed.

As you can see in Figure 4.17, Peace of Mind tests the following:

- RAM (SIMMs and the address bus)
- Video RAM (if present)
- A QuickDraw accelerator (if present)
- All attached monitors
- The SCSI controller and devices connected to the native SCSI bus (but not devices connected to a NuBus SCSI card)
- Processors (CPU, FPU, and MMU)
- Sound
- Keyboard
- Mouse
- Floppy drives
- Printers
- Clocks (CPU and real-time)
- PRAM
- Printer and serial ports

In addition, it computes a number of standard system benchmarks that can be used to compare system performance over time.

In-depth control over the testing is provided by the "Power User" interface (see

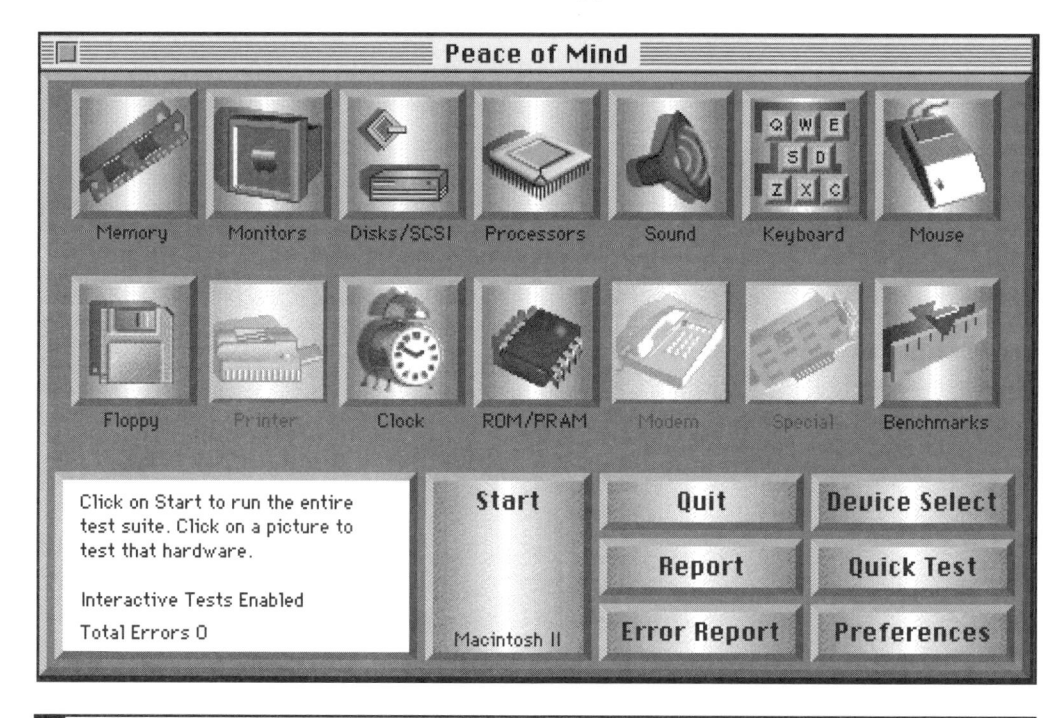

Figure 4.17 Peace of Mind's "Normal" interface

Figure 4.18). From this display, which works very much like a System 7 disk directory listing, you can choose specifically which tests you want to perform and execute them individually or in groups.

Peace of Mind's "interactive" tests require user participation. These include tests such as the keyboard test (see Figure 4.19), for which the user presses each key. Peace of Mind detects keys that stick as well as keys that don't return properly ("Key Bounce"). Many of the sound tests also require user input to determine whether the sound generated by the Macintosh was adequate.

Peace of Mind provides a looping function that repeats tests for a specified length of time. This feature is very useful for catching intermittent errors.

Peace of Mind comes with two emergency disks, one for 800K drives and one for 1.4Mb drives. Although these disks aren't big enough to provide the entire Peace of Mind test suite, they will let you test main memory and devices connected to the native SCSI bus.

MacTest Pro

MacTest Pro is the latest version of a software diagnostic utility from Apple. Prior to the spring of 1993, it was available only to authorized Apple service technicians. However, it can now be

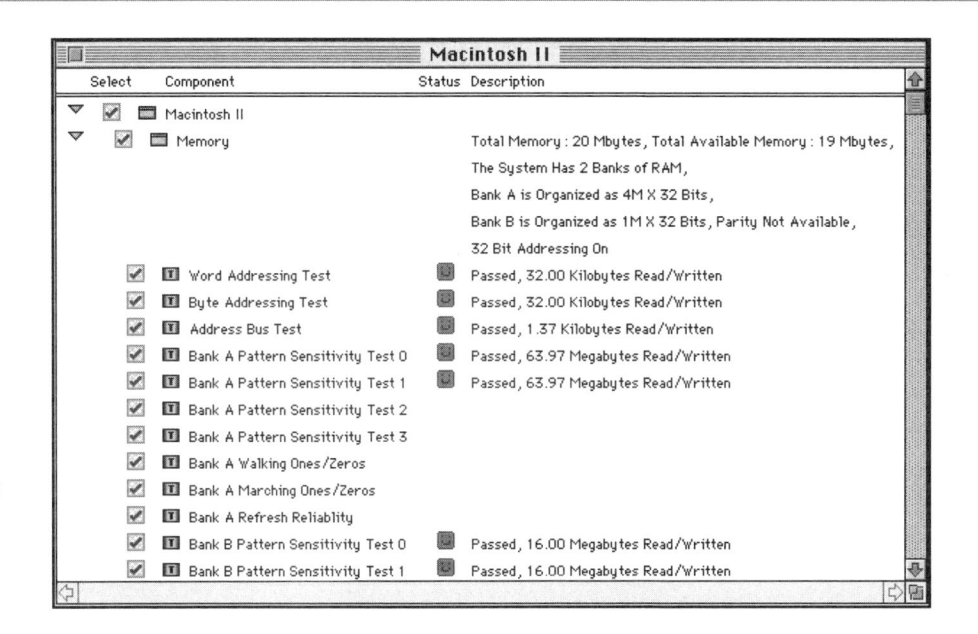

Figure 4.18 Peace of Mind's "Power User" interface

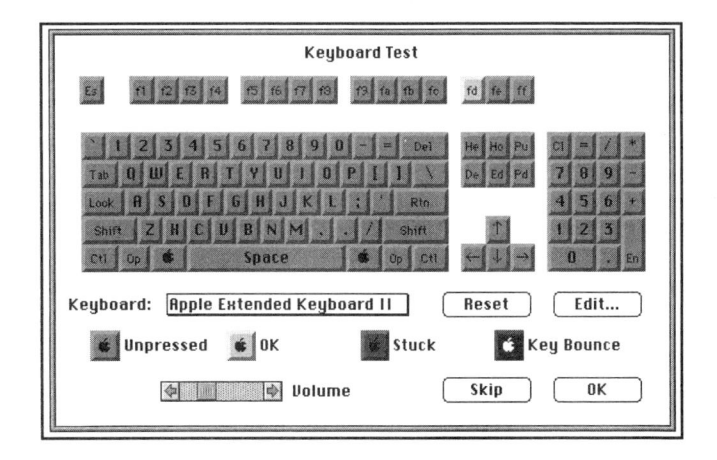

Figure 4.19 Peace of Mind's keyboard test

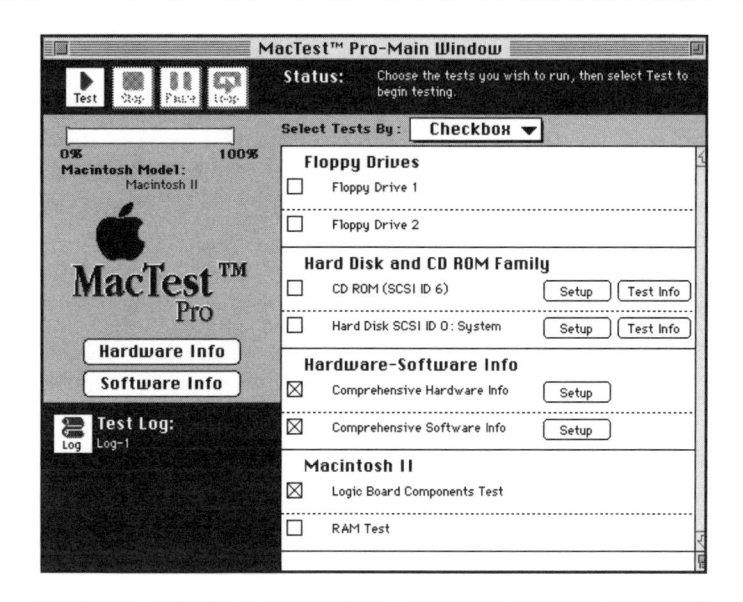

Figure 4.20 Tests performed by MacTest Pro

purchased by anyone at a price competitive with both MacEKG and Snooper.

Because MacTest Pro was originally directed at people servicing Apple brand products, its tests focus on Apple equipment. It tests a wide range of Apple hardware, including Macintosh logic board circuits, hard drives, monitors, video boards, floppy drives, and CD-ROM players. Although it can recognize that hardware made by a company other than Apple is installed in a Macintosh, it can't test the third-party products.

In general, MacTest Pro tests all installed floppy drives, any Apple hard disks, any Apple CD-ROM players, logic board components, video RAM, RAM, Apple video boards, and Apple monitors. It also provides an in-depth profile of the hardware and software installed in a Macintosh. The specific tests, however, depend exactly on the Macintosh model being tested. The tests are provided as individual modules, so that the program can be customized for specific models. The tests shown in Figure 4.20, for example, are for a Macintosh II, IIx, and IIcx.

MacTest Pro modules are grouped into "CPU Tests" (with versions for various Macintosh models), "Hard Disk, CD ROM Tests," "Floppy Drive Tests," "Apple Video Card Tests," and "Communication Ports Tests." As an example, the CPU test suite for the largest group of Macintosh models (II, IIx, IIcx, IIfx, IIvi, IIvx, LC, LC II, LC III, SE/30, Performa 200, Performa 400, Performa 600, Classic II, Color Classic) can be found in Table 4.1. A more extensive set of CPU tests is available for the Quadras and Centrises; PowerBook CPU tests are also available.

The hard drive tests can be used on any Macintosh with an Apple-brand hard drive (internal or external). They scan for bad areas on the disk, check the ability of the drive to access the entire disk, and verify the ability of the drive to write to the disk. The CD-ROM tests require a special CD-ROM for testing and stereo headphones. Performance of the drive is verified by listening to the test CD-ROM and noting the sounds.

Floppy drive tests work with Apple 800K or 1.4Mb drives. They can verify the formatting on a floppy disk and the integrity of the disk media. They can also verify that the drive can access the entire disk.

To help identify intermittent problems, MacTest Pro provides a looping feature. Looping repeats a group of tests a specific number of times or until the user clicks the mouse button. Both the number of times the tests are repeated and the specific tests included in the looping are under user control.

Diagnostics When the Machine Won't Boot

The diagnostic techniques you have read about so far are useful as long as you can get your Mac to boot. However, if it won't even boot (in other words, you never reach the desktop), then you need to resort to other techniques to try to isolate the problem.

What to Do When Your Startup Hard Disk Is Corrupted

When a Mac won't boot because the hard disk is corrupted, the cause can be the software on the disk, the disk surface, or the mechanics of the disk drive. Fortunately, disk drives are relatively reliable and most problems are with either the software or the disk surface (in other words, bad sectors). The general strategy for diagnosing and solving this type of problem is to assume the best (a software or disk surface problem) and attempt to solve the problem. If you can't, then in all likelihood the problem is mechanical.

Table 4.1 MacTest Pro Tests for the II, IIx, IIcx, IIfx, IIvi, IIvx, LC, LC II, LC III, SE/30, Performa 200, Performa 400, Performa 600, Classic II, and Color Classic

II IIx IIcx	IIfx	IIvx Perf. 600	IIvi LC, LC II LC III Color Classic Perf. 400	Classic II Perf. 200	SE/30	Test
						Logic board component tests
		✔	✔	✔	✔	I/O processor
		✔	✔	✔		Color lookup table (CLUT)
✔	✔	✔	✔	✔	✔	FPU
✔	✔	✔	✔	✔	✔	ROM
✔	✔	✔	✔	✔	✔	SCSI
✔		✔	✔	✔	✔	SCC
		✔				Cache
✔	✔	✔	✔	✔	✔	RAM
		✔	✔		✔	Video RAM
		✔	✔	✔	✔	Display test patterns

During the boot process, the small portion of the Macintosh operating system that is in ROM searches installed disks, looking for a System folder. It looks first at the internal floppy drive(s), ejecting any floppies from which it can't boot. If your Mac has a port for an external floppy drive (or serial hard drive, in older Macs), it checks any disks that are attached to that port. Failing to find a System folder on a floppy or serial hard drive, it turns to the SCSI port. Unless you have indicated otherwise through the Startup Disk control panel, it checks SCSI devices from the highest address down (6 down to 0).

By the way: The first hard disk available from Apple for the Macintosh was a serial hard disk (the HD 20) that plugged into the external floppy drive port; an external floppy drive could be daisy-chained from the hard drive. The Macintosh Plus can use the HD 20, but newer Macs with external floppy drive ports cannot. (Before you laugh at the thought of a slow, 20Mb drive, you should know that some of those drives, purchased in 1985, are still working without error.)

There is one major indication that you have a problem with your startup hard disk: The Mac can't find a System folder anywhere. In that case, it displays the icon of a floppy disk with a question mark in it. Alternatively, a happy Mac may flash on and off. In addition, the Mac may tell you that you can't read a particular disk and ask whether you want to reformat it.

When this happens, don't panic—and don't reformat anything! There are several reasons for a problem with your startup disk, ranging from a corrupted System file to bad sectors on the hard disk. You may be able to fix the problem without reformatting.

To find (and hopefully fix) the problem, you first need to be able to boot the computer. That means you've got to have a floppy from which you can boot. If you are running System 6, create a minimal System disk and place on it any diagnostic software you will be using. (Diagnostic software is discussed earlier in this chapter and in Chapter 10.) You'll need to be very selective about what you put on an 800K disk. However, if you install just a minimal set of System files, you should have enough room to add one or two repair tools.

If you are running System 7, you'll need to use a 1.44Mb floppy for your repair disk. (The System file is just too big to leave you any usable room on an 800K disk.) You can find a minimal System 7 on the Disk Tools disk that comes as part of the

System 7 installation set. Copy the System folder from Disk Tools (it takes up about 1.1Mb) and then add your repair software. Because space is limited, you will probably be limited to only one or two tools.

If you have more than one hard disk or a large hard disk that is partitioned into multiple volumes and the problem is only with the startup volume, then gaining access to any repair software on your hard disks can be a lot easier than you thought. You can install a System folder on a volume other than your damaged startup volume, reboot, and gain access to all your repair software. This procedure assumes that you have the operating system and your repair tools on floppy disk. To get started do the following:

1. Insert the operating system Install disk into a floppy drive and boot the computer. If the Mac asks you if you want to reformat the damaged hard disk volume, respond "no."

2. When the desktop appears, install at least a minimal system on an undamaged hard disk volume. If at all possible, this volume should be on another hard drive.

3. Once the installation is complete, return to the desktop. Use the Startup Disk control panel to make the volume containing the new System folder the startup disk.

4. Reboot.

5. If necessary, install your repair tools on the new startup disk. You are then ready to try to recover the damaged hard disk.

If you have only one hard disk volume, then you're limited to whatever you can fit on your repair disk. To get your machine up and running, insert the repair floppy into a floppy disk drive and reboot the computer. If the Mac asks you if you want to reformat the damaged hard disk volume, respond "no."

At this point, you have several options. You can certainly reformat the damaged disk volume and reinstall software from backups. However, it may be possible to repair the damage with software such as Norton Utilities or HDT ToolKit. (You will find more about disk diagnostic and repair utilities in Chapter 10.) Using disk repair tools is faster (and easier) than the reformat and restore route, but it is not always as effective.

You may also want to delete the System folder from the damaged disk and install a clean set of System files. In that case, you should reinstall fonts, INITs, and other startup items from your backup copies. (What? No backup copies? Tsk, tsk, tsk. Backups are the only insurance you can really count on in case of system failure. However, we're all human and it

Fix Your Own Mac: *Upgrading and Troubleshooting*

Figure 4.21 A friendly backup reminder

often takes getting burned once to convince someone of the necessity of keeping recent backups. If you can't remember, try making a photocopy of Figure 4.21 and taping it in a strategic location.)

If the preceding doesn't work, then you are probably looking at a physical problem with the hard disk or with your SCSI bus. For more information on how to handle such problems, see Chapter 10.

What to Do When INIT Conflicts Prevent Booting

Sometimes an INIT problem is so bad that the Mac hangs during the boot process and never makes it to the desktop. To handle this problem do the following:

1. Insert your repair floppy into a floppy drive and reboot the machine.
2. Remove all INITs that you absolutely don't need to reach the desktop from the System folder on your hard disk.
3. Eject the repair floppy.
4. Reboot. Your machine should reach the desktop successfully.

At this point, you can begin replacing INITs, one by one. When the boot process hangs, you'll have identified the offending INIT. Return to the repair floppy to gain access to the computer so you can remove that INIT once more. Alternatively, use one of the programs discussed earlier in this chapter (for example, Startup Manager or Conflict Catcher) to make the process of identifying the offending INIT easier. Once you've identified which INIT is the culprit, you'll either have to live without it or get an upgrade from the manufacturer.

What It Means When You See the Sad Mac

The first thing a Mac does when you power it up is to run a series of hardware diagnostic tests. The program that does these tests is located in ROM. If the computer fails any of those tests, the ROM displays a "sad Mac" on the screen (see Figure 4.22). Because these tests are performed *before* the program in ROM checks for system software on a disk, a sad Mac usually indicates some major hardware problem.

Underneath the sad Mac are some codes that indicate the nature of the failure. The codes are displayed in *hexadecimal.* Hexadecimal, or base 16, is a numbering system often used as a shorthand for binary (base 2). Whereas each number position in the decimal system represents a power of 10 and can accept the values 0 through 9, each hexadecimal number position represents a power of 16 and can accept the values 0 through 15. Therefore each hexadecimal digit can take the place of four binary digits. We don't have single digits for the values 10 through 15, so hexadecimal includes the letters *A* through *F* to stand for those values ($A = 10$, $B = 11$, $C = 12$, $D = 13$, $E = 14$, $F = 15$).

The sad Mac codes for Macintoshes with a 68000 CPU (Table 4.2) are six digits. The leftmost two, the "class code," indicate which part of the diagnostic program identified a problem. The rightmost four digits, the "subclass code," indicate what type of problem was found. Class code 01 indicates a problem with ROM. When that occurs on a Macintosh out of warranty, your only recourse is to try to find a set of replacement ROMs. Either you can purchase a replacement motherboard from an Apple dealer or a used-Macintosh dealer or you can attempt to find a set of ROMs from a used-Macintosh dealer.

Class codes 02 through 05 indicate problems with RAM. The subclass codes actually identify which RAM chip is bad. If you see one of these class codes, be sure to note the subclass code. Then head for your nearest service center.

Class code 0F represents a *software exception* (a catastrophic error in a program from which the Macintosh cannot recover). Software exceptions rarely appear as a result of the diagnostics performed while a Mac is booting. However, you may see one if you accidentally hit the interrupt button (the rear button on the programmers switch) during the boot process. If that should occur, simply press the reset button or turn the machine off and then on to begin booting all over again.

By the way: Software exceptions can occur when programs are running. However, the most common result is a bomb box rather than a sad Mac code.

The Sad Mac codes were expanded when the Mac II appeared to accommodate the computer's 32-bit architecture. The software exception codes are the same as those in the original codes but are displayed in two rows of eight digits. For example, the following codes indicate a divide by zero error:

0000000F
00000004

The codes produced by the boot-time diagnostics have the following format:

XXXXYYYY
ZZZZZZZZ

The XXXX contains information about the state of the internal test manager;

Figure 4.22 The dilemma of a sad Mac

> **Table 4.2** Sad Mac Codes for the 68000 Macintoshes

Class Code	Meaning	Subclass Code
01	ROM test failed	Not used
02	Memory test—bus subtest	Location of bad RAM chip as follows:
		0001 (bad RAM chip at location F5)
		0002 (bad RAM chip at location F6)
		0004 (bad RAM chip at location F7)
		0008 (bad RAM chip at location F8)
		0010 (bad RAM chip at location F9)
		0020 (bad RAM chip at location F10)
		0040 (bad RAM chip at location F11)
		0080 (bad RAM chip at location F12)
		0100 (bad RAM chip at location G5)
		0200 (bad RAM chip at location G6)
		0400 (bad RAM chip at location G7)
		0800 (bad RAM chip at location G8)
		1000 (bad RAM chip at location G9)
		2000 (bad RAM chip at location G10)
		4000 (bad RAM chip at location G11)
		8000 (bad RAM chip at location G12)
03	Memory test—byte write	0008 (problem is with SIMMs 1 and 3)
		0800 (problem is with SIMMs 2 and 4)
04	Memory test—Mod3 test	Location of bad RAM chip as above
05	Memory test—address uniqueness	Location of bad RAM chip as above
0F	Software Exception	0001 (bus error)
		0002 (address error)
		0003 (illegal instruction)
		0004 (divide by zero)
		0005 (check instruction)
		0006 (traps instruction)
		0007 (privilege violation)
		0008 (trace)
		0009 (line 1010 unimplemented instruction)*
		000A (bad partition map on hard drive)
		000B (other exception)
		000C (not used)
		000D (interrupt button on programmer's switch has been pressed)
		0064 (couldn't read System file into memory; System software is probably incompatible with computer)

*This exception is actually not an error, but is part of the mechanism used to access routines in the Mac's ROM ToolBox.

you can ignore those digits. The YYYY indicates either a software exception (000F) or a hardware diagnostic failure. In some cases, the eight Z digits provide additional information about the problem.

The sad Mac codes for Macintoshes from the II onward can be found in Table 4.3. Notice that they identify which chip failed the startup diagnostics. When an error of this type occurs, jot down the entire sad Mac code and have it handy when you talk to a service technician.

Snooper's NuBus Board

There is yet another diagnostic tool available for use with a Macintosh that won't boot: Snooper's NuBus diagnostic board. If your Mac can use NuBus boards, then this board may be able to identify the major component that has failed. The way in which this board operates is similar to some of the diagnostic tools used by authorized service technicians. However, it is easier to use and costs considerably less.

By the way: Although the Snooper board is compatible with the IIsi, the orientation of the IIsi's slot makes it difficult to see the lights on the board. In addition, Macs with only one NuBus slot make it impossible to test for NuBus cards that are drawing too much power.

As you can see in Figure 4.23, the board has seven lights across the top. The leftmost three are used to test the voltages coming from the Macintosh's power supply. Problems with these lights indicate either a faulty power supply, NuBus cards that are faulty or drawing too much power, or an internal hard drive that is drawing too much power. By removing NuBus cards one at a time and disconnecting the internal hard drive, the board can be used to identify exactly which component is affecting the computer's internal power.

The light labeled *clock* tests the NuBus clock. This is a 10MHz clock the operates much like the CPU's internal clock; it sends regular pulses down the NuBus to synchronize access to it. Problems with this light could indicate a problem with a NuBus card or a major failure of the NuBus clock itself. To find out, you simply remove the NuBus cards one by one. (Be sure the Macintosh is turned off when you are removing or inserting boards!) If all cards are removed and the Snooper board still indicates a problem, then the source of the problem is probably on the motherboard. In that case, take a deep breath and be prepared to replace the motherboard.

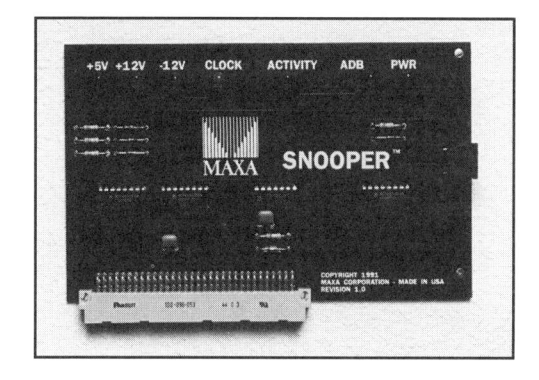

Figure 4.23 Snooper's NuBus Board

Table 4.3 Sad Mac Codes for the 32-bit Macintoshes

YYYY Code	Meaning	Use of Z Digits
0001	ROM checksum failure	Not used
0002	RAM failure in Bank B*	Identifies which bits failed
0003	RAM failure in Bank B	Identifies which bits failed
0004	RAM failure in Bank A	Identifies which bits failed
0005	Address bus failure	Identifies which line in the address bus failed
0006	Can't access VIA1 chip	Not used
0007	Can't access VIA2 chip	Not used
0008	Can't access Font Desk Bus	Not used
0009	Can't access MMU	Not used
000A	Can't access NuBus	Not used
000B	Can't access SCSI chip	Not used
000C	Can't access IWM chip	Not used
000D	Can't access SCC chip	Not used
000E	Data bus failure†	Identifies which line in the data bus failed
000F	(unused)	
FFxx	Software exception where xx can be:	

01 (bus error)
02 (address error)
03 (illegal instruction)
04 (divide by zero)
05 (check instruction)
06 (cpTrap CC, Trap CC, Trap V)
07 (privilege violation)
08 (trace)
09 (line 1010 unimplemented instruction)‡
0A (line 1111 unimplemented instruction)§
0B (unused)
0C (CP protocol violation)
0D (format exception)
0E (spurious interrupt)
0F (Trap 0-15 exception)
10 (Interrupt Level 1)
11 (Interrupt Level 2)
12 (Interrupt Level 3)
13 (Interrupt Level 4)
14 (Interrupt Level 5)
15 (Interrupt Level 6)
16 (Interrupt Level 7)
17 (FPU branch or set on unordered condition)
18 (FPU inexact result)
19 (FPU divide by zero)
1A (FPU underflow)
1B (FPU operand error)
1C (FPU overflow)
1D (FPU not-a-number error)
1E (PMMU configuration error)
1F (PMMU illegal operation)
20 (PMMU access level violation)

*The SIMM slots in many Macintoshes are grouped into "banks." All slots in a bank must either be filled with SIMMs of the same size and speed or be completely empty. The Mac II, IIx, and IIfx, for example, have two banks of four slots each.
†This error may also be caused by a bad SIMM.
‡This is actually not an error but part of the mechanism used to access routines in the Macintosh's ROM.
§This is actually not an error but part of the mechanism used to access an FPU.

The light labeled *activity* looks for activity on the NuBus. If one NuBus board is malfunctioning, it may interfere with normal activity on the NuBus. The technique for identifying the problem is the same as that for identifying a faulty clock: Remove NuBus boards one by one. If all boards have been removed and the Snooper board still reports a problem, then the motherboard is probably at fault.

When the Snooper board is connected to an ADB port, the rightmost two lights can test for and identify ADB problems. By disconnecting ADB devices one by one, you can determine whether the problem is caused by a VIA failure, a failed ADB fuse, or a faulty ADB device. If the VIA has failed or the ADB fuse has blown, you must either replace the motherboard or find someone who can do board-level repairs to replace the chip. If the problem is with an ADB device, you can replace it or send it back to the manufacturer for repair. Since most ADB devices are relatively inexpensive and are, at the same time, essential for the operation of the computer, you may decide that it's most cost effective to just replace the offending component.

By the way: The ADB fuse is soldered to the motherboard. It's not the plug-in type that can easily be replaced.

Chapter 4: Troubleshooting Techniques

THE APPLE TECHSTEP

The ultimate Macintosh hardware diagnostic tool is a hand-held device from Apple called TechStep (see Figure 4.24). Formerly available only to authorized service technicians, TechStep can now be purchased by anyone who wants to pay the $995 price. Although TechStep's price probably is probably more than most individual Macintosh owners want to spend, it can save a business with many Macintoshes a great deal in diagnostic and repair costs.

TechStep connects to the Macintosh through cables to the ADB, modem, printer, audio, and SCSI ports. The tests it performs are controlled by software in ROM. Like MacTest Pro, the tests in a ROM pack are geared toward one group of Macintosh CPUs or type of peripheral. (The TechStep can hold two ROM packs at once.) Operation of the device and the results of the tests it performs appear on a four-line LCD screen. Results are also saved inside the TechStep and can be downloaded to a Macintosh via a serial cable (either the printer or modem port) for later printing or permanent storage.

TechStep provides a wider range of tests and more in-depth testing than any other Macintosh diagnostic tool. For example, the initial ROM packs—which

Figure 4.24 The Apple TechStep

handle the Classic, SE, SE/30, II, IIx, and IIcx—test the components in Table 4.4. The SCSI hard drive tests provided by the SCSI HD Tests ROM pack can identify bad areas on the disk and in many cases can actually recover data stored on those bad spots. TechStep also provides a looping function that repeats one or more tests to help identify intermittent problems.

Fix Your Own Mac: Upgrading and Troubleshooting

Table 4.4 *Tests Provided for the Apple TechStep in Its CPU Tests, Volume 1, and SCSI HD Tests ROM Packs*

II/IIx	IIcx	SE/30	SE	Classic	Tests
✔	✔	✔	✔	✔	Power supply voltage
✔					Battery voltage
	✔				Power-up voltage
✔	✔	✔	✔	✔	ROM*
✔	✔	✔	✔	✔	Base RAM (first 33K)†
✔	✔	✔	✔	✔	RAM size‡
✔	✔	✔	✔	✔	Read and write RAM performance
		✔			Video RAM
✔	✔	✔	✔	✔	VIA
✔	✔	✔	✔	✔	Real-time clock chip
✔	✔	✔	✔	✔	PRAM
✔	✔	✔	✔	✔	SCC
✔	✔	✔	✔	✔	SCSI controller
✔	✔	✔	✔	✔	SWIM/IWM
✔	✔	✔			FPU
✔	✔	✔	✔	✔	Sound
✔	✔	✔	✔	✔	ADB
✔	✔	✔			Apple video card(s) in NuBus slot(s)§
✔	✔	✔	✔	✔	Floppy drives
					SCSI functions
✔	✔	✔	✔	✔	Termination voltage
✔	✔	✔	✔	✔	Correctness of termination
✔	✔	✔	✔	✔	Bus scan to identify all attached devices
✔	✔	✔	✔	✔	Positioning of read/write heads
✔	✔	✔	✔	✔	Write
✔	✔	✔	✔	✔	Self-test (initiate test built into drive)
✔	✔	✔	✔	✔	Check for bad spots on the disk surface

*On a Macintosh II or SE, this test identifies only that there is a ROM problem, not which ROM chip is bad. To identify the specific ROM, you would need to swap ROM chips one at a time and repeat the test.

†The TechStep needs a portion of the first 33K of Macintosh RAM to perform many of its tests and therefore must verify that this region of RAM is OK before proceeding to other diagnostics.

‡This test not only reports the total amount of RAM installed, but indicates whether the SIMMs in each bank are all of the same size and speed and whether SIMM sizes are appropriate to the banks in which they have been installed.

§TechStep tests only Apple video cards because third-party boards don't have the information that TechStep needs to identify the boards.

Adding Memory

One of the best upgrades you can give your Mac is more memory. In most cases, it gives you the biggest gain in computing power for your money. Although installing memory in a Macintosh is relatively easy, making sure you get the right type of memory and the right amount of memory can be a challenge. Each Macintosh model has memory peculiarities that determine how much memory it can access, what type of memory it requires, how that memory can be configured, and how fast that memory must be. Therefore before getting to machine specifics, this chapter helps you understand what determines how much memory a Macintosh can access. It also tries to answer the question, "Just how much memory do I need?"

How Much Memory Do I Need?

The quick, flippant answer to the question of how much memory you need is, "As much as you can afford, up to the maximum RAM supported by your Macintosh." How much do you *really* need? That depends on the type of software you use.

One way to get a handle on how much you need is to pay attention to the way you use software. Jot down how much RAM the operating system takes up. (If you're using System 7, that will usually be something between 2 and 3Mb.) Then, over a period of several days, keep track of each application you use and how much memory is allocated to it. Note every time you have to quit an application so that you have enough memory to run another. Add up the memory requirements of all those applications that you wanted to be able to run at the same time but couldn't because you didn't have enough RAM. Be sure also to include any extra RAM you wished you could allocate to a program but couldn't. To that total add the amount of RAM used by the operating system. That's the amount of RAM you need for daily processing. To allow for growth, increase your total by at least 50%. This produces a good measure of the amount of RAM you should have installed in your Macintosh.

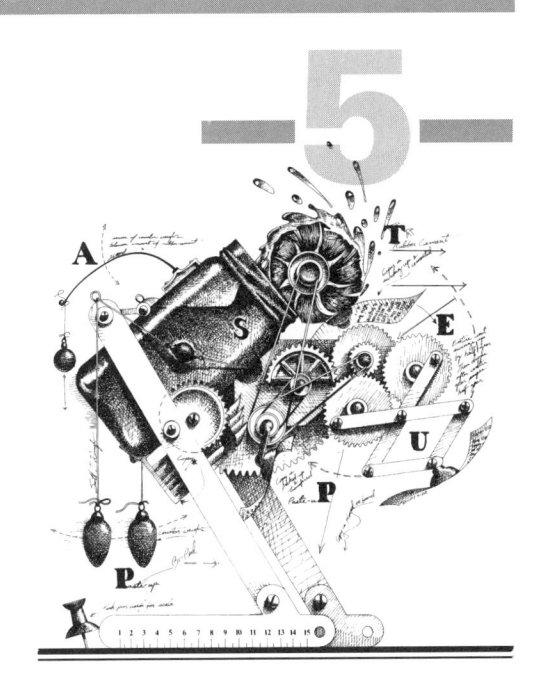

> **By the way:** If the amount of RAM you need is more than the total RAM your Macintosh can use, you have three choices. You can live with the maximum RAM your Mac can accept, you can add a CPU accelerator board that raises the RAM limit (an option for only some of the Compact Macs), or you can purchase a Mac with a higher RAM limit.

Hardware and Software Limits to RAM Expansion

The amount of RAM that you can install in your Macintosh is determined by both hardware and software factors. The total number of bytes that a computer can access (its *address space*) is related to the size of a portion of the computer's system bus. The proportion of that address space that can be used for RAM is determined by the amount of RAM soldered to the motherboard, the size and type of SIMMs that the computer can accept, and the way in which the system software allocates portions of the address space.

Memory and the System Bus

As you read in Chapter 1, the system bus carries signals from one component of the computer to another. To understand how the bus and memory are related, you have to look at the construction of the bus. A bus is actually a collection of circuits, called *lines*, running in parallel.

A drawing of a portion of a typical Macintosh bus appears in Figure 5.1. Each line in the bus is assigned a special purpose. Some lines carry addresses, in which case they are part of the *address bus*. Lines that carry data are part of the *data bus*. The remaining lines carry control signals, such as timing pulses from the CPU's internal clock and instructions to the computer's components (for example, "read" or "write").

Each line in the address and data buses represents 1 bit. A Macintosh address bus has either 24 or 32 lines. When the lines are viewed together as the bits of a binary number, a 32-bit address bus can carry values from 0 through 2^{32-1} (4,294,967,296, or 4Gb), each of which corresponds to a numbered byte. The maximum amount of memory that any Macintosh can address is therefore 4Gb.

However, Macintoshes with a 68000 microprocessor have only a 24-bit address bus, even though the CPU operates internally on 32-bit quantities. A 24-bit address bus can access 2^{24-1} bytes (16,777,215, or 16Mb). In the early days of the Macintosh, no one imagined that the Macintosh operating environment would need anywhere near a 16Mb address space; people thought that there was plenty of excess capacity.

Because they thought the missing 8 upper bits of the address bus would never be used, many programmers used those extra 8 bits for purposes other than addressing main memory. Programs that do this will bomb when used in an environment that expects 32-bit rather than 24-bit addresses and are often called *32-bit dirty*. Programs that don't play tricks with the upper 8 bits and run without a problem in a 32-bit environment are known as *32-bit clean*.

Whether your Macintosh can use 32-bit addressing depends on several things. First, it must have at least a 68020 microprocessor, which ensures that it has a 32-bit address bus. Second, it must have 32-bit-clean ROMs or software that compensates for the presence of 32-bit-dirty ROMs. Macintoshes from the LC onward have 32-bit clean ROMs. Other 68020 or 68030 Macintoshes need to install Mode32, an INIT developed by Connectix Corp.

By the way: Apple has licensed Mode32 for free distribution to owners of 68020 or 68030 Macs with dirty ROMs. To obtain a copy, call the Apple Customer Assistance Center at 1-800-776-2333.

By the way: System 7.1 comes with a system extension that theoretically replaces Mode32. However, users report numerous problems with the system extension. Mode32 works beautifully. Therefore you may want to stick with it at least until the bugs have been worked out of the Apple-written extension.

Regardless of whether your Macintosh can use 24- or 32-bit addressing, not all the address space can be allocated to RAM. ROM must have its own unique set of addresses. In addition, the Macintosh uses *memory-mapped I/O*. When a program wants to perform some input or output, it reads from or writes to a main memory address, rather than to a specific I/O device. These addresses don't physically correspond to RAM or ROM; instead they provide a mechanism for *device-independent I/O*. A program simply reads from or writes to the main memory addresses set aside for the device, using the same input and output commands regardless of the type of device. The actual input and output are handled by a *device driver*, software written specifically for each I/O device that handles the physical transfer of data. The beauty of this arrangement is that a Macintosh needs only one device driver for each I/O device, supplied either as a part of the Macintosh operating system

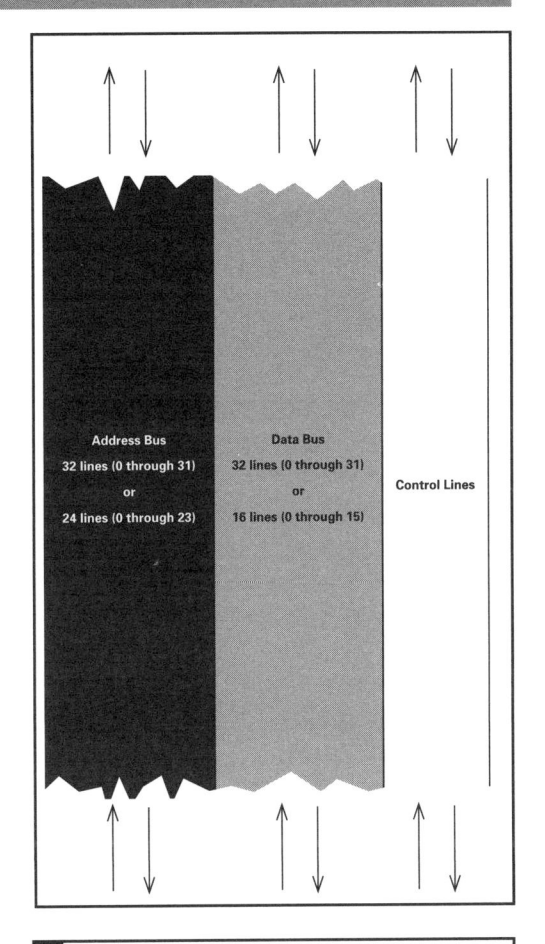

Figure 5.1 The parts of a Macintosh system bus

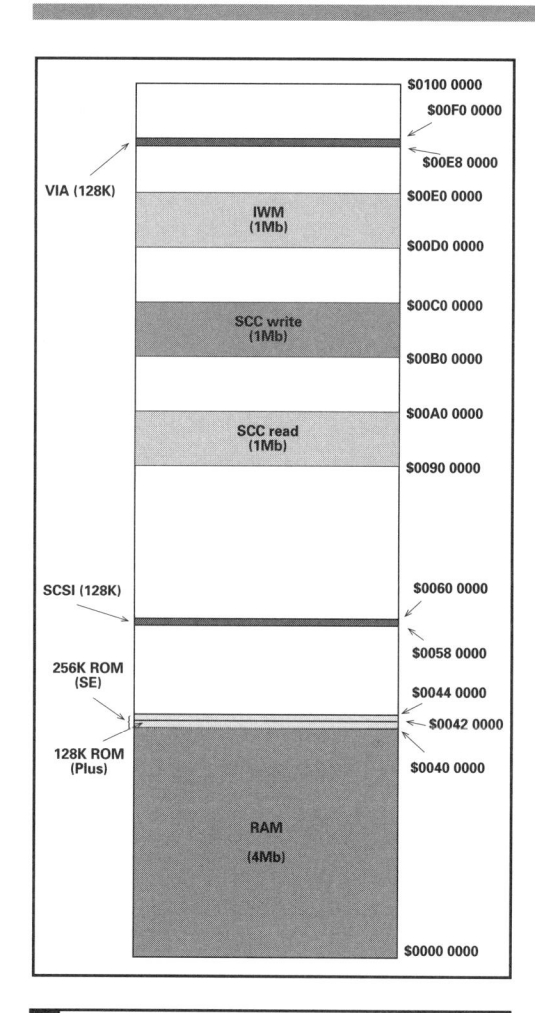

Fix Your Own Mac: Upgrading and Troubleshooting

Figure 5.2 Memory map for 68000 Macintoshes

[Memory map showing addresses from $0000 0000 to $0100 0000, with regions labeled: RAM (4Mb), 128K ROM (Plus), 256K ROM (SE), SCSI (128K), SCC read (1Mb), SCC write (1Mb), IWM (1Mb), VIA (128K)]

(for example, the LaserWriter driver) or by the manufacturer of the I/O device.

By the way: If you've ever installed software on an MS-DOS computer, you'll remember that each piece of MS-DOS software supplies its own set of device drivers.

By the same token, a programmer doesn't need to write a device driver or, in many cases, even to be concerned with the specific I/O device that the program will ultimately use. For example, most Macintosh software will run on any size monitor with any number of colors, without having to install a device driver for the specific monitor attached to the computer. (The major exceptions to this statement are some games and high-end graphics software that require a specific number of colors or shades of gray.)

The 68000 compact Macintoshes generally allocate RAM as in Figure 5.2. Note that the addresses that appear at the right of the figure are expressed in hexadecimal (indicated by the dollar sign preceding the number). The maximum address—$0100 0000—is equal to 16Mb. RAM is allocated to the address range $0000 0000 through $0040 0000, a total of 4Mb. That is why the maximum RAM that a compact Macintosh such as the Plus, Classic, or SE can use is 4Mb; the rest of the address space is allocated to ROM, I/O devices, and expansion slots.

The Macintosh II line, LC III, and 68040 Macintoshes use a general RAM allocation like that in Figure 5.3. RAM is given the first 1Gb of space, even though the maximum RAM that any current Macintosh can use is 256Mb. Just as with the 68000 Macs, the remaining address space is used by ROM, expansion slots, and I/O devices.

When a 32-bit Macintosh is used in 24-bit mode, the operating system translates 24-bit addresses into 32-bit addresses, using an allocation like that in Figure 5.4. Notice that 8Mb are allocated to RAM, producing the 8Mb RAM limit for Macintoshes with a 32-bit address bus that are operating in 24-bit mode. The 6Mb expansion slot space was originally designed for the Mac II, providing 1Mb of RAM for each NuBus slot.

By the way: Some software, such as Virtual from Connectix, can take the address space allocated to unused expansion slots and use it for virtual memory addresses. With Virtual, a 68020 Macintosh (equipped with a PMMU), 68030 Macintosh, or 68040 Macintosh can address up to 15Mb RAM when using virtual memory in 24-bit mode. The limit of 8Mb of physical RAM is still present.

Chapter 5: Adding Memory

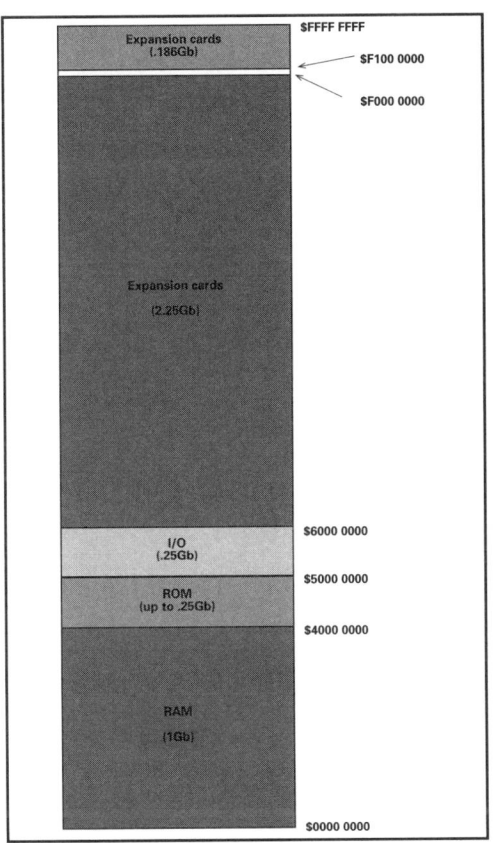

Figure 5.3 *32-bit RAM allocation*

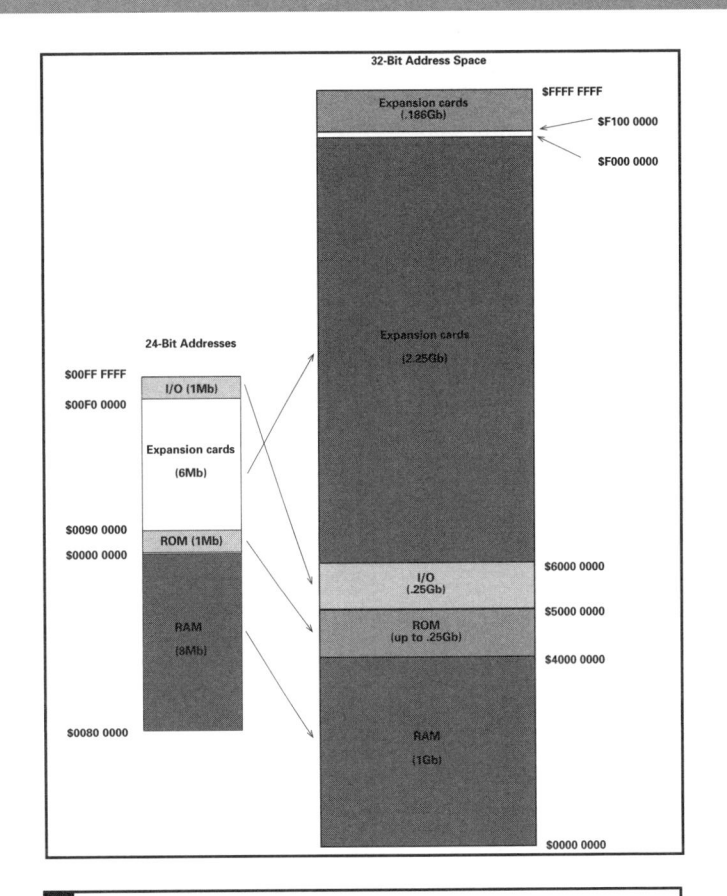

Figure 5.4 *Translating 24-bit to 32-bit addresses*

Although the remaining Macintoshes (LC, LC II, Classic II, Performa 200, Color Classic) have 32-bit address buses, they allocate their RAM differently from the rest of the 32-bit Macintoshes. As you can see in Figure 5.5, this memory mapping provides only 10Mb for RAM. Even though it may be possible to install more than 10Mb of physical RAM in one of these machines, the computer will only access 10Mb.

Notice in Figure 5.5 that 384K of RAM has been set aside as video RAM. If no

VRAM SIMM is installed in the computer's VRAM slot, the Macintosh can use this space for storing the memory map of the display screen. However, using regular RAM instead of VRAM limits you to a 13-inch monochrome monitor.

The remaining factors in determining how much RAM your Macintosh can use are the amount of RAM soldered to the motherboard and the number and type of SIMM slots.

UNDERSTANDING SIMMs

A *single in-line memory module* (SIMM) is a small circuit board that contains RAM chips. Memory is added to all Macintoshes except the 512Ke, 512K, and 128K by plugging a SIMM into a special SIMM slot on the computer's motherboard. However, all SIMMs are not alike. They differ not only in the type of chips on the SIMM, but in the speed of the SIMM.

Types of SIMMs

The types of SIMMs are summarized in Table 5.1. As you can see in Figure 5.6, as well as having different electronic characteristics, they look somewhat different. To complicate matters further, the Mac Portable and PowerBooks can accept only one RAM expansion card rather than the SIMMs used in desktop models. They therefore use a variety of RAM expansion boards with varying capacities.

SIMMs are made up of *dynamic RAM* (DRAM) chips. DRAM is both cheaper and slower than the *static RAM* that is used in cache memory. Once static RAM is given a

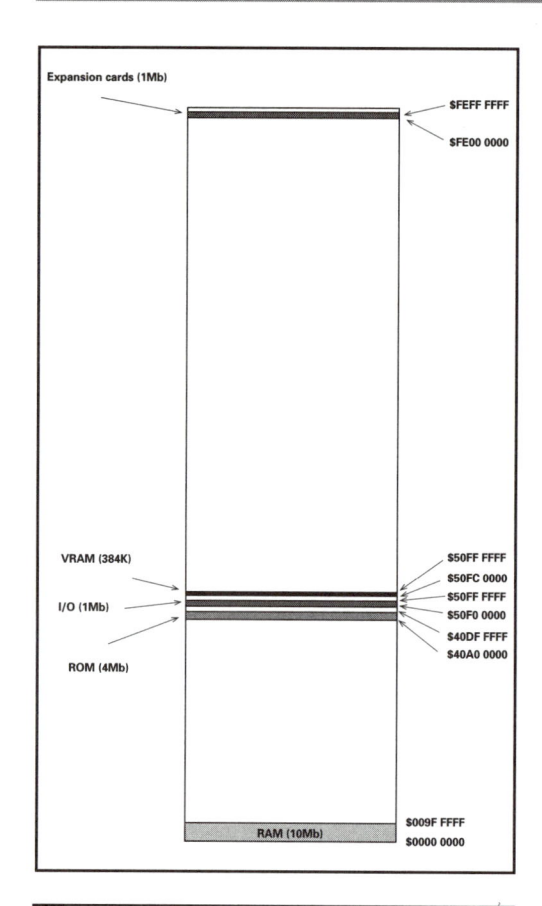

Figure 5.5 Address allocation for 32-bit Macintoshes with a 10Mb RAM limit

Table 5.1 Types of Macintosh SIMMs

Type of SIMM	Macintosh Model	Capacities
Parity (9-bit)	IIfx	256K,* 1Mb, 4Mb, 16Mb
72-pin (32-bit)	LC III, Centris 610, Centris 650, Centris 660av, Quadra 800, Quadra 840av	1Mb, 2Mb, 4Mb, 8Mb, 16Mb, 32Mb
30-pin with PAL™ logic	II, IIx[†]	4Mb
30-pin (8-bit)	All other Macintoshes	256K, 1Mb, 2Mb, 4Mb, 8Mb, 16Mb

*Although 256K SIMMs were used extensively in the 1980s, the price of 1Mb SIMMs has dropped so low and Macintosh memory needs have risen so high that most vendors aren't offering 256K SIMMs any more.

[†]The II and IIx require PAL logic in 4Mb SIMMs; any other SIMMs used in those machines are standard 30-pin SIMMs.

value, it retains that value even if the electrical signal that set that value is withdrawn. (This does not mean that electricity is removed from the computer; it simply means that the static RAM circuit is no longer receiving input.) However, the electrical signal that gives DRAM a value must be retransmitted periodically. Otherwise, the DRAM "forgets" the value it is supposed to retain. Nonetheless, static RAM is simply too expensive to use for general-purpose RAM storage.

SIMM Banks

Except for the newest Macs (LC III, Centris 610, Centris 650, Centris 660av, Quadra 800, Quadra 840av), SIMMs must be installed in groups known as *banks*. A bank is one, two, or four SIMMs. The reason for the difference lies in the type of chips used to construct the SIMMs and the size of the computer's data bus.

Standard 30-pin SIMMs use chips that supply 8 bits at a time. In Macs that have a 16-bit data bus (the 68000 Macs, LC, LC II), 1 byte is taken from each of two SIMMs to provide the entire 16 bits. Therefore such machines require banks of two SIMMs. This is also why all SIMMs in a bank must be of the same size and speed. Although it is technically possible to pull 16 bits from one SIMM, RAM access is much faster if the 16 bits can be taken from two SIMMs at the same time, rather than in two steps from the same SIMM. Macs that have a 32-bit data bus need to access four SIMMs at a time to assemble an entire 32-bit word. Their banks are therefore made up of four SIMMs.

The 72-pin SIMMs used in the newest Macs supply a full 32 bits at one time. That means that the computer needs to access only one SIMM to obtain a word of data. Therefore each SIMM slot functions as a bank, making it possible to add SIMMs one at a time.

SIMM Speeds

SIMM speeds are measured in *nanoseconds* (abbreviated *ns*). A nanosecond is equal to 10^{-9} seconds. The lower the speed of a SIMM, the faster the Macintosh can access the memory contained in that SIMM. Each Macintosh model has a maximum speed it can use. For example, the Macintosh Plus can use SIMMs as slow as 150ns, whereas the Quadra 950 requires 80ns SIMMs. In some circumstances, you can use SIMMs of different speeds in the same computer. However, when SIMMs must be installed in rows or banks, then all SIMMs within the same row or bank must be of the same speed. You will find model-specific information about the type and speed of SIMM required for specific Mac models throughout this chapter.

8-bit 30-pin SIMM

9-bit 30-pin SIMM

72-pin SIMM

PowerBook Memory Expansion board

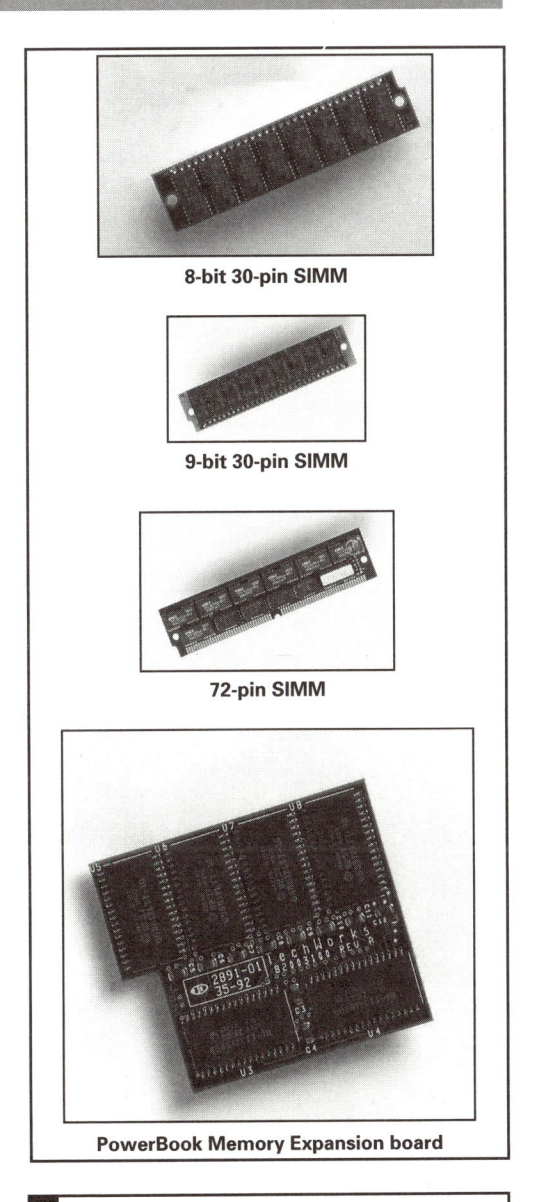

▶ **Figure 5.6** *Macintosh SIMMs*

> **By the way:** The late Grace Hopper, who is generally acknowledged as the first computer programmer, used to describe a nanosecond by producing a piece of thin wire approximately 18 inches long. She said that the wire represented the distance that light would travel in a nanosecond.

Anatomy of a SIMM Slot

A SIMM slot is an opening on the motherboard designed to accept an expansion board containing RAM chips. The slot contains thin wire fingers that make contact with the gold connectors on the SIMM. It also has posts at either end. These posts contain tabs that must be inserted through the holes at either end of the SIMM. In early Macintoshes, the posts are made of plastic; in later models, they are made of metal.

The construction of a SIMM slot makes it vulnerable to damage if SIMMs aren't inserted or removed carefully. Forcing a SIMM into a slot can bend the metal fingers. Forcing a SIMM in or out can also break the posts or the tabs on the posts. In either case, the SIMM won't be able to make good contact with the slot, and the RAM on the SIMM won't be accessible. Once the pins are bent or the posts damaged, the only solution is either to replace the motherboard or to hope you can find someone who does board-level repairs and can replace just the slot.

Where to Get SIMMs

SIMMs are sold by virtually every merchandiser who handles Macintosh products. However, the price varies considerably, depending on whether you're purchasing from a dealer or from a mail-order firm. Dealer prices tend to be higher than mail-order prices. Should you order mail order? The answer is definitely "yes" if you plan to install your own SIMMs. The answer is "maybe" if you plan to have a dealer install them. If a dealer will install the SIMMs you purchase from the store for free, then it may cost less overall to buy from the dealer. However, if the charge to install SIMMs is the same, regardless of where they are purchased, then it is probably cheaper to purchase them through the mail and then take them and the computer to the dealer for installation.

The names and phone numbers of some of the many reputable mail-order firms that sell SIMMs can be found in Appendix B. Although most of these firms advertise in major publications such as MacUser, MacWorld, and MacWEEK, you should always call to check for current prices. SIMM prices change from week to week, and often the prices in advertisements are out of date.

General SIMM Installation Procedure

The process for installing SIMMs is more or less the same, regardless of the type of Mac. (Where there are specific instructions for a model, you will find them later in this chapter.) Keep in mind that installing SIMMs means opening the Macintosh's case. Pay special attention to avoiding static electricity. (See Chapter 3 for some suggestions.)

To install SIMMs:

1. Open the Macintosh's case and expose the SIMM slots. (In some cases, exposing the SIMM slots requires removing the motherboard; in others you may need to remove the disk drive platform.)

2. Center a SIMM over a SIMM slot.

WARNING Handle SIMMs only at the top and sides; don't touch the gold connectors on the bottom. If you do, you will transfer oil from your fingers to the connectors, coating them so they can't make a good connection with the slot.

3. Angle the SIMM into the slot at about a 45-degree angle and press gently (see Figure 5.7).

4. Continue applying gentle pressure until you hear the SIMM click into place. In modular Macs, the SIMM will sit upright. In others, such as compact Macs, it will remain at an angle.

5. If necessary, click the tabs in the upright posts that hold the SIMMs into the holes on either edge of the SIMM.

6. Repeat steps 1 through 4 for each SIMM.

7. Plug in the power cord and turn on the computer. If the computer boots normally (you hear no strange sounds), turn off the computer. Reassemble the Macintosh's case and replace all cords and cables. If you hear any strange sounds (in particular, a four-tone musical chime), then the SIMMs haven't been installed properly.

Some SIMM installations require you to remove existing SIMMs before installing new ones. You can remove a SIMM by hand by gently pulling it away from the tabs that hold it. Then tip the SIMM to about a 45-degree angle to disengage it from the slot. At that point, you can lift it out. However, manual SIMM extraction runs the risk of damaging the tabs. (If the tabs are damaged, SIMMs will not be held securely and may not make a good connection with the metal fingers in the slot.) To be safe, use a SIMM extractor like that in Figure 5.8.

Figure 5.7 Installing a SIMM

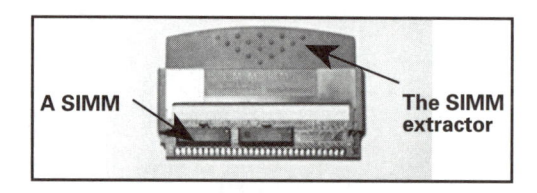

Figure 5.8 A SIMM extractor

What Can Go Wrong

Four problems can occur when you are installing SIMMs:

- **Damage to the wires inside the SIMM slot:** If you press too hard when you are attempting to insert a SIMM into a slot, you can bend the fine wires that are inside the SIMM slot. If this occurs, the only solution is either to replace the entire motherboard or to try to find someone who can do board-level repairs and is willing to replace the slot. To avoid bending the wires, be sure the SIMM is centered directly over the slot before you attempt to insert it. Second, apply only gentle pressure when inserting a SIMM. If you meet more than gentle resistance, don't force it. Pull the SIMM back and recenter it over the slot before trying again.

- **Damage to the posts or the tabs on the posts:** When SIMMs are inserted and removed from the same slots many times, the posts and/or the tabs on the posts can become damaged. Older Macs, in which the posts are made of plastic, are particularly vulnerable to this problem. If the posts or tabs are badly damaged, a SIMM won't seat firmly in its slot and can't make adequate contact with the slot. As with damaged slot wires, the only solution to posts and/or tabs that have been damaged is to replace the motherboard or find someone who can replace the slot. To avoid damaging the posts and tabs, use a SIMM extractor to remove SIMMs. When inserting SIMMs, use only the minimal amount of pressure necessary to insert the tabs through the holes in the SIMMs.

- **Improperly seated SIMM:** If a SIMM isn't inserted all the way into its slot, it won't make complete contact with the slot. If you hear the chimes when you turn the Mac on immediately after inserting a SIMM, the most likely cause is an improperly seated SIMM. When this occurs, turn off the computer and remove the power cord. Then check each SIMM to locate any that aren't inserted completely into their slots. Apply gentle pressure to each incompletely seated SIMM to insert it properly in the slot. In some cases, you may need to remove the incompletely seated SIMM and begin the installation again.

- **Damaged SIMM connectors:** If a SIMM is repeatedly inserted or removed from SIMM slots, the gold connectors that make the connection with the slot can become damaged. When that occurs, the SIMM can't make a good connection with the slot. SIMM connectors can also become coated with oils from human hands.

If the SIMM connectors are damaged, there isn't much you can do; the SIMM is useless. However, if the connectors are merely oily, clean them gently with a lint-free swab that has been wetted with a bit of rubbing alcohol.

> **By the way:** You can recover the chips on a SIMM with damaged connectors by purchasing an empty SIMM board and moving the chips from the damaged board to the new one. However, doing so requires dealing with soldered chips and therefore should be attempted by someone with experience.

> **By the way:** Improperly installed SIMMs aren't the only reason you might hear chimes when you power up your Mac. However, when the chimes occur immediately after installing SIMMs, an improperly seated SIMM is the most likely cause.

RAM AND THE 68000 COMPACT MACS

At the time the Macintosh Plus was introduced, its 1Mb of RAM seemed wonderfully generous. A limit of 4Mb seemed like more than any Mac user would ever need. Little did we know.... This section looks at the RAM configurations and installation procedures for the 68000 compact Macs. These machines all have a limit of 4Mb of physical RAM. Because they have a 68000 CPU, they cannot use virtual memory to extend that total. (As you will see in Chapter 6, you can add a CPU accelerator board to your 68000 Mac that does provide access to as much as 16Mb RAM.)

Adding RAM to a compact Mac means that you have to remove the motherboard from the computer. To do that you need to disconnect the floppy drive, any internal hard drive that may have been installed, the power supply, and the speaker. This is one of those procedures that you should leave to a service technician if playing around inside your computer makes you the least bit uneasy.

Mac Plus RAM Configurations

The Macintosh Plus has four SIMM slots, organized in two rows. It accepts 30-pin SIMMs of speeds less than or equal to 150ns. RAM must be added two SIMMs at a time: a row (the Mac Plus term for a bank) can contain two SIMMs, or it can contain zero SIMMs. The SIMMs in each row must be of the same speed and capacity. All available memory configurations can be found in Table 5.2.

Fix Your Own Mac: Upgrading and Troubleshooting

> **By the way:** Apple's documentation says you can fill Row 1 with 256K SIMMs and leave Row 2 empty, for a total of 512K RAM. The question is, "Why would anybody want to do that?"

The Plus motherboard contains two RAM size resistors that signal the computer how much RAM is installed. The first resistor (R8) is labeled "256K bit"; the second (R9) is labeled "One Row." In the default 1Mb configuration, the 256K-bit resistor is present; the One Row resistor is not installed. The 2Mb configuration requires the resistors in the opposite configuration. Nonetheless, 2Mb is a rarely used configuration because it discards some of the SIMMs shipped with the machine; when adding two 1Mb SIMMs, you might as well keep two of the 256K SIMMs to give you 2.5Mb. Notice that for the 2.5Mb and 4Mb configurations, no resistor is installed. In practical terms that means you may have to snip the 256K-bit resistor when adding RAM to a Plus.

Macintosh SE RAM Configurations

The Macintosh SE has the same memory configurations as the Macintosh Plus, although the two rows of SIMM slots are side by side rather than on top of one another (see Table 5.3). The only other difference is that in the 2Mb configuration, slots 1 and 2 are empty (as opposed to slots 3 and 4 in the Plus); the two 1Mb SIMMs are placed in slots 3 and 4. Also keep in mind that there are two versions of the SE motherboard. Earlier SEs have RAM-sized resistors just like the Mac Plus. Later SEs have a RAM-sized

Table 5.2 RAM Configurations for the Mac Plus

Configuration		Size	Total RAM
	Row 1 (SIMMs 1 and 2)	256K	1Mb
	Row 2 (SIMMs 3 and 4)	256K	
	Resistors:		
	256K bit (R8)	150 ohms	
	One Row (R9)	Not installed	
	Row 1 (SIMMs 1 and 2)	1Mb	2Mb
	Row 2 (SIMMs 3 and 4)	Empty	
	Resistors:		
	256K bit (R8)	Not installed	
	One Row (R9)	150 ohms	
	Row 1 (SIMMs 1 and 2)	1Mb	2.5Mb
	Row 2 (SIMMs 3 and 4)	256K	
	Resistors:		
	256K bit (R8)	Not installed	
	One Row (R9)	Not installed	
	Row 1 (SIMMs 1 and 2)	1Mb	4Mb
	Row 2 (SIMMs 3 and 4)	1Mb	
	Resistors:		
	256K bit (R8)	Not installed	
	One Row (R9)	Not installed	

Chapter 5: Adding Memory

jumper, located just above SIMM 1 (the top left SIMM).

Installing RAM in the Macintosh Plus and SE

As mentioned earlier, installing SIMMs in a compact Mac means that you not only have to take the case apart, but must unplug internal hard and floppy drive connectors and then remove the motherboard to gain access to the SIMM slots. This actually isn't as difficult as it may sound.

> **By the way:** The Mac Plus was not designed to accept an internal hard drive. However, several third-party manufacturers made drives that could be mounted inside a Mac Plus.

The process for installing the SIMMs in the Plus or SE is as follows:

1. Open the computer's case. (See Chapter 3 for details.)

2. Note the orientation of the floppy drive connector, power supply connector, and speaker connector. If you think you won't be able to remember the way a connector goes, mark the edge closest to you with a felt-tip pen.

3. Unplug the connectors from the motherboard. (See the top view of an SE in Figure 5.9.)

4. Lay the computer face down on a soft, lint-free cloth.

5. Remove the radio frequency shield from an SE (see Figure 5.10). (The Plus has no radio frequency shield.)

Table 5.3 RAM Configurations for the Macintosh SE

Configuration		Size	Total RAM
	Row 1 (SIMMs 1 & 2)	256K	1Mb
	Row 2 (SIMMs 3 & 4)	256K	
	Resistors:		
	256K bit (R35)	150 ohms	
	One Row (R36)	Not installed	
	Jumper: on 1M		
	Row 1 (SIMMs 1 & 2)	1Mb	2Mb
	Row 2 (SIMMs 3 & 4)	Empty	
	Resistors:		
	256K bit (R35)	Not installed	
	One Row (R36)	150 ohms	
	Jumper: on 2/4M		
	Row 1 (SIMMs 1 & 2)	1Mb	2.5Mb
	Row 2 (SIMMs 3 & 4)	256K	
	Resistors:		
	256K bit (R35)	Not installed	
	One Row (R36)	Not installed	
	Jumper: off		
	Row 1 (SIMMs 1 & 2)	1Mb	4Mb
	Row 2 (SIMMs 3 & 4)	1 Mb	
	Resistors:		
	256K bit (R35)	Not installed	
	One Row (R36)	Not installed	
	Jumper: off		

115

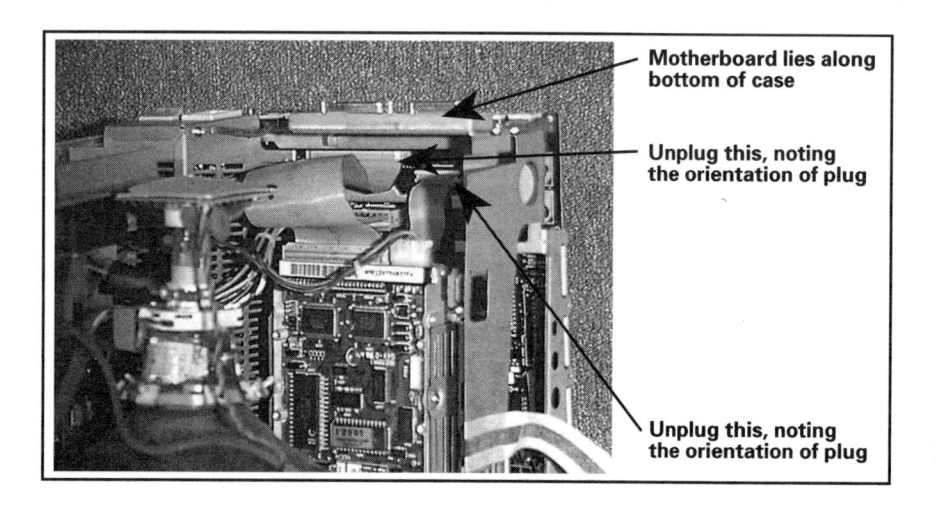

Fix Your Own Mac: *Upgrading and Troubleshooting*

Figure 5.9 Disconnecting cables from the Mac SE

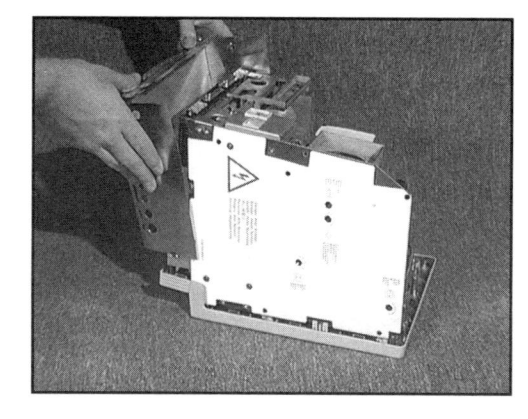

- Motherboard lies along bottom of case
- Unplug this, noting the orientation of plug
- Unplug this, noting the orientation of plug

Figure 5.10 Removing the radio frequency shield from an SE

6. Gently remove the motherboard from the computer and lay it on the table, as in Figure 5.11. The SIMM slots are located at the edge of the motherboard *opposite* the ports (see Figure 5.12).

7. If necessary, remove SIMMs that either are in the wrong row or will not be used.

8. Install the new SIMMs.

9. If necessary, clip a resistor or move a jumper to indicate the memory configuration. (See Table 5.2 for the resistor status with each Mac Plus RAM configuration; see Table 5.3 for the resistor/jumper status for each SE configuration.)

10. Replace the motherboard.

11. Reconnect the internal components.

12. Replace the Mac's case.

Macintosh Classic RAM Configurations

The Macintosh Classic doesn't have standard SIMM slots like the Plus and SE. Instead it has 1Mb of RAM soldered on the motherboard. Additional RAM is provided on an expansion board. At a minimum, the expansion board has 1Mb of soldered RAM. It also has two SIMM slots that can accept 256K or 1Mb SIMMs (150ns or faster); both slots must be either completely empty or filled with SIMMs of the same size and speed.

Figure 5.11 Removing the motherboard from a Macintosh Plus or SE

Chapter 5: Adding Memory

The possible configurations can be found in Table 5.4.

Installing SIMMs in a Classic

The design of the Classic is a bit different from that of the other compact Macs. Its motherboard sits a bit above the bottom of the computer. To install SIMMs in the Classic do the following:

1. Open the computer's case. (See Chapter 3 for details.)
2. Note the orientation of the hard disk connector, floppy drive connector, power supply connector, and speaker connector. If you think you won't be able to remember the way a connector goes, mark the edge closest to you with a felt-tip pen.
3. Unplug the components.
4. Place the computer face down on a soft, lint-free surface. *
5. Slide the motherboard up and out of the computer (see Figure 5.13).
6. Lay the motherboard flat on a table. The Classic's RAM expansion slot can be found at the far left of the motherboard (see Figure 5.14).
7. What you do next depends on the current RAM configuration of the computer. If the computer has no RAM expansion board, simply plug the board into the RAM expansion

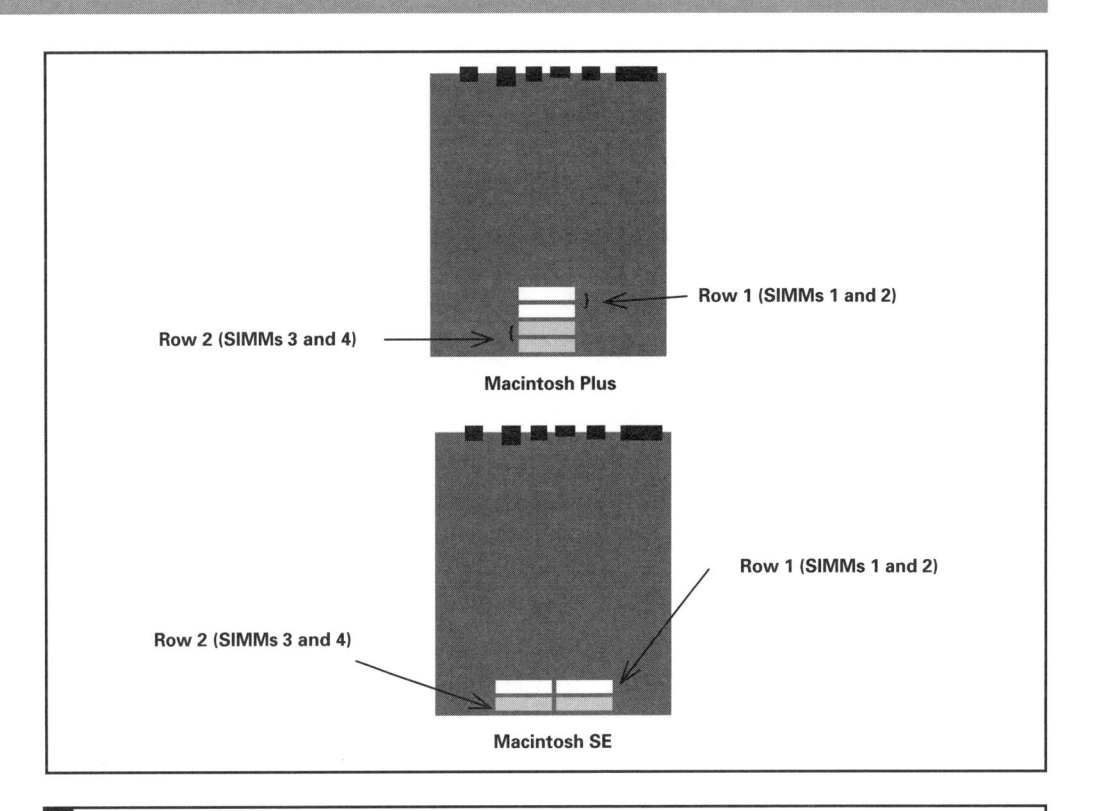

Figure 5.12 Location of SIMM slots on the Mac Plus and SE motherboards

Table 5.4 RAM Configurations for the Macintosh Classic

Soldered on Motherboard	Soldered on RAM Expansion Card	SIMM Size on Expansion Card	Total RAM
1Mb	Not installed		1Mb
1Mb	1Mb	Empty	2Mb
1Mb	1Mb	256K Jumper: SIMM installed	2.5Mb
1Mb	1Mb	1Mb Jumper: SIMM installed	4Mb

Fix Your Own Mac: Upgrading and Troubleshooting

Figure 5.13 Removing the motherboard from a Mac Classic

Table 5.5 *RAM Configurations for Macintoshes with two 30-pin SIMM Slots*

Configuration	Soldered on Motherboard	SIMM Size	Total RAM
	2Mb	SIMM slots empty	2Mb
	2Mb	1Mb	4Mb
	2Mb	2Mb	6Mb
	2Mb	4Mb	10Mb

slot. If you are adding SIMMs to an existing RAM expansion board, remove the RAM expansion board from the logic board. Remove any SIMMs that won't be remaining on the board.

8. Install the new SIMMs. Plug the RAM expansion board back into the logic board.

9. Replace the motherboard in the computer. Plug in the disk drives and other components.

10. Close the Macintosh's case and reconnect all cords and cables.

RAM AND MACINTOSHES WITH TWO 30-PIN SIMM SLOTS

Several Macintosh models—Classic II, Color Classic, LC, LC II, Performa 400, Performa 405, Performa 430—have two 30-pin SIMM slots. These slots can be filled with 1Mb, 2Mb, or 4Mb SIMMs, 100ns or faster. (Although these computers can physically accept 8Mb or 16Mb SIMMs, the RAM limit of 10Mb makes using SIMMs larger than 4Mb a waste of money.)

RAM Configurations for Macs with Two 30-Pin SIMM Slots

The possible RAM configurations can be found in Table 5.5. Keep in mind that each of these machines has 2Mb of RAM soldered to the motherboard. The total installed RAM is therefore equal to whatever is present in the SIMM slots plus the soldered RAM. Also notice that both SIMM slots must be filled with SIMMs of the same size and speed.

Chapter 5: *Adding Memory*

Figure 5.14 The location of the RAM expansion slot on the Classic motherboard

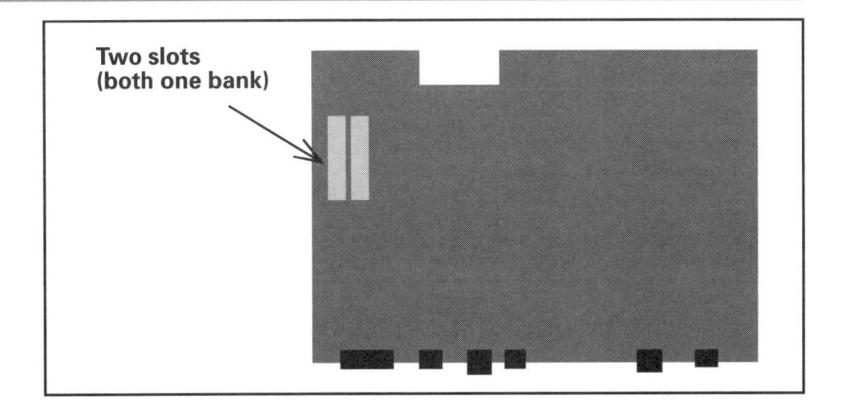

Figure 5.15 Location of SIMM slots in the LC, LC II, Peforma 400, Performa 405, and Performa 430

Installing SIMMS in the LC, LC II, Performa 400, Performa 405, and Performa 430

The LC, LC II, Performa 400, Performa 405, and Performa 430 are typical of desktop Macs. To install SIMMs, follow the procedures in the section "General SIMM Installation Procedure." In all five of these computers, the SIMMs slots can be found along the left edge of the motherboard (assuming the ports are facing you, as in Figure 5.15).

Installing SIMMs in a Classic II/Performa 200

The design of the Classic II/Performa 200 is a bit different from that of the other compact Macs. Its motherboard sits a bit above the bottom of the computer. To install SIMMs in the Classic II/Performa 200:

1. Open the computer's case. (See Chapter 3 for details.)

2. Note the orientation of the hard disk connector, floppy drive connector, power supply connector, and speaker connector. If you think you won't be able to remember the way a connector goes, mark the edge closest to you with a felt-tip pen.

3. Unplug the components.

4. Place the computer face down on a soft, lint-free surface.

5. Slide the motherboard up and out of the computer (see Figure 5.16).

Figure 5.16 Removing the motherboard from a Mac Classic II

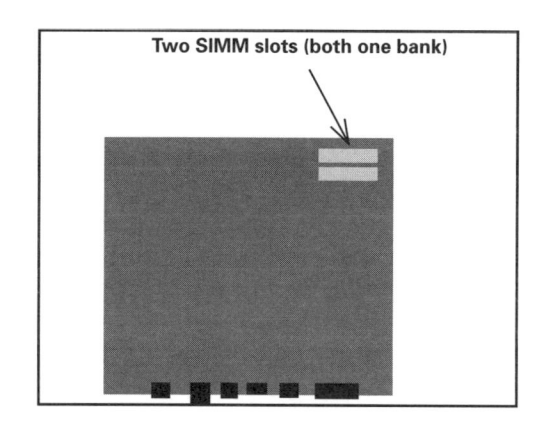

Figure 5.17 The location of SIMM slots on the Classic II/Performa 200 motherboard

6. Lay the motherboard flat on a table. With the ports facing you, the Classic II/Performa 200's SIMM slots are at the top right corner of the motherboard (see Figure 5.17).

7. Remove any SIMMs that won't remain in the computer.

8. Install the new SIMMs.

9. Replace the motherboard in the computer. Plug in the disk drives and other components.

10. Close the Macintosh's case and reconnect all cords and cables.

Installing SIMMs in the Color Classic

Although the Color Classic is a compact Mac, you don't need to take its case apart completely to gain access to its motherboard. To install SIMMs in the Color Classic:

1. Open the computer's case. (See Chapter 3 for details.)

2. Place the computer face down on a soft, lint-free cloth.

3. Gently pull the motherboard toward you, out of the case (see Figure 5.18).

4. Place the motherboard flat on a table.

5. Install the SIMMs. With the ports facing you, the SIMM slots are on the left edge of the motherboard (see Figure 5.19).

6. Replace the motherboard.

7. Close the case.

RAM AND MACINTOSHES WITH FOUR 30-PIN SIMM SLOTS

Five Macintosh models—IIsi, IIvx, IIvi, Performa 600, Quadra 700—have four 30-pin SIMM slots. Each can accept 1Mb, 4Mb, or 16Mb SIMMs; some can also use 2Mb SIMMs. However, the minimum acceptable SIMM speed varies between these models, as does the amount of RAM soldered on the motherboard.

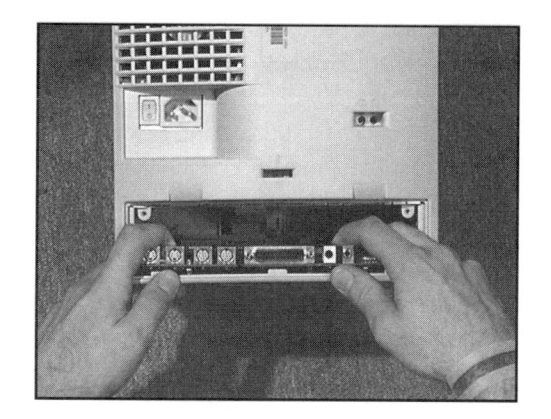

Figure 5.18 Removing the motherboard from the Color Classic

Chapter 5: Adding Memory

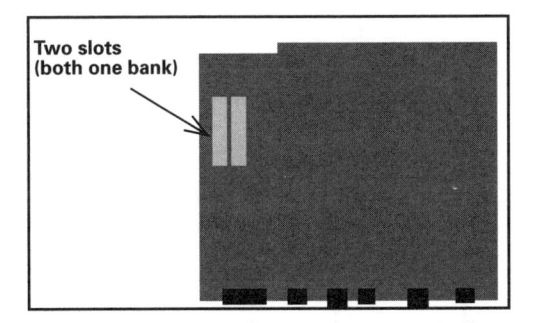

Figure 5.19 Location of SIMMs on the Color Classic motherboard

By the way: To be completely accurate, each of these machines can also use 256K SIMMs. However, the price of 1Mb SIMMs has dropped so low that many vendors aren't even offering 256K SIMMs for sale any more. For that reason, 256K SIMM configurations haven't been included in the configuration tables.

RAM Configurations for the Macintosh IIsi

The IIsi comes with 1Mb of soldered RAM. Coupled with the four SIMM slots, that gives it a maximum RAM capacity of 65Mb, using any of the configurations in Table 5.6. The IIsi requires SIMMs of 100ns or faster. All four SIMM slots must either be empty or be filled with SIMMs of the same size and speed.

Table 5.6 RAM Configurations for the Macintosh IIsi

Configuration	Soldered on Motherboard	SIMM Size	Total RAM
	1Mb	(SIMM slots empty)	1Mb
	1Mb	1Mb	5Mb
	1Mb	2Mb	9Mb
	1Mb	4Mb	17Mb
	1Mb	16Mb	65Mb

Installing RAM in the Macintosh IIsi

The IIsi is typical of modular Macs. To install SIMMs, follow the procedures in the section "General SIMM Installation Procedure." With the ports facing you, the SIMM slots are located in the lower left-hand corner of the motherboard (see Figure 5.20).

RAM Configurations for the Macintosh IIvx, IIvi, and Performa 600

The IIvx, IIvi, and Performa 600 have 4Mb RAM soldered on their mother-

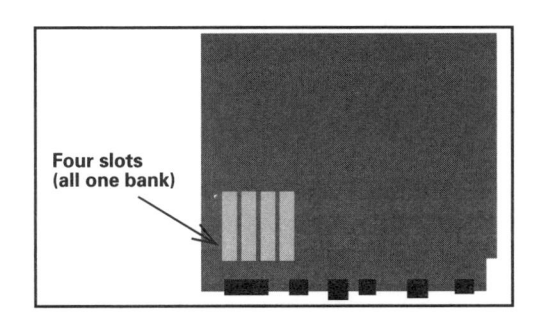

Figure 5.20 Location of SIMM slots on the Macintosh IIsi

Fix Your Own Mac: *Upgrading and Troubleshooting*

Table 5.7 RAM Configurations for the Macintosh IIvx, IIvi, and Performa 600

Configuration	Soldered on Motherboard	SIMM Size	Total RAM
	4Mb	(SIMM slots empty)	1Mb
	4Mb	1Mb	8Mb
	4Mb	2Mb	12Mb
	4Mb	4Mb	20Mb
	4Mb	16Mb	68Mb

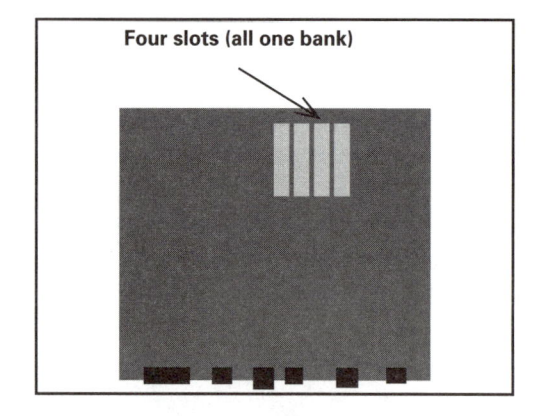

Figure 5.21 Location of SIMM slots in the Macintosh IIvi, IIvx, and Performa 600

boards. They can use 1Mb, 2Mb, 4Mb, and 16Mb SIMMs of 80ns or faster. The 4Mb of soldered RAM give them a maximum RAM capacity of 68Mb, which can be configured as in Table 5.7. Keep in mind that all four SIMM slots must either be empty or be filled with SIMMs of the same size and speed.

Installing RAM in the IIvx, IIvi, and Performa 600

The IIIvx, IIvi, and Performa 600 are typical of desktop Macs. To install SIMMs, follow the procedures in the section "General SIMM Installation Procedure."

In all three computers, the SIMM slots are just right of center at the edge of the computer, away from the ports (see Figure 5.21).

RAM Configurations for the Quadra 700

The Quadra 700 comes with 4Mb RAM soldered on the motherboard. However, unlike the other Macintoshes with four 30-pin SIMM slots, it can't use 2Mb SIMMs. Its possible RAM configurations—using 80ns SIMMs—are therefore those found in Table 5.8. When ordering 16Mb SIMMs for the Quadra 700, be sure that you are very clear about the Macintosh model. The Quadra 700's SIMM slots are underneath its disk drives. It therefore requires special low-profile 16Mb SIMMs.

Installing RAM in the Quadra 700

The design of the Quadra 700 is similar to that of the Mac II, IIx, and IIfx in that its SIMM slots are hidden under its disk drive platform. Before you can install SIMMs you must remove the disk drives. There are two ways to do this: You can unplug the internal disk drives and completely remove the disk drive platform from the computer, or you can flip it over on top of the power supply. The first method is generally

Chapter 5: Adding Memory

Table 5.8 RAM Configurations for the Quadra 700

Configuration	Soldered on Motherboard	SIMM Size	Total RAM
	4Mb	(SIMM slots empty)	1Mb
	4Mb	1Mb	8Mb
	4Mb	4Mb	20Mb
	4Mb	16Mb	68Mb

what SIMM vendors recommend in their instructions; the second method is easier.

To move the disk drives so that the SIMM slots are accessible:

1. Unscrew the screws at the corners of the disk drive platform. (These screws attach the platform to the posts that hold it up over the motherboard.) Place the screws in a safe place.

2. If you are planning to remove the disk drive platform from the computer, note the orientation of the hard disk and floppy drive connectors. If you don't think you can remember which way the plugs are placed in their connectors, mark the end closest to you with a dot from a felt-tip pen.

3. Unplug the disk drive connectors.

4. Gently lift the disk drive platform out of the computer and place it in a safe, lint- and static-free location. The SIMM slots are now accessible. Assuming that the ports are facing you, the SIMM slots are at the upper right of the motherboard (see Figure 5.22).

If you aren't planning to remove the disk drive platform, unscrew it as in the preceding Step 1. Then gently flip it over onto the power supply. The SIMM slots will be accessible.

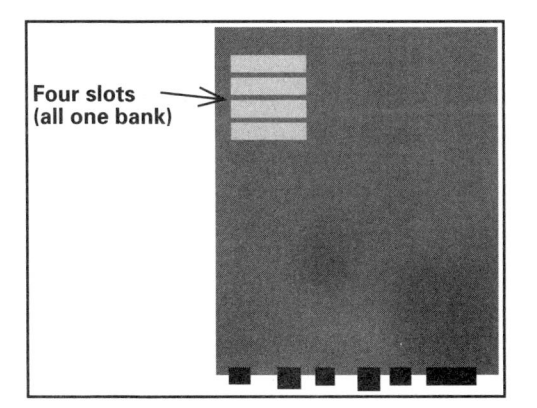

Four slots (all one bank)

Figure 5.22 Location of SIMM slots in a Quadra 700

123

Fix Your Own Mac: Upgrading and Troubleshooting

Table 5.9 Basic RAM Configurations for Macintoshes with eight SIMM slots

Configuration		SIMM Size	Total RAM
	Bank A	256K	1Mb
	Bank B	Empty	
	Bank A	256K	2Mb
	Bank B	256K	
	Bank A	1Mb	4Mb
	Bank B	Empty	
	Bank A	1Mb	5Mb
	Bank B	256K	
	Bank A	1Mb	8Mb
	Bank B	1Mb	

RAM AND MACINTOSHES WITH EIGHT 30-PIN SIMM SLOTS

There are six Macintosh models with eight SIMM slots (SE/30, II, IIx, IIfx, IIcx, IIci). Although the rules for where SIMMs can be placed vary somewhat among the models, the configuration options are similar. The basic configurations, using 256K and 1Mb SIMMs, can be found in Table 5.9. There are a number of options for high-capacity memory configurations; some of the most popular appear in Table 5.10.

As you may have noticed in Tables 5.9 and 5.10, the eight SIMM slots are organized in two "banks," labeled A and B. A bank must be completely empty or completely filled with SIMMs of the same size and speed. That means that you must add four SIMMs at a time to a Mac with eight 30-pin SIMM slots.

Installing RAM in the SE/30

The SE/30 accepts standard 30-pin SIMMs of 120ns or faster. Because this computer has 32-bit dirty ROMs, you must install either Mode32 or the System 7 extension to access more than 8Mb RAM.

As mentioned earlier, installing SIMMs in a compact Mac means that you not only must take the case apart, but also

Chapter 5: Adding Memory

must unplug internal hard and floppy drive connectors and then remove the motherboard to gain access to the SIMM slots. This actually isn't as difficult as it may sound.

The process for installing the SIMMs in the SE/30 is as follows:

1. Open the computer's case. (See Chapter 3 for details.)

2. Note the orientation of the floppy drive connector, power supply connector, and speaker connector. If you think you won't be able to remember the way a connector goes, mark the edge closest to you with a felt-tip pen.

3. Unplug the connectors from the motherboard (see the top view in Figure 5.23).

4. Lay the computer face down on a soft, lint-free cloth.

5. Remove its radio frequency shield (see Figure 5.24).

6. Gently remove the motherboard from the computer and lay it on the table, as in Figure 5.25. If you place the motherboard with the ports facing you, the SIMM slots are in the upper right corner (see Figure 5.26).

Table 5.10 *Sample high-capacity memory configurations for Macintoshes with eight SIMM slots*

Configuration		SIMM Size	Total RAM
	Bank A	1Mb	20Mb
	Bank B	4Mb	
	Bank A	4Mb	32Mb
	Bank B	16Mb	
	Bank A	1Mb	68Mb
	Bank B	16Mb	
	Bank A	1Mb	96Mb
	Bank B	16Mb	
	Bank A	16Mb	128Mb
	Bank B	16Mb	

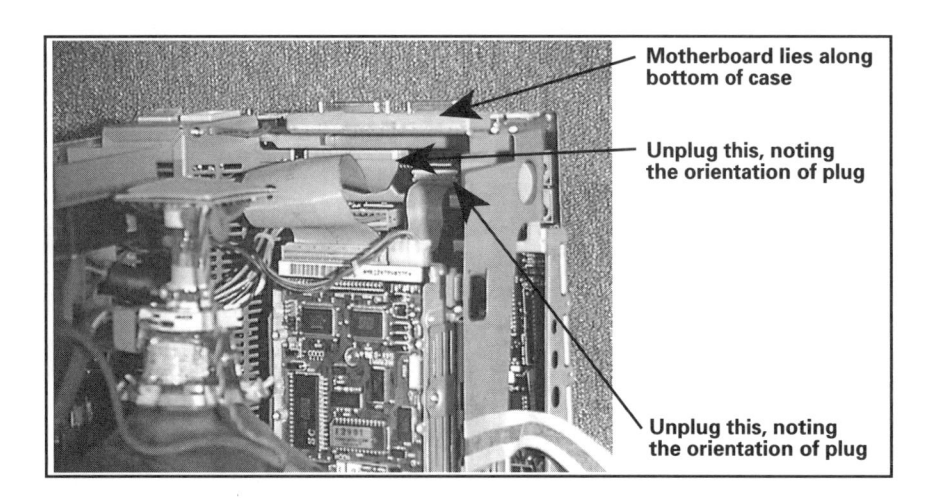

Fix Your Own Mac: *Upgrading and Troubleshooting*

Figure 5.23 *Disconnecting cables from the Mac SE/30*

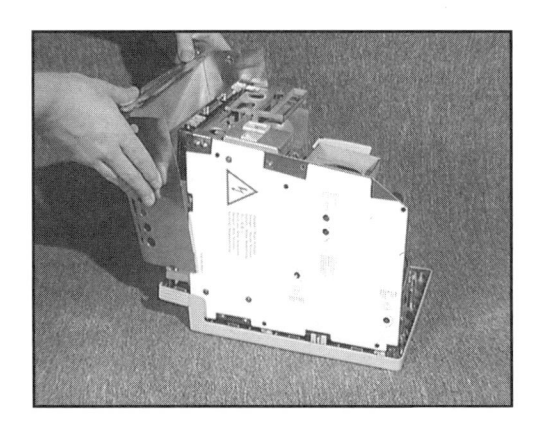

Figure 5.24 *Removing the radio frequency shield*

Figure 5.25 *Removing the motherboard from a Macintosh SE/30*

7. If necessary, remove SIMMs that are in the wrong row or that will not be used.

8. Install the new SIMMs.

9. Replace the motherboard.

10. Reconnect the internal components.

11. Replace the Mac's case.

Macintosh II RAM Considerations

There is a lot of confusion about exactly how much RAM you can put in a Mac II. Here's the real story:

- An unmodified Mac II, without any special software to compensate for 32-bit dirty ROMs, is limited to 8Mb RAM, the limit for any machine using 24-bit addresses.

- If you add Mode32 or Apple's System 7 extension that compensates for 32-bit dirty ROMs to an unmodified Mac II, you can use 32-bit addresses and therefore access more than 8Mb RAM. However, because of a problem with the Mac II ROMs, Bank A can't accept SIMMs larger than 1Mb. That means that you can install 20 or 68Mb RAM. The 20Mb configuration has 4Mb SIMMs in Bank B and 1Mb SIMMs in Bank A; the 68Mb configuration has 16Mb SIMMs in Bank B and 1Mb SIMMs in Bank A.

- To get more than 68Mb RAM in a Mac II, you need to replace the Mac II ROMs with the IIx ROMs. This upgrade, which includes an internal SuperDrive, allows the Mac II to handle 4Mb and 16Mb SIMMs in Bank A as well as in Bank B, making it possible to install up to 128Mb RAM (16Mb SIMMs in all eight slots). If you have a Mac II, don't wait too long to add the SuperDrive and IIx ROMs, even if you don't plan to add more than 68Mb RAM right now. Although the upgrade is currently still available, the Mac II is a relatively old machine and there is no guarantee how long Apple will provide the upgrade.

The Macintosh II requires SIMMs of 120ns or faster. Any 4Mb SIMMs used in the II must also include "PAL" logic chips; 16Mb SIMMs must be "low profile" because they must fit under the disk drive platform. Therefore when ordering high-capacity SIMMs for a Mac II, be sure that you specify the precise machine for which you need the RAM. (Be prepared to pay a bit more as well.)

Macintosh IIx RAM Considerations

Assuming that it is equipped with either Mode32 or the System 7 extension that compensates for 32-bit dirty ROMs, an unmodified Mac IIx can handle a full 128Mb of RAM. However, like the Mac II, 4Mb SIMMs must include the PAL logic chips; 16Mb SIMMs must be "low profile" so that they will fit under the disk drive platform. All SIMMs must be 120ns or faster.

Mac IIfx RAM Considerations

Many things about the IIfx make it unique in the Macintosh line. This includes the type of SIMMs it uses. To be completely accurate, Mac IIfx SIMMs are actually 64-pin. In addition, Mac IIfx SIMMs must include *parity logic*. Parity is a method of error checking. Although there are many ways to implement parity checking, it generally involves adding an extra bit to a byte, making it 9 bits rather than 8.

The two most common parity-checking schemes are *odd parity* and *even parity*. In either case, the computer counts the number of 1s in a byte. If the computer is using odd parity, then the *parity bit* (the ninth bit that is added to the byte) is 1 if the number of 1s is odd but 0 if the number of 1s is even. If the computer is using even parity, then the parity bit is 1 if the number of 1s is even but 0 if the number of 1s is odd. For example, consider the byte 10011011, which contains five 1s and three 0s. With odd parity, the parity bit is 1; with even parity, the parity bit is 0.

▶ **Figure 5.26** Location of SIMM slots on the SE/30 motherboard

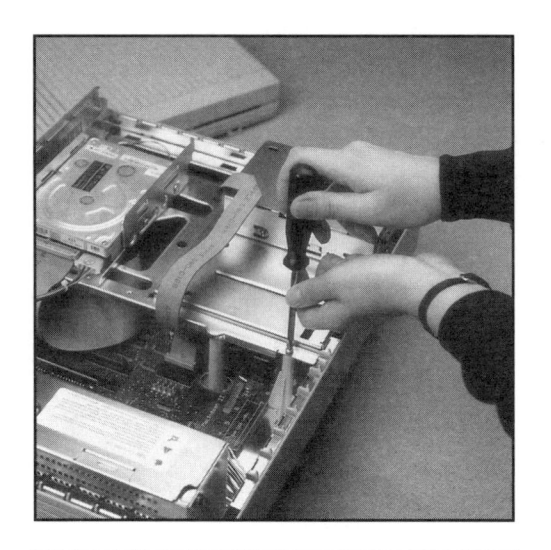

Fix Your Own Mac: Upgrading and Troubleshooting

Figure 5.27 *Removing the screws from the disk drive platform*

The parity bit is added whenever a byte is stored in memory. It is then transmitted with the byte as it moves throughout the computer. When the byte reaches its destination, the parity bit is recomputed from the first 8 bits in the byte. If the parity bit that came with the byte doesn't match what was recomputed, then there has been an error in the transmission of the byte.

Parity SIMMs (9-bit) cost a bit more than the standard 8-bit SIMMs. However, parity checking catches about half the byte transmission errors. Why only half? Because parity checking can only detect an error when an odd number of bits have changed. Assume that you are working with the byte you saw earlier (10011011). If one bit changes, as in 11011011, then the number of 1s is even, causing a change in the parity bit. The same thing happens if three bits change, 11101011; the number of 1s has again switched from odd to even. However, if two bits change to something like 11111011, the number of 1s remains odd. This remains true for any even number of bit changes.

Installing RAM in the Macintosh II, IIx, and IIfx

As mentioned earlier, the SIMM slots in the II, IIx, and IIfx are underneath the disk drive platform. To access them you must either completely remove the drive platform from the computer or place it upside down on the power supply. Vendors who sell SIMMs recommend the first method; the second method is easier.

To move the disk drives so that the SIMM slots are accessible, do the following:

1. Unscrew the screws at the corners of the disk drive platform (see Figure 5.27). (These screws attach the platform to the posts that hold it up over the motherboard.) Place the screws in a safe place.

2. If you are planning to remove the disk drive platform from the computer, note the orientation of the hard disk and floppy drive connectors. If you don't think you can remember which way the plugs are placed in their connectors, mark the end closest to you with a dot from a felt-tip pen.

3. Unplug the disk drive connectors.

4. Gently lift the disk drive platform out of the computer and place it in a safe, lint- and static-free location. The SIMM slots are now accessible.

If you aren't planning to remove the disk drive platform, unscrew it as in the preceding Step 1. Then gently flip it over onto the power supply. The SIMM slots will be accessible. In the II and IIx, the

SIMM slots are at the lower left corner of the motherboard (see Figure 5.28). Notice that Bank A, which must be filled first, is the inner bank. In the IIfx, the SIMM slots are rotated 90 degrees from those in the II and IIx; notice in Figure 5.28 that bank A, which must be filled first, is below bank B.

Installing RAM in the IIcx and IIci

The Macintosh IIcx can accept standard 30-pin SIMMs of 120ns or faster. The IIci accepts standard 30-pin SIMMs of 80ns or faster. Because these computers have 32-bit dirty ROMs, you must install either Mode32 or the System 7 extension to access more than 8Mb RAM.

The IIcx and IIci are typical of the desktop Macs. To install SIMMs in either, see the section "General SIMM Installation Procedure." The two banks of SIMMs are centered at the top edge of the motherboard (see Figure 5.29).

RAM AND THE 16-SLOT QUADRAS

The Quadra 900 and 950 have 16 SIMM slots, organized into four banks of four. As with the other Macs that use 30-pin SIMMs, any given bank must be completely empty or completely filled with SIMMs of the same size and speed (80ns or faster).

RAM Configurations for the Quadra 900 and 950

Using 1Mb, 4Mb, and 16Mb (80ns or faster) SIMMs, there are a number of possible RAM configurations, a sampling of which can be found in Table 5.11. The four SIMM banks are lettered A through

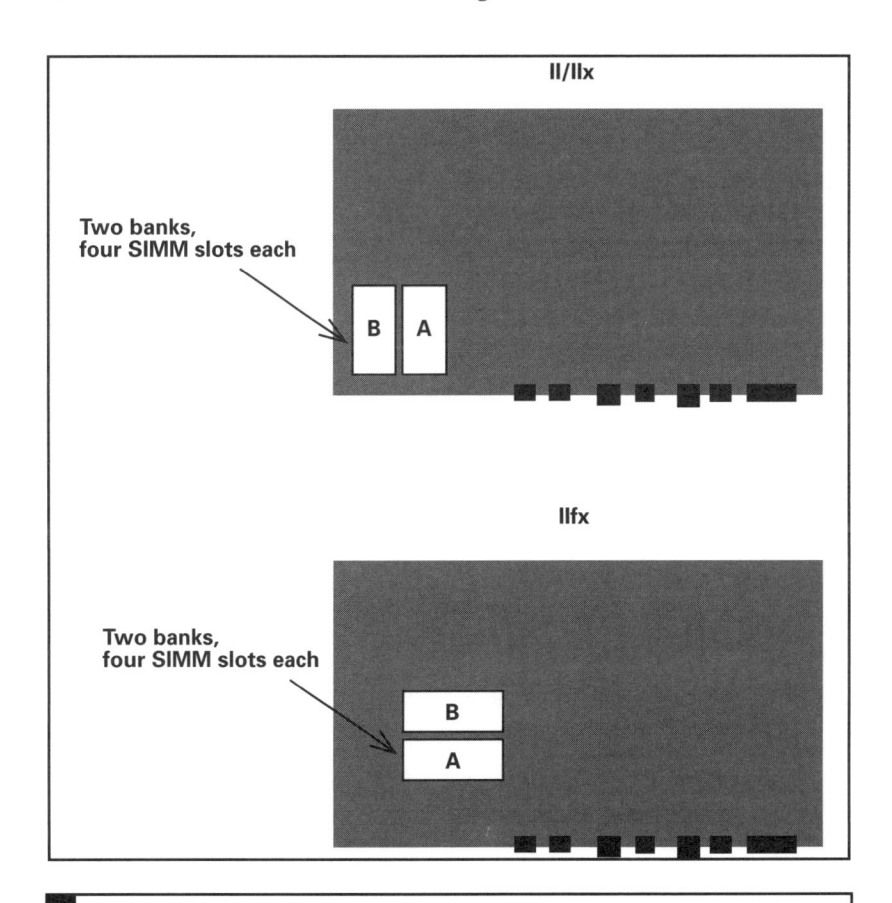

Figure 5.28 *Location of SIMM slots in the Macintosh II, IIx, and IIfx*

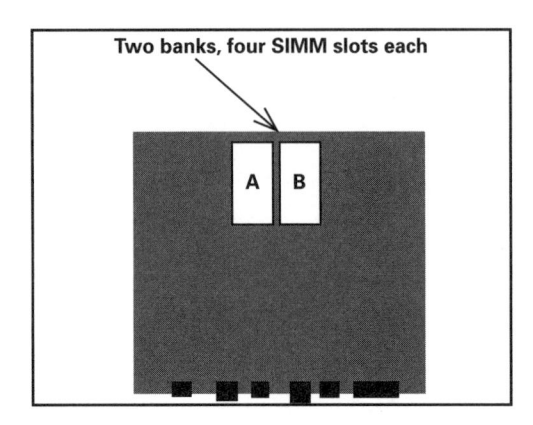

Fix Your Own Mac: Upgrading and Troubleshooting

Figure 5.29 *Location of SIMM slots in the Macintosh IIcx and IIci*

Table 5.11 *Sample RAM Configurations for the Quadra 900 and 950*

Configuration		SIMM Size	Total RAM
	Bank A	1Mb	16Mb
	Bank B	1Mb	
	Bank C	1Mb	
	Bank D	1Mb	
	Bank A	1Mb	40Mb
	Bank B	1Mb	
	Bank C	4Mb	
	Bank D	4Mb	
	Bank A	4Mb	64Mb
	Bank B	4Mb	
	Bank C	4Mb	
	Bank D	4Mb	
	Bank A	1Mb	136Mb
	Bank B	1Mb	
	Bank C	16Mb	
	Bank D	16Mb	
	Bank A	4Mb	160Mb
	Bank B	4Mb	
	Bank C	16Mb	
	Bank D	16Mb	
	Bank A	16Mb	256Mb
	Bank B	16Mb	
	Bank C	16Mb	
	Bank D	16Mb	

D, moving from left to right. Note that although the configurations in Table 5.11 use all four banks, not every bank needs to be filled. For example, the Quadra 900 and 950 can handle as little as 4Mb RAM (1Mb SIMMs in the four slots in Bank A).

Installing RAM in the Quadra 900 and 950

The Quadra 900 and Quadra 950 are typical of other modular Macs. To install SIMMs in either, see the section "General SIMM Installation Procedure." The SIMM slots in each bank are arranged in two rows of two slots each (see Figure 5.30).

RAM AND MACINTOSHES WITH 72-PIN SIMM SLOTS

As you read earlier, the LC III, Centris 610, Centris 650, Centris 660av, Quadra 800, and Quadra 840av use 72-pin SIMMs that can supply a full 32 bits at a time. This means that you can add SIMMs one at a time to these Macintoshes. Even if the Macintosh has more than one SIMM slot, the SIMMs don't have to be the same size or speed. The 72-pin SIMMs are available in 1Mb, 2Mb, 4Mb, 8Mb, 16Mb, and 32Mb sizes. These computers all require SIMMs of 80ns or faster.

Each SIMM board has two banks, one on each side of the board. For example, the 4Mb and 8Mb SIMMs actually use the same size RAM chips. However, the 4Mb SIMM has chips on one side of the board, while the 8Mb SIMM has chips on both. In other words, there are actually only three types of RAM chips used to make 72-pin SIMMs: those used in the 1Mb and 2Mb SIMMs, those used in the 4Mb and 8Mb SIMMs, and those used in the 16Mb and 32Mb SIMMs.

RAM Configurations for the Macintosh LC III and Performa 450

The LC III/Performa 450 has 4Mb of RAM soldered to the motherboard and one 72-pin SIMM slot that can accept up to a 32Mb SIMM. The possible RAM configurations are therefore those found in Table 5.12.

RAM Configurations for the Centris 610 and 660av

Like the LC III, the Centris 610 and 660av have 4Mb of RAM soldered on their motherboards. However, they have two (rather than one) SIMM slots. Because the SIMMs in the two slots can be of different sizes, there are many RAM configurations, with capacities ranging from 4Mb to 68Mb. Some sample configurations can be found in Table 5.13.

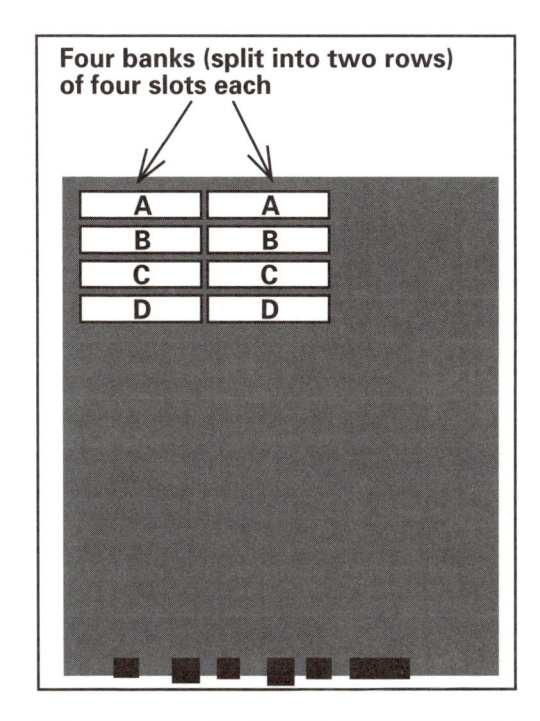

Figure 5.30 Location of SIMM slots in the Quadra 900 and 950

Fix Your Own Mac: Upgrading and Troubleshooting

▶ **Table 5.12** RAM Configurations for the Macintosh LC III

Configuration	Soldered on Motherboard	SIMM Size	Total RAM
	4Mb		4Mb
▬	4Mb	1Mb	5Mb
▦	4Mb	2Mb	6Mb
▬	4Mb	4Mb	8Mb
▨	4Mb	8Mb	12Mb
▥	4Mb	16Mb	20Mb
▩	4Mb	32Mb	36Mb

▶ **Table 5.13** Sample RAM Configurations for the Centris 610 and 660av

Configuration	Soldered on Motherboard	SIMM Size	Total RAM
	4Mb		4Mb
▬	4Mb	1Mb	6Mb
▦	4Mb	2Mb	8Mb
▬	4Mb	4Mb	12Mb
▦	4Mb	4Mb / 8Mb	16Mb
▨	4Mb	8Mb	20Mb
▥	4Mb	16Mb	36Mb
▩	4Mb	32Mb	68Mb

RAM Configurations for the Centris 650, Quadra 800, and Quadra 840av

The Centris 650, Quadra 800, and Quadra 840av each have four 72-pin SIMM slots. All three computers are available with 8Mb of RAM soldered to the motherboard; the Centris 650 also has a 4Mb soldered configuration. The four SIMM slots provide a range of RAM for 4Mb to 132Mb (4Mb soldered) or 8Mb to 136Mb (8Mb soldered). As with any Macintosh that uses 72-pin SIMMs, the sizes of SIMMs can be mixed, providing a wide variety of possible configurations. Sample configurations for the Centris 650 with 4Mb soldered on the motherboard can be found in Table 5.14; sample configurations for the Centris 650 with 8Mb soldered on the motherboard and for the Quadra 800 and 840av appear in Table 5.15.

Table 5.14 Sample RAM configurations for the Centris 650 with 4Mb soldered on the motherboard

Configuration	Soldered on Motherboard	SIMM Size	Total RAM
	4Mb		4Mb
	4Mb	1Mb	8Mb
	4Mb	2Mb	12Mb
	4Mb	2Mb 4Mb	16Mb
	4Mb	4Mb	20Mb
	4Mb	4Mb 16Mb	44Mb
	4Mb	16Mb	68Mb
	4Mb	32Mb	132Mb

Fix Your Own Mac: Upgrading and Troubleshooting

Table 5.15 Sample RAM Configurations for the Quadra 800, Quadra 840av and Centris 650 with 8Mb Soldered on the Motherboard

Configuration	Soldered on Motherboard	SIMM Size	Total RAM
	8Mb		8Mb
	8Mb	1Mb	12Mb
	8Mb	2Mb	16Mb
	8Mb	2Mb 4Mb	20Mb
	8Mb	4Mb	24Mb
	8M	4Mb 16Mb	48Mb
	8Mb	16Mb	72Mb
	8Mb	32Mb	136Mb

Installing SIMMs in Macintoshes with 72-Pin SIMM Slots

The LC III, Centris 610, Centris 650, and Quadra 800 are typical of other modular Macs. To install SIMMs, see the section "General SIMM Installation Procedure." The location of SIMM slots in these computers can be found in Figure 5.31. Keep in mind that unlike other desktop Macintoshes, each of the slots represents an entire SIMM bank.

RAM AND THE PORTABLES AND POWERBOOKS

The Macintosh Portables and PowerBooks add RAM differently from desktop models. Rather than having SIMM slots, they have a single expansion slot for RAM. The board that fits into that slot accepts a variety of RAM configurations. Keep in mind that because there is only one RAM expansion slot, upgrading RAM means replacing the existing RAM expansion board with a new one.

Chapter 5: Adding Memory

RAM Configurations for the Macintosh Portables

There are two models of the Macintosh Portable, the initial model without a backlit screen and the upgraded model with a backlit screen. Both computers have 1Mb of RAM soldered to the motherboard and one RAM expansion slot. The original Portable can accept expansion cards with 1Mb to 4Mb RAM; the backlit Portable can accept expansion cards with 1 to 3Mb RAM. If the Portable's processor direct slot isn't used by another card, a second RAM expansion board can be placed in that slot, producing configurations like that in Table 5.16. Note that the maximum RAM for the original Portable is therefore 9Mb but only 8Mb for the backlit Portable. All RAM chips must be 100ns or faster.

One SIMM slot, a bank by itself

LC III/Performa 450

Two SIMM slots, each a separate bank

Centris 610 and 660av

Four SIMM slots, each a separate bank

Centris 650, Quadra 800, and Quadra 840av

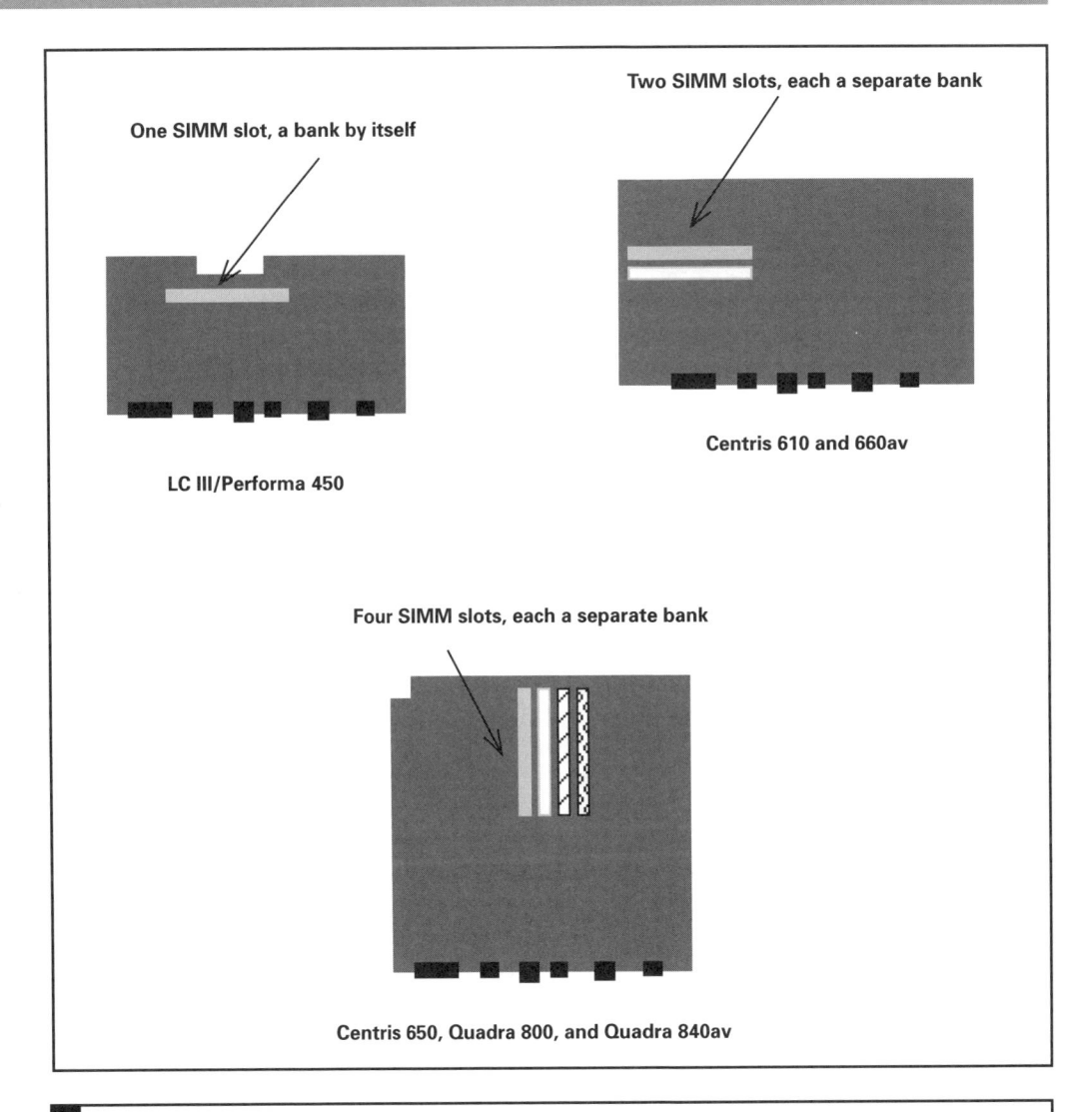

▶ *Figure 5.31* Location of SIMM slots in the LC III/Performa 450, Centris 610, Centris 650, Centris 660av, Quadra 800, and Quadra 840av

Fix Your Own Mac: Upgrading and Troubleshooting

Table 5.16 RAM Configurations for the Original Macintosh Portable and the Backlit Macintosh Portable

Soldered on Motherboard	RAM Expansion Slot	Processor Direct Slot	Total RAM
1Mb	Empty	Empty	1Mb
1Mb	1Mb	Empty	2Mb
1Mb	2Mb	Empty	3Mb
1Mb	3Mb	Empty	4Mb
1Mb	3Mb	1Mb	5Mb
1Mb	4Mb	Empty	5Mb*
1Mb	4Mb	1Mb	6Mb*
1Mb	3Mb	2Mb	6Mb
1Mb	4Mb	2Mb	7Mb*
1Mb	3Mb	3Mb	7Mb
1Mb	4Mb	4Mb	8Mb*
1Mb	3Mb	4Mb	8Mb
1Mb	4Mb	4Mb	9Mb*

*This configuration is available only with the original Macintosh Portable (no backlit screen).

Installing RAM in the Macintosh Portable

Because RAM is added on an expansion board rather than on a SIMM, installing RAM in a Macintosh Portable is similar to adding any other expansion board. To install a RAM expansion card, do the following:

1. Open the Portable's case. (See Chapter 3 for details.) The back portion of the inside of the Portable is exposed. As you can see in Figure 5.32, there are four slots: the PDS, RAM expansion slot, ROM expansion slot, and modem expansion slot.

2. If present, remove the existing RAM expansion card.

3. Insert the new RAM expansion card.

4. Replace the cover.

RAM Configurations for the PowerBook 100, 140, 145, and 170

The PowerBook 100, 140, 145, and 170 use 100ns or faster RAM on a single ex-

Chapter 5: Adding Memory

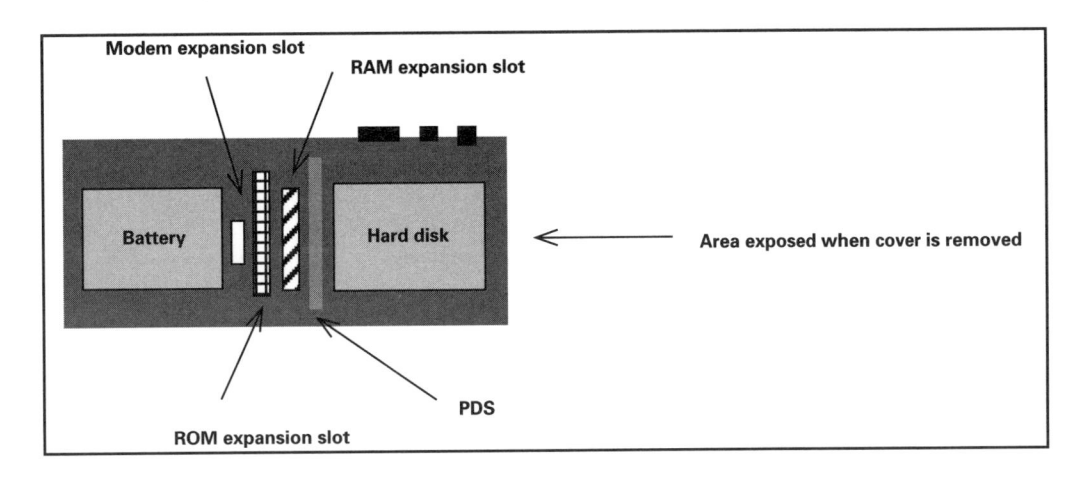

Figure 5.32 *Location of expansion slots in the Macintosh Portables*

pansion board. All four laptops have 2Mb of RAM soldered on the motherboard and can handle expansion board capacities of 2Mb, 4Mb, or 6Mb, providing the RAM configurations in Table 5.17.

RAM Configurations for the PowerBook 160, 165c, 180, 180c

The PowerBook 160, 165c, 180, and 180c require 85ns RAM on a single expansion board. All four have 4Mb of RAM soldered on the motherboard and can handle expansion board capacities of 2Mb, 4Mb, 6Mb, or 10Mb, providing the RAM configurations in Table 5.18.

The 160, 165c, 180, and 180c can actually use RAM expansion cards designed for the 100, 140, 145, and 170. However, because these cards contain slower RAM than those designed specifically for the 160,

Table 5.17 *RAM Configurations for the PowerBook 100, 140, 145, and 170*

Soldered on Motherboard	RAM Expansion Slot	Total RAM
2Mb	Empty	2Mb
2Mb	2Mb	4Mb
2Mb	4Mb	6Mb
2Mb	6Mb	8Mb

▶ **Table 5.18** RAM Configurations for the PowerBook 160, 165c, 180, and 180c

Soldered on Motherboard	RAM Expansion Slot	Total RAM
4Mb	Empty	4Mb
4Mb	2Mb	6Mb
4Mb	4Mb	8Mb
4Mb	6Mb	10Mb

▶ **Table 5.19** RAM Configurations for the PowerBook Duo 210 and 230

Soldered on Motherboard	RAM Expansion Slot	Total RAM
4Mb	Empty	4Mb
4Mb	4Mb	8Mb
4Mb	8Mb	12Mb
4Mb	20Mb	24Mb

165c, 180, and 180c, their use slows down the overall performance of the computer.

RAM Configurations for the PowerBook Duos

The PowerBook Duos have 4Mb RAM soldered to their motherboards. Duo 210 RAM is has a speed of 80ns; Duo 230 RAM has a speed of 70ns. Each computer also has a single RAM expansion slot that can handle between 4 and 20Mb, providing RAM configurations like those in Table 5.19.

Installing PowerBook RAM

As you have read, PowerBook RAM is installed on a RAM expansion board rather than in SIMM slots. It therefore is installed like any other expansion board:

1. Open the PowerBook. (See Chapter 3 for details.)

2. Locate the RAM expansion slot. As you can see in Figure 5.33, all the PowerBooks except the 100 and the Duos have a similar internal organization. The RAM expansion slot is on the secondary logic board at the upper left of the computer. In the 100, it is located to the left of the CPU board. The Duos' RAM expansion slot is at the right edge of the logic board.

3. If a RAM expansion board is present, remove it.

4. Install the new RAM expansion board.

5. Replace the computer's top and the three screws that hold the case together.

Chapter 5: Adding Memory

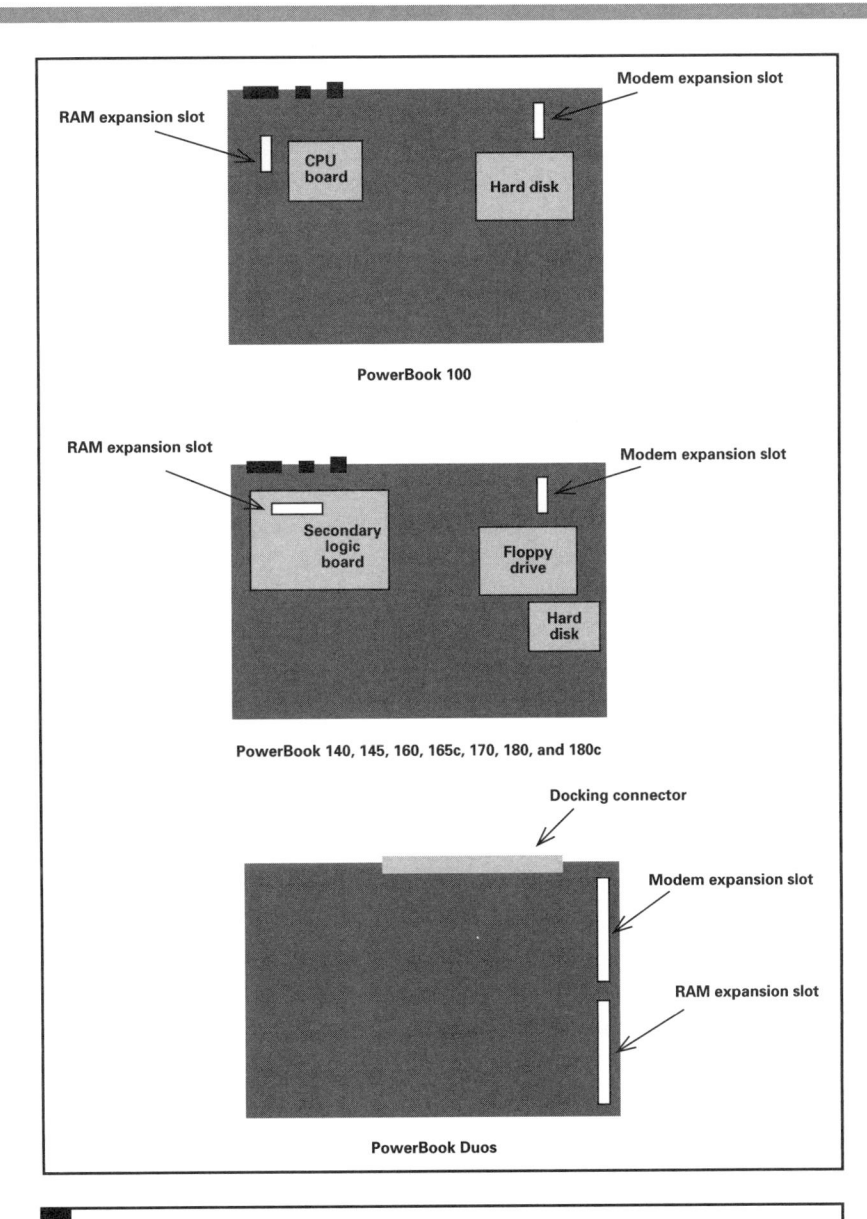

Figure 5.33 Location of the RAM expansion slot in PowerBooks

CPU Accelerators

When you need more raw processing speed, you probably should consider upgrading the CPU in your Mac (see Figure 6.1). CPU upgrades, often called *accelerator boards* because they are supplied on circuit boards, either replace or provide an alternate to the CPU that came with your computer. Although accelerator boards are among the most expensive upgrades, in some cases they can be significantly cheaper than purchasing a new computer yet provide processing speed near that found in the Quadra line.

> **By the way:** One alternative to a CPU accelerator is a logic board upgrade. For details, see Chapter 8.

Today's accelerator boards contain either a 68030 or 68040 CPU, running from 16 to 50Mhz. A 68030 board may also include an FPU. For example, the accelerator in Figure 6.2 contains a 68030 CPU (the big chip at the center top) and an FPU (directly to the right of the CPU). Notice that the accelerator board has a connector at the bottom that connects to a processor direct slot.

The 68040 comes in two versions. The standard 68040 has a built-in FPU. However, some accelerators use the 68LC040, a lower-cost version of the 68040 that has no FPU or provision to accept one. The 68LC040 is found in the Centris 610, for example.

Accelerator boards for older Macs may include SIMM slots to let you add more memory than the computer was originally built to accept. Some combination boards for Macintoshes without expansion slots also include adapter circuits for an external monitor.

Deciding which CPU upgrade to install can be challenging. There are literally hundreds of them available, offering different microprocessors, speeds, and other features. Comparing them can be difficult. For example, if you have a choice between a 50MHz 68030 and a 40MHz 68040, which should you buy? If everything else is equal and you're looking for the fastest CPU, then a 40MHz 68040 is the best choice. It's actually

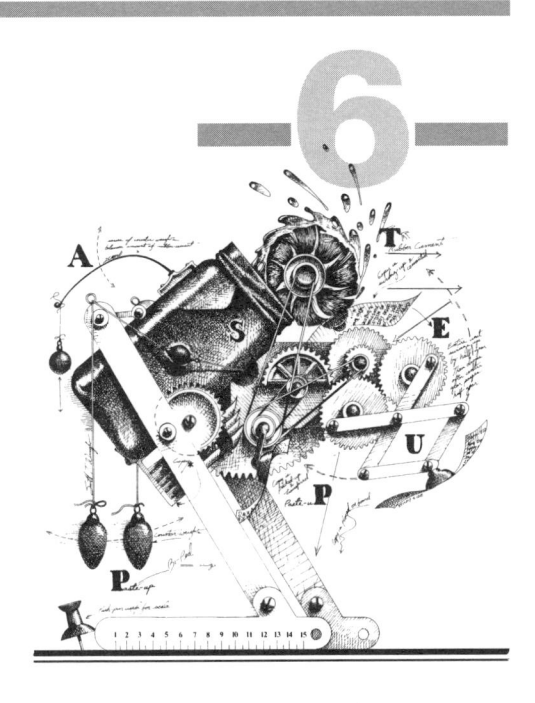

Figure 6.1 The accelerated Mac—a solution to processing bottlenecks

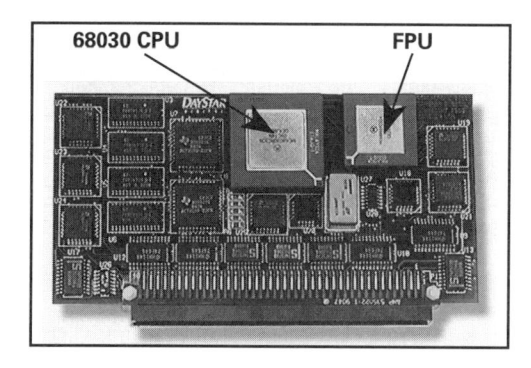

Figure 6.2 A CPU accelerator (DayStar PowerCache) with an FPU

faster than the 50MHz 68030. To understand why this is so, you need to know something about how computers execute the instructions that make up their programs and the internals of the Motorola CPUs.

CPU Structure and Program Execution

A computer program is nothing more than a series of instructions that a computer executes. As you read in Chapter 1, a CPU has a finite number of things it knows how to do (its instruction set). All programs must therefore be written using only the instructions in the CPU's instruction set. Because the 68000, 68020, 68030, and 68040 are all part of the same microprocessor family, their instruction sets are almost identical. (The higher-numbered CPUs have a few instructions the lower-numbered CPUs don't, making their instruction sets downward compatible.)

By the way: Although it has never been used in a Macintosh, there is a 68010 microprocessor. It was used, for example, in the AT&T 3B1 (once known as the AT&T UNIX PC).

By the way: CPUs in different microprocessor families, such as the Intel 80x86 family, have instruction sets that are fundamentally different from the Motorola 680x0 instruction set. This is one of the major reasons that you can't take an executable program from an MS-DOS computer and run it directly on a Macintosh. Emulators such as SoftPC take instructions from the Intel instruction set and translate them to the corresponding Motorola instruction, which the Macintosh can then execute.

The instructions in the instruction set are represented by binary codes. Programs written in languages such as assembly language, BASIC, Pascal, or C must be translated into those binary codes before the computer can understand and execute them. The process of executing a program therefore consists of bringing an instruction into the CPU (a *fetch*), figuring out what the instruction is telling the CPU to do (the *decode*), and then actually performing the requested action (an *execute*). This sequence, known as the *fetch-decode-execute cycle*, occurs for every instruction in a program.

Chapter 6: CPU Accelerators

> **By the way:** Assembly language programs are translated to binary by an *assembler*.
> Other programs are translated by either an *interpreter*, which performs the translation line by line while the program is running, or a *compiler*, which translates the entire program before it is run.

The execute phase of the fetch-decode-execute cycle may require another fetch. This typically occurs when the instruction needs to operate on some data stored in memory, either simply moving it from one location to another or using it in an arithmetic or logical operation. Suppose, for example, a program encounters an instruction to add a value stored in main memory to a value already present in the CPU. As you can see from Figure 6.3, the CPU first retrieves the next instruction. It then decodes it into two parts, one that indicates the action it should perform and a second that indicates where the data on which the instruction will operate can be found. The CPU's decode circuitry realizes that one of the numbers needed for the addition operation is still in main memory. Therefore, when the execute portion of the cycle begins, the CPU performs another fetch to retrieve the data prior to performing the addition.

From where does the instruction come? That depends on which CPU is executing

Fetch → Get next instruction

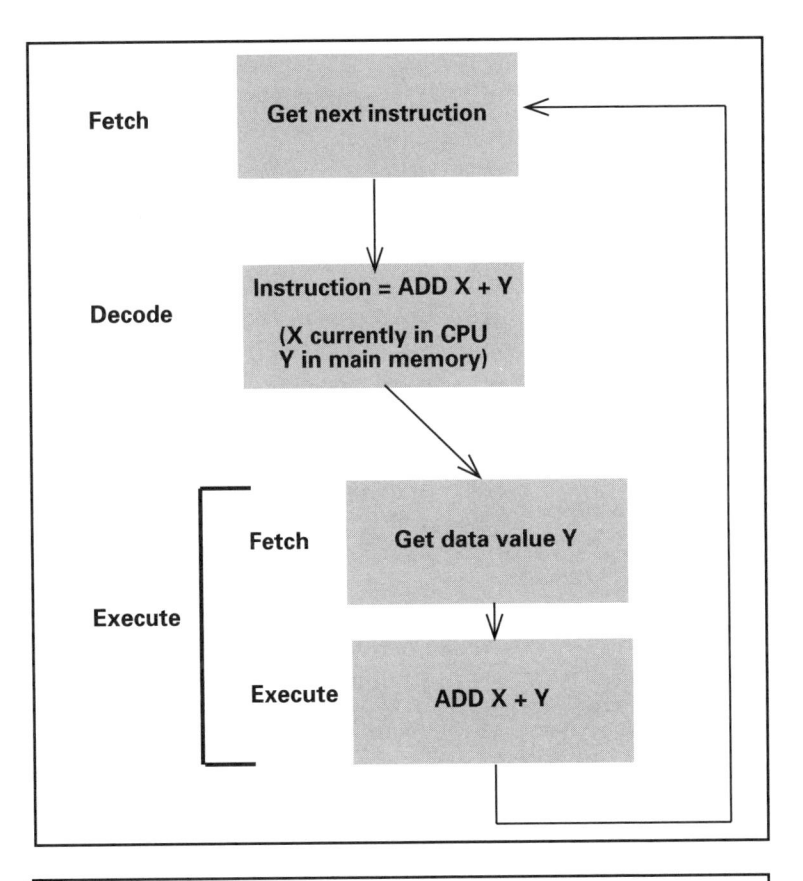

Decode → Instruction = ADD X + Y
(X currently in CPU
Y in main memory)

Execute:
- Fetch → Get data value Y
- Execute → ADD X + Y

▶ *Figure 6.3* The fetch-decode-execute cycle

the instruction. The 68000 must fetch each instruction directly from main memory. However, the 68020, 68030, and 68040 have caches for instructions. (As you probably remember, a cache is a holding area for instructions or data.) The 68020 and 68030 have 256-byte instruction caches; the 68040's instruction cache hold 4K bytes.

Instruction caches hold several instructions at a time. Main memory loads the instruction cache at its own pace, even when the CPU is executing an instruction; the CPU empties it as it needs instructions. Because the type of memory used to create an instruction cache is faster than regular main memory, fetching an instruction from the cache is faster than fetching it from main memory. (This is one reason that CPUs with caches are faster than the 68000.)

Each step in the fetch-decode-execute cycle is performed by a different part of the CPU. As you can see from the block diagram of the 68030 in Figure 6.4, the CPU has its own internal buses that connects its various parts. These are connected to the system bus by the data pads (connected to the system bus's data lines), the address pads (connected to the system bus's address lines), and the bus controller (connected to the system bus's control lines). There are two internal CPU caches, one for data, one for instructions. The 68030's data cache holds 256 bytes; the 68040's holds 4K bytes. (The 68020 has an instruction cache but no data cache.)

By the way: The internal CPU caches are distinct from instruction caches that can be added to some Macintoshes on expansion boards. You will find more information about adding caches in Chapter 7.

The execution unit has three parts, one for handling data, one for handling memory addresses, and one for keeping track of which instruction to execute next (the *program counter*). The decode circuitry in the 68020 and 68030 is made up of four stages (cache holding register, stage B, stage C, and stage D); the 68040 has six stages. The 68020, 68030, and 68040 have been designed to take advantage of this fact. Although common wisdom states that a CPU can only do one thing at once, each *part* of the CPU can only do one thing at once. This means that a CPU can have more than one instruction in the decode phase at the same time.

The technique of having multiple instructions in different stages of the decode phase is known as *pipelining*. The more instructions a CPU can have in its pipeline at one time, the faster the CPU

Chapter 6: CPU Accelerators

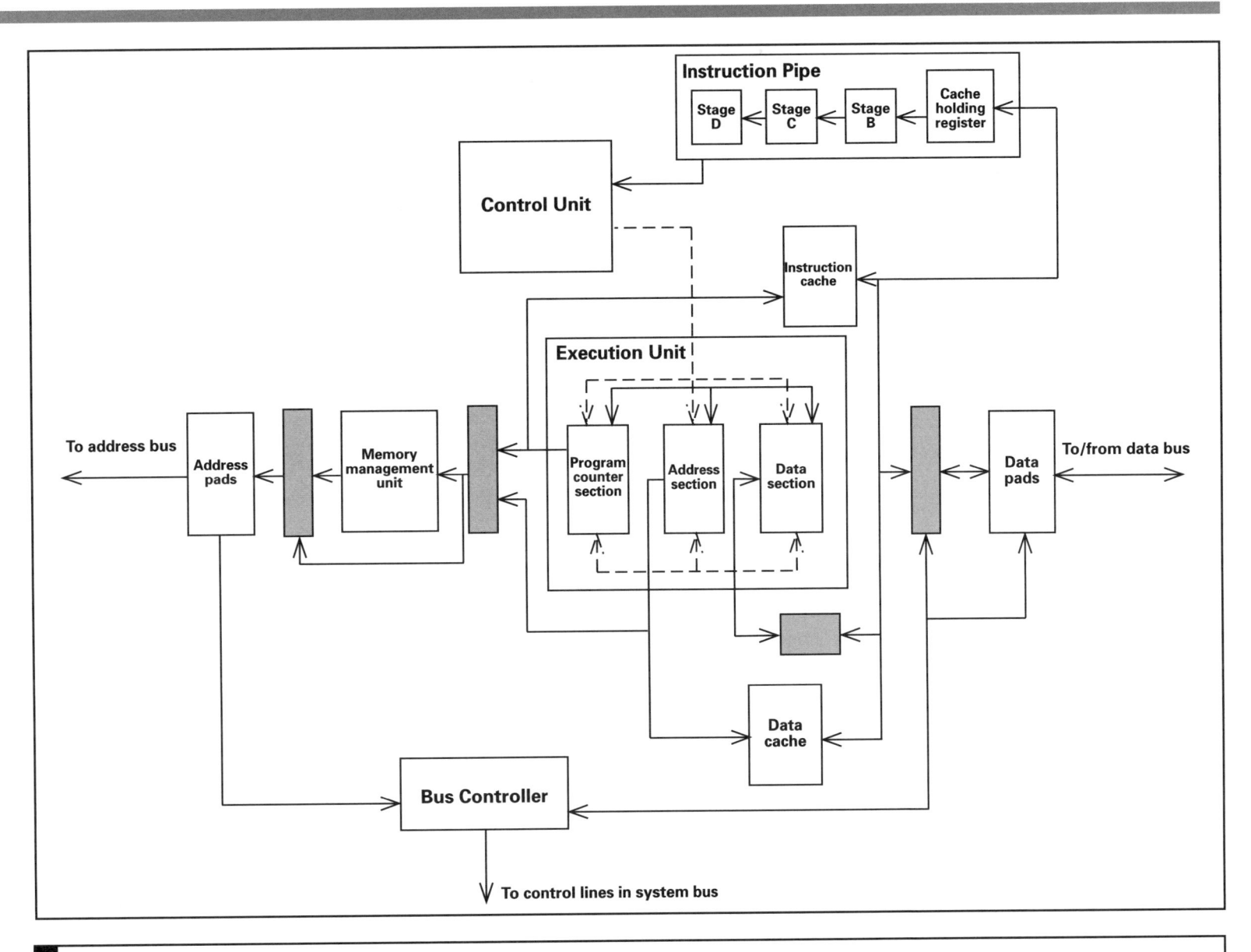

Figure 6.4 Block diagram of the Motorola 68030 68040 microprocessor

145

can run. Because they have four stages in their decode circuitry, the 68020 and 68030 can pipeline four instructions; the 68040 can pipeline six. Coupled with its larger instruction and data caches, the six-instruction pipeline makes a 68040 faster than a 68030 of the same or even higher speed. This is why the 40MHz 68040 is faster than the 50MHz 68030. (The 33MHz 68040 is also faster than the 50MHz 68030.)

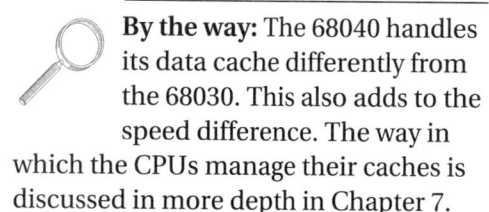

> **By the way:** The 68040 handles its data cache differently from the 68030. This also adds to the speed difference. The way in which the CPUs manage their caches is discussed in more depth in Chapter 7.

Choosing an Accelerator

Because so many CPU accelerators are available, it can be difficult to decide which to purchase. Like so many things in computing, there are trade-offs between power, features, price, ease of use, and ease of installation.

Type of Microprocessor

A CPU accelerator has either a 68030 or a 68040 microprocessor. The 68040 accelerators are considerably more expensive than those based on the 68030. They are also more likely to be subject to software and hardware incompatibilities, although most of the incompatibilities that arose when the 68040 debuted have been removed by upgrades from software manufacturers. (See the section on compatibility for more details.) On the other hand, the 68040 provides the fastest performance of any CPU currently available for the Macintosh.

Although 68030 accelerators are available for every Mac from the 512K onward, 68040 accelerators are generally limited to Macintoshes with 32-bit address and data buses. Although this may not seem fair, keep in mind that CPU speed isn't the only thing that determines how fast your Mac runs. Macs with a 16-bit data bus need two bus cycles to transfer one 32-bit word of data, regardless of which type of CPU is receiving the data. A 68040 in such a computer would spend so much time waiting for data to arrive that the advantage gained by the faster microprocessor would be lost.

Which should you buy? If a 68040 is available for your machine and you can afford it, purchase it. Even if a 68040 isn't available or you can't or don't want to spend that much money, a 68030 can provide significant performance increases. The increase in performance brought by a 68030 will be particularly dramatic if you are upgrading a 68000 Mac.

Microprocessor Speed

There are 68030 CPU accelerators available that operate at 16, 25, 33, 40, and 50MHz; 68040 CPU accelerators run at either 25, 33, or 40MHz. Within a processor line, the higher the clock speed, the faster the accelerator runs. However, keep in mind that the 68040 is faster than a 68030, even one with a higher clock speed. By the same token, as the speed of the CPU goes up, so does the price of the accelerator board.

Which should you buy? The general wisdom is to purchase the fastest CPU you can afford. For example, although you may not think that you need more than a 33MHz 68030 right now, your computing needs are likely to increase over time. If you can afford the 40 or 50MHz, go ahead and give yourself the extra capacity.

FPU

The 68030 microprocessor works with the 68882 FPU to speed up floating-point operations. In most cases, an FPU is an option with a 68030 accelerator. If you do a lot of spreadsheet work, statistics, data analysis, or other application that requires extensive manipulation of floating-point quantities, then you should purchase an FPU along with your 68030 accelerator. On the other hand, if you don't do much number crunching, then you may be able to get along without one. If cost is a major factor in your choice of an accelerator, then you may be able to cut corners by skipping the FPU.

An FPU is built into the 68040. (This is one reason that a 68040 accelerator costs more than a 68030.) When you purchase a 68040 accelerator, you get the FPU, regardless of whether you need it.

> **By the way:** To be completely accurate, there is a version of the 68040—the 68LC040 used in the Centris 610 and the low-end Centris 650—that does not include an FPU and cannot accept an add-on FPU.

Effect on SIMM Requirements

The 68000 Macintoshes can use slower SIMMs than other Macintoshes. That means that in some cases you may need to replace your existing SIMMs with faster RAM that will work with the new CPU. This is particularly true in Macs such as the Plus and SE, which can accept 150ns SIMMs. The 68030, however, generally requires 80ns or faster SIMMs. This need to replace existing SIMMs is one of the hidden costs in adding a CPU accelerator.

Video Adapter Circuitry

One of the major limitations to the older compact Macs is that they have no expansion slots. To get around that problem, several manufacturers of accelerator boards for the older compact Macs have included adapter circuits for an external monitor on the same circuit board as the new CPU. Such boards cost more than those without the video circuitry but provide added functionality to the computer.

Should you purchase such a board? The answer boils down to cost. If you plan to upgrade the CPU and add an external monitor at the same time, it may be more cost effective to replace the computer with something like an LC III. However, if you plan to upgrade incrementally (a little bit at a time), then you can add the combination board and get immediate benefits from the new CPU. You can add the external monitor later, when you can afford it. Although your total cost may be close to what you'd pay for a new computer, by going the upgrade route you don't need to lay out all the money at once.

Type of Installation

An accelerator installs in one of four ways. It can plug into a processor direct slot (perhaps the Mac's only slot), plug into a NuBus slot, replace the Mac's original CPU, or be clipped around the existing CPU, which remains on the motherboard. (The latter is the case for most of the accelerators for compact Macs without slots.)

If your Mac has only one slot, a CPU accelerator that uses that slot prevents you from adding any other boards to the machine. If you want to preserve the use of that slot for something like a network board, then you may want an accelerator that plugs directly into the motherboard. Alternatively, look for an accelerator that installs on an adapter board that provides a pass-through" slot. In other words, the accelerator board plugs into your computer's only slot. However, the accelerator board has a slot on it that can be used as if the accelerator board wasn't there.

One benefit of accelerators that plug into slots is that they can be turned off," so that you can use the computer's original CPU. If the accelerator replaces the original CPU, then you have no choice but always to use the accelerator.

CPU accelerators that use a processor direct slot are faster than those that use a NuBus slot. This is because the processor direct slot is connected directly to all the address, data, and control lines in the bus. On the other hand, NuBus slots aren't connected directly to the system bus. Instead NuBus signals pass through NuBus controller and transceiver circuits, which in turn are connected to the bus. The processing performed by the NuBus controller and transceiver circuits and competition from other NuBus boards needing access to the NuBus circuitry slows down the passage of data to and from boards installed in NuBus slots.

Installation Procedures

Some accelerator boards can be installed by the user. This generally applies to accelerators that plug into slots. Some accelerators that replace the original CPU on the motherboard can also be installed by a user who has a reasonably steady hand. As with any other type of upgrade, if playing with the insides of your computer makes you the least bit uneasy, it pays to let a service technician do the work.

Other accelerator boards should be installed by a service technician. In particular, accelerators for the Plus, SE, and Classic, which have no slots, require modifications to the motherboard. Unless you are very skilled with circuit board modifications, you shouldn't try to install such accelerators yourself. In fact, some manufacturers of accelerators for the older compact Macs ask you to ship the entire computer to them for installation.

By the way: You never know when you might need to ship your Mac somewhere. It therefore always pays to keep the original shipping materials, boxes, styrofoam, and all. (Keep the boxes closed; some cats, dogs, and children like to chew on styrofoam.)

Upgradability

If you purchase a 68030 accelerator today, can it be upgraded to a 68040? Some accelerators are designed to be easily upgraded. For example, the DayStar Universal PowerCache board plugs into an adapter. (The adapter either uses a processor direct slot or replaces the original CPU on the motherboard, depending on the type of Macintosh.) The PowerCache board can be upgraded by simply unplugging the board and inserting another with a more powerful CPU into the adapter.

If you purchase an accelerator with a 68LC040, you will be unable to add an FPU. If you later need one, the only option is to replace the CPU with a standard 68040. Some manufacturers of

68LC040 accelerators discount the cost of their 68040 products for purchasers of their 68LC040 products.

Upgrade prices and policies vary widely. If upgradability is important to you, talk to the manufacturer about such issues before you make your purchase decision.

Compatibility

Most existing software is compatible with 68030 accelerators. Although there were software problems when the 68040 debuted, most incompatibilities with application software have been eliminated. However, incompatibilities still exist between some brands of 68040 CPU accelerators and parts of the Macintosh operating system. In particular, the Radius Rocket boards are known to have problems with file sharing, AppleTalk Remote Access, and QuickTime under System 7 and with the entire System 7.1 release. The RocketWare software that is shipped with each Radius Rocket, however, seems to handle all these problems except those with QuickTime.

In general, 68030 accelerators are also compatible with existing hardware. The same is true for 68040 accelerators, with one major exception. Some NuBus boards use a technique called *byte smearing*. Byte smearing involves the way in which the computer and a NuBus board exchange information. Each board has a 32-bit (one word) storage area (a *register*) for data moving into and out of the board. Those 32 bits are divided into 4 bytes (8 bits = 1 byte). When a board needs to transfer only 1 byte, it can place it in any of the 4 bytes in the register. If the board uses byte smearing, then a single byte is copied (or smeared") into all 4 bytes of the register. The computer can then pluck the data out of any byte in the board's register. By the same token, a 2-byte transfer (16 bits) can also be smeared, creating two copies of the 16 bits.

Most 68040 accelerator boards aren't compatible with NuBus boards that use byte smearing. Even though Apple has warned hardware developers not to use the technique, some boards that use byte smearing exist. Unfortunately, there's no way to tell if any of your NuBus boards use byte smearing. The only way to do so is to talk to the board's manufacturer. If technical support personnel don't know what you're talking about, insist on talking to someone who does.

Warranty and Support Policies

Warranties on CPU accelerators vary a great deal, from one year, to five years, to a lifetime (as long as you own your computer"). Does a longer warranty bring enough benefit that you should pay more for it? Probably not. In general, electronics tend to fail early in their lives (in other words, within the first year) or last an acceptably long time (three to five years or more). However, if everything else is equal (including cost), then there's no reason not to go for the security of a longer warranty.

When purchasing a CPU accelerator, you should also consider how and where you get technical support. This is especially important if you will be installing the board yourself. Look at the days and hours tech support is provided; also consider whether or not the call is toll-free. If your board is installed by a dealer, consider whether the dealer will continue to provide tech support or if you will need to consult the manufacturer for help after the board is installed.

WHERE TO GET AN ACCELERATOR

CPU accelerators can be purchased from dealers, mail-order firms, or in some cases, directly from the manufacturer. Mail-order purchases are generally the cheapest but provide no support other than replacing a defective board; tech support usually comes from the manufacturer. Dealer purchases are the most costly but may include free installation and tech support. When purchasing from a dealer, make sure that all costs are clearly spelled out. (Nobody likes costly surprises, such as an added charge for installation.)

Some manufacturers sell direct to users. If you are purchasing a new accelerator (as opposed to upgrading one already installed), the price is likely to be close to that charged by a dealer; manufacturers who sell direct typically don't give the discounts found when shopping mail order. However, upgrades are usually available only from the manufacturer.

By the way: There is one major exception to the statement that manufacturers don't give significant discounts when they are selling direct to users. That occurs at trade shows such as the Macworld Expo, where everybody seems to be discounting everything. Attending trade shows is great for comparison shopping and for finding both hardware and software at good prices.

ACCELERATOR SURVEY

There are many types of CPU accelerators. The specific CPUs, CPU speeds, and additional features vary considerably from one manufacturer and Macintosh model to another. This section therefore looks at a sampling of accelerator boards available from a variety of manufacturers. As you look through it, keep in mind that it truly is just a sampling and makes no attempt to be comprehensive. New, faster CPU accelerators are available all the time; others are discontinued as they are superseded by new technology.

Once you find accelerators in which you are interested, find the manufacturer's address and phone number in Appendix B. Then call the manufacturer for more information. For comparative information, check out the comprehensive review of more than 100 accelerators that can be found in the April 1993 issue of *MacUser* magazine. The best way to find the most recent product information is to look at the advertisements in current issues of Macintosh publications such as *MacWorld*, *MacUser*, and *MacWEEK*.

Accelerators for 68000 Compact Macs

A CPU accelerator brings the most dramatic speed improvement to a 68000 Mac. However, because the Plus and Classic have no slots, installing an accelerator in any of these models is difficult. CPU accelerators designed for 68000 Macintoshes feature a 68030 CPU; 68040 accelerators are not available. Most also include four SIMM slots for RAM up to 16Mb. However, because the 68000 machines are built to handle only 4Mb of RAM, software such as Virtual by Connectix is required to access the additional RAM. (Virtual is included with many of those accelerators that offer the added memory support.) The upgraded Mac thinks" that the RAM above 4Mb is *virtual memory* (simulated memory that usually uses a disk file to represent RAM that isn't physically present in a computer). The computer manipulates and accesses the added RAM as if it were virtual memory. However, because in this case the virtual memory is actually physical RAM, access is much faster than virtual memory that uses a disk file. As you may remember, the 16Mb limit is imposed by the computer's 24-bit address bus.

When pricing CPU accelerators for 68000 compact Macs, don't forget to include the cost of added RAM. A full 16Mb (four 4Mb SIMMs) adds around $600 to the cost of upgrading. Although you certainly can function with less than the full 16Mb RAM, you'll need a minimum of 4Mb to run System 7; high-end graphics and multimedia applications routinely require more.

Macintosh Plus Accelerators

Accelerators for the Macintosh Plus (see Table 6.1) must either be soldered or clipped onto the motherboard. In some cases, the computer must be sent to the accelerator manufacturer for installation. In others, the accelerator is technically installable by the user. However, if you aren't comfortable with pulling and inserting chips, don't attempt to install such an upgrade yourself. Spend the money to have an authorized service technician do the installation.

Notice in Table 6.1 that many Mac Plus accelerators provide video support. This means that the expansion board contains adapter circuitry and a port for a large, external monitor. Keep in mind, however, that even using adapter

▶ *Table 6.1 Accelerators for the Macintosh Plus*

Manufacturer	Model	CPU	Clock Speed	FPU	How Installed	Warranty	Other Features
MacProducts	RailGun030	68030	16MHz	Included	Clips onto motherboard	1 year	RAM to 16Mb
MacProducts	RailGun030	68030	25MHz	Included	Clips onto motherboard	1 year	RAM to 16Mb
MacProducts	RailGun030	68030	25MHz	Included	Clips onto motherboard	1 year	RAM to 16Mb
MacProducts	RailGun030 Pro	68030	16MHz	Included	Clips onto motherboard	1 year	RAM to 16Mb, video support
MacProducts	RailGun030 Pro	68030	25MHz	Included	Clips onto motherboard	1 year	RAM to 16Mb video support
MacProducts	RailGun030 Pro	68030	25MHz	Included	Clips onto motherboard	1 year	RAM to 16Mb video support
NewLife	NewLife 25	68030	25MHz	Included	Clips onto motherboard	2 years	RAM to 16Mb, video support, fan
NewLife	NewLife 33c	68030	33MHz	Included	Clips onto motherboard	2 years	RAM to 16Mb, video support, fan
Novy Systems	ImagePro	68030	16MHz	Optional	Clips onto motherboard	2 years	RAM to 16Mb, video support, fan
Novy Systems	ImagePro	68030	25MHz	Optional	Clips onto motherboard	2 years	RAM to 16Mb, video support, fan
Novy Systems	ImagePro	68030	33MHz	Optional	Clips onto motherboard	2 years	RAM to 16Mb, video support, fan

circuitry on an expansion board, the Mac Plus can only support a monochrome monitor.

Macintosh SE Accelerators

Like the Mac Plus, the 68000-based SE shows tremendous speed improvements when enhanced with a CPU accelerator (see Table 6.2). However, because the SE has a PDS, accelerators can be easier to install. Any accelerator that uses the PDS can be installed by a user with a relatively steady hand. (Nonetheless, if you don't feel comfortable opening the SE's case and removing its motherboard, find someone else to do the installation.)

If you want to add an external monitor to your SE, keep in mind that once you place an accelerator in the PDS, it can't be used for a video board. Therefore, look for an accelerator that includes video support. The video circuitry on CPU accelerators for the SE supports a variety of monochrome monitors; regardless of what circuitry you add, the SE can't generate grayscale or color signals.

Using the SE's PDS for an accelerator board also precludes using that slot for any other type of expansion board (for example, an Ethernet board). If you need to add a specialized network adapter or some other expansion board, look for a CPU accelerator board with a PDS pass-through. Such accelerator boards plug into the SE's PDS but also provide a PDS on the accelerator board itself.

Macintosh Classic Accelerators

Many manufacturers make accelerators for the original Classic (see Table 6.3). In most cases, they clip onto the motherboard around the computer's original CPU. In fact, installing a CPU accelerator in a Classic is very much like installing one in a Macintosh Plus. Clip-on installations are theoretically installable by the user. However, use your judgment in deciding whether you feel comfortable taking your Classic apart and removing its motherboard.

A number of Classic accelerators provide support for an external monitor. Such monitors are available in a variety of sizes. However, they are monochrome only; grayscale and color are not available.

Chapter 6: CPU Accelerators

Table 6.2 *Accelerators for the Macintosh SE*

Manufacturer	Model	CPU	Clock Speed	FPU	How Installed	Warranty	Other Features
Applied Eng.	TransWarp SE	68030	16MHz	Optional	Replaces original CPU	1 year	RAM to 16Mb
Applied Eng.	TransWarp SE	68030	25MHz	Optional	Replaces original CPU	1 year	RAM to 16Mb, 32K RAM cache
Applied Eng.	TransWarp SE	68030	40MHz	Optional	Replaces original CPU	1 year	RAM to 16Mb, 32K RAM cache
DayStar	Universal PowerCache	68030	33MHz	Optional	PDS	3 years	RAM to 16Mb
DayStar	Universal PowerCache	68030	40MHz	Optional	PDS	3 years	RAM to 16Mb
DayStar	Universal PowerCache	68030	50MHz	Optional	PDS	3 years	RAM to 16Mb
Extreme Systems	Vandal	68030	33MHz	Included	PDS	3 years	RAM to 16Mb, video support
Extreme Systems	Vandal	68030	40MHz	Included	PDS	3 years	RAM to 16Mb, video support
Extreme Systems	Vandal	68030	50MHz	Included	PDS	3 years	RAM to 16Mb, video support
MacProducts	RailGun030	68030	16MHz	Included	PDS	1 year	RAM to 16Mb
MacProducts	RailGun030	68030	25MHz	Included	PDS	1 year	RAM to 16Mb
MacProducts	RailGun030	68030	25MHz	Included	PDS	1 year	RAM to 16Mb
MacProducts	RailGun030 Pro	68030	16MHz	Included	PDS	1 year	RAM to 16Mb, video support
MacProducts	RailGun030 Pro	68030	25MHz	Included	PDS	1 year	RAM to 16Mb, video support
MacProducts	RailGun030 Pro	68030	25MHz	Included	PDS	1 year	RAM to 16Mb, video support
Mobius	030 Accelerator	68030	25MHz	Optional	PDS	3 years	RAM to 16Mb, video support
NewLife	*Accelerator!* SE	68030	16MHz	Optional	PDS	2 years	Virtual memory to 16Mb, video support
NewLife	NewLife 33	68030	33MHz	Optional	PDS	2 years	RAM to 16Mb, video support PDS pass-through slot
Novy Systems	ImagePro	68030	16MHz	Optional	Clips onto motherboard	2 years	RAM to 16Mb, video support
Novy Systems	ImagePro	68030	25MHz	Optional	Clips onto motherboard	2 years	RAM to 16Mb, video support
Novy Systems	ImagePro	68030	33MHz	Optional	Clips onto motherboard	2 years	RAM to 16Mb, video support

Table 6.3 Accelerators for the Macintosh Classic

Manufacturer	Model	CPU	Clock Speed	FPU	How Installed	Warranty	Other Features
DayStar	Universal PowerCache	68030	33MHz	Optional	Clips onto motherboard	3 years	RAM to 16Mb
DayStar	Universal PowerCache	68030	40MHz	Optional	Clips onto motherboard	3 years	RAM to 16Mb
DayStar	Universal PowerCache	68030	50MHz	Optional	Clips onto motherboard	3 years	RAM to 16Mb
MacProducts	RailGun030	68030	16MHz	Included	Clips onto motherboard	1 year	RAM to 16Mb
MacProducts	RailGun030	68030	25MHz	Included	Clips onto motherboard	1 year	RAM to 16Mb
MacProducts	RailGun030	68030	25MHz	Included	Clips onto motherboard	1 year	RAM to 16Mb
MacProducts	RailGun030 Pro	68030	16MHz	Included	Clips onto motherboard	1 year	RAM to 16Mb, video support
MacProducts	RailGun030 Pro	68030	25MHz	Included	Clips onto motherboard	1 year	RAM to 16Mb, video support
MacProducts	RailGun030 Pro	68030	25MHz	Included	Clips onto motherboard	1 year	RAM to 16Mb, video support
Mobius	030 Accelerator	68030	25MHz	Optional	Clips onto motherboard	3 years	RAM up to 16Mb, video support
NewLife	*Accelerator!* Classic	68030	16MHz	Optional	Clips onto motherboard	2 years	RAM to 16Mb, video support
Novy Systems	ImagePro	68030	16MHz	Optional	Clips onto motherboard	2 years	RAM to 16Mb, video support
Novy Systems	ImagePro	68030	25MHz	Optional	Clips onto motherboard	2 years	RAM to 16Mb, video support
Novy Systems	ImagePro	68030	33MHz	Optional	Clips onto motherboard	2 years	RAM to 16Mb, video support

Accelerators for 68020 Macs

Although the 68020 was a tremendous speed improvement when it first appeared in a Mac in 1987, it seems unbearably slow when compared to the 68030 and 68040. In many cases, a machine with a 68020 is just too slow to run many of today's programs satisfactorily. Therefore, if you intend to keep your Mac II or LC, you'll want to install a CPU accelerator or new logic board. (Logic board upgrade options are discussed in Chapter 8.)

Macintosh II Accelerators

One of the two most useful upgrades you can add to a Mac II is a CPU accelerator (see Table 6.4). Although a logic board upgrade is available to turn the Mac II into a IIfx, the cost of that upgrade is three to five times more than an accelerator. (Keep in mind that the IIfx logic board upgrade requires new SIMMs and SCSI terminators.)

There are two types of Mac II ROM, A and B. A number of accelerator boards are incompatible with Mac IIs with the A ROMs (those built before December 1987). Fortunately, a free upgrade to the B ROMs is available from an authorized Macintosh dealer.

Because the Macintosh II doesn't have a PDS, installing a CPU upgrade often means removing the original CPU and replacing it with an adapter containing a PDS. This can be done by a user with a steady hand. However, if you aren't comfortable with pulling and replacing chips, don't attempt this type of installation on your own. A bent pin means a ruined adapter; the only solution is to replace it.

Some CPU accelerators for the Mac II are designed to use NuBus slots. Such accelerators are easy to install but generally don't perform as well as those that use a PDS on adapter cards.

Macintosh LC Accelerators

The LC's 68020 is certainly slow in terms of today's currently Macintosh models. It can be upgraded with either a 68030 or a 68040 (see Table 6.5). Most LC accelerators use the computer's PDS. However, others install directly on the motherboard, replacing the original CPU with an adapter. The advantage of the latter is that it leaves the PDS open for another expansion board. On the other hand, an accelerator that uses the PDS is much easier to install than one that requires pulling the original CPU and installing an adapter.

When considering a CPU upgrade, keep in mind that the LC III logic board upgrade available at a reasonable price. The logic board is also upgradable to 36Mb RAM, whereas the LC can only handle

Table 6.4 Accelerators for the Macintosh II

Manufacturer	Model	CPU	Clock Speed	FPU	How Installed	Warranty	Other Features
DayStar	Universal PowerCache	68030	33MHz	Optional	Replaces original CPU*	3 years	
DayStar	Universal PowerCache	68030	40MHz	Optional	Replaces original CPU*	3 years	
DayStar	Universal PowerCache	68030	50MHz	Optional	Replaces original CPU*	3 years	
DayStar	Turbo 040	68040	25MHz	Included	Replaces original CPU*	3 years	128K RAM cache
DayStar	Turbo 040	68040	33MHz	Included	Replaces original CPU*	3 years	128K RAM cache
DayStar	Turbo 040	68040	40MHz	Included	Replaces original CPU*	3 years	128K RAM cache
Mobius	Speedster 25i	68LC040	25MHz	Not available	Plug-in[†]	3 years	Static RAM cache
Mobius	Speedster 25	68040	25MHz	Included	Plug-in[†]	3 years	Static RAM cache
Mobius	Speedster 33i	68LC040	33MHz	Not available	Plug-in[†]	3 years	Static RAM cache
Mobius	Speedster 33	68040	33MHz	Included	Plug-in[†]	3 years	Static RAM cache
Mobius	Speedster 40i	68LC040	40MHz	Not available	Plug-in[†]	3 years	Static RAM cache
Mobius	Speedster 40	68040	40MHz	Included	Plug-in[†]	3 years	Static RAM cache
Radius	Rocket 25i	68LC040	25MHz	Not available	NuBus	1 year	PDS RAM to 128Mb
Radius	Rocket	68040	25MHz	Included	NuBus	1 year	PDS RAM to 128Mb
Radius	Rocket 33	68040	33Mhz	Included	NuBus	1 year	PDS RAM to 128Mb

*Requires installation of an adapter card that replaces the computer's original CPU and creates a PDS.
[†]Adapter replaces original CPU; original CPU is installed in adapter card, making both original CPU and accelerator CPU available.

Chapter 6: CPU Accelerators

Table 6.5 *Accelerators for the Macintosh LC*

Manufacturer	Model	CPU	Clock Speed	FPU	How Installed	Warranty	Other Features
Applied Eng.	TransWarp LC	68030	25MHz	Optional	PDS	1 year	32K RAM cache
Applied Eng.	TransWarp LC	68030	33MHz	Optional	PDS	1 year	32K RAM cache
Applied Eng.	TransWarp LC	68030	40MHz	Optional	PDS	1 year	32K RAM cache
Applied Eng.	TransWarp LC	68030	50MHz	Optional	PDS	1 year	32K RAM cache
DayStar	Universal PowerCache	68030	33MHz	Optional	PDS	3 years	
DayStar	Universal PowerCache	68030	40MHz	Optional	PDS	3 years	
DayStar	Universal PowerCache	68030	50MHz	Optional	PDS	3 years	
DayStar	Turbo 040	68040	25MHz	Included	PDS	3 years	128K RAM cache
DayStar	Turbo 040	68040	33MHz	Included	PDS	3 years	128K RAM cache
Extreme Systems	Impact 030	68030	32MHz	Optional	PDS	3 years	32K RAM cache
Fusion	TokaMac ELC	68LC040	25MHz	Not available	PDS	1 year	
Fusion	TokaMac LC	68040	25MHz	Included	PDS	1 year	
Mobius	Speedster 25i	68LC040	25MHz	Not available	Plug-in*	3 years	RAM cache
Mobius	Speedster 25	68040	25MHz	Included	Plug-in*	3 years	RAM cache
Mobius	Speedster 33i	68LC040	33MHz	Not available	Plug-in*	3 years	RAM cache
Mobius	Speedster 33	68040	33MHz	Included	Plug-in*	3 years	RAM cache
Mobius	Speedster 40i	68LC040	40MHz	Not available	Plug-in*	3 years	RAM cache
Mobius	Speedster 40	68040	40MHz	Included	Plug-in*	3 years	RAM cache

*Adapter replaces original CPU; original CPU is installed in adapter card, making both original CPU and accelerator CPU available.

10Mb. The logic board upgrade, however, requires all new SIMMs. Although 4Mb RAM are soldered to the LC III motherboard, that isn't enough RAM for much computing under System 7.

Accelerators for 68030 Macs

At first thought, it might seem that a 68030 Macintosh wouldn't need a CPU upgrade. However, many 68030 Macs run at clock speeds considerably slower than those available with the CPU's on today's accelerators. A CPU upgrade can therefore add both performance and longevity to a 68030 machine.

Macintosh SE/30 Accelerators

The SE/30 is still an extremely useful machine. When equipped with a video board in its single processor direct slot, it can produce grayscale and color images on a variety of sizes of external monitors. However, its 16MHz CPU is too slow for processor-intensive operations such as statistics or three-dimensional graphics rendering. If you intend to use your SE/30 for much more than light office work, you should probably add a faster and/or more powerful CPU (see Table 6.6).

When choosing a CPU accelerator for the SE/30, keep in mind that if you select one that installs in a PDS, you will be unable to add any other expansion boards unless the accelerator board contains a PDS pass-through. Alternatively, look for an accelerator that replaces the original CPU, rather than using the PDS. A CPU accelerator that replaces the original CPU, however, is more difficult to install than one that plugs into the PDS because it requires modifications to the motherboard.

Macintosh Classic II Note

As of the date this book went to press, there were no CPU accelerators available for the Classic II. This machine has a design different from other compact Macs, making it impossible to clip an accelerator around the computer's CPU.

Macintosh LC II/Performa 4XX Series Accelerators

Despite having a 68030 CPU, the LC II/Performa 4xx isn't a particularly peppy machine. If you plan to use it for processor-intensive operations that involving high-end graphics or number crunching, then you should seriously consider adding a CPU accelerator (see Table 6.7).

CPU accelerators for the LC II/Performa 4xx either use the computer's PDS or replace the original CPU. The advantage of the latter design is that it leaves the PDS free for other expansion boards. Nonetheless, if you don't intend to add any other boards, keep in mind that a PDS accelerator is easier to install than one that requires modification of the motherboard.

Chapter 6: CPU Accelerators

Table 6.6 *Accelerators for the Macintosh SE/30*

Manufacturer	Model	CPU	Clock Speed	FPU	How Installed	Warranty	Other Features
DayStar	Universal PowerCache	68030	33MHz	Optional	PDS	3 years	PDS pass-through
DayStar	Universal PowerCache	68030	40MHz	Optional	PDS	3 years	PDS pass-through
DayStar	Universal PowerCache	68030	50MHz	Optional	PDS	3 years	PDS pass-through
DayStar	Turbo 040	68040	25MHz	Included	PDS	3 years	128K RAM cache, PDS pass-through
DayStar	Turbo 040	68040	33MHz	Included	PDS	3 years	128K RAM cache, PDS pass-through
DayStar	Turbo 040	68040	40MHz	Included	PDS	3 years	128K RAM cache, PDS pass-through
Fusion	TokaMac SX 25i	68LC040	25MHz	Not available	PDS	1 year	
Fusion	TokaMac SX 25	68040	25MHz	Included	PDS	1 year	
Mobius	Speedster 25i	68LC040	25MHz	Not available	Plug-in*	3 years	Static RAM cache
Mobius	Speedster 25	68040	25MHz	Included	Plug-in*	3 years	Static RAM cache
Mobius	Speedster 33i	68LC040	33MHz	Not available	Plug-in*	3 years	Static RAM cache
Mobius	Speedster 33	68040	33MHz	Included	Plug-in*	3 years	Static RAM cache
Mobius	Speedster 40i	68LC040	40MHz	Not available	Plug-in*	3 years	Static RAM cache
Mobius	Speedster 40	68040	40MHz	Included	Plug-in*	3 years	Static RAM cache

*Adapter replaces original CPU; original CPU is installed in adapter card, making both original CPU and accelerator CPU available.

The LC II/Performa 4xx can also be upgraded with an LC III motherboard. Although the logic board upgrade is actually less expensive than most accelerator boards, its CPU is slower than that found on most accelerators. The logic board upgrade also requires new SIMMs to expand the computer's RAM beyond the 4Mb soldered onto the LC III motherboard.

Table 6.7 *Accelerators for the Macintosh LC II/Performa 4xx Series*

Manufacturer	Model	CPU	Clock Speed	FPU	How Installed	Warranty	Other Features
DayStar	Universal PowerCache	68030	33MHz	Optional	PDS	3 years	
DayStar	Universal PowerCache	68030	40MHz	Optional	PDS	3 years	
DayStar	Universal PowerCache	68030	50MHz	Optional	PDS	3 years	
DayStar	Turbo 040	68040	25MHz	Included	PDS	3 years	128K RAM cache
DayStar	Turbo 040	68040	33MHz	Included	PDS	3 years	128K RAM cache
Extreme Systems	Impact 030	68030	32MHz	Optional	PDS	3 years	32K RAM cache
Fusion	TokaMac ELC	68LC040	25MHz	Not available	PDS	1 year	
Fusion	TokaMac LC	68040	25MHz	Included	PDS	1 year	
Mobius	Speedster 25i	68LC040	25MHz	Not available	Plug-in*	3 years	Static RAM cache
Mobius	Speedster 25	68040	25MHz	Included	Plug-in*	3 years	Static RAM cache
Mobius	Speedster 33i	68LC040	33MHz	Not available	Plug-in*	3 years	Static RAM cache
Mobius	Speedster 33	68040	33MHz	Included	Plug-in*	3 years	Static RAM cache
Mobius	Speedster 40i	68LC040	40MHz	Not available	Plug-in*	3 years	Static RAM cache
Mobius	Speedster 40	68040	40MHz	Included	Plug-in*	3 years	Static RAM cache

*Adapter replaces original CPU; original CPU is installed in adapter card, making both original CPU and accelerator CPU available.

Macintosh IIx Accelerators

The Macintosh IIx is essentially a Macintosh II with a 68030 CPU and a SuperDrive. Like the SE/30, its 68030 is slow by today's standards. Because the Mac IIx has six NuBus slots, room for at least three internal drives (two floppy, one hard), and a robust power supply, it usually makes good sense to keep the computer and upgrade it (see Table 6.8). CPU accelerators for the IIx either create their own PDS by using an adapter that replaces the original CPU or install in a NuBus slot. A NuBus accelerator is easier to install than one that replaces the original CPU, but it runs somewhat slower.

In the interest of full disclosure, it seems fair to remind you that a logic board upgrade to a IIfx is available for the Mac IIx. However, the logic board upgrade costs three to five times the price of a CPU accelerator. In addition, it requires all new

Table 6.8 Accelerators for the Macintosh IIx

Manufacturer	Model	CPU	Clock Speed	FPU	How Installed	Warranty	Other Features
DayStar	Universal PowerCache	68030	33MHz	Optional	Replaces original CPU*	3 years	
DayStar	Universal PowerCache	68030	40MHz	Optional	Replaces original CPU*	3 years	
DayStar	Universal PowerCache	68030	50MHz	Optional	Replaces original CPU*	3 years	
DayStar	Turbo 040	68040	25MHz	Included	Replaces original CPU*	3 years	128K RAM cache
DayStar	Turbo 040	68040	33MHz	Included	Replaces original CPU*	3 years	128K RAM cache
DayStar	Turbo 040	68040	40MHz	Included	Replaces original CPU*	3 years	128K RAM cache
Radius	Rocket 25i	68LC040	25MHz	Not available	NuBus	1 year	PDS, RAM to 128Mb
Radius	Rocket	68040	25MHz	Included	NuBus	1 year	PDS, RAM to 128Mb
Radius	Rocket 33	68040	33Mhz	Included	NuBus	1 year	PDS, RAM to 128Mb

*Requires installation of an adapter card that replaces the computer's original CPU and creates a PDS.

SIMMs and SCSI terminators. Given the availability of 68040 accelerators for less than the cost of the logic board upgrade, the IIfx logic board upgrade doesn't seem particularly attractive.

Macintosh IIcx Accelerators

The IIcx, the first modular Mac in a small box, is a smaller version of the Macintosh IIx. It has only three NuBus slots and no PDS. If you intend to add a CPU accelerator (see Table 6.9), then you can choose from among those that create a PDS with an adapter that plugs into the motherboard (replacing the original CPU) or those that occupy a NuBus slot.

Notice in Table 6.9 that the Radius Rocket series provides an interesting alternative. Although the boards install in a NuBus slot, they provide a PDS for other expansion boards. Using one of these accelerators therefore has less impact on the overall expandability of the computer than using a NuBus accelerator that simply occupies a slot.

Although a plug-in accelerator is harder to install than a NuBus board, it does leave all three NuBus slots available for other boards. (Don't forget that the IIcx has no on-board video and must therefore use at least one of its three slots for a video card.) There is, however, one complication associated with installing a plug-in CPU accelerator in a IIcx: Most IIcx's have a soldered, not socketed, CPU. If you have such a IIcx, then you won't be able to remove the original CPU yourself to replace it with an adapter for a plug-in accelerator board. You will need either to have the accelerator installed by an authorized service technician or to send the motherboard to the accelerator manufacturer to have a CPU socket installed. Which of those options is available depends on the manufacturer from whom you purchased the accelerator.

How do you know which type of CPU your IIcx has? In most cases, the top of the soldered CPU is all black; the top of the socketed CPU is gold with a 0.25-inch black border. To be certain, you should also look at the side of the CPU. If it sits flush with the motherboard, then it is soldered. If there is a 0.25-inch-high socket between the CPU and the motherboard, then it is definitely socketed. Whatever you do, don't try to remove a soldered CPU from the motherboard yourself; you could seriously damage both the CPU and the motherboard.

Chapter 6: CPU Accelerators

Table 6.9 *Accelerators for the Macintosh IIcx*

Manufacturer	Model	CPU	Clock Speed	FPU	How Installed	Warranty	Other Features
DayStar	Universal PowerCache	68030	33MHz	Optional	Replaces original CPU	3 years	
DayStar	Universal PowerCache	68030	40MHz	Optional	Replaces original CPU	3 years	
DayStar	Universal PowerCache	68030	50MHz	Optional	Replaces original CPU	3 years	
DayStar	Turbo 040	68040	25MHz	Included	Replaces original CPU	3 years	128K RAM cache
DayStar	Turbo 040	68040	33MHz	Included	Replaces original CPU	3 years	128K RAM cache
DayStar	Turbo 040	68040	40MHz	Included	Replaces original CPU	3 years	128K RAM cache
Mobius	Speedster 25i	68LC040	25MHz	Not available	Plug-in*	3 years	Static RAM cache
Mobius	Speedster 25	68040	25MHz	Included	Plug-in*	3 years	Static RAM cache
Mobius	Speedster 33i	68LC040	33MHz	Not available	Plug-in*	3 years	Static RAM cache
Mobius	Speedster 33	68040	33MHz	Included	Plug-in*	3 years	Static RAM cache
Mobius	Speedster 40i	68LC040	40MHz	Not available	Plug-in*	3 years	Static RAM cache
Mobius	Speedster 40	68040	40MHz	Included	Plug-in*	3 years	Static RAM cache
Radius	Rocket 25i	68LC040	25MHz	Not available	NuBus	1 year	PDS, RAM to 128Mb
Radius	Rocket	68040	25MHz	Included	NuBus	1 year	PDS, RAM to 128Mb
Radius	Rocket 33	68040	33Mhz	Included	NuBus	1 year	PDS, RAM to 128Mb

*Adapter replaces original CPU; original CPU is installed in adapter card, making both original CPU and accelerator CPU available.

Macintosh IIsi Accelerators

The IIsi, with its single PDS, is easy to expand. Keep in mind, however, that if you install an accelerator card in that slot, you may lose any other expansion capabilities. As you can see from Table 6.10, some IIsi accelerators do use a PDS; of those, two provide PDS pass-through slots so that you can add another board even though the original slot is occupied.

An alternative to using the IIsi's single slot is an accelerator that plugs into the motherboard. Because the installation of a plug-in accelerator requires removing the computer's original CPU and installing an adapter, a plug-in accelerator is more difficult to install than one that uses a slot. (Such accelerators nonetheless can be installed by someone with a steady hand.) However, the plug-in accelerator leaves the PDS free to accept another expansion board.

Macintosh IIci Accelerators

Until the release of the Centris Macintoshes, the IIci was considered the low-cost Macintosh of choice for high-end work. Today, however, the IIci has been surpassed in both price and performance not only by the Centrises, but by the LC III as well. (The LC III, however, is less expandable.)

The IIci has three NuBus slots, a PDS, and a slot for a cache card. You can purchase a CPU accelerator that uses any of those slots or one that plugs directly into the motherboard, replacing the original CPU (see Table 6.11). Installing an accelerator that plugs into the motherboard is more difficult than installing one that plugs into a slot because you must remove the original CPU and replace it with an adapter card for the accelerator board. Nonetheless, using a plug-in accelerator leaves other slots available for further expansion.

Notice in Table 6.11 that some of the accelerator boards that install in slots include PDS pass-throughs and slots for RAM caches. Such boards can help retain your IIci's expandability even after a CPU accelerator has been installed.

Chapter 6: CPU Accelerators

Table 6.10 Accelerators for the Macintosh IIsi

Manufacturer	Model	CPU	Clock Speed	FPU	How Installed	Warranty	Other Features
DayStar	Universal PowerCache	68030	33MHz	Optional	PDS	3 years	
DayStar	Universal PowerCache	68030	40MHz	Optional	PDS	3 years	
DayStar	Universal PowerCache	68030	50MHz	Optional	PDS	3 years	
DayStar	Turbo 040	68040	25MHz	Included	PDS	3 years	128K RAM cache
DayStar	Turbo 040	68040	33MHz	Included	PDS	3 years	128K RAM cache
DayStar	Turbo 040	68040	40MHz	Included	PDS	3 years	128K RAM cache, PDS pass-through
Extreme Systems	Accomplice	68030	50MHz	Included	PDS	3 years	PDS pass-through, 32K RAM cache
Fusion	TokaMac SX 25i	68LC040	25MHz	Not included	PDS	1 year	
Fusion	TokaMac SX 25	68040	25MHz	Included	PDS	1 year	
Mobius	Speedster 25i	68LC040	25MHz	Not available	Plug-in*	3 years	Static RAM cache
Mobius	Speedster 25	68040	25MHz	Included	Plug-in*	3 years	Static RAM cache
Mobius	Speedster 33i	68LC040	33MHz	Not available	Plug-in*	3 years	Static RAM cache
Mobius	Speedster 33	68040	33MHz	Included	Plug-in*	3 years	Static RAM cache
Mobius	Speedster 40i	68LC040	40MHz	Not available	Plug-in*	3 years	Static RAM cache
Mobius	Speedster 40	68040	40MHz	Included	Plug-in*	3 years	Static RAM cache

*Adapter replaces original CPU; original CPU is installed in adapter card, making both original CPU and accelerator CPU available.

Table 6.11 Accelerators for the Macintosh IIci

Manufacturer	Model	CPU	Clock Speed	FPU	How Installed	Warranty	Other Features
Applied Eng.	TransWarp CI	68030	50MHz	Optional	Cache slot	1 year	64K RAM cache
DayStar	Universal PowerCache	68030	33MHz	Optional	PDS	3 years	
DayStar	Universal PowerCache	68030	40MHz	Optional	PDS	3 years	
DayStar	Universal PowerCache	68030	50MHz	Optional	PDS	3 years	
DayStar	Turbo 040	68040	25MHz	Included	PDS	3 years	128K RAM cache
DayStar	Turbo 040	68040	33MHz	Included	PDS	3 years	128K RAM cache
DayStar	Turbo 040	68040	40MHz	Included	PDS	3 years	128K RAM cache, PDS pass-through
Fusion	TokaMac CI 25i	68LC040	25MHz	Not included	Cache slot	1 year	
Fusion	TokaMac CI 25	68040	25MHz	Included	Cache slot	1 year	
Fusion	TokaMac 33	68040	33MHz	Included	Cache slot	1 year	
Fusion	TokaMac 33c	68040	33MHz	Included	Cache slot	1 year	128K RAM cache
Mobius	Speedster 25i	68LC040	25MHz	Not available	Plug-in*	3 years	Static RAM cache
Mobius	Speedster 25	68040	25MHz	Included	Plug-in*	3 years	Static RAM cache
Mobius	Speedster 33i	68LC040	33MHz	Not available	Plug-in*	3 years	Static RAM cache
Mobius	Speedster 33	68040	33MHz	Included	Plug-in*	3 years	Static RAM cache
Mobius	Speedster 40i	68LC040	40MHz	Not available	Plug-in*	3 years	Static RAM cache
Mobius	Speedster 40	68040	40MHz	Included	Plug-in*	3 years	Static RAM cache
Radius	Rocket 25i	68LC040	25MHz	Not available	NuBus	1 year	PDS, RAM to 128Mb
Radius	Rocket	68040	25MHz	Included	NuBus	1 year	PDS, RAM to 128Mb
Radius	Rocket 33	68040	33Mhz	Included	NuBus	1 year	PDS, RAM to 128Mb

*Adapter replaces original CPU; original CPU is installed in adapter card, making both original CPU and accelerator CPU available.

Macintosh IIvi Accelerators

The Macintosh IIvi, the first machine designed for multimedia use, seems an ideal candidate for a CPU accelerator. (Multimedia production generally needs as much horsepower as it can get.) Nonetheless, accelerator options are somewhat limited. As you can see in Table 6.12, only one manufacturer (DayStar) makes IIvi-compatible CPU accelerators. These accelerators install in the computer's PDS and are therefore installable by the user.

Macintosh IIvx/Performa 600 Accelerators

The Macintosh IIvx/Performa 600 is the successor to the IIvi. The multimedia use for which it was designed usually requires a significant amount of processing power. If you are working with video or audio production or manipulating photographic-quality images, then a CPU accelerator can speed up the development process.

By the way: A CPU accelerator can't eliminate all the performance bottlenecks in multimedia work. The speed of a multimedia presentation relies as much on video speed and I/O speed as on CPU speed. For intensive multimedia use, consider also a video accelerator (see Chapter 11) and/or a SCSI accelerator (see Chapter 10).

Table 6.12 Accelerators for the Macintosh IIvi

Manufacturer	Model	CPU	Clock Speed	FPU	How Installed	Warranty	Other Features
DayStar	Universal PowerCache	68030	33MHz	Optional	PDS	3 years	
DayStar	Universal PowerCache	68030	40MHz	Optional	PDS	3 years	
DayStar	Universal PowerCache	68030	50MHz	Optional	PDS	3 years	
DayStar	Turbo 040	68040	25MHz	Included	PDS	3 years	128K RAM cache
DayStar	Turbo 040	68040	33MHz	Included	PDS	3 years	128K RAM cache
DayStar	Turbo 040	68040	40MHz	Included	PDS	3 years	128K RAM cache

As you can see in Table 6.13, a number of manufacturers produce both 68030 and 68040 accelerators for the machine. Some use the computer's PDS; others replace the original CPU with an adapter into which the accelerator is plugged. Accelerators that use the PDS are easier to install than those that require removing the original CPU and installing an adapter board for the CPU accelerator. Because the IIvx has NuBus slots, there is little disadvantage in using the PDS for an accelerator.

Macintosh IIfx Accelerators

Even though the Macintosh IIfx was the fastest Mac II, it is slower than the Quadra 800. If you are using a IIfx for high-end

Table 6.13 Accelerators for the Macintosh IIvx/Performa 600

Manufacturer	Model	CPU	Clock Speed	FPU	How Installed	Warranty	Other Features
DayStar	Universal PowerCache	68030	33MHz	Optional	PDS	3 years	
DayStar	Universal PowerCache	68030	40MHz	Optional	PDS	3 years	
DayStar	Universal PowerCache	68030	50MHz	Optional	PDS	3 years	
DayStar	Turbo 040	68040	25MHz	Included	PDS	3 years	128K RAM cache
DayStar	Turbo 040	68040	33MHz	Included	PDS	3 years	128K RAM cache
DayStar	Turbo 040	68040	40MHz	Included	PDS	3 years	128K RAM cache
Mobius	Speedster 25i	68LC040	25MHz	Not available	Plug-in*	3 years	Static RAM cache
Mobius	Speedster 25	68040	25MHz	Included	Plug-in*	3 years	Static RAM cache
Mobius	Speedster 33i	68LC040	33MHz	Not available	Plug-in*	3 years	Static RAM cache
Mobius	Speedster 33	68040	33MHz	Included	Plug-in*	3 years	Static RAM cache
Mobius	Speedster 40i	68LC040	40MHz	Not available	Plug-in*	3 years	Static RAM cache
Mobius	Speedster 40	68040	40MHz	Included	Plug-in*	3 years	Static RAM cache

*Adapter replaces original CPU; original CPU is installed in adapter card, making both original CPU and accelerator CPU available.

graphics work or heavy-duty number crunching, you may want to exchange its 68030 for a 68040. Because the IIfx has no PDS, an accelerator must plug into the motherboard. As you can see from Table 6.14, the Fusion TokaMac IIFX requires that the motherboard be sent to the manufacturer for installation. The DayStar Turbo 040 is installable by the user but does require pulling the original CPU and plugging in an adapter card that creates a PDS for the CPU accelerator.

PowerBook Accelerators

Few CPU accelerators are available for PowerBooks. Digital Eclipse does provide a 25MHz 68030 for the PowerBook 140, giving the computer the processing power of a 170, and a 33MHz 68030 for the 160, giving the computer the processing power of a 180 (see Table 6.15). Neither of these accelerators can be installed by the user; the PowerBook must be shipped to Digital Eclipse for installation.

Table 6.14 *Accelerators for the Macintosh IIfx*

Manufacturer	Model	CPU	Clock Speed	FPU	How Installed	Warranty	Other Features
DayStar	Turbo 040	68040	25MHz	Included	Replaces original CPU*	3 years	128K RAM cache
DayStar	Turbo 040	68040	33MHz	Included	Replaces original CPU*	3 years	128K RAM cache
Fusion	TokaMac IIFX	68040	33MHz	Included	PDS[†]	1 year	128K RAM cache

*Requires installation of an adapter card that replaces the computer's original CPU and creates a PDS slot.
[†]Motherboard must be shipped to manufacturer for installation.

Table 6.15 *Powerbook Accelerators*

Manufacturer	Model	CPU	Clock Speed	FPU	PowerBook Model	Warranty	Other Features
Digital Eclipse	F/25	68030	25MHz	Included	140	1 year	
Digital Eclipse	F/33	68030	33MHz	Included	160	1 year	

Caches, PMMUs, and Math Coprocessors (FPUs)

You can add three types of upgrades to a Macintosh to speed performance or extend main memory. Caches and math coprocessors can enhance computation speed in some circumstances; *paged memory management units* (PMMUs) are essential for virtual memory, a technique used to extend main memory without adding more physical RAM. This chapter looks at all three types of upgrades, including why you might want to add the upgrade and the specific Macintosh models for which such an upgrade is needed and/or available.

Caches

By definition, a cache is a small place in which something is stored. Computers use caches to hold instructions or data (see Figure 7.1). In many circumstances, caches can speed the operations of a computer. The Macintosh actually uses three types of caches. The first, a *disk cache*, is implemented by the operating system. It sets aside a section of RAM to use as a holding area for programs or data to speed transfers between the disk and main memory. Because this type of cache uses dynamic RAM and is controlled by the operating system, it isn't the type of cache you add as an upgrade. (In fact, you control the operation and size of the disk cache with System 7's Memory control panel.)

An *instruction cache*, made from high-speed static RAM, works directly with the CPU, holding a small number of program instructions. A *data cache* is also made from high-speed static RAM. It, too, works directly with the CPU, holding a small amount of data on which the CPU is likely to perform some arithmetic or logical operation. The 68020 has an internal instruction cache; the 68030 and 68040 have both internal instruction caches and internal data caches.

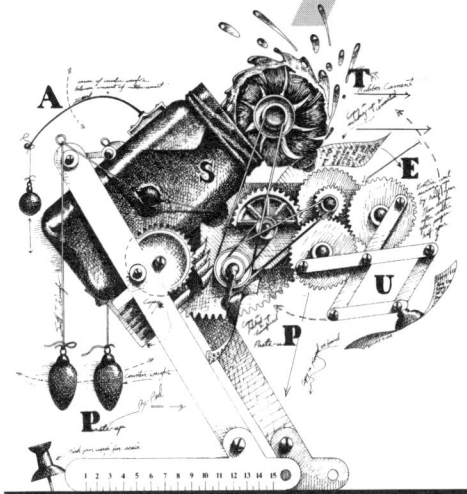

When a cache-equipped CPU executes a program, it first looks for the "next" program instruction in its instruction cache. If the instruction is in cache memory (a *cache hit*), then the CPU can pull the instruction directly from the cache, an operation that is much faster than reading the instruction from main memory. However, if the instruction isn't in the instruction cache (a *cache miss*), the CPU must fetch the instruction from RAM.

An instruction is fetched from RAM into the instruction cache. To make room for the incoming instruction, the CPU must overwrite one of the instructions that is already in the cache. The instruction that is overwritten (and thus deleted from the cache) is the instruction that is least likely to be used next. The CPU assumes that this is the least recently used instruction. (There has been a great deal of research into identifying which instruction in a cache is least likely to be used next; the strategy used by the Motorola CPUs is the most effective.)

Fetching an instruction from the instruction cache is approximately 33% faster than fetching an instruction from main memory. Even with the small, 256-byte instruction caches found in the 68020 and 68030, the hit ratio is usually between 40% and 70%. This means that it really doesn't take a lot of cache memory to produce noticeable speed improvements. In addition to speeding up the fetch operation, while the CPU is reading the cache it can simultaneously be fetching something from main memory. That main memory fetch might be loading the data cache, for example.

Figure 7.1 *A cache—holding data or instructions*

Data caches operate much like instruction caches. When a CPU needs a piece of data to use in a program instruction, it first checks to see if the piece of data is present in the data cache. If it is, the CPU can avoid reading the data from main memory, thus speeding up access to that data.

Write-Through Versus Write-Back Caches

There are two ways in which a cache-equipped CPU can handle operations that require writing to RAM. If the data being modified are in the data cache, then the CPU can make the modification to both the copy in the cache and the copy in main memory (a *write-through cache*). This is the strategy used in the 68030. The major drawback to a write-through cache is that performing the write to RAM negates some of the speed benefits of the data cache. On the other hand, the data in RAM are always correct.

The alternative to a write-through cache is a *write-back*, or *copy-back*, cache. When a write-back cache makes a modification to data stored in its data cache, it makes the modification to the cache only; the modification is not written to main memory. The modification is written to main memory only when the CPU needs to overwrite the modified data in the cache, with other data being brought into the cache from main memory. Because every write to a write-back cache doesn't involve a write to RAM, the write-back cache operates faster than a write-through cache. This strategy is used by the 68040. The drawback to this strategy is that data in RAM can be incorrect; only the modified data in the cache are guaranteed to be up to date.

When 68040 Macintoshes first appeared, there were software incompatibilities with the write-back cache. Although Apple supplied a control panel device that turned off 68040 caching completely, that solution negated much of the performance benefits of the 68040. At this point, most software vendors have updated their software to handle the 68040's caching requirements.

Cache Availability

You can speed up some Macintoshes by adding additional cache memory. Such caches, used as instruction caches, come on expansion boards that plug into a processor direct slot or a special-purpose cache slot. You may also be able to add cache memory to a CPU accelerator board.

All IIcis sold since 1991 and the IIvx have slots specifically intended for installation of a cache card. You can also install cache cards in the PDS of a IIsi or Quadra. In addition, some 68030 and 68040 accelerator boards have cache memory or slots for cache cards.

A sample of cache options for Macintosh computers can be found in Table 7.1. Keep in mind that although the sizes of these caches appear very small when compared to typically main memory

Table 7.1 Cache Cards for Macintosh Computers

Manufacturer	Macintosh Model(s)	Product	Size
Apple Computer	IIci	IIci Cache Card	32K
Applied Eng.	IIci IIsi	QuickSilver CacheIn	32K
DayStar	IIci IIsi Quadras	FastCache	32K to 128K
DayStar	SE SE/30 Classic LC, LC II, LC III II IIx IIcx IIci IIsi IIvx	Universal PowerCache	32K, 64K*
Logica Research	IIci IIsi	LogiCache	64K

*The Universal PowerCache is a CPU accelerator that includes cache memory.

sizes, it doesn't take much cache memory to provide a noticeable speed improvement.

Should you add an external instruction cache? If you need the fastest processing possible, coupling an instruction cache with a fast CPU can help. Instruction caches are moderately priced ($200 to $500). They therefore make good sense for a Quadra, which already has a 68040 CPU. A cache card can also speed up a IIci or IIsi for less than the cost of a CPU accelerator. However, keep in mind that you need both a fast CPU *and* a cache card to obtain the maximum processing speed.

PAGED MEMORY MANAGEMENT UNITS

A PMMU provides support for *virtual memory*. Virtual memory is a technique that uses disk storage as simulated RAM. (In the computer world, the word *virtual* means "simulated.") Only the 68020, 68030, and 68040 support virtual memory. In addition, you must be using System 7 or Connectix's Virtual (an INIT that provides virtual memory under later versions of System 6).

When working in a virtual memory system, the computer has two address spaces. The *real address space* represents memory that is physically present in the computer. The *virtual address space* represents the memory being simulated. To run, a program must be in real memory. Therefore, the role of the PMMU is to translate between real addresses and virtual addresses and to control the movement of programs and data between disk and main memory.

In a virtual memory scheme, real memory (physically installed RAM) is divided into fixed-size blocks known as *page frames*. The disk file that simulates the virtual memory address space is also divided into blocks of the same size (*pages*). With the Macintosh, pages and page frames are 4K. The operating system swaps pages from real memory page frames to disk and back again as pages are needed in real memory for program execution. The PMMU takes care of locating pages both in real memory and in the virtual memory disk file.

By the way: To be completely accurate, a virtual memory scheme doesn't have to allocate memory in fixed size blocks. When the blocks vary in size, they are known as *segments*. Segmented virtual memory is more difficult to manage than paged virtual memory and isn't used widely on microcomputers.

Chapter 7: Caches, PMMUs, and Math Coprocessors (FPUs)

In the sample in Figure 7.2, real memory has four page frames. However, the virtual address space has room for 16 pages. Therefore, only four pages can be in main memory at one time. (Of course, the actual number of page frames in any given Macintosh depends on the amount of physical RAM installed.) Notice that a virtual page can be loaded into any available page frame. That means that the parts of a program might be scattered all over main memory. The operating system, working with the PMMU, however, handles the program as if it were in one contiguous block of main memory.

> **By the way:** Virtual memory adds considerable complexity to an operating system, especially one that supports *multitasking* (more than one program in the execution phase at a time). The operating system must not only keep track of what is in which page frame and work with the hardware to perform address translation, but also know the program to which each page frame belongs. In addition, it must protect real memory used by one program from real memory used by another.

The amount of RAM you can simulate with virtual memory is limited by the

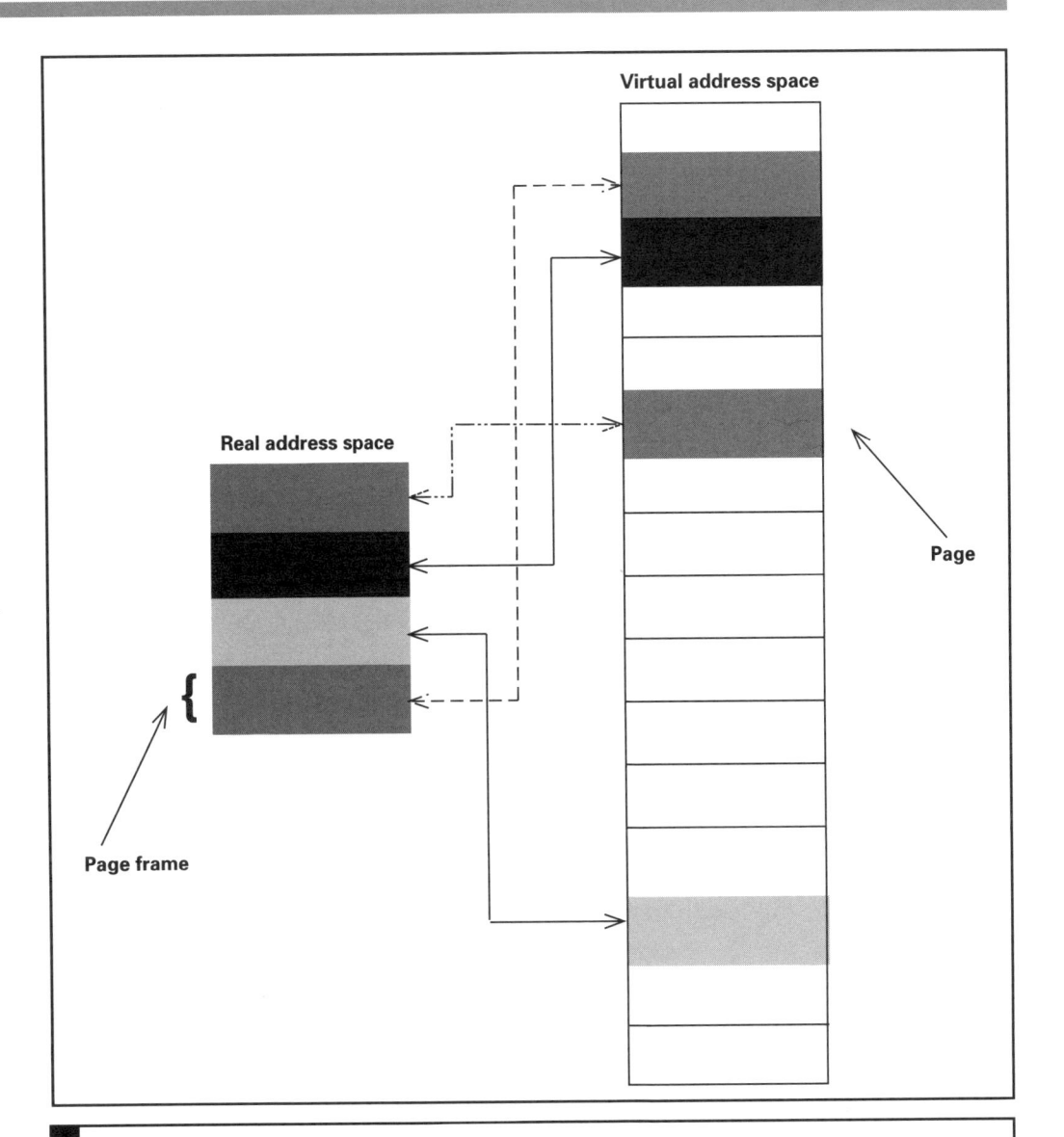

Figure 7.2 Mapping real memory to virtual memory

Figure 7.3 A Motorola 68851 PMMU

maximum amount of RAM your Mac can access and by how much free disk space you have. To implement virtual memory, the Macintosh needs a file as big as the entire virtual address space. When a page is swapped from real memory to disk, it is written to the virtual memory file in the location that corresponds to the page's virtual address. In essence, the virtual memory file is a picture of the contents of the entire virtual address space.

PMMU circuitry is built into the 68030 and 68040. However, if you want to use virtual memory with a 68020 Mac, you must add a PMMU as a separate coprocessor like that in Figure 7.3. Note that although the LC uses a 68020, it cannot accept a PMMU. Therefore, the only machine that actually needs a PMMU is a Mac II.

Some CPU accelerators for the Mac II can take advantage of the PMMU circuitry in the 68030 or 68040 and therefore do not require a PMMU on the Mac II motherboard to support virtual memory. When you consider a Mac II accelerator, be sure to check with the manufacturer to find out whether you need a PMMU chip in addition to the new CPU on the accelerator board.

Although Motorola is no longer making the PMMU for the 68020, Mac II PMMUs are available for under $100 from most vendors that sell SIMMs. (They are selling existing stock or PMMUs made by companies other than Motorola.) Installation requires removing the existing memory management unit (a socketed chip) from the motherboard and inserting the PMMU. This upgrade is installable by the user who has a steady hand and isn't afraid to pull and insert chips. If you aren't comfortable with making chip modifications to your motherboard, then let a service technician do it; bent pins make the PMMU useless and may damage the PMMU socket.

Math Coprocessors

A math coprocessor, or *floating-point unit* (FPU), is a processor designed to handle operations on floating-point numbers. Floating-point numbers are decimal fractions that are multiplied by some base number raised to a power (the *exponent*). For example, the floating-point number 2.456×10^{18} has a base of 10 and an exponent of 18. The number is therefore actually 2.456 (the *mantissa*, or *significand*) multiplied by 10 raised to the 18th power (1 followed by 18 zeros). Typically, such numbers are formatted so that there is only one digit to the left of the decimal point; the rest of the number is a decimal fraction. Because floating-point numbers are so complex, it takes a special internal format to store them. In turn, that special format requires special software to manipulate the numbers.

> **By the way:** When the base to which the exponent is raised is 10, a floating-point number is often said to be in *scientific notation*, since this type of number formatting is commonly used to express very large or very small scientific quantities.

Storing Floating-Point Numbers

Computers can't manipulate base 10 numbers directly. Instead, everything is converted to binary. Therefore, floating-point numbers used by a computer use an exponent base that is a power of 2. For example, the floating-point storage format used by the Macintosh uses 2 for its base, although it could just as easily have used 4, 8, or even 16. The base is the same for every floating-point number in any given computer. For that reason, the computer doesn't need to store the base. It therefore stores only the sign of the mantissa, the mantissa itself, and the exponent.

To contain all that information, each Macintosh floating-point number requires 80 bits, or 10 bytes, of storage. Bit 79 (the most significant bit of an 80-bit space) is used for the sign of the mantissa.

It holds a 0 if the mantissa a positive, a 1 if it is negative. The exponent is 15 bits long, stored in bits 64 through 78. Bits 0 through 63 are reserved for the mantissa.

Floating-point exponents are stored as binary integers. They are the power to which 2 (the base) is raised and then multiplied by the mantissa. However, exponents can be both positive and negative. (A negative exponent, $-n$, represents a fraction between 0 and 1, such as 0.5 or 0.025. To find the value of a base raised to a negative exponent, take the reciprocal of the base raised to the exponent. For example, 2^{-1} is $1 \div 2^1$, or 0.5; 2^{-3} is $1 \div 2^3$, or 0.125.) A floating-point format must therefore also account for the sign of the exponent.

One way to handle the problem would be to use the most significant bit of the 15-bit exponent to hold the sign of the exponent. The resulting 14-bit exponent would have the range ±16,383. The drawback to this solution is that the computer must then perform arithmetic on the exponent as a signed quantity. Arithmetic would be faster if the computer could work with the exponent if it were a positive integer, without having to worry about handling the bit that has been set aside as the sign.

The solution to this problem is a technique known as *excess notation*. Excess notation means that some fixed quantity is added to every value of the exponent. The exact value of the excess varies from one computer to another but is always enough to make the smallest exponent value 0. The Macintosh uses an excess of 16,384 (2^{14}, the place value of the most significant bit in the 15-bit exponent). In binary, the excess is 100 0000 0000 0000.

The smallest exponent that can be represented in 15 bits is –16,384. That quantity is actually stored as 0 (–16,384 plus the excess of 16,384). The highest exponent values is +16,383. To store this maximum value, the 15 bits of the exponent are all filled with 1, producing 32,767 ($2^{15}-1$), the maximum value that can be stored in 15 bits. The actual value of the exponent, however, is the stored value minus the excess: 32,767–16,384, or 16,383.

Given an exponent range of –16,384 through +16,383, the Macintosh can store floating-point numbers in the range $2^{-16,384}$ through $2^{+16,383}$. This is an enormous range, well beyond that demanded by all but the most intensive scientific and statistical applications.

The mantissa of a floating-point number is also a binary value. The most significant bit (bit 63) always has the value 1. There is an implied binary point directly between bits 62 and 63; bits 0 through 62 contain the fractional portion of the mantissa.

As an example, consider the decimal number 32. In binary, 32 is represented as 100000. This value is also equal to 100000.0×2^0. (Remember that any base raised to the 0 power is always 1.) At this point, the mantissa (100000.0) isn't in the right format to be stored. The binary point must be moved so that it is to the right of the most significant 1. Each time the binary point is moved one place to the left, the exponent increases by 1. In other words, 100000.0×2^0 is the same number as 1.000000×2^5.

Now that the mantissa has been placed in the proper format, the exponent can be handled. The 5 is translated to binary (101) and added to the excess (100 0000 0000 0000), producing a final exponent of 100 0000 0000 0101. The final floating-point format looks like Figure 7.4.

The left-most bit is the sign of the mantissa; the following 15 bits are the expo-

> **Figure 7.4** *Final floating point format*

0100 0000 0000 0101 1000 0000 0000 0000 0000 0000 0000 0000 0000 0000 0000 0000 0000 0000 0000 0000

nent, including the excess. The remaining 64 bits are the mantissa.

Deciding When an FPU Is Necessary

A CPU is designed to have circuitry for manipulating integers (whole numbers without decimal fractions). However, it doesn't have circuits for handling floating-point numbers. Instead, floating-point operations are handled by software. Such software handles the parts of the floating-point number—the exponent and the mantissa—separately. In that way, it can manipulate each as an integer, using the CPU's integer arithmetic circuits.

Because floating-point operations are implemented in software, they are processor-intensive tasks. If the CPU must handle floating-point manipulations as well as all other computer operations, programs that perform a high volume of calculations run rather slowly. An FPU, however, can relieve the CPU of some of its burden by assuming the task of handling floating-point numbers.

Any Macintosh that is regularly used for number crunching (see Figure 7.5) is a good candidate for an FPU. The performance of large spreadsheets, statistics programs, and data analysis programs will all benefit from an FPU.

An FPU isn't an expensive upgrade (they're generally less than $200). Should you add one? If you need the added number-processing power, then do so. Otherwise, it probably doesn't pay to spend the money. Unfortunately, not every Macintosh that needs an FPU can accept one.

FPU Availability

No matter how much you might need one, you can't add an FPU to a 68000 or 68LC040 Mac. On the other hand, the 68040 has an FPU built in. FPU availability for the Macintosh product line is summarized in Table 7.2.

Types of FPUs

An FPU is tailored specifically to the type of CPU with which it will be working. The 68020 uses a 68881 FPU; the 68030 uses a 68882 FPU. When purchasing an FPU for either a 68020 or 68030 Macintosh, be sure to specify exactly what type of computer you have so that you receive the correct FPU.

Figure 7.5 *Number crunching (?)*

Table 7.2 *Macintosh FPU Availability*

Model	FPU Availability	Comments
Plus	Not available	
SE	Not available	
SE/30	Included	
Classic	Not available	
Classic II/Performa 200	Not available	
Color Classic	Optional	FPU board installs in PDS
LC	Optional	FPU board installs in PDS
LC II/Performa 400, 405, 430	Optional	FPU board installs in PDS
LC III/Performa 450	Optional	Installs in socket; does not take up PDS
II	Included	
IIx	Included	
IIcx	Included	
IIci	Included	
IIsi	Included	
IIvi	Included	
IIvx	Included	
Performa 600	Optional	
IIfx	Included	
Centris 610	Not available	
Centris 650	Not available	Low-end configuration (4Mb RAM, 80Mb hard disk)
Centris 650	Included	All other configurations
Quadra 700	Included	
Quadra 800	Included	
Quadra 900	Included	
Quadra 950	Included	
Portable	Not available	
PowerBook 100	Not available	
PowerBook 140	Optional	
PowerBook 145	Optional	
PowerBook 160	Optional	
PowerBook 165c	Optional	
PowerBook 170	Included	
PowerBook 180	Included	

Logic Boards

A logic board upgrade is an alternative to adding several individual upgrades to a Macintosh. If giving your Mac a CPU accelerator is like a brain transplant, then swapping the motherboard is a multiorgan transplant (Figure 8.1)!

Whether replacing the logic board makes sense is largely a matter of cost: Is the cost of the new logic board less than the cost of individual upgrades? Do the benefits of adding the logic board upgrade justify the cost? This chapter looks at the available logic board upgrades and helps you decide whether their cost is justified. It also discusses troubleshooting logic board problems and identifies situations where the only repair alternative is a motherboard replacement.

What You Get with a New Logic Board

A new logic board includes the following:

- **New CPU:** A logic board upgrade includes a faster CPU. The new logic board therefore can take the place of a CPU accelerator.

- **New ROMs:** A logic board may include newer ROMs than those on the original motherboard. With the exception of the ROM/1.4Mb floppy drive upgrade available for the Macintosh II, this is the only way to get upgraded ROMs.

  By the way: Some used Macintosh dealers may have ROMs for sale that are not part of a motherboard. However, it is rare to find such ROMs available, and when you can find them, they are usually not state-of-the art.

- **New bus:** A logic board upgrade also means a new bus. That means your computer may gain additional expansion slots and/or wider data and address buses. In addition, the new logic board may have more SIMM slots, providing room to install more RAM.

Additional benefits can include a socketed rather than a soldered battery (early Mac IIs have soldered batteries) and a

Figure 8.1 *The logic board upgrade—giving your Mac a multiorgan transplant*

socketed rather than a soldered CPU (some Mac IIcis have soldered CPUs).

AVAILABLE LOGIC BOARD UPGRADES

There are two sources for Macintosh logic boards: Apple Computer and used Macintosh dealers. Used Macintosh dealers can supply logic board replacements if your current logic board is defective; in some cases they may also have motherboards from older Macs that are actually an upgrade to your current Mac. For example, a 128K, 512K, or 512Ke Mac can be upgraded with a Mac Plus motherboard. Such motherboards are usually not new, but reconditioned.

By the way: When you look into the purchase of parts for discontinued Macintoshes, always ask if the part is new or reconditioned. A reconditioned part can be as reliable as a new part. However, to protect yourself, always inquire about a warranty whenever investigating the purchase of reconditioned hardware.

Logic upgrades to current Mac models, however, are available only from Apple. That means that they are sold only through Apple dealers. As a result, don't expect significant discounts from the suggested retail price.

The following logic board upgrades are available:

- **Classic II:** This upgrade transforms a Classic into a Classic II, including 2Mb RAM, a microphone, and a new case. The cost of the upgrade (just over $600) is less than the cost of purchasing a new computer and less than the cost of some CPU accelerators, but the Classic II is essentially a dead-end machine. Once you transform your Classic into a Classic II, it will be difficult to upgrade it further. For example, there aren't any CPU accelerators for the Classic II because of its unusual design. In addition, the Classic II motherboard's CPU runs only at 16MHz. For the same $600, you can purchase a 33MHz CPU accelerator, some of which can access RAM up to 16Mb. In most cases, you will be better off adding a CPU accelerator that has room for SIMMs than exchanging the Classic motherboard for a Classic II motherboard.

- **LC II:** This upgrade transforms an LC into an LC II. It includes 2Mb RAM and a new top for the computer. At a retail cost of just over $700, this logic board upgrade doesn't make much sense. The upgrade to an LC III costs less!

- **LC III:** This upgrade transforms an LC or LC II into an LC III. It includes 4Mb RAM, 512K VRAM, and a new case. Given its cost of only $600, this particular logic board upgrade is a good value. The only drawback is that you won't be able to use any of your existing SIMMs. However, adding a 4Mb SIMM to bring the machine to a respectable 8Mb should cost no more than another $150, bringing your entire upgrade cost to less than $750.

- **IIfx:** This upgrade transforms a II or IIx into a IIfx. No RAM is included. Although the IIfx is a very fast computer, there are some significant drawbacks to this upgrade. First, it is very expensive (around $2,300). Second, you won't be able to use any of your existing SIMMs; the IIfx requires special parity RAM. Third, you won't be able to use any existing SCSI terminators; the IIfx uses a type of termination not found in any other Macintosh. In most cases, it makes more sense to add a CPU accelerator to a II or IIx rather than to exchange its motherboard for a IIfx motherboard.

- **Centris 650:** This upgrade turns a IIvx into a Centris 650. It includes 8Mb RAM, 512K VRAM, Ethernet adapter, and FPU. Costing about $1600, its cost is approximately equal to adding a 68040 CPU accelerator and Ethernet board.

- **Quadra 700:** This upgrade turns a IIcx or IIci into a Quadra 700. The $3,100 price includes 4Mb RAM, a microphone, and a new case. The three NuBus slots in the IIcx or IIci are replaced by two NuBus slots and a PDS, providing a bit more expansion flexibility. In essence, however, the only thing you really gain with this upgrade is the 25MHz 68040. The same microprocessor can be purchased as a CPU upgrade for about half the cost. In addition, because its SIMM slots are underneath the disk drive platform, it can be difficult to find the low-profile 16Mb SIMMs that fit in the Quadra 700, whereas the IIcx and IIci can use standard 16Mb SIMMs.

- **Quadra 950:** This upgrade turns a Quadra 900 into a Quadra 950. It doesn't include any RAM, but can use the RAM previously in the Quadra 900. Costing around $2,600, the new logic board contains a 33MHz 68040 rather than the 25MHz 68040 found in the 900. A CPU accelerator would be less expensive, but at this point, none are available for the Quadra line. Therefore if you want the maximum performance form your 900, then the logic board upgrade is your only alternative.

- **Centris 660av:** This upgrade turns a Centris 610 into a Centris 660av. Although expensive, the 660av logic board does provide the video and speech capabilities of the newer machine.

- **Quadra 840av:** This upgrade turns a Quadra 800 into a Quadra 840av. If you need the 840av's multimedia capabilities, then the upgrade may be worth the cost.

Logic Board Upgrade Installation Issues

A replacement logic board can be installed by an end-user. However, before you attempt such an upgrade, keep in mind that first you will need to

- remove all SIMMs,
- unplug and remove all internal disk drives,
- remove all expansion boards,
- unplug and remove the power supply.

Once everything is unplugged, you will be able to remove the original motherboard and replace it with the new one. Then you will have to replace all the components you removed. This is definitely not a procedure that should be attempted by a novice. Unless you are relatively skilled, you should let a service technician perform a logic board swap.

By the way: If you are replacing your motherboard because your existing motherboard is damaged, you may be able to purchase the replacement without ROMSs and save some money. In that case, installation requires moving your ROMs from the old motherboard to the new.

There is one other important issue associated with logic board upgrades. Apple is very concerned about what happens to its ROM chips, especially current ones. When you purchase a logic board upgrade to bring an older Mac up to a current model (as opposed to replacing an older motherboard with a used motherboard), the original logic board must be returned to Apple. Therefore upgrades to current logic boards are available only from authorized Apple dealers and must be installed by authorized service technicians.

Troubleshooting Logic Board Problems

A number of problems can arise with the circuits on a Macintosh motherboard. As you will remember from Chapter 5, many can be identified with diagnostic software. These include ROM problems, some RAM failures, and major chip failures. In addition, the Macintosh's internal ROM diagnostic programs identify many logic board problems and, when necessary, display the appropriate sad Mac code.

Unfortunately, there are some logic board problems that diagnostic software can't identify. In particular, such problems include broken or weak solder, slot failures, and other bus problems.

Cold Solder Problems

Although the CPU and FPU are generally plugged into sockets in the motherboard, most of the other chips are soldered onto the motherboard to provide a stable connection between the chip carrier's pins and the motherboard's printed circuits. Over time, especially if the computer is moved frequently, solder can break off or become weak. The result is a chip that doesn't make a good connection with the motherboard.

Such problems usually occur when the solder is cold (in other words, when the Mac is first booted). As the machine heats up, the solder melts a bit and makes a complete connection. The usual indication that you have a cold solder problem is system crashes or other irregular behavior during the first 15 minutes of system operation. Once the computer warms up, it operates properly.

If you suspect a cold solder problem, keep in mind that the motherboard isn't the only place where chips are soldered onto circuit boards. Any expansion boards that may be installed in your Macintosh also have soldered chips. Therefore before blaming the problem on the motherboard, you need to eliminate expansion boards as the source of the problem. There are two techniques for isolating the problem source:

- If your Mac can operate without the expansion board, remove the expansion board. Boot the machine and wait to see if the problem occurs. If the problem doesn't, then the expansion board is the culprit. Otherwise, the problem is probably on the motherboard.

- If your Mac can't operate without the expansion board (for example, a video board in a Mac that has no built-in video support), then remove the expansion board and install it in another Mac. If the second Mac exhibits the problem that occurred on your computer, then the problem is with the expansion board. If the second Mac doesn't have any problems with the board, then it's probably your motherboard that's at fault.

Cold solder problems can be fixed. The repair involves removing the bad solder and applying new. However, before the problem can be repaired, the location of the bad solder must be found. In most cases, finding the problem location requires someone who can do board-level repairs. That means you must remove the logic board from the Macintosh and send it to the repair person. While the board is out for repair, your Macintosh is, of course, useless. There is also no guarantee that the problem actually can be found and fixed. In addition, a repair may be very costly, depending on how much time it takes the repair person to locate the site of the bad solder. If you are paying for labor by the hour, then such low-level troubleshooting can become very costly. (At last check, the going rate for service technician time was around $65 an hour.)

The only alternative is to replace the logic board. This may be more expensive than getting the logic board repaired, but it is certainly quick and the cost for parts and labor can be identified before any work begins. You can purchase the replacement motherboard from a dealer in used Macintosh parts (the most cost-effective source) and either install it yourself or take it to an authorized service center for installation. You can also purchase the replacement logic board from an Apple dealer.

By the way: It's very true that dealers in used Macintosh parts don't have replacement logic boards for newer models. However, now that Apple provides a one-year warranty on its computers, if a logic board should fail in a newer Mac, you can always take it to an authorized service center for a free warranty repair.

Bus and Slot Problems

Most diagnostic software cannot detect electrical problems with the Macintosh's bus. You should suspect a bus and/or slot problem when expansion boards aren't behaving properly. To isolate the problem, try the following:

- If your Macintosh has a board in its PDS, remove the board and install it in a second Mac. If the second Mac exhibits the irregular behavior that occurred in your computer, then the problem is with the board, not the bus or slot. However, if the board functions properly, then either the PDS or the system bus is the problem.

- If your Mac has only one NuBus slot, remove the NuBus board and install it in a second Mac. If the board doesn't work properly in the second Mac, then the board is the problem. Otherwise, the NuBus slot or the bus are probably at fault.

- If your Mac has more than one NuBus slot, remove all expansion boards except one. Test the performance of the board. Repeat the process, reinstalling each board in turn in its original slot. If more than one of the boards exhibits problems, then it is likely that the cause is the system bus. However, to be sure, test any boards that don't operate properly in more than one slot. If they continue to exhibit problems, then you can be relatively certain that the bus is bad in some way.

On the other hand, if only one expansion board produces problems, either the slot or the board is at fault. To isolate which it is, move the board to another slot. If the board behaves properly in another slot, then the original slot is the most likely source of the problems.

There is only one viable solution to a bus or slot problem: Replace the motherboard. Although it may be possible to find someone who can repair a bad slot, it may not be cost effective to do so. On the other hand, bus problems can't be fixed.

Problems with On-Board Video

Diagnostic software often cannot detect problems with built-in video support. Because the circuitry is part of the motherboard, it can't be repaired by simply replacing an expansion board. Diagnosing such problems is also a bit trickier than identifying problems where expansion boards are involved.

If you have a Macintosh with built-in video and your monitor doesn't display its normal image, the source of the problem could either be the monitor itself, the cable connecting the monitor to the computer, or the on-board video circuitry. To isolate which component is at fault,

- Try another monitor on your computer or try your monitor on another Mac. If the second monitor works properly or your monitor exhibits the same problems on another Mac, then your monitor is the problem. Apple monitors are usually repaired by authorized Apple service centers. If you have a monitor made by a company other than Apple, contact the manufacturer for repair instructions.

- If your monitor isn't the problem, replace the cable that connects the monitor to the computer. If this doesn't solve the problem, then you're probably facing a problem with the video circuitry on the motherboard.

Video circuitry can be repaired by someone who does board-level repairs by actually replacing the video chips. However, in most cases it will be more expedient (although not necessarily cheaper) to replace the motherboard.

Power Supplies and Power Protection

Power is the life blood of a computer; without it, the computer is nothing more than an expensive doorstop. A Macintosh owner needs to think about power in three different circumstances: when adding upgrades to a Mac that will draw power from the computer's power supply, when adding input devices that draw power from the ADB controller, and when plugging in the computer to draw power from the local power company.

This chapter looks at a variety of issues surrounding power supplies, including the size of the power supply in each Macintosh and how to identify power supply problems. One section of the chapter is devoted to power supply problems in older Macs (Plus and earlier), since those models not only exhibit different symptoms when their power supplies are failing but are notorious for power supply problems. The second section of the chapter looks at ADB chains and how the power drawn by ADB devices affects the number of devices you can have in a given chain. Finally, this chapter looks at ways to protect your computer from damage that travels down electric lines.

Internal Power Supplies

Every desktop computer has an internal power supply. All the components on the motherboard as well as internal disk drives and expansion boards draw power from that power supply. A monitor plugged into the system unit, however, does not. Nonetheless, as you add internal disk drives and expansion boards, the drain on the internal power supply increases. Some Macintoshes have enough power to operate fully loaded (all slots full) without a problem (see Figure 9.1). Others, however, are underpowered and may show performance irregularities when equipped with a full complement of internal devices.

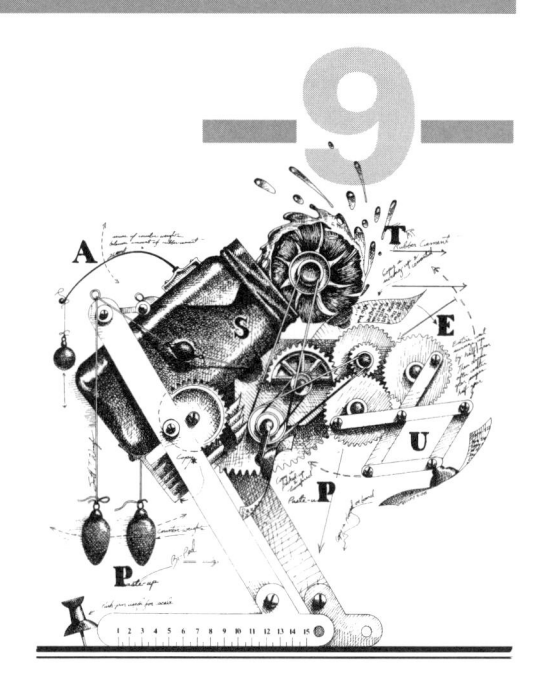

Figure 9.1 Full-powered Macs—able to heft any components

Standard Macintosh Power Supplies

The output of a Macintosh's internal power supply is measured in watts. The wattage of the power supplies found in unmodified Macintoshes can be found in Table 9.1. Notice that some power supplies are "switching" power supplies. These types of power supplies automatically sense whether the incoming current is 110V or 220V and handle the current accordingly. They can also handle either 50Hz or 60Hz current. (Just as MHz means "megahertz," Hz means "hertz," or cycles per second.) That means that Macintoshes equipped with switching power supplies can be used in countries with 220V/50Hz current with only a change of the plug; a step-down transformer isn't required.

The power supply in a desktop Macintosh takes the AC coming from the wall and converts it into the DC voltages required by the computer's components. The Portable and PowerBooks, however, have a different type of power arrangement. When a Portable or PowerBook is running off its battery, the computer draws DC directly from the battery. However, if the Portable or PowerBook is plugged into the wall, the computer either takes DC from the battery or from the battery charger, which performs the AC to DC conversion. Notice in Table 9.1 that the Portable and PowerBooks can be charged from either 110V/60 Hz current or 220V/50Hz current.

Power Requirements of Internal Devices

As you begin to install CPU accelerators, large internal hard disks, and other expansion boards in your Macintosh, you need to pay attention to how much power your components are drawing. In Table 9.2 you will find some sample power requirements for a variety of Macintosh components. Keep in mind, however, that power requirements vary considerably from one model and manufacturer to another.

Troubleshooting Power Supply Problems

Power supply problems can be very hard to troubleshoot. This is because power supply problems are often intermittent, showing up irregularly under many different circumstances. Nonetheless, there are some signs that can indicate that the power supply is the source of hardware misbehavior:

- The computer crashes when trying to access the internal hard disk.

- The internal hard disk powers down and then backs up.

Chapter 9: Power Supplies and Power Protection

Table 9.1 Wattage of Power Supplies in Unmodified Macintoshes

Model	Watts	Switching?
Plus	60	No
SE	100	Yes
Classic	100	No
Classic II	100	No
Color Classic	100	Yes
LC	50	Yes
LC III	30	Yes
II	230	Yes
IIx	230	Yes
IIcx	90	Yes
IIci	90	Yes
SE/30	75	Yes
IIsi	100	No
IIvi	112	Yes
IIvx	112	Yes
IIfx	230	Yes
Centris 610	86	Yes
Centris 650	112	Yes
Quadra 700	50	Yes
Quadra 800	200	Yes
Quadra 900	303	Yes
Quadra 950	303	Yes
Portable	N/a	Yes
PowerBook 100	N/a	Yes
PowerBook 140	N/a	Yes
PowerBook 145	N/a	Yes
PowerBook 160	N/a	Yes
PowerBook 165c	N/a	Yes
PowerBook 170	N/a	Yes
PowerBook 180	N/a	Yes
PowerBook Duo 210	N/a	Yes
PowerBook Duo 230	N/a	Yes

Table 9.2 Power Requirements of Macintosh Components

Component	Watts
Internal hard disks for desktop Macs	
50Mb	6.0
100Mb	6.0
200Mb	4.5
240Mb	6.0
425Mb	12.0
480Mb	12.0
600Mb	32.0
1,050Mb	42.0
1,200Mb	54.0
2,000Mb	28.0
2,800Mb	66.0*
4,000Mb	60.0*
Internal hard disks for PowerBooks	
80Mb	1.7
120Mb	1.5
200Mb	4.5
CPU accelerators	
NewLife 33	17.0
NewLife 25	8.0
NewLife 33c	5.0
Fusion TokaMac (in IIfx)	10.0
(in IIci)	5.0
(in SE/30)	7.0
(in LC)	4.0
Extreme Vandal (with video in SE)	6.9
Extreme Impact 030 (in LC, LC II)	3.9
DayStar Universal PowerCache	8.0
Video boards	
SuperMac	
Spectrum/8 (in LC)	4.0

Continues...

Table 9.2 ...Continued

	Watts
(in si)	7.5
(all others)	9.45
Spectrum/24	10.0
Lapis	
ProColorServer 8 16 (in LC)	5.0
(in II)	7.0
ProColorServer 24 (in LC)	7.0
(in II)	10.0
Cache cards	
DayStar FastCache (32K)	5.5
(64K)	3.9
DayStar FastCache Quadra	5.0
SCSI accelerators	
DayStar Disk Runner	9.5

*These drives are usually only available as internal devices for the Quadra 900 and 950 because of their heavy power requirements.

- The computer can't boot because the hard disk won't spin fast enough.

- Expansion boards aren't functioning properly.

Some software diagnostic programs, including MacEKG, can detect power supply problems. MacEKG's ReActivator function, when used in conjunction with a smart power strip called PowerKey, automatically starts a Macintosh, runs the MacEKG tests, and then reboots the computer. Automated repetitive testing is an ideal way to isolate the cause of intermittent problems.

Macintosh Plus Power Supply Problems

The Macintosh Plus—like its predecessors the 128K, 512K, and 512Ke—is notorious for having power supply problems. In fact, if you plan to upgrade and keep your Plus, then you should seriously consider replacing the power supply at the time you install any upgrades.

As strange as it might seem, the first symptom that your Plus's power supply has a problem is difficulty with the monitor. In fact, if your monitor looks like any of those in Figure 9.2, then you should suspect a power supply problem. The reason that a bad power supply causes video problems is that the power supply and video circuitry are not on the motherboard, but on a second circuit board (the *analog board*). When the voltage coming from the power supply is abnormal, a circuit in the Plus shorts out the power supply and stops the *flyback transformer*. The flyback transformer is involved in stepping up the voltage coming from the power supply so that the voltage is high enough to generate an image on the CRT.

By the way: Other compact Macintoshes also have their video circuitry on the analog board. However, their power supplies have not been the sources of problems like those in 128K, 512K, 512Ke, and Plus.

| Herringbone pattern | Image skewed with white streaks | No image |

Figure 9.2 Macintosh Plus screen images that indicate a power supply problem

ADB CHAINS AND POWER REQUIREMENTS

Power drawn through an ADB port is measured in milliamps. The maximum

power that can be handled by the ADB chip in each Macintosh model can be found in Table 9.3. Keep in mind that even if your Macintosh has two ADB ports, both are managed by a single ADB chip. Therefore the total milliamps drawn by ADB devices is the sum of the devices in all ADB chains. Although most of the time you will be able to use three ADB devices, in some cases you may be limited to one or two. For example, the PowerBook 145's ADB chip can handle only 10 milliamps, just enough for a very-low-power mouse.

By the way: The theoretical limit to an ADB chain is 16 devices. However, when more than three are installed, the power drain is often such that none of the devices function properly.

Notice in Table 9.3 that three Macintoshes don't have ADB ports. The Plus was released before the Apple Desktop Bus became a part of the Macintosh design. The PowerBook Duos, which also have no ADB ports, nonetheless can gain access to an ADB port when they are docked in either the Duo Dock or the Duo MiniDock.

The power requirements of some typical ADB devices can be found in Table 9.4.

Table 9.3 Maximum ADB Power Draw

Model	Milliamps
Plus	N/a
SE	500
Classic	500
Classic II	500
Color Classic	500
LC	200
LC II	200
LC III	200
II	500
IIx	500
IIcx	500
IIci	500
SE/30	500
IIsi	500
IIvi	500
IIvx	500
Centris 610	500
Centris 650	500
Centris 660av	500
Quadra 700	200
Quadra 800	500
Quadra 840av	500
Quadra 900	500
Quadra 950	500
Portable	100
PowerBook 100	50
PowerBook 140	50
PowerBook 145	10
PowerBook 160	200
PowerBook 165c	200
PowerBook 170	50
PowerBook 180, 180c	200
PowerBook Duo 210	Unavailable
PowerBook Duo 230	Unavailable

Table 9.4 Power Requirements of Some ADB Devices

Type of Device	Milliamps
Mouse	10–80
Trackball	10–150
Standard keyboard	25
Extended keyboard	80
Graphics tablet	200

Notice that there is a wide range of power requirements for a given type of component. For example, a mouse can draw between 10 and 80 milliamps. That means that if you are looking for a mouse for the PowerBook 145, which can only handle 10 milliamps in an ADB chain, you must use an extremely low-power mouse. You also won't be able to use any other ADB devices on that chain.

Some devices, such as graphics tablets, draw a lot of ADB power. For all practical purposes, you will need a desktop Mac other than an LC to handle one (in other words, a Mac that can handle 500 milliamps of ADB power). The moral to the story is that when you purchase an ADB device, pay attention to how much power it draws and how much ADB power your Mac supports.

Electric Power Problems

If you want your Macintosh to last as long as possible, you need to feed it the cleanest, most stable electrical power you can. Computers are susceptible to changes in electrical voltages, particularly if the changes come as sudden spikes, known as *surges*. A power surge is a sudden increase in voltage, which generally raises the voltage above the level that the computer's components can tolerate. If allowed to make its way to a computer, a power surge can literally fry the components throughout the machine.

By the way: Most computer insurance policies cover damage from power surges. However, if your Macintosh is in your home, don't simply assume that it is covered under your homeowner's policy. Many homeowner's policies place a limit on the amount of computer equipment, if any, they will cover. You may need to take out a rider on your policy. Alternatively, consider taking out a policy with a company such as Safeware, which specializes in providing coverage for computer equipment.

Although less damaging, computers also react to low voltages (often called brownouts). If the incoming voltage drops too low, the computer acts as if it had been turned off, causing you to lose all work in progress that hasn't been saved to a disk. Of course, the same occurs when the electric power is suddenly removed from a computer. Someone may have tripped over a cord and unplugged the computer or flipped the wrong circuit breaker in the building, or there could be a power problem outside the building. Any of these things can cause you to lose your work in progress. In addition, a Macintosh that isn't shut down gracefully using the Finder's Shutdown command may leave its hard disk in a vulnerable position (for example, the read/write heads haven't been moved to a safe position and the data structures that keep track of where things are on disk haven't been updated). (See Chapter 10 for details.)

The bottom line is that your Macintosh needs some sort of power protection. There are three general solutions, increasing in price and the amount of protection provided:

- **Surge protector:** A surge protector, which usually contains four to six electrical outlets, is designed to stop power surges before they reach your computer.

- **Line conditioner:** A line conditioner not only provides surge protection, but compensates for low incoming voltages. It can keep a computer from powering down during brownout conditions.

- **Uninterruptible power supply (UPS):** A UPS provides a backup battery in case of a total loss of electrical power. There are two types of UPSs. The first—a standby UPS—runs the computer off the electric lines until a power loss is detected. Then it automatically switches to battery power. Depending on the model, it may or may not provide surge protection and line conditioning. The second type of UPS—a continuous UPS—always runs off the battery, avoiding the cutover time; power coming from the electric line is used to charge the battery. This type of UPS provides surge and brownout protection to the computer because the battery always supplies a constant voltage.

UPSs are not designed to let you operate for long periods of time off backup battery power. Instead, they provide an average of 10 minutes of power, allowing you to shut down the system gracefully until electric power is restored. Note that the amount of power provided by a UPS battery depends on the size of the UPS (how many watts it produces) and the power draw of the devices connected to it.

The type of power protection in which you should invest depends on several things, including the stability of electrical power in your area, the frequency of thunderstorms in your area, and the importance of never losing even a few minutes of work. At the very least, you should have some sort of surge protection.

Surge protectors have become very inexpensive (less than $10). However, be wary of any surge protector that doesn't have an indicator that the surge protection circuits are still functional. Inexpensive surge protectors do work—at least once. However, damping a major power surge can burn out the surge protection circuits, and without some type of indicator, there is no way for you to know that the surge protector is no longer functional. It will continue to work as a multioutlet strip, but not as a surge protector. Basic surge protectors with surge indicator lights cost between $15 and $50. This is one instance where saving money on a cheap piece of equipment could end up costing you much more in the long run.

There are a number of sources of power surges, including lightning strikes, power-up and power-down of equipment throughout a building, and return of electricity after a blackout. A surge protector can isolate your Macintosh from many of those surges. However, to be completely safe, there are some things you can do to protect yourself:

- If you are in one of the areas of the country where heavy thunderstorms occur, pay attention to the weather broadcasts on the radio and television. When thunderstorms are in your area, shut down your computers and unplug them from the wall until the storms have passed. You may also want to unplug the computer equipment at night, on weekends, and over holidays. (If the preceding isn't feasible, then you need more power protection than a simple surge protector.)

- Place equipment that draws a lot of power (for example, a photocopier or an electric dryer) on a different electrical circuit from that used by computing equipment. If possible, power up the power-hungry equipment before you turn on the computers.

- When a blackout occurs, unplug all computer equipment until the power is restored. You can leave a light turned on to tell you when the power is back.

By the way: Power surges also travel down telephone lines. You should therefore also consider a surge protector for the telephone lines entering modems and fax machines.

If the voltage on your electrical lines is irregular, then you should consider a line conditioner. A line conditioner has a capacitor that stores electricity. If the voltage coming from the wall drops, the capacitor discharges some of its stored power, bringing the voltage entering your computer back up to normal. Most also include surge protection; high-end models also correct for high as well as low voltages.

A line conditioner is rated in watts to indicate the maximum amount of power draw it can handle. For example, a 600-watt line conditioner can support a Macintosh with an internal hard drive and its monitor. It may also be able to handle a printer. (Laser printers draw considerably more power than ink-jet or dot-matrix printers.) When you start to add external devices with their own power supplies (for example, scanners, tape drives, and CD-ROM players), you'll probably need a 1,200-watt line conditioner. Prices run from about $90 to $250, depending on the wattage the line conditioner can handle.

As mentioned earlier, line conditioners are only effective for small voltage drops. When the power drops more than about 5%, a line conditioner is useless. If you can't afford to lose even a moment of data, then you need some type of battery backup—a UPS. Most UPSs sold today are standby UPSs, which cut over to battery power when a voltage drop is detected. They are less expensive than those that provide continuous battery power; cutover times have become so short (around 2 milliseconds or less) that the computer doesn't even notice that a change has occurred.

Because UPSs are relatively expensive (400 watts standby with surge protection, $200; 400 watts standby with surge protection and line conditioning, $325; 400 watts continuous, $475), only computers, monitors, and disk drives are connected to them. If a printer or scanner goes down because of a power loss, you can always restart the work; there really won't be a loss of data. Therefore you can get by with a smaller UPS than line conditioner.

UPSs are usually installed in businesses. If your Macintosh is used for home and recreational purposes, you probably don't need a UPS. In most cases, you'll need a good surge protector. However, if the power voltage coming into your home varies a great deal, consider a line conditioner; it will help extend the life of your computer. Business users should weigh the cost of a UPS versus the cost of recovering data lost by a sudden blackout. A UPS for servers often makes sense; you may also want to put a UPS on critical workstations.

Disk Storage

It seems you can never have enough disk storage. No matter how big your hard disk is, the time will come when it fills up and you need even more storage space. (The old adage, "Work expands to fill the time available" might be rewritten as, "Stored files expand to fill the disk space available.") In particular, if you work with color or grayscale graphics or video images, you are likely to run out of disk space much sooner than later. (It's not unusual for a single grayscale image to occupy more than 2Mb of disk space!)

Because we rely on disk storage so heavily, it's vital that the disk drives installed in or connected to a Macintosh have enough space to store all needed files and that the drives and media work with minimal problems. Unfortunately, disk drives fail. The media on which programs and data are stored run out of available space and sometimes become damaged. This chapter therefore looks at a variety of disk storage issues, including how disk drives work, options for upgrading disk storage, and disk drive troubleshooting techniques.

An Introduction to Disk Storage

Disks used by computers for storage are flat, circular media made of plastic or metal. Today's disk drives use two basic storage technologies: magnetic and/or optical. Regardless of the storage technology, data are laid out and accessed in much the same way.

By the way: Magnetic and optical storage technologies aren't mutually exclusive. In particular, *floptical* drives use magnetic storage media coupled with lasers to increase storage density.

A disk storage system needs both the disk drive mechanism to read and write data and some storage media. The media may be permanently installed in the drive, as is typical with most of today's hard disks, or it may be removable. Removable media include floppy disks, cartridge hard disks, and most forms of optical storage.

Each disk that forms a part of the media placed in a drive is known as a *platter*. If the platter is magnetic media, data can be stored on both sides. If the platter is optical media, data are usually stored on only one side.

When storage media are made up of more than one platter, as is the case with large hard disks, the platters are placed on a central core known as a *spindle*. Data are usually written on all surfaces, although sometimes the very top and bottom aren't used. The disk drive in Figure 10.1, for example, has four platters.

Data are stored on the bottom of the top platter, both sides of the two interior platters, and the top of the bottom platter.

Read/Write Heads

Data are stored and retrieved with a *read/write head*. There is one read/write head for each disk surface on which data are stored. Each head is attached to an *access arm*, all of which are attached to a single *boom*. For example, in Figure 10.1, there are three access arms, each of which has two read/write heads, one for the surface above and one for the surface below.

It takes two types of movement to bring the read/write heads over the entire surfaces on which data are stored. First, the platters spin at a high rate of speed. Hard disks, for example, spin at a fixed speed between 3,600 and 7,200 RPM (although the exact speed varies from one drive to another, the speed of a given drive is fixed). Second, the boom moves in and out, from the outer edge of the platters toward the spindle and back again. This movement, known as a *seek*, represents the largest part of the time needed to access data on a disk.

Figure 10.1 *The anatomy of a multiple-platter disk drive*

> **By the way:** Because floppy disks are made of a flexible plastic, they can't spin as rapidly as hard disks, which are

made of metal. (The plastic loses its rigidity at high speeds.) This is one reason why access to data on a floppy disk is slower than access to data on a hard disk.

> **By the way:** When 3.5-inch floppy disks were first introduced, many people confused them with hard disks, because they were used to the 5.25-inch floppies that were placed in a flexible carrier. The rigid plastic case around the 3.5-inch floppy disk led them to think it was a "hard" disk.

The read/write heads float above the surface of a hard disk on a very thin cushion of air; they never make physical contact with the disk. (Floppy disk read/write reads do make physical contact with the disk.) If something should cause the air cushion to break, the read/write heads plunge onto the disk surface (a *head crash*). Given that the platters are rotating between 3,600 and 7,200 RPM, a head crash does a great deal of damage to a disk. It can take a visible gouge out of a hard disk!

There are two major causes of disk head crashes. The first is something that jars the disk drive, such as bumping up against it or dropping it while it is turned on. Although disk drives are much less sensitive than many people would lead you to believe, you should never move a disk drive while it is spinning, and you should avoid bumping or jarring it. In addition, you should always use the Finder's Shutdown command before powering down your Mac. This action *parks the heads* of all mounted disk drives. Parking moves the access arms to a safe area in the center of the platters so that the read/write heads are no longer over disk surfaces containing data. Then if the drive is moved, there is virtually no chance that a damaging head crash can occur.

The second major cause of a head crash and other types of media damage is atmospheric contaminants. Small specks of dust or even smoke can get between the read/write reads and the disk surface, breaking the air cushion. Most hard disks are sealed in their cases to prevent contaminants from getting in. You must be careful, however, with drives that use removable media, including floppy drives and cartridge drives.

Physical Disk Organization

Each surface on which data are stored is divided into concentric circles called *tracks*. The tracks are numbered, beginning with 0, starting from the outside edge of the disk. At the same time, each surface is divided into pie-shaped sections known as *sectors*. As you can see in Figure 10.2, a single sector is therefore a

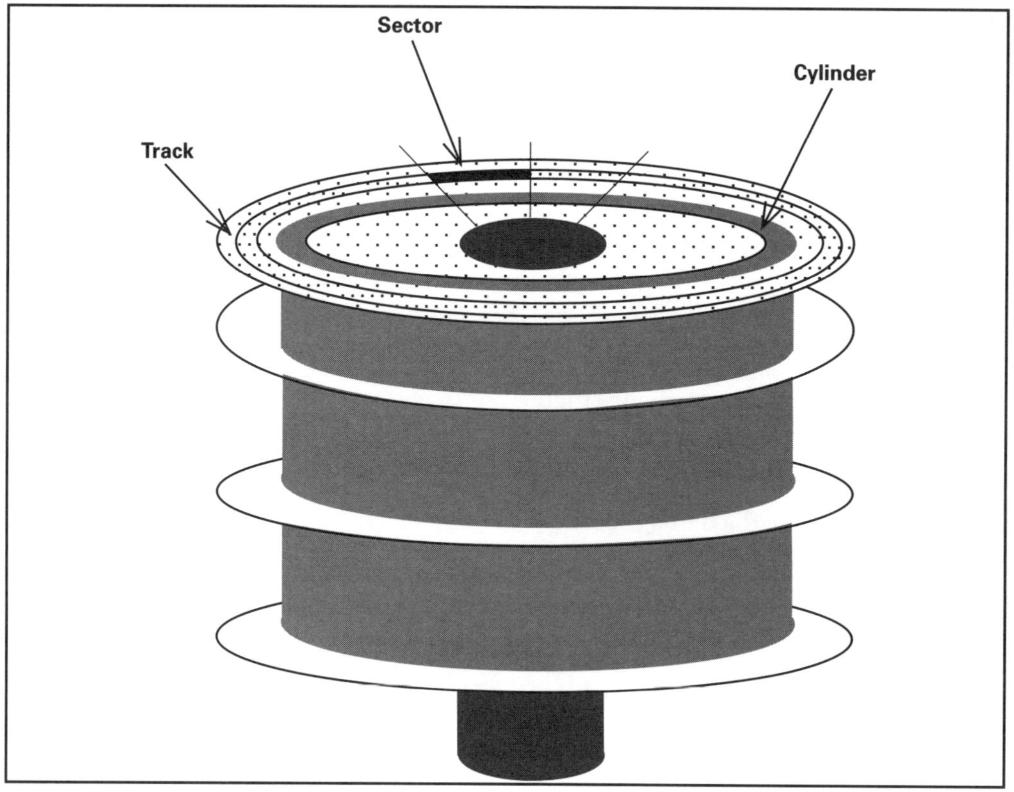

Figure 10.2 *The organization of a disk*

portion of a single track. On Macintosh disks, each sector is 512 bytes in size.

The movement of the boom takes the read/write heads from one track to another. The spinning of the platters brings sectors under the read/write heads. Because seek time is the largest portion of disk access time, disk drives store data in such a way as to minimize read/write head movement. Therefore when a track is filled with data, the next data are stored on the same track on a different disk surface, rather than on a different track on the same disk surface. The same track through all the surfaces in a disk drive is known as a *cylinder*. On a floppy disk or a single-platter hard disk, a cylinder is the same track on the top and bottom of the disk surface. On a multiple-platter hard disk, a cylinder cuts through all the platters in the stack.

Disk Rotation Speeds

As mentioned earlier, the media in a disk drive spins at a high rate of speed, bringing the sectors on a given track under the read/write heads. In traditional disk drives, the platters always spin at the same rate of speed. Although the same amount of data is stored on each track, the density of the data is higher at inner tracks (those nearer the spindle) than at the outer tracks. To see why this is so, look at Figure 10.3. Notice that the same angular rotation produces movement from A to A´ on the inner track and B to B´ on the outer track. The outer track travels further than the inner track. To store the same amount of data in the same rotational area, the data on the outer track must be stored farther apart than the data on the inner track.

Although most disk drives spin at a constant rate of speed, Macintosh 400K and 800K floppy drives do not. These variable-speed drives break the disk surface into zones, each of which is a group of adjacent tracks. The storage density within each zone is the same. The drive changes speed—slowing down as the read/write heads move to outer tracks—to access data that are stored more densely than those on single-speed drives. As a result, variable-speed floppy drives store more on a disk than single-speed drives. A single-speed drive can only store 360K on a single-sided disk and 720K on a double-sided disk.

SCSI drives also break disk surfaces into zones, placing more sectors in outer tracks than the inner. However, SCSI controllers are able to read the variable storage densities without changing speed.

Data Encoding and Disk Compatibility

As you know, everything in a computer is represented as some sort of binary code. That includes the data that are stored on a disk. On a magnetic disk, 0s and 1s are stored as changes in the direction of the magnetic field on the disk. However, there is more than one way to indicate when the bit pattern of the data changes from a 0 to a 1 and back again.

The Macintosh uses *group-code recording* (GCR) along with *non-return-to-zero, inverted* (NRZI) encoding to store data on a Macintosh-format disk. NRZI encoding changes the direction of the magnetic field whenever a 1 appears in the data. It makes no change whenever a 0 appears. The problem with this is that there is no way to identify groups of more than two 0s. In other words, groups of three or more 0s are encoded just like two 0s. The solution is the GCR, which precedes a string of 0s with a count of how many 0s are in the group. As a result, it takes four 8-bit patterns to represent 3 bytes of data.

MS-DOS floppy disks use an alternate data-encoding scheme known as *modified frequency modulation* (MFM). Using MFM, the direction of the magnetic fields changes whenever the data contain a 1 or two adjacent 0s; no direction change occurs for a 0 by itself. The Macintosh SuperDrive is designed to read and write MFM disks as well as GCR disks; this is what makes it compatible with 720K and 1.4Mb MS-DOS disks.

> **By the way:** Apple has announced that in early 1994 it will be introducing a low-cost line of Macintoshes that use disk drives that use only MFM encoding. These single-speed disk drives, the same

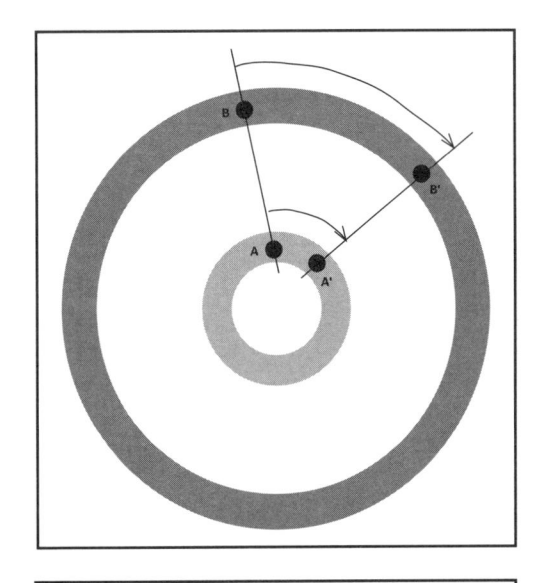

Figure 10.3 *Storage density with a single-speed disk drive*

as those used in most MS-DOS computers, store 720K on a double-sided disk and 1.4Mb on a high-density disk. They also sell for about one-third the cost of the SuperDrive. Apple is therefore suggesting that software developers begin distributing software on 1.4Mb disks, which can be read by both the SuperDrive and the lower-cost MFM drives. As a result, any Macintosh without a SuperDrive will soon be at a considerable disadvantage.

Disk Formatting

When you purchase an unformatted magnetic disk, it is truly a blank surface—it has no tracks or sectors. Most magnetic disks are sold in this way because they can then be formatted to the specifications of the drive in which they will be used. *Formatting* a disk does the following:

- *Lays down the pattern of tracks and sectors.* The more tracks on a disk (the more densely the tracks are packed), the more data can be stored on the disk. For example, 1.4Mb disks have more tracks than 800K disks, even though both use the same 3.5-inch media.

  By the way: Because the tracks are packed so tightly on a 1.4Mb disk, the media must be of higher quality than 800K media. (Manufacturing standards are more exacting for 1.4Mb media.) Although it is possible to drill a second hole in an 800K disk and reformat it to hold 1.4Mb, you shouldn't do so. You run the risk of media failure and the loss of all the data on the disk.

- *Initializes track 0 (the outermost track) to hold data structures that describe the contents of the disk.* Because formatting creates a new set of these data structures, reformatting a disk makes any existing files on the disk inaccessible. It does not, however, actually erase those files.

- *Checks for and marks bad sectors.* Sectors that are damaged are flagged so they won't be used.

  By the way: If you accidentally reformat a disk, don't panic—and don't make any changes to the disk. As long as you don't write to a reformatted disk, your chances of recovering its contents are good. To effect the recovery, you'll need a disk utility such as Norton Utilities that can examine the disk and reconstruct the original data structures that describe the disk's contents.

- *Sets the disk interleave.* The interleave determines whether data in a given track are written to adjacent sectors, every other sector, or every third sector. The reason behind interleaving is discussed shortly.

Formatting a disk is not the same as "erasing" a disk. When you choose **Erase Disk** from the Finder's special menu, the Macintosh operating system doesn't reformat the disk; it initializes the disk volume by re-creating the data structures that describe the contents of the disk, effectively making the files on the disk inaccessible. Unlike formatting, it doesn't check for bad blocks, lay down tracks and sectors, or set the interleave.

By the way: The Macintosh operating system uses the word *initialize* as a synonym for *format*. However, most third-party disk management utilities use the term *format*.

Interleaving

Hard disks spin at the same speed, regardless of the type of Macintosh on which they are being used. However, not all Macintoshes can accept data at the same rate. Assume, for example, that data are stored in adjacent tracks (an interleave of 1:1), as in Figure 10.4. A file begins in sector 0. If it is bigger than a sector, it grows into sector 1, sector 2, and so on, until the track is full. Because the tracks in which the file are stored are adjacent to one another, they travel under the read/write head at the maximum possible speed (the rotation speed of the disk). If the computer can't accept data at that rate, then the disk must make a full rotation between data transfers. In other words, the disk drive reads sector 0, spins completely around, and then reads sector 1. This slows down data access unnecessarily.

The alternative is to space out the sectors in which a file is stored. Then the time it takes to spin the disk to the next sector in a file corresponds more closely to the speed at which the computer can accept data, thus avoiding the delay of another disk rotation. Faster Macs can use the 1:1 interleave, but slower Macs use either a 1:2 interleave (see Figure 10.5) or a 1:3 interleave (see Figure 10.6).

The Macintosh operating system automatically sets the correct interleave for the computer to which the disk drive is connected when you format a disk. However, some disk management utilities give you the chance to specify the interleave. Older Macs, such as the Plus, use a 1:3 interleave; newer Macs (from the Mac II onward) can use the 1:1. If you move a disk drive to another Macintosh and discover that the performance of the drive degrades immediately, you may need to reformat the drive to

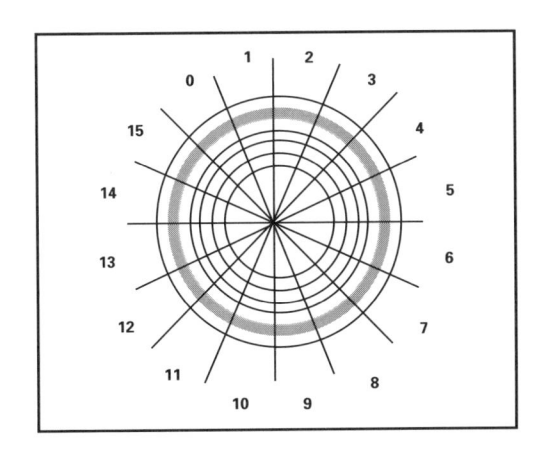

▶ **Figure 10.4** 1:1 disk interleaving

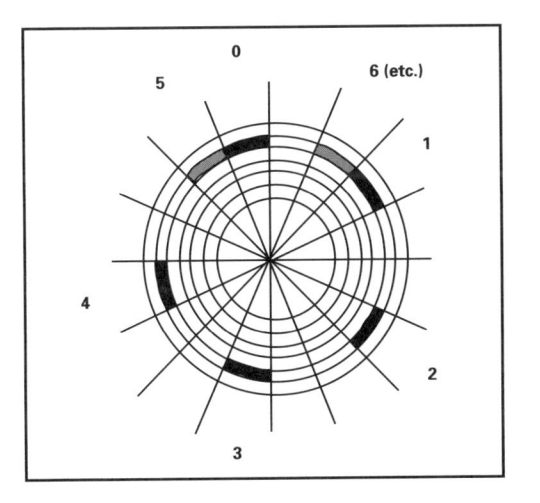

▶ **Figure 10.5** 1:2 disk interleaving

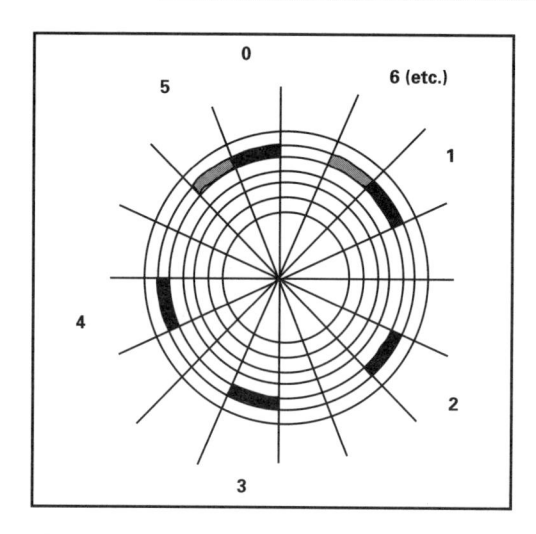

Figure 10.6 *1:3 disk interleaving*

get the correct interleave. However, don't forget that reformatting makes the files on the disk inaccessible. Be sure to back up your disk before reformatting!

Logical Disk Organization

Each hard disk is divided in logical blocks of 512 bytes. To make it easier to work with disk space, *logical blocks* are grouped together into *allocation blocks*. An allocation block is some multiple of the logical block size. For example, an allocation block might be 1,024 bytes. The size of an allocation block is set when a disk is formatted; it cannot be changed without reformatting. It is the smallest amount of space that can be added to a file at one time by any program. As you will see later in this chapter, the size of the allocation block is related to the size of the drive.

To make it easier to allocate contiguous space on a disk, allocation blocks are grouped together into larger units called *clumps*. A clump is the smallest amount of space added to a file whenever a program needs more space than is currently available. The clump size can be set by an application program, which means that different programs can allocate space in different-sized chunks (although never less than an allocation block).

Disk Partitioning

Once a hard disk is formatted, it can be partitioned. (Floppy disks cannot be partitioned.) A *partition* is a section of a hard disk that appears on the Macintosh desktop as a separate disk volume. In most cases, you can speed up disk operations by partitioning a large hard disk (generally, one greater than 200Mb). Each partition has its own desktop file. Because the desktop file is smaller, locating and copying files is faster. In addition, partitions can make it easier to organize and back up files, especially if the sizes of the partitions are multiples of the size of your backup media.

Partitions on the same hard disk can be formatted for use by different operating systems. For example, one hard disk can be used for both Macintosh operating system and A/UX volumes. The structure of A/UX hard disk volumes is different from that of Macintosh operating system volumes and can't be mounted by the Macintosh operating system. However, A/UX can mount both its own partitions (there are several types) and Macintosh operating system partitions.

Disk Volume Organization

Each volume has an organization similar to that in Figure 10.7. (Don't forget that a volume can be an entire disk or a disk partition.) Notice that the logical blocks are numbered beginning with the first physical blocks on the volume. However, allocation blocks actually begin their numbering with the fourth physical block. The contents of each area on a volume are described in the following sections.

> **By the way:** The Desktop file, which keeps track of things like file/folder icons and the comments entered in a file/folder's Get Info box isn't a part of the disk organization. Instead it's a file used and maintained by the Finder.

Boot Blocks

The first two logical blocks of each disk volume are filled with system startup information. These *boot blocks* may contain information needed to boot the computer from the disk. If the volume isn't a startup volume (in other words, it contains no System folder), then the boot blocks are filled with 0s.

The boot blocks contain information such as the following:

- name of the System file
- name of the Finder file
- name of the file containing the startup screen
- name of the startup program, the program to be run when the computer is booted (usually the Finder)
- name of the system scrap file (usually the Clipboard)

Chapter 10: Disk Storage

Logical block		Allocation block
0	System startup information	
1		
2	Master directory block (MDB)	
3	Volume bit map	0
n ↓	Catalog file	m ↓
	Extents overflow file	
	All other files and unused space	
	Alternate MDB	
	Unused space	

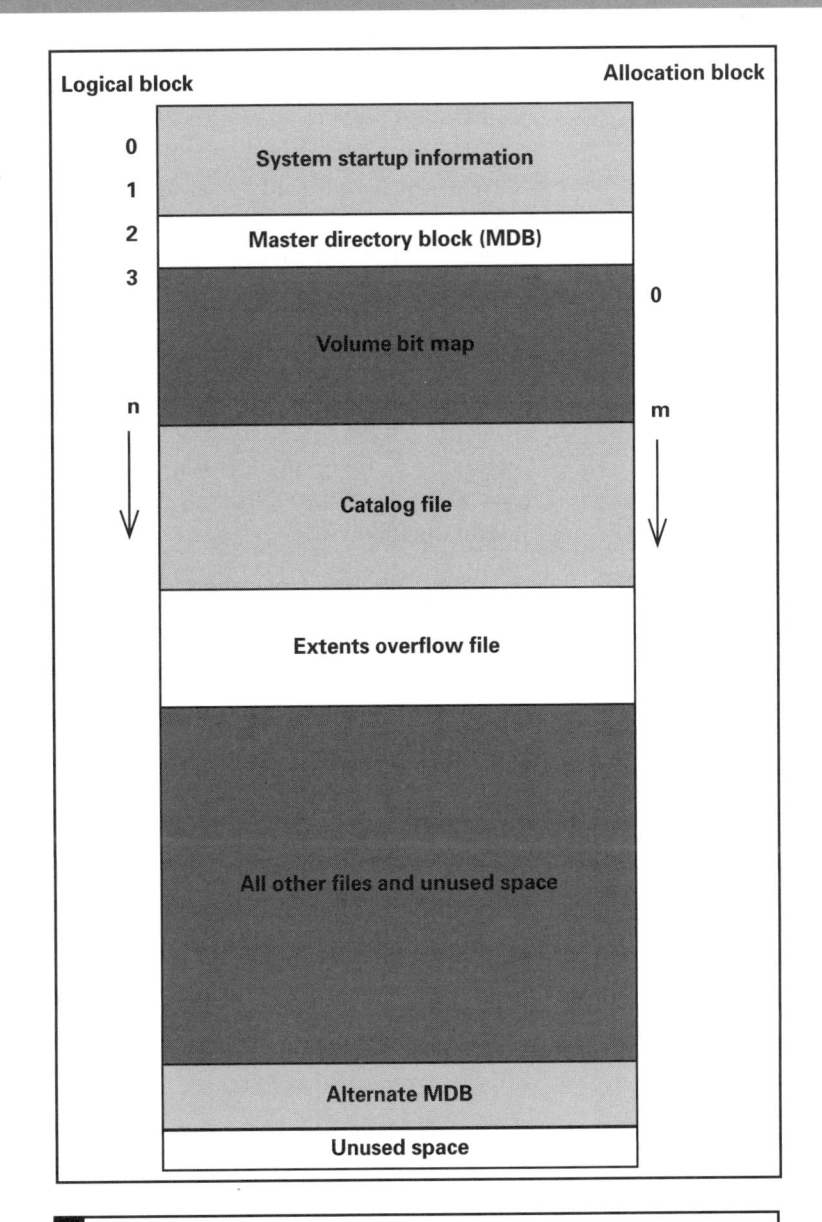

▶ *Figure 10.7 The organization of a Macintosh disk volume*

209

- memory configuration parameters

The boot blocks actually also include program code that can be used to execute the System file and start up the computer. However, in most cases the computer boots from program code that is part of the System file.

Master Directory Blocks

A *master directory block* (MDB), or *volume information block* (VIB), contains a wide range of information about what is stored on the volume. Its contents include the following:

- date and time when the volume was created
- date and time when the volume was last modified
- attributes that indicate whether the volume is locked by hardware or software and whether it was mounted successfully
- number of files and directories in the top-level directory

> **By the way:** The Macintosh operating system refers to disk directories as folders.

- number of directories and files on the volume
- location of the first block in the volume bit-map (discussed shortly)
- location of the first block in the catalog file (discussed shortly)
- size of allocation blocks
- number of allocation blocks in the volume
- clump size to use unless a program instructs otherwise
- size of catalog and extents overflow files (discussed shortly)
- volume name

Each Macintosh volume maintains a copy of the MDB in the next-to-the-last block on the volume. This copy is for use by disk utility programs (especially those that are designed to recover accidentally deleted files or reformatted disks).

Volume Bit-map

The volume bit-map keeps track of which allocation blocks are in use and which are available. It contains 1 bit for every allocation block on the volume. If an allocation block is in use, its bit in the volume bit-map is 1; if an allocation block is available, its bit in the volume bit-map is 0. Note that this says nothing about which files are occupying the allocation blocks.

The size of the volume bit-map depends on the size of the disk and the size of the disk's allocation blocks. However, it has a maximum size of 65,535 bits. That means that there can't be more than

65,535 allocation blocks on a disk volume. If the allocation block size is equal to the logical block size (512 bytes), then a volume can be no larger than 32Mb. Larger disk volumes (up to a maximum of 2Gb) are supported by increasing the size of the allocation block. For example, if the allocation block is four logical blocks (2,048 bytes), then the maximum volume size is 128Mb.

There is one drawback to larger allocation blocks. Even if a program needs to store only 1 byte beyond the end of its current file, it must expand the file by an entire allocation block. The result can be wasted space. You can keep the allocation block size relatively small by partitioning a large hard disk. This can help avoid the wasted space of large allocation block sizes as well as speed up disk access.

Catalog File and Extents Overflow File

The actual structure of the files and directories on a disk is maintained in the catalog file. In addition to storing the relationships between files and directories, the catalog file stores the following information about each file and directory:

- type of catalog entry (for example, file or directory)
- date and time file or directory was created
- date and time file or directory was last modified
- first allocation block in a file
- location of the end of the file
- name of the file or directory
- identification of the directory containing the file or directory (its *parent* directory)
- the first three *extents* allocated to the file (an extent is another word for a group of allocation blocks used by a file)

If the list of blocks used by a file becomes too long to fit into the catalog file, it can overflow into the extents overflow file.

Floppy Drive Upgrades

Since late 1989, all Macintoshes have been equipped with 1.4Mb floppy disk drives. Such Macintoshes aren't candidates for floppy drive upgrades. However, all Mac Pluses, early SEs, and all Mac IIs were shipped with 800K drives. In addition, the SE and the Mac II, IIx, and IIfx have room for a second internal floppy drive. This section therefore looks at adding a second floppy drive as well as upgrading an 800K drive to a 1.4Mb drive.

By the way: Many Macintosh models have a port for an external floppy disk drive. If you have a need for a second floppy drive and your Mac doesn't have room inside for one, consider purchasing an external floppy from a third-party manufacturer.

Adding a Second Internal Floppy Drive

As you just read, the SE and the six-slot desktop Macs can accept a second internal floppy drive. Apple currently provides a 1.4Mb drive that can be installed as a second internal drive. Should you add the extra drive? The answer depends on your computing needs and on which Macintosh model you have.

The major reason for installing a second floppy drive is to ease copying between floppy disks. Without a second floppy, you must either copy the contents of the floppy being copied to a hard disk temporarily or perform an unbearable number of disk swaps. Therefore if you find yourself frequently making copies of floppy disks, consider adding a second drive. Otherwise, it probably shouldn't be high on your list of computer purchases.

If you install a second floppy drive in an SE, there won't be room for an internal hard drive. Although you can certainly attach external hard drives to the SCSI port, if you transport the computer frequently, moving an external hard drive can be inconvenient. Therefore if you need a second floppy drive on an SE, you are probably better off with an external drive.

The six-slot Macs (II, IIx, and IIfx) don't have a connector for an external floppy drive. Fortunately, they do have enough room for two internal floppy drives and an internal hard disk. If you need a second floppy drive, there is no physical reason you can't install one. Keep in mind, however, that the Mac II needs a ROM upgrade before it can access a 1.4Mb drive.

Upgrading to a SuperDrive

The Plus, early SEs, and Mac IIs are all candidates for upgrading their 800K drives to 1.4Mb drives. Because software manufacturers are moving to shipping software on 1.4Mb disks, it's important that a Mac be equipped with the high-density drive.

The Macintosh Plus cannot be upgraded to accept an internal 1.4Mb drive. However, all is not lost. Several manufacturers provide external SCSI 1.4Mb drives (for example, the DaynaFile from Dayna or the SuperFloppy from PLI). Although such drives are slower than the internal 1.4Mb drives, they do give the Plus access to Macintosh high-density disks and the ability to read and write MS-DOS format disks.

By the way: Not all 1.4Mb external floppy drives can read and write 400K and 800K disks. When purchasing such a drive, be sure that you know exactly which formats it can handle.

A 1.4Mb floppy drive is one upgrade that should be performed on any SE or Mac II you intend to keep. Both need a ROM upgrade to handle the 1.4Mb drive. For that reason, the upgrade kits must be purchased from Apple. They should also be installed by an authorized service technician, who can return your computer's original ROMs to Apple. If the original ROMs aren't returned, you will end up paying significantly more for the upgrade. (More than the cost of the installation!)

By the way: Don't wait too much longer to upgrade the ROMs and internal floppy drive in your SE or Mac II. There is absolutely no way to predict how much longer Apple will continue to make the upgrade available.

DIAGNOSING FLOPPY DRIVE PROBLEMS

Floppy disk media is considerably less reliable than hard disk media. It is not unusual for the media to become damaged from extended use, making it impossible to read from or write to the disk. Although you can use disk recovery software to attempt to access the files on the disk, in most cases you just throw the damaged floppy away. However, not all floppy read and write problems are caused by bad media. Some can be caused by the drive itself.

Misalignment

When operating properly, a read/write head is centered in the track in which it is currently writing. However, over time the alignment of the heads may change, resulting in data that aren't centered in the tracks that were created when the disk was formatted (see Figure 10.8).

There are two signs that your floppy drive might be misaligned. First, you have trouble reading disks that were written in other floppy drives, although you have no trouble reading those that you wrote. Second, disks written in your drive can't be read in other floppy drives. Eventually, the misalignment can become so bad that you won't be able to read the disks on which commercial software is shipped.

Aligning a floppy disk drive takes a fair amount of equipment (including an oscilloscope) and about a half hour of work. Nonetheless, because new Apple floppy drives are still relatively expensive

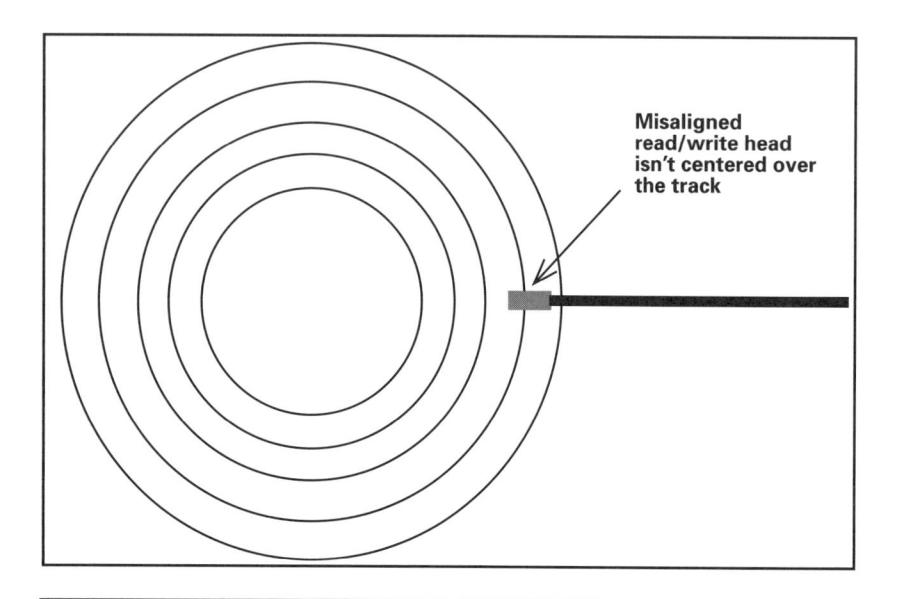

Misaligned read/write head isn't centered over the track

Figure 10.8 Misaligned floppy disk drive

($150–$200), it often makes sense to have the drive realigned unless the drive is very old or exhibiting other problems. Unless you already have access to the necessary equipment, take your drive to a repair technician to have the work done.

Before deciding to have a floppy drive realigned, there is one major drawback you should consider: The realigned drive won't be able to read any floppy disks written prior to the realignment. You might therefore want to replace the misaligned drive with a new drive and then install the misaligned drive mechanism in a case to use as an external drive, at least until you can transfer data from floppies written by the misaligned drive. Alternatively, place the files you have on floppy on some type of mass storage device (a hard disk or cartridge drive) until the drive is aligned and then copy the files back to floppy.

Dirt

Apple's floppy disk drives don't have doors across the opening into which you insert the disk. That means that dirt and oils can easily enter the drive. Dirty read/write heads can be the cause of intermittent problems with reading and writing that aren't connected to specific disks. If disks that your floppy drive can't read and/or write work fine in another disk drive, then it's very likely that you have a dirt problem.

By the way: You can prevent a lot of dirt and oil from entering a Macintosh floppy drive by always leaving a disk hanging out of the drive. Don't actually seat the disk in the drive; just leave it about half way out.

The solution to a dirt problem is to clean the read/write heads. The easiest way is to use a commercial head cleaning kit. These kits contain a floppy disk case filled with a disk made of cloth. You place a few drops of cleaning fluid (supplied with the kit) on the cloth disk and insert it into the drive. As the Macintosh attempts to mount the cleaning disk, the heads make contact with the cleaning cloth and dirt and oils are wiped from the heads to the cloth.

Some people think that head cleaning kits are too abrasive. The alternative is to clean the drive manually. To do this, you need to open the computer and the floppy drive itself so that you have access to the heads. Then you need a lint-free swab (available at most computer stores and in most computer cleaning kits) and some alcohol. The cleaning process involves gently wiping each read/write head with an alcohol-moistened swab. As with many other procedures that require getting inside the computer, you shouldn't attempt this if taking your computer apart makes you at all nervous.

HARD DISK UPGRADES

You are going to run out of hard disk space; sooner or later, it's going to happen. This section therefore looks at alternatives for upgrading your mass storage. Today's technology offers both magnetic and optical media options.

Adding More Mass Storage

Despite the technological advances in removable magnetic and optical media, the most widely used mass storage device on a Macintosh is still the *fixed hard disk* (a hard disk sealed in a case). Fixed hard drives provide the fastest data access and the highest storage capacities of any disk type. In most cases, they also are the cheapest, when cost is measured in dollars per megabyte. However, buying a fixed hard disk can be expensive because you must purchase the entire disk at one time. Some of today's removable media (for example, cartridge hard drives and optical drives), although they cost more per megabyte initially, present a lower initial cost with additional incremental costs as you add media. Removable media provide theoretically unlimited capacity that you pay for in small chunks as you need it.

Comparing the Types of Mass Storage

The fixed hard disk that is part of every current Macintosh has some advantages:

- fast access
- low cost per megabyte
- availability of all files on-line at the same time
- reliability (sealed case keeps out atmospheric contaminants)

A fixed hard disk's biggest drawback is that its storage capacity isn't expandable. To get more space you must replace the drive with a larger one or invest in an additional drive, incurring a significant up-front cost.

Removable media avoid the drawbacks of a fixed disk. Their advantages include the following:

- low initial cost
- unlimited storage capacity
- low incremental upgrade costs for media

However, drives that use removable media generally provide slower access speeds than fixed hard disks and are more susceptible to atmospheric contamination because the disk isn't sealed in the drive. In addition, only those files on media currently mounted in the drive are accessible. In essence, working with removable media is like working with gigantic floppy disks.

There are four kinds of removable media in widespread use today: *floptical, magneto-optical* (or simply *optical*), *cartridge,* and CD-ROM. Although we are used to thinking of CD-ROM as a read-only medium, drives are now available that can write and master CD-ROMs.

A floptical is a combination of a high-capacity floppy disk and laser technology. Similar to a floppy disk, the medium is placed in a rigid plastic cartridge. Flopticals, which store just over 20Mb on a 3.5-inch cartridge, achieve such high storage densities by embedding data that allow the read/write heads to position themselves into the disk surface. Because the laser can use the embedded positioning data to position the reads precisely, the track density on a floptical can be many times greater than that on a typical floppy disk. Flopticals certainly have a higher storage capacity than floppy disks, but they are nonetheless magnetic media and therefore tend to wear much like floppy disks. They are useful for semipermanent data storage and transfer but typically aren't a solution for mass storage needs.

By the way: An alternative high-density floppy drive is the *Bernoulli* drive. Manufactured by the Iomega Corporation, Bernoulli cartridges store either 44Mb or 90Mb. They are relatively inexpensive and as reliable as any floppy-based media can be.

A magneto-optical drive (see Figure 10.9), however, can provide an alternative to a fixed hard disk for permanent mass storage. The drive uses a laser to change the direction of a magnetic field embedded in an optical disk. Writing is done in two steps. During the first step, the laser heats the media and lets the read/write align all the magnetic particles in the same direction, effectively erasing whatever was previously stored. For the second step, the laser heats only those places where data need to be stored; therefore when the read/write head passes over the heated areas, the direction of the magnetic field changes only in those spots. As a result, space on a magneto-optical cartridge can be reused, just like other magnetic media. The 3.5-inch cartridges store 128Mb; 5.25-inch cartridges store as much as 640Mb.

Cartridge drives (see Figure 10.10) use hard drives that are placed in a rigid plastic case. Most such drives use mechanisms made by SyQuest and are often simply called *SyQuest drives*. SyQuest sells the drive mechanisms to disk drive manufacturers, who place them in cases and add appropriate cabling and software. You will therefore find SyQuest drives sold under many manufacturer's labels. Nonetheless, if you look for or ask for a SyQuest drive, most people will know exactly what you mean.

The two older SyQuest formats use 5.25-inch cartridges that store either 44Mb or 88Mb. Drives made to handle the 44Mb cartridges are limited to only that cartridge. The 88Mb drive can read 44Mb cartridges but cannot write or format them. The latest version of these drives, the 88c, can read and write both 44Mb

Figure 10.9 A magneto-optical drive

Figure 10.10 A cartridge hard drive

and 88Mb; however, it cannot format 44Mb cartridges (you must purchase them preformatted). These drives are standard throughout the computing industry and are frequently used for exchanging files when floppy disks don't have enough capacity.

A newer 3.5-inch cartridge stores 105Mb. However, because so many people already have drivers for the larger, lower-capacity cartridges, the 105Mb version is not as widely used. If you will be exchanging files with someone, then you should probably avoid the 105Mb SyQuest. If you are going to use it only for your own storage purposes, then this larger drive is a viable option, especially because its cartridges cost less per megabyte than the smaller cartridges.

By the way: Other manufacturers do make mechanisms for cartridge hard drives. However, they may not be compatible with the SyQuest drives. If you are going to be exchanging cartridges with someone, make sure you both have the same type of drive.

By the way: Prior to the summer of 1993, only SyQuest manufactured cartridges for SyQuest drives. Although the "compatible" cartridges do work in SyQuest drives, SyQuest insists that non-SyQuest cartridges may damage the drives.

CD-ROM first came to our desktops as a read-only medium. It is typically used for high-capacity (500Mb–600Mb) file distribution. It's great for data that don't change, such as encyclopedias or collections of clip art. Until recently, you couldn't economically write to a CD-ROM. Although it costs only about $2 to duplicate a CD-ROM from a master, mastering equipment cost well over $15,000; paying someone else to master your CD-ROM for you cost nearly $1,500. That situation has changed dramatically. The CD-ROM drive in Figure 10.11 sells for under $4,000; it can be used to write single-copy CD-ROMs (blanks cost less than $40) or to master CD-ROMs for mass duplication. This type of drive is ideal for uses where large quantities of data must be stored and kept unchanged for indefinite periods. For example, it might be used by a county Bureau of Records to store birth, death, and marriage data as well as to record real estate transactions. It is also useful for any company, such as a software company, that needs to master CD-ROMs for duplication. Once you've mastered more than three discs, the drive has paid for itself. Although they are not for everyone, recordable CD-ROMs will become more common and less costly in the near future.

Deciding How Much and What Type of Mass Storage You Need

How much mass storage do you need? What type of mass storage should you purchase? The answer isn't quite as simple as figuring out how much RAM you should have. There are several factors to consider:

- What size is your current drive? If your current drive is small (for example, less than 200Mb), then a replacement or second fixed hard drive usually makes sense. You should at least double the size of your existing drive. On the other hand, if you are already using a drive that is 1Gb or more, then you are faced with a significant cost for a larger disk. You can go to a 2Gb drive or look into the even larger disk arrays. For owners of mid-sized fixed hard drives (200Mb–600Mb), the choice isn't clear based solely on the size of the current drive; consider some of the following issues.

By the way: The largest fixed hard drive storage capacities are found in *redundant arrays of inexpensive disks* (RAIDs). RAIDs are made up of high-capacity fixed hard drives that are cabled together and accessed as if they were one disk. Disk arrays are very expensive (compared to the cost of other fixed disk storage) and typically used only with network and database servers.

Figure 10.11 A recordable CD-ROM drive

- How long did it take you to fill up your current drive? If it took you three years or more to fill up your current drive, then moving to a larger fixed hard disk will probably be economical.

- Are your storage needs likely to continue to grow at the same pace? If your mass storage needs will continue to increase at the same rate or more and you filled up your current drive in less than three years, then a fixed hard drive may not be a good alternative. You will be facing a never-ending spiral of hard disk replacements.

- Do you need all your files on-line at all times? If you need all your files accessible all the time, then a fixed hard drive is your best alternative. However, if you need only a portion of your files at any one time, then removable media are a good option. For example, if you have large collections of clip art, it usually works well to place them on cartridge hard disks or optical disks. By the same token, if your work divides neatly into unrelated projects, you can place the files for each project on removable media. On the other hand, if you are configuring a Macintosh for use as a network or database server, then a large fixed hard disk may be the only alternative because the entire software collection must be available all the time.

DIAGNOSING HARD DRIVE PROBLEMS

Problems with hard disks come from two general sources: the hardware and how data are stored and organized on the disk. Hardware problems usually require repair by the manufacturer of the disk drive or a service technician; you can usually handle problems with disk contents yourself.

Problems with Disk Contents

The contents of a hard disk include the files that you store on the disk and data that the operating system maintains to keep track of the disk's contents. Either can become damaged.

Damage to User Files

The files that you store on disk can become damaged in many ways, including the following:

- The system crashes while you are saving a file.

- An application program corrupts a file during a save operation. Such an application probably contains significant bugs and shouldn't be used unless you have absolutely no alternative.

- A file is written to a physically damaged disk sector. If there are only one or two files damaged by bad sectors, give them names with the extension "bad." (The "bad" files need to remain on disk as a band-aid over the damaged sectors, preventing an application or the operating system from using them.) Then restore the originals from a backup copy. However, if there are a significant number of bad sectors on the disk, you should probably reformat it. Reformatting marks damaged sectors as bad so they won't be used for storage. This technique obviously requires that you have a current backup copy of your disk!

- You accidentally delete a file or reformat a disk volume. As long as you don't write to the disk after the accidental deletion or reformatting, you can usually recover it using a utility program designed for that purpose. A sample of disk diagnosis and repair utilities can be found a bit later in this chapter.

Damage to Data About Disk Contents

As you read earlier, a hard disk contains information about what is stored on the disk as well as the files you have placed on it. Over time, this information can become corrupted:

- **Catalog:** The disk catalog may have lost track of files or how files are connected to directories.

- **Volume bit-map:** The volume bit-map may inaccurately reflect which blocks are used and which are unused.

- **Master directory block:** Any of the information in the MDB may be inaccurate.

These problems can often be fixed by a disk repair utility without damaging any disk contents or requiring disk reformatting. (Disk repair utilities are discussed later in this chapter.)

In addition to problems with the disk's directory structures, a disk may also end up with *cross-linked files*. Two files that are cross-linked are sharing the same space on disk. In all likelihood, one or both of the files is inaccessible. The solution is to delete all cross-linked files and to restore them from a backup copy.

Media Damage

Even though a hard disk's metal surface is much more durable than a floppy disk's plastic surface, it can still be damaged. The most common type of media damage is a block that becomes slightly marred, making it unusable. Bad blocks usually manifest themselves when a file has been saved onto one and later can't be read. This occurs because most application software can't detect a bad block while writing to the disk. However, when the application attempts to read the file, it can't.

Bad blocks aren't a major problem, as long as you have a recent backup of your disk. One solution is to reformat the disk and restore its contents from the backup. Formatting will flag the damaged blocks so they won't be used. Alternatively, you can use a disk repair utility that can flag bad blocks without reformatting. After the repair, you will need to restore those files that occupied bad blocks from your backup.

By the way: Under System 7 (but not any earlier versions of the Macintosh operating system), formatting a floppy disk also marks bad blocks so they won't be used.

On the other hand, a head crash is a very serious problem. When a read/write head makes contact with the disk surface, the very least that happens is that the read/write head gouges the disk surface. The disk is most likely spinning when the crash occurs; therefore pieces of metal can break off the read/write head and/or the disk and fly around the disk's case, causing additional damage.

If you've had a head crash, you can either repair or replace the drive. Repairing the drive usually means replacing the drive mechanism. It may also be possible—especially with large, multiplatter drives—to replace just the damaged components. Most drive repairs are performed by the manufacturer of the drive. Assuming the damaged drive is not the internal drive that came with your Macintosh, you should call the manufacturer's technical support and obtain a return authorization number. Then package the drive and ship it off for repairs. If the damaged drive is the internal drive that came with your Macintosh, then repairs are usually handled by an authorized Apple service technician.

By the way: There are authorized Apple dealers and there are companies that sell Macintoshes. The former are licensed by Apple to sell and service Apple products. The latter are part of what is known as the *gray market*. An authorized Apple dealer will not perform free warranty repair on a machine purchased from a gray market dealer. Although the price of the computer through a gray market dealer may be less than that from an authorized dealer, you will need to return the machine to the company from which you bought it for warranty repairs. (The warranty is actually offered by the gray market dealer, not Apple.)

Before deciding to have the drive repaired, check the cost of having the manufacturer or service technician replace the drive mechanism (the worst-case scenario) against the purchase price of a new drive. Also consider your current and future storage needs. If your hard disk was nearly full before the head crash, then it may not make sense to repair the drive but instead to go ahead and purchase a larger one. You may even be able to save $100–$200 on the cost of a replacement external drive by purchasing an internal drive mechanism that will fit inside the case of the damaged drive.

> **By the way:** Although used hard disks are available, general wisdom holds that you should avoid them. The same is true with used cartridges for SyQuest or optical drives. Even if the drive and/or media are under warranty, the best warranty in the world doesn't do you much good after you've lost your data.

Other Drive Problems

Other, less serious problems can affect hard disks without actually damaging data. These involve the mechanics of the drive. If your drive is intermittently spinning up and spinning down, for example, you may have a problem with the drive's power supply or the motor that causes the drive's spindle to turn.

Such problems can usually be fixed by the manufacturer of the drive or a service technician for a reasonable cost. (A replacement power supply in a 640Mb drive recently cost around $150.) To obtain such a repair for a third-party drive, call the drive manufacturer's technical support number and describe the drive's symptoms. In most cases, they will give you a return authorization number and instructions for shipping the drive. To obtain such repair for the internal drive that came with your Macintosh, contact an Apple dealer.

Disk Diagnostic and Repair Software

Short of media damage or a mechanical drive problem, you can do a great deal of disk repair yourself using software designed for the purpose. You can also use disk utility software to diagnose a wide variety of disk problems. Two such programs with very different capabilities are Norton Utilities from Symantec and Hard Disk ToolKit from FWB.

Norton Utilities

Norton Utilities is a collection of disk utility programs that, among other things, can diagnose and repair a number of disk problems. In addition, in many cases it can recover accidentally deleted files or files from a disk that has been accidentally reformatted. It can handle floppy disks, SCSI disks attached to the Macintosh's native SCSI bus, and SCSI disks attached to a SCSI accelerator card in a NuBus slot or PDS. (SCSI accelerators are discussed later in this chapter.) All its modules are user-friendly; all except one can be used successfully by any knowledgeable Macintosh user. (The Disk Editor module can be used by anyone to view disk info, but using it to modify disk contents is so potentially destructive that it should be used only by an expert.)

Norton Utilities' distribution disks include two "emergency disks." These disks contain a copy of Norton Utilities and a System file (version 6.0.4 on the 800K disk and version 7.0.1 on the 1.4Mb disk). You can use these disks when your startup hard disk won't boot.

Disk Doctor (see Figure 10.12) scans a hard disk to identify problems with the disk catalog, volume bit-map, and master directory block. For example, in Figure 10.13 Disk Doctor has discovered that the boot blocks are empty, indicating that the computer can't be booted from the disk. As in all cases where it detects a problem, Disk Doctor gives the user the choice of whether to make the repair; no repairs are done automatically.

Disk Doctor also locates files that have been disconnected from the directory hierarchy, are inaccessible (probably due to a bad block), or have become cross-linked. It can reconnect lost files but cannot fix inaccessible or cross-linked files. You may be able to recover cross-linked files by deleting all files that Disk Doctor has identified as cross-linked and restoring them from a backup copy. If that doesn't work, you should back up all files that aren't cross-linked and reformat the disk. The good files can

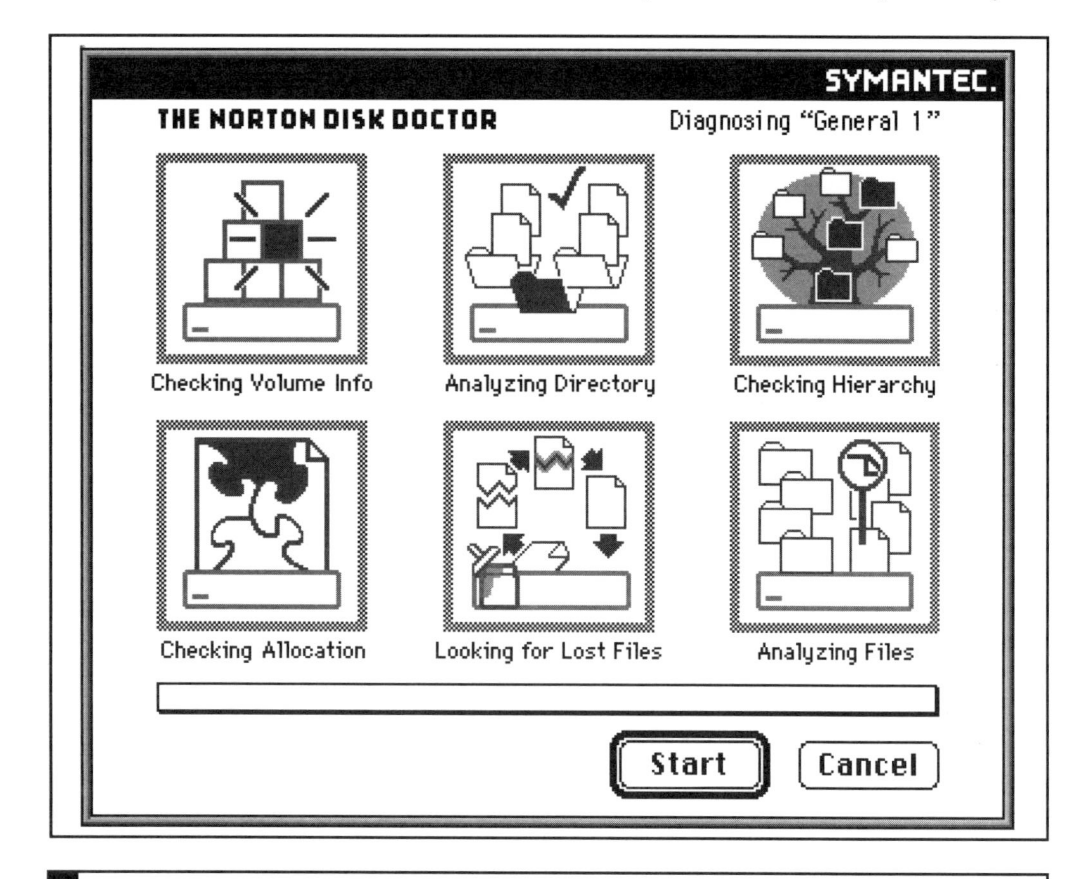

Figure 10.12 Norton Disk Doctor

be restored from the backup just made; the cross-linked files must come from a backup made before the cross-linking occurred. Inaccessible files should be restored from a backup. If that doesn't work, you should reformat the disk to map out bad blocks.

Files that have been accidentally deleted can usually be recovered as long as you haven't written to the disk since the file was deleted. If you have written to the disk, you will only be able to recover the file if the space used by the file hasn't been reused in any way. The UnErase module (see Figure 10.14) has three methods of recovering files: Quick UnErase, scanning by file type, and searching for strings of text that are contained in a file. QuickErase works best if Norton's FileSaver INIT, which keeps track of file activity on a disk, has been installed.

Once UnErase has examined the disk volume, it presents a list of deleted files along with an estimate of their recovery potential. In most cases, you'll be able to recover files that haven't been overwritten by other files. You may also be able to recover parts of files whose contents have been overwritten.

A disk that been accidentally reformatted or a disk that is so badly damaged that Disk Doctor can't fix it can often be recovered with Volume Recover. If

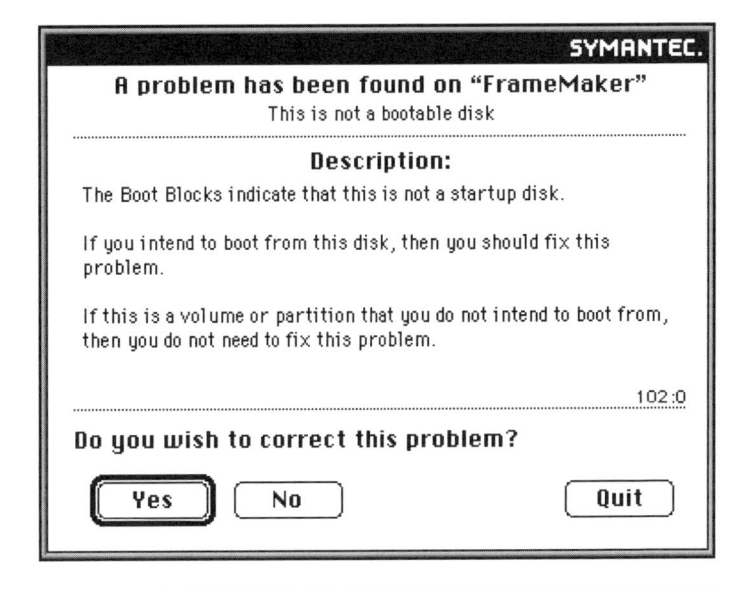

Figure 10.13 A possible problem discovered by Norton Disk Doctor

FileSaver has been installed, Volume Recover uses it to identify what files were on the disk (see Figure 10.15). Otherwise, it can scan the disk to look for disk directory information or look for markers that indicate a specific type of file. Once files have been located, Volume Recover works much like UnErase, giving the user a chance to indicate which files should be saved. Because Volume Recover can only be effective if a disk hasn't been written to after the damage or accidental format occurred, you cannot recover files to the disk you are recovering. This means you must have some other disk (floppy, removable, or fixed hard) to which you can save the recovered files.

The most powerful and potentially dangerous module in the Norton Utilities package is the Norton Disk Editor. The Disk Editor allows a user to view and modify the contents of a disk on the bit and byte level. Using it to look at a disk does no damage, but be very careful when using it to modify disk contents. It's not difficult to corrupt a file in such a way that it becomes inaccessible. If you want to experiment, be sure you do it with a copy of the file rather than the original.

The Disk Editor can provide a fascinating view of disk contents. For example, in Figure 10.16, you can see the contents of a disk's boot blocks. Because this particular disk—named System—contains a system folder, its boot blocks have data in them. Clicking on each entry in the display produces a description of what the parameter means. In Figure 10.16, for example, you can see a description of the disk's Signature Bytes.

Disk Editor can also show you the contents of the Catalog and Extents files as well as the master directory block (called the *Volume Info Block* by Norton Utilities). In fact, the scroll bar at the top left of the window (under the words *Absolute Sector*) can step you

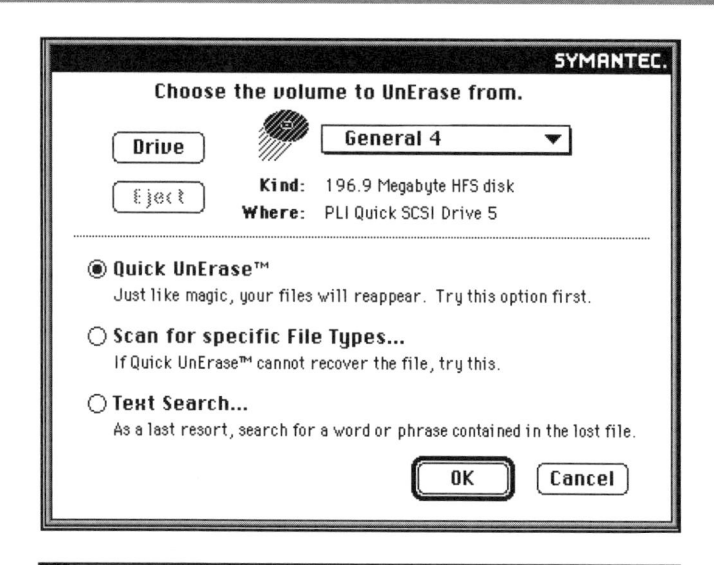

Figure 10.14 Recovering deleted files

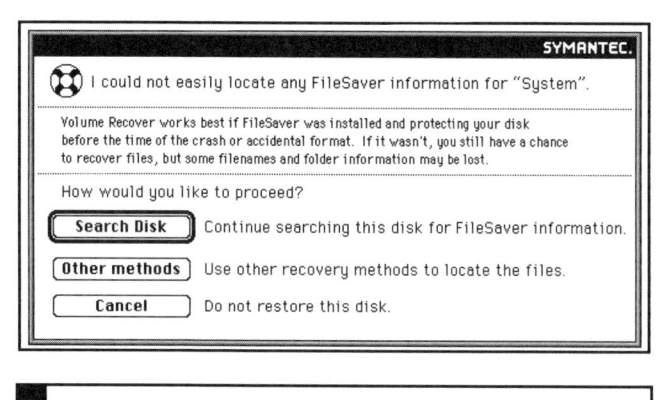

Figure 10.15 Recovering a damaged or accidentally formatted volume

through the disk sector by sector. It's a great way to learn about the structure of a disk.

Other than the disk directory files, the contents of a disk appear as their hexadecimal and character equivalents. In Figure 10.17, for example, you can see a portion of a word processing file. The two left columns are the offsets of each row of bytes within the file. The next four columns are the hexadecimal representations of the file's contents. Those values are translated into characters in the right column. As you can see, the first part of the file consists of header information that doesn't make much sense except to the word processor. The actual content of the document begins with "For most...."

Editing the file is dangerously easy. All you need to do is click on a byte—a "00" is highlighted in Figure 10.17—and type its new contents. You certainly could change the text of the document without damaging anything, but if you were to change the header information, the document might be unrecognizable to the program that created it. Because a disk editor is so potentially destructive, use such tools with great care.

In addition to its disk diagnostic, repair, and recovery features, Norton Utilities provides several other disk management utilities, including the following:

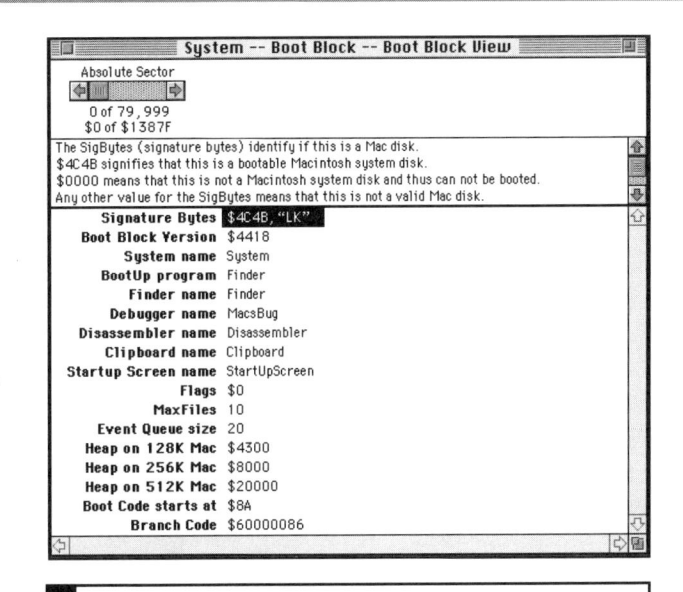

Figure 10.16 Examining the contents of the boot blocks

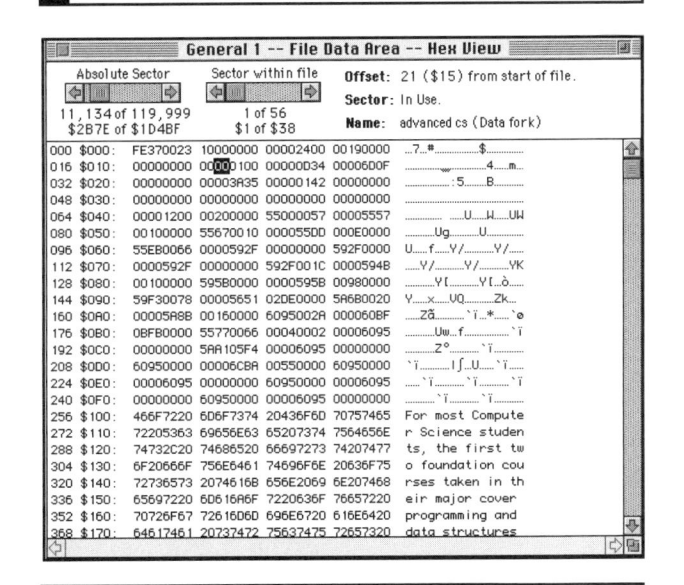

Figure 10.17 Editing the contents of a disk

- **Directory Assistance II** (customizes the Open File and Save File dialog boxes)
- **Fast Find** (searches for files and folders)
- **Floppier** (copies floppy disks)
- **DiskLight** (monitors disk I/O activity)
- **Speed Disk** (defragments and optimizes disks)
- **Norton Partition** (partitions hard disks)
- **Norton Backup** (makes backup copies onto floppies, cartridges, or other hard disks)
- **Wipe Info** (physically erases a disk)
- **Norton Encrypt** (encrypts data to provide security for files)

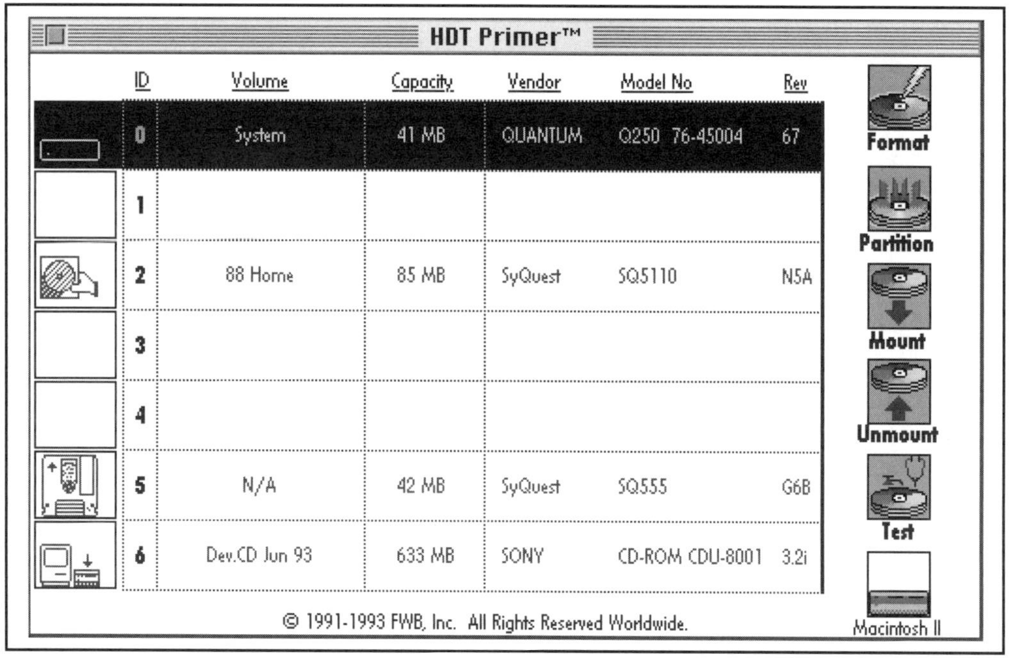

Hard Disk ToolKit

FWB's Hard Disk ToolKit (HDT) provides a set of utilities to diagnose, repair, and control SCSI devices connected to the Macintosh's native SCSI bus. (It cannot access devices connected to NuBus or PDS SCSI accelerator cards.) The central utility—HDT Primer—can be used by knowledgeable Macintosh users to format, partition, test, and in some cases repair fixed and cartridge hard drives. Low-level control SCSI control is provided by the World Control module, which is aimed at expert users.

HDT recognizes all SCSI devices on the Macintosh's native SCSI bus. For example, the SCSI bus in Figure 10.18 has an internal hard drive (ID 0), an 88Mb SyQuest drive with a cartridge named "88 Home" (ID 2), a 44Mb SyQuest drive in which no cartridge is mounted (ID 5), and a CD-ROM player with a disc named Dev.CD Jun 93 (ID 6). Read-only devices such as the CD-ROM player can be mounted or unmounted, but not formatted, partitioned, or tested.

Figure 10.18 The HDT Primer main screen

HDT Primer's suite of tests (see Figure 10.19) includes four types of tests:

- **Read:** A read test reads data from a disk without making any changes.

- **Write:** A write test reads data from the disk and then writes the data it just read. Theoretically, this shouldn't destroy any data, but if there are bad blocks on the disk, HDT Primer won't be able to read and/or write those files. The test could also damage the data on a disk if power fails during the test. A complete backup of a disk is therefore a wise safeguard before performing any diagnostic that modifies a disk.

- **Verify:** Verification checks the disk without moving data into the computer.

- **Seek:** A seek test checks the positioning of the read/write heads over a block of data.

In addition, HDT Primer can initiate the SCSI self-test built into a SCSI drive to test the mechanics of the drive itself and test the RAM in those drives that have it.

HDT Primer can take care of bad blocks without reformatting the drive. When it encounters a bad block, it marks the block as bad and reallocates the space to an undamaged portion of the disk.

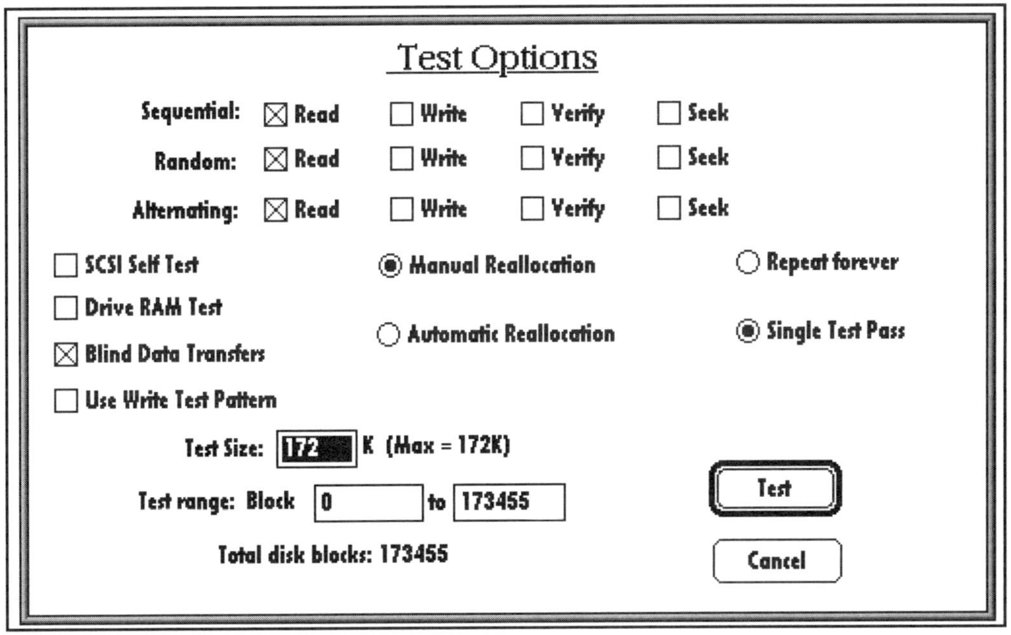

Figure 10.19 HDT Primer's disk drive test options

Although any data on the bad blocks may be lost, you won't need to go through the formatting process. (HDT's documentation suggests that if a drive has more than 10 bad blocks, you probably should reformat it anyway.)

World Control provides low-level access to a wide range of SCSI-1 and SCSI-2 parameters. Its Info option displays the drive's "geometry." As you can see in Figure 10.20, the data include the size of the disk's sectors, the number of sectors per track, its interleave, the total number of cylinders, the number of read/write heads, and the number of tracks per zone. (As you may remember, a zone is a group of tracks that have the same storage density.)

Changing SCSI parameters like those in Figure 10.21 with World Control can optimize the performance of a SCSI disk drive. However, you shouldn't attempt such modifications unless you are thoroughly familiar with their effect on the drive.

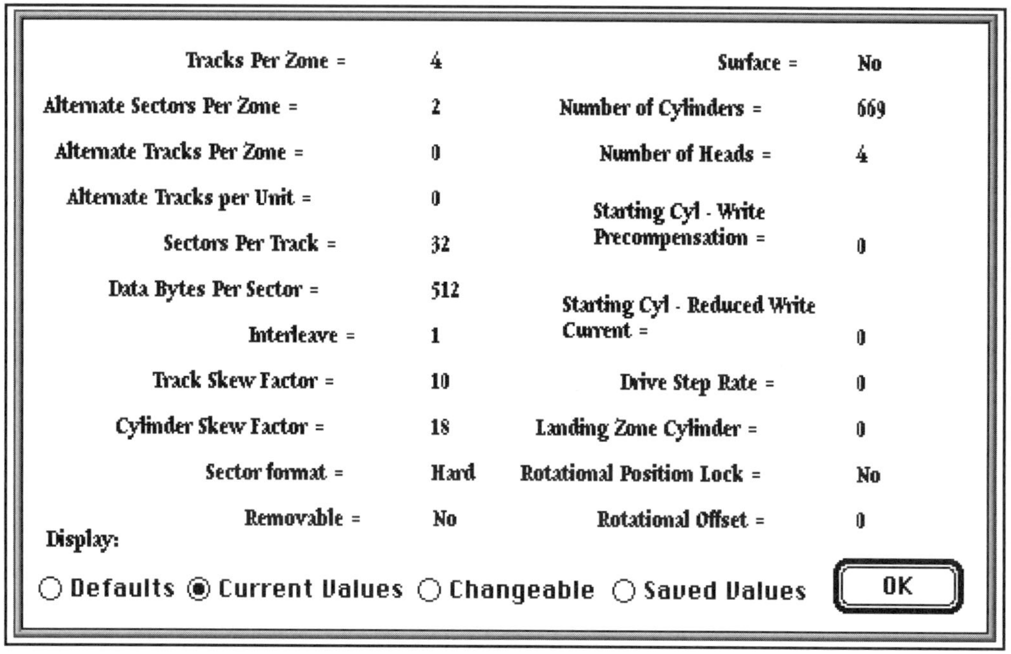

Tracks Per Zone =	4	Surface =	No
Alternate Sectors Per Zone =	2	Number of Cylinders =	669
Alternate Tracks Per Zone =	0	Number of Heads =	4
Alternate Tracks per Unit =	0	Starting Cyl - Write Precompensation =	0
Sectors Per Track =	32		
Data Bytes Per Sector =	512	Starting Cyl - Reduced Write Current =	0
Interleave =	1		
Track Skew Factor =	10	Drive Step Rate =	0
Cylinder Skew Factor =	18	Landing Zone Cylinder =	0
Sector format =	Hard	Rotational Position Lock =	No
Removable =	No	Rotational Offset =	0

Display: ○ Defaults ● Current Values ○ Changeable ○ Saved Values   [OK]

Figure 10.20 *Disk drive "geometry" displayed by HDT World Control*

In addition to HDT Primer and World Control, the Hard Drive ToolKit contains the following utilities:

- **HDT LightShow:** an INIT that monitors disk drive activity
- **HDT BenchTest:** a program that performs benchmark tests on hard disks, floppy disks, RAM disks, CD-ROM discs, optical drives, and disk drives accessible over a network. Although not precisely diagnostic tests, benchmarks collected over a period of time can indicate patterns in a drive's performance. Significant performance decreases are often an indicator of a problem.
- **HDT Util:** a program that copy-protects files
- **HDT Prober:** a control panel device for resetting the SCSI bus, mounting SCSI devices, and getting information about SCSI drives
- **HDT Extension:** an INIT that configures the way the Macintosh checks for SCSI drives during the system startup process. For example, it can instruct the Macintosh to wait while a SCSI drive spins up to full speed.

PROBLEMS WITH THE SCSI BUS

Some problems with reading from and writing to disks have nothing to do with

Chapter 10: Disk Storage

the disk itself. They arise from problems with the way in which SCSI devices are chained together. Creating a reliable SCSI chain like that in Figure 10.22 is more of an art than a science. In fact, it is often called "SCSI voodoo." Four factors can affect how well a SCSI chain operates: physical position in the chain, total length of cables in the chain, the SCSI ID numbers assigned to devices in the chain, and termination.

Physical Position in the Chain

Theoretically, it shouldn't matter where a device is physically placed in a SCSI chain. The Macintosh uses the device's SCSI ID to locate it. However, in reality, some devices are very fussy about where they are placed. CD-ROM drives and SCSI floppy drives are among the biggest culprits. If at all possible, try to place these types of devices in the middle of a SCSI chain, rather than at the end.

Total Length of Cabling

Theoretically, you can place up to seven SCSI devices in a single chain, although getting a chain of more than three devices to work reliably can often be a challenge. The total length of cable in the chain shouldn't exceed 18 feet; in most cases, you should try to keep it under 12 feet. When you are dealing with a chain of more than four devices, espe-

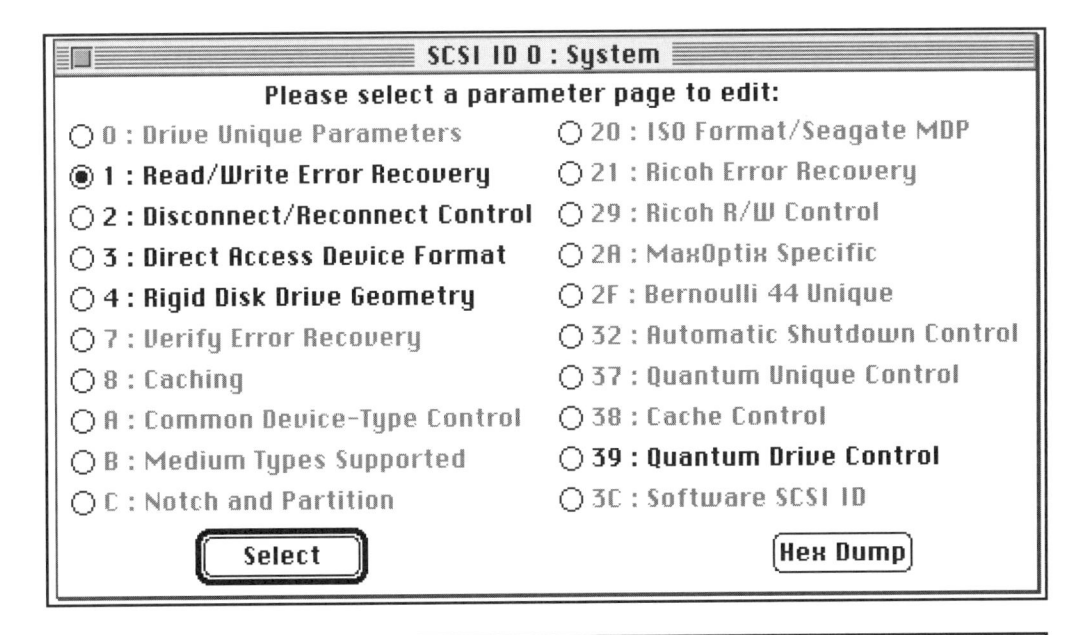

Figure 10.21 SCSI parameters accessible with HDT World Control

cially if you have termination problems, keeping the cable length short can be very difficult.

SCSI IDs

Each device in a SCSI chain has a unique SCSI ID number. If your Macintosh has an internal hard drive, that drive will always be device 0. All other devices must have unique numbers between 1 and 6. (The Macintosh itself is device number 7.) Notice in Figure 10.22, however, that SCSI addresses don't need to correspond to the physical placement of the device

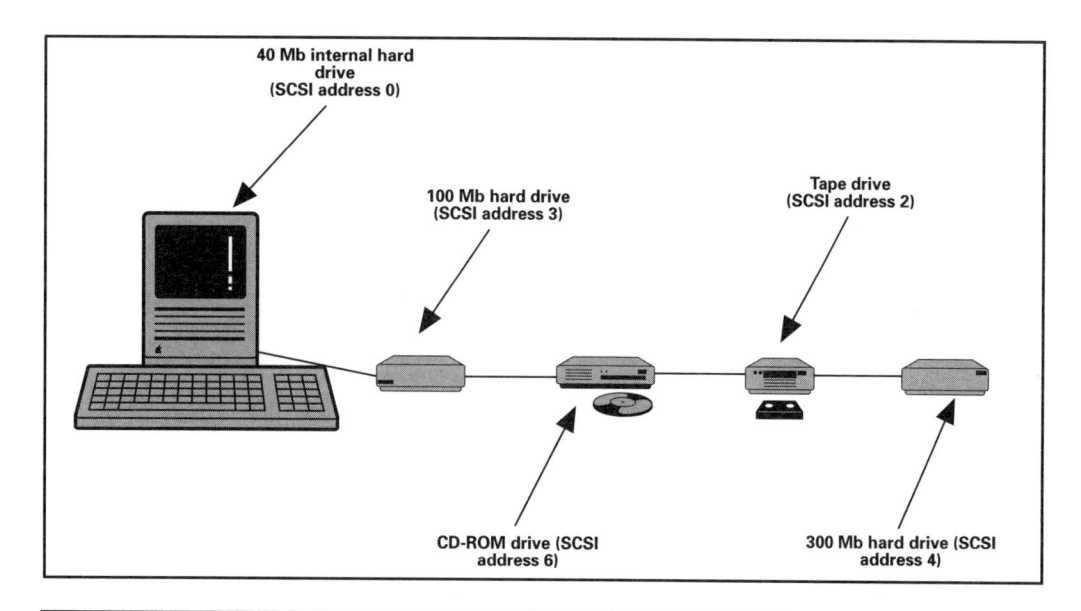

Figure 10.22 A SCSI chain

in the chain; the two are completely independent.

If you boot your Macintosh and see multiple icons for the same disk, then you should suspect duplicate SCSI IDs. The solution is to reset the SCSI IDs so that no two devices have the same ID. Most of today's SCSI devices have some external method for setting the SCSI ID, either a push-button or *dual in-line pin* (DIP) switches. In the case of DIP switches, you must often configure the switches so that they represent the binary equivalent of the SCSI ID you want to assign to the device.

SCSI Termination

SCSI terminators are small pieces of hardware that plug into SCSI devices to absorb signals that echo along the chain. Providing proper termination is usually the most difficult aspect of setting up a reliable SCSI chain. Termination problems can also be hard to diagnose, because SCSI chains that have worked reliably for some time can suddenly begin to exhibit read/write errors for no readily apparent reason. You should suspect termination problems when a SCSI chain begins to misbehave after a period of reliable performance, especially if no changes have been made to any part of the SCSI chain.

SCSI terminators can be external or internal. External terminators plug into one of the SCSI ports on a SCSI device and provide a connector for a SCSI cable. Internally terminated SCSI devices have the termination technology inside their cases. With most of today's SCSI devices, internal termination can be removed by pulling some resistors (easy to do) or setting DIP switches on the outside of the case. However, you may encounter an internally terminated device from which termination cannot be removed.

There are three different sets of rules for termination. The first applies to those

Macs that can handle only one internal SCSI device (all SCSI-equipped Macs except the IIvx and Performa 600, Quadra 800, 840av, 900, and 950 and the Centrises). General wisdom holds that only the first and last devices in a SCSI chain should be terminated. Some sample configurations can be found in Figure 10.23. If your Mac has only an internal drive (see Figure 10.23a), then that drive is terminated inside the computer. If you have only an external drive connected to a Mac without an internal drive (see Figure 10.23b), then the external drive should be terminated. In other words, if there is only one SCSI device on the chain, it should be terminated with a single terminator; a second terminator isn't required.

A Mac that has both an internal SCSI drive and a single external SCSI device (see Figure 10.23c) should have both devices terminated. Because the termination on the internal hard drive is installed when the drive is installed, you only need to worry about the external device. By the same token, a Mac with no internal hard drive and two external devices (see Figure 10.23d) should have both external devices terminated.

A typical configuration, however, usually includes an internal hard drive and several external devices (see Figure 10.23e). In that case, the last device in the chain

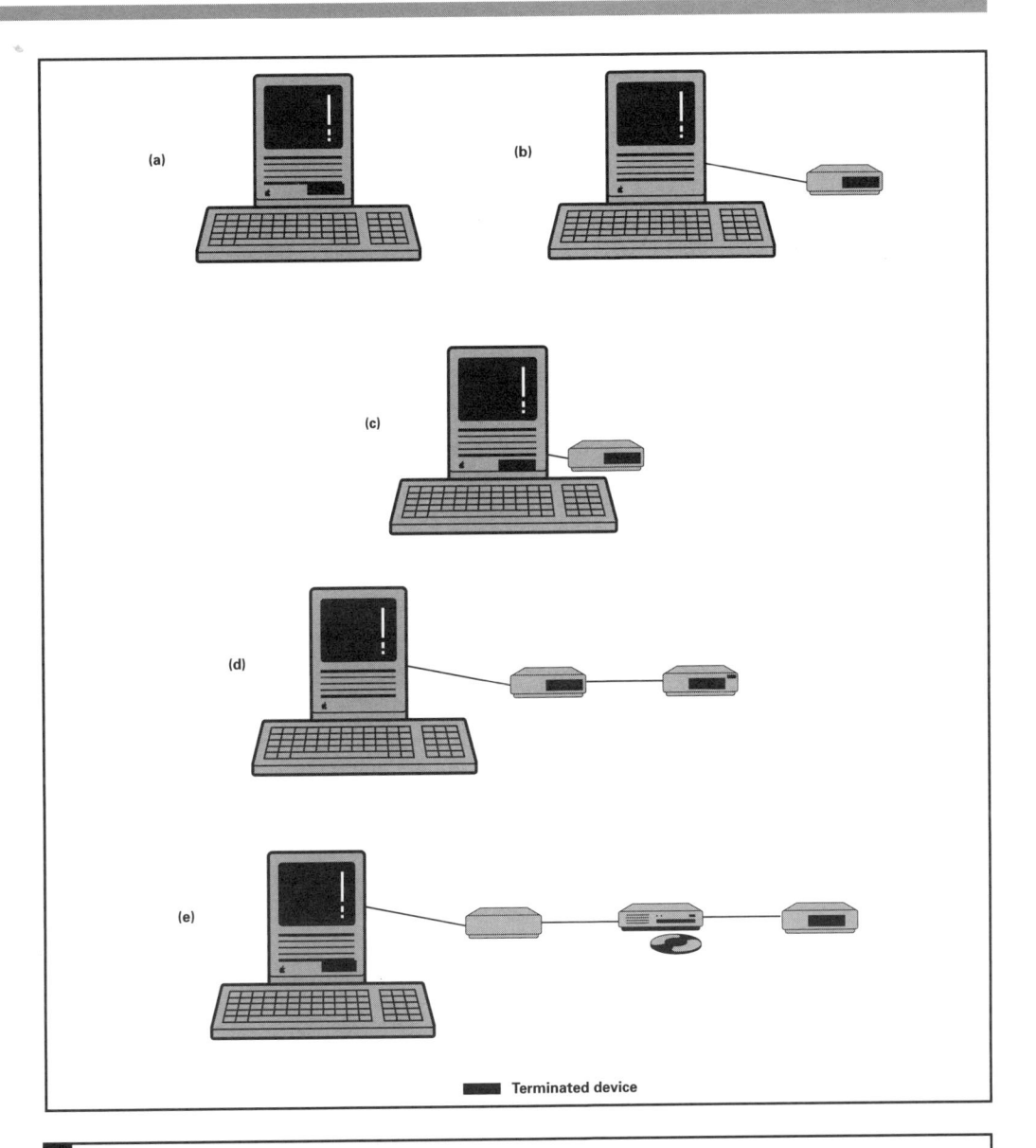

Figure 10.23 SCSI termination configurations

is terminated; the termination on the internal hard drive takes care of the termination requirements of the other end of the chain.

It is possible (although a bit tricky) to place three terminated devices on a SCSI chain. This situation can arise if you have an internal hard disk and two internally terminated external SCSI devices from which termination cannot be removed. To get such a chain to work reliably, the two terminated external devices must be the last two devices in the chain. The last device must be connected to the next-to-the-last device by a 6-foot cable; the next-to-the-last device must be connected to the device that precedes it in the chain or the computer (if there are no other SCSI devices) by another 6-foot cable. As you can see, you are already running into the limit on overall cable length.

By the way: Don't try to put more than three terminated SCSI devices in a chain; you won't be able to get it to work.

The Quadra 900 and 950 have two SCSI controller circuits, one for internal devices and one for external devices. Note that the Quadra 900 and 950 see all SCSI devices as one SCSI chain, limiting you to a total of seven devices, just like any other Mac. The internal SCSI cable is terminated at both ends; in other words, you don't need to add terminators when you add internal devices. The external portion of the SCSI chain is also terminated inside the computer. That means you need to terminate only the last external device.

The remaining Macs (IIv and Performa 600, Quadra 800, Quadra 840av, and the Centrises) use only one integrated circuit to handle both internal and external SCSI devices. The beginning of the internal portion of the SCSI chain is permanently terminated. If no external devices are present, the Mac automatically terminates the end of the internal SCSI chain. However, if an external device is present, the Mac detects it during the boot process and disables the second internal terminator.

The Macs that have the automatic terminator are very sensitive to the number of terminators on the internal portion of the SCSI chain. If no internal device is terminated, the computer won't function properly. If more than one internal device is terminated, there is a risk of damage to the logic board.

Not every type of Mac uses the same type of SCSI terminator. The IIfx uses terminators not found in any other Mac. If you have a IIfx or are considering upgrading a II or IIx to the IIfx, keep in mind that you will be unable to use internally terminated devices from which termination cannot be removed. In addition, if you are upgrading a II or IIx, you will need to replace all your existing external terminators.

SCSI Accelerators and SCSI-2

Given the speed of today's CPUs, one of the biggest bottlenecks in Macintosh performance is the rate at which data travel through the SCSI controller. One way to speed up your Mac therefore is to add a SCSI accelerator. Some SCSI accelerators can also provide you with a second SCSI chain, letting you attach 14 rather than seven SCSI devices. SCSI accelerators are primarily NuBus, although some do install in a PDS. Most are bus master boards that provide DMA capabilities.

The design of a SCSI controller is governed by a standard set of specifications. The Macintosh's internal SCSI bus is based on the SCSI-1 standard. The SCSI-2 standard, however, provides for significantly faster data transfer. Most SCSI accelerators therefore are based on all or part of the SCSI-2 standard.

SCSI-2 boards do work with SCSI-1 disk drives (the typical external SCSI drives you purchase for your Mac). However, they can't benefit from much of the speed improvement that SCSI-2 can bring, including Fast SCSI-2 (doubles the maximum data transfer rate, providing transfer rates of up to 10 megabits per second) and Wide SCSI-2 (transfers 16 rather than 8 bits at a time, providing transfer rates of up to 20 megabits per second). Ironically, there currently aren't any Macintosh-compatible disk drives that are built to the Wide SCSI-2 standard. However, Fast SCSI-2 drives are available (for example, from FWB). Coupling a SCSI accelerator that supports Fast SCSI-2 with a Fast SCSI-2 drive provides the fastest disk access with using a single disk (as opposed to a disk array).

Not all SCSI devices can be used with a SCSI accelerator. In most cases, you will be able to attach fixed hard disks and SyQuest drives. The other types of devices that are supported vary from one product to another.

A sampling of SCSI accelerators can be found in Table 10.1. Unless otherwise noted, all boards in the table are compatible with any NuBus-equipped Mac. Most of the boards in Table 10.1 sell for around $1,000. The major exception is the PLI QuickSCSI card. Although it supports only a few SCSI-2 features, it provides a controller for a second SCSI chain and some speed improvements for about $500.

Many SCSI accelerators come with software that allows you to set up *disk mirroring*, a technique for instantaneous backup. Disk mirroring requires two disk drives, one of which is maintained as the mirror image of the other. Everything that is written to the primary drive is also written to the mirror drive. The benefit of disk mirroring is that you always have a current backup of any work. However, because all disk output is written twice, it does slow down disk write activities.

Table 10.1 SCSI Accelerators

			FEATURES				
Manufacturer	*Model*	*Slot*	**Bus Master**	***Fast SCSI-2***	***Wide SCSI-2***	***Dual bus***	***Other***
ATTO Technologies	Silicon Express II	NuBus	Yes	Yes	No	Yes	
Dynatek	Mach II	NuBus	Yes	Yes	No	Yes	
FWB	SCSI Jackhammer	NuBus	Yes	Yes	Yes	Yes	128K RAM cache
Loviel	SCSI Bolt*	PDS	Yes	Yes	Yes	Yes	
Loviel	Arrow	NuBus	Yes	Yes	Yes	Yes	
MacProducts USA	Magic SCSI II	NuBus	Yes	Yes	No	Yes	
Mass Microsystems	Fast SCSI-2 Board	NuBus	Yes	Yes	Yes	No	
MicroNet Technology	SS series	NuBus	No	Yes	No	No	
MicroNet Technology	SB series	NuBus	No	Yes	No	No	
PLI	QuickSCSI	NuBus	No	No	No	Yes	
ProCom Technology	Nu 32 SCSI	NuBus	Yes	Yes	Yes	Yes	
Storage Dimensions	Data Cannon PDS	PDS	Yes	Yes[†]	Yes[‡]	No	

*This SCSI accelerator works only in the IIfx.
[†]Supported on versions for the Quadra and IIfx.
[‡]Supported on Quadra version only.

Video

Without some type of video screen, a Macintosh just isn't a Macintosh. Our primary mode of access to the Macintosh is visual; that's what makes its graphic user interface possible. Most Macintosh users are therefore concerned about the quality, size, and number of colors or grays that appear on their screens. This chapter begins by exploring the technology of the types of monitors used with Macintoshes, how colors and shades of gray are represented, and the relationship between video RAM and monitor capabilities. (Such a background will make it easier for you to evaluate monitors that you are considering for purchase.) This chapter then looks at video acceleration to provide faster screen redraws and at the addition of video RAM.

Monitor Technology

There are two types of monitors used with Macintoshes—*cathode ray tube* (CRT), found on desktop machines, and *liquid crystal display* (LCD), used in portables. Each has its own benefits and drawbacks that make it most suitable for a specific type of computer. Nonetheless, much of the terminology used to describe monitor characteristics is the same. This section therefore first looks at some of the terms used to describe monitors and their images and then turns to the technology of CRTs and LCDs.

Describing Monitors

Monitors are described in terms of their size and the sharpness of the image they can display. As with many things where computers are concerned, there is confusion and misinformation surrounding the way in which monitors are described.

Monitor size is expressed in terms of the diagonal measurement of the monitor, just as it is with television sets. For example, the monochrome monitor built into all compact Macs except the Color Classic has a 9-inch diagonal. The Color Classic's screen is measured as 10 inches. Nonetheless, the actual image area has the same 9-inch diagonal as the original monochrome. Why the measurement difference? Prior to the past few years,

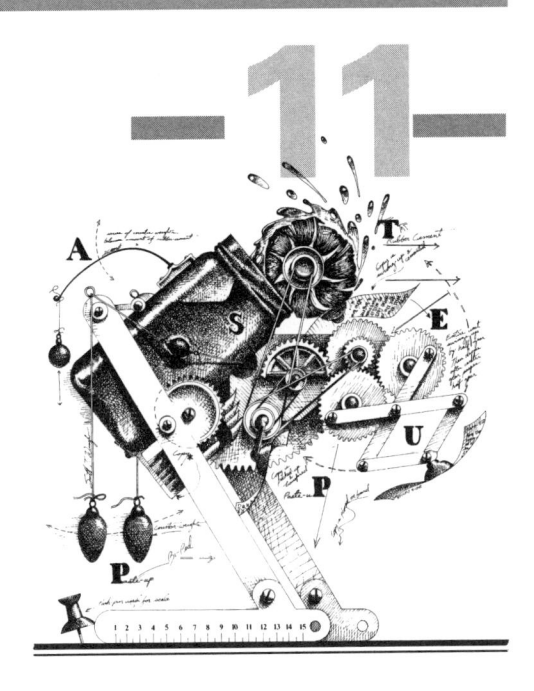

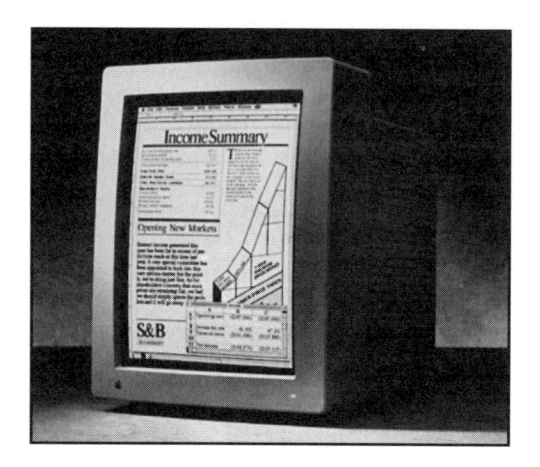

Figure 11.1 A full-page display

Figure 11.2 A 21-inch two-page display

U.S. manufacturers were required to indicate the diagonal of the image of a monitor; however, throughout the rest of the world, screen diagonal included all the glass visible in the monitor's case. Today, U.S. manufacturers are using the larger measurement. That means that most monitors that are advertised as 20-inch actually display an image with a 19-inch diagonal measurement. By the same token, 13- and 14-inch monitors generally have the same image area; a 12-inch monitor has a smaller image area.

A monitor with a 15-inch diagonal such as that in Figure 11.1 can display one full 8.5- × 11-inch page. It is therefore often called a *full-page display*; it is also known as a *portrait display* because the page is displayed in upright, or portrait, orientation.

To see a full two pages of text, you need a 21-inch monitor (Figure 11.2); monitors with 19-inch diagonal images display slightly less than two pages. (Nonetheless, 19-, 20-, and 21-inch monitors are all known as *two-page displays*.) Smaller monitors, such as the 13-inch in Figure 11.3, can generally display the full width of a page but less than the full length.

By the way: The bigger a monitor, the heavier it gets. A 13-inch color monitor weighs up to 35 pounds, light enough to sit on the top of a modular Mac. However, a 20-inch color monitor weighs nearly 90 pounds. If you are contemplating purchasing a two-page display, make sure you have enough desk space for it; don't count on being able to put it on top of your system unit.

Regardless of the technology used to create the display on a monitor's screen, the image is created from a pattern of dots. Because the dots are very small, the human eye perceives the pattern as objects rather than as individual dots. (Yes, this is exactly the same as the principle behind dot matrix and laser printers.)

Each dot on a monitor screen is known as a *picture element*, or *pixel*. The closer together the pixels (in other words, the higher the pixel density), the better the quality of the image. Pixel density, measured in *dots per inch* (dpi), identifies the *resolution* of the monitor. The most common resolution used by Macintosh monitors is 72 dpi. (This is the same resolution that you get when you print on an ImageWriter printer; laser printers generally print at either 300 or 600 dpi.)

Resolution is one of those terms that is often misunderstood and misused. It should be used to describe pixel density. However, it is also misused to describe the total pixels on a monitor. The problem with this is that two monitors with the same number of pixels will have different resolutions if they are of different sizes. For example, a 13-inch monitor that is 640 x 480 pixels will have a higher resolution than a 16-inch monitor with the same number of pixels. Therefore when looking at a monitor's specifications, consider both the pixel density (resolution) and the total number of pixels (overall size of the image relative to the resolution).

By the way: Some Macintosh monitors can switch between multiple resolutions. Such monitors use the higher resolutions to provide a larger Desktop with lower quality images.

CRT Displays

The displays used with desktop Macintoshes are based on CRTs. A CRT provides a brighter, crisper image than an LCD. However, the CRT requires much more power and is much larger and heavier, making it ideal for a desktop machine but unsuitable for a portable.

A CRT display takes its name from the big tube on which an image is displayed (what we often call a *picture tube*). The tube's interior is a vacuum. The inside of its screen is coated with chemicals known as *phosphors*, which light up when they are struck by an electron beam. The other end of the tube (the narrow end) therefore has a source of electrons (a gun).

Monochrome and Grayscale CRTs

Monochrome and grayscale monitor screens are coated with a single color phosphor. They also have one electron gun (see Figure 11.4). The beam of electrons is shot through a thin metal plate

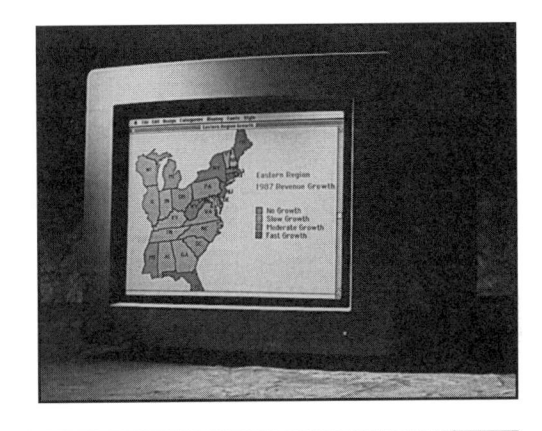

Figure 11.3 A 13-inch display

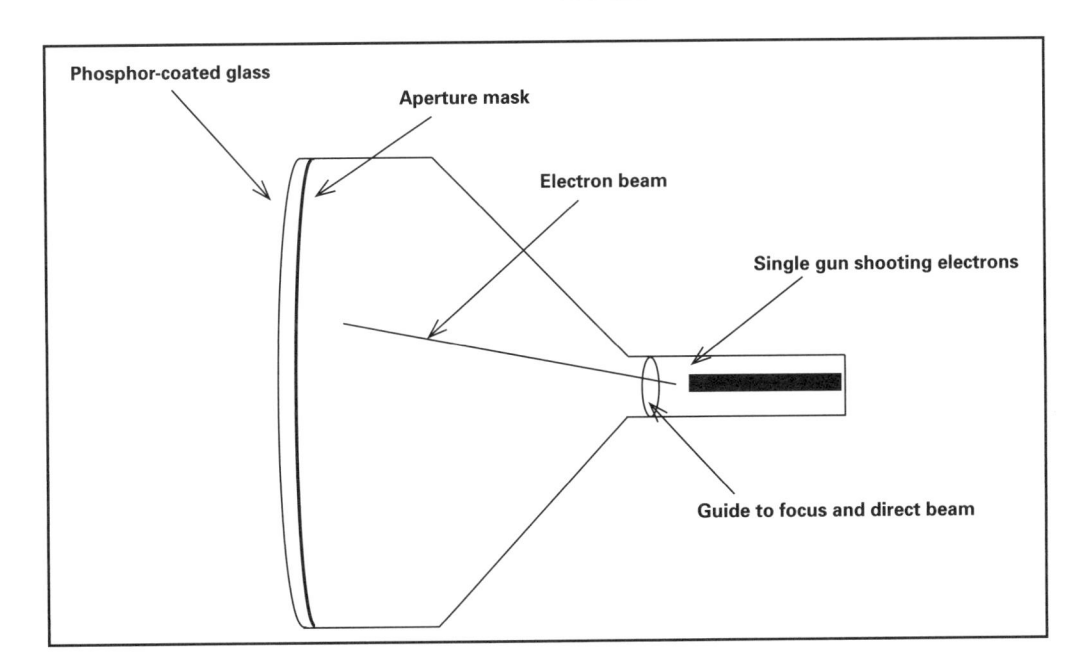

Figure 11.4 A monochrome/grayscale CRT

Fix Your Own Mac: *Upgrading and Troubleshooting*

(the *shadow mask* or *aperture mask*) that is punctured with tiny holes. Each hole represents a pixel. When the electron beam passes over a hole in the shadow mask, it reaches through it to a phosphor on the monitor screen, lighting that phosphor. For a monochrome monitor, the electron beam always has the same intensity; for a grayscale monitor, the electron beam varies in intensity, thus changing the brightness with which the phosphor glows.

The electron beam can light only one pixel at a time. It therefore moves across the screen from the screen's right to the screen's left (see Figure 11.5), lighting only those pixels necessary to create the screen image. When the electron beam reaches the left edge of the screen, it is turned off and moved back to the right edge (a *retrace*), where it begins the right to left sweep again, one pixel below the previous line. (The retrace movement is much faster than creating part of the screen image.) Creating a screen image in this way is known as *raster scanning*.

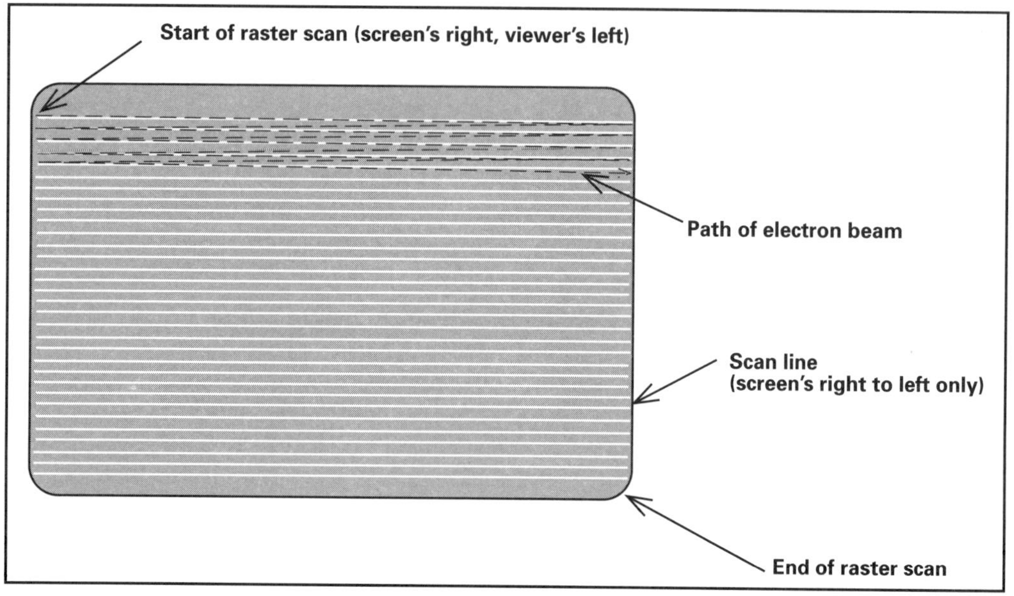

Unfortunately, phosphors don't retain their glow; they begin to fade very quickly once the electron beam is removed. Therefore the pattern on the screen must be refreshed frequently (30 to 60 times a second) so that the image on the screen remains visible, without fading. When the electron beam reaches the lower left corner of the screen, it is turned off and moved to the top right corner, from where it can begin the raster scan again. The time interval to move the electron beam from bottom left to top right is known as a *frame*.

By the way: The resolution of television sets is usually expressed in terms of "lines of resolution." This refers to the number of raster scan lines on the screen. Given the same size of screen, the more scan lines, the closer together

Figure 11.5 *Raster scanning*

the lines will be and the higher the resolution. (Although there's no reason television resolution couldn't be described in terms of dots per inch, it simply isn't.)

The size of the holes in a monitor's shadow mask is related to the monitor's resolution: The smaller the holes, the higher the resolution. Hole size is expressed in terms of a ratio called *dot pitch*. A high-resolution monitor will have a dot pitch of .28 millimeters or less.

Color CRTs

The image on a color CRT is created with the same raster scan movement as that on a monochrome or grayscale monitor. However, the inside of the CRT screen is coated with phosphors of three colors rather than with a single color.

A color image is created by mixing varying amounts of the primary colors red, green, and blue (which is why color monitors are often called *RGB monitors*). If you are used to mixing colors with crayons or paints, then this probably contradicts what you know about primary colors (red, blue, and yellow). When you mix colors with crayons or paints, the colors are *added* to one another to form a new color. For example, yellow and blue form green. If you mix all colors together, you form black; if no colors are present, you have white (the absence of color).

However, when you project a color onto a screen, placing one color on top of another blocks light, *subtracting* one color from another. For example, red and green on top of one another form yellow. If all three primary colors are present in the same intensity, all light is blocked, producing white (all colors); if no colors are present, all light gets through, producing black.

A color monitor therefore has red, green, and blue phosphors, one set of three for each pixel. The shape of those phosphors and the way in which they are lit depends on the type of monitor. Conventional color monitors use three electron guns, one focused on each color phosphor (Figure 11.6). The beams themselves are colorless; the actual color is formed by the intensity of each beam, which determines the percentage of each color that makes up a given pixel.

To provide a good color image, the three electron guns in a conventional color CRT must be focused precisely together on each pixel (*convergence*). If they aren't, you may see ghosts of the color that is out of alignment beside images on the screen. Diagnostic software such as Snooper tests convergence. You can then use controls (generally located on the back or side of a monitor) to adjust the monitor, watching the test pattern displayed by the diagnostic software change until the convergence is correct.

Figure 11.6 A three-gun color CRT

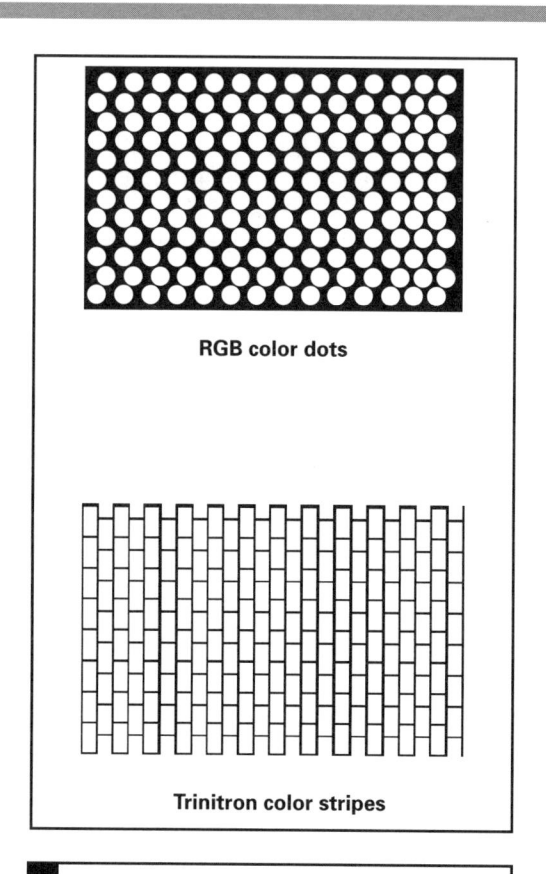

Figure 11.7 Color dots versus color

The major alternative to conventional color CRTs is the Trinitron CRT. Developed by Sony, the Trinitron uses only a single electron gun, just like a monochrome or grayscale monitor. However, instead of a shadow mask, it has an *aperture grill* that focuses the single electron beam on rectangular color stripes. Because there is only one electron gun, convergence isn't an issue. Because the color stripes and the holes in the aperture grill are rectangular, there is less wasted space between pixels on the screen than there is with the round holes in an aperture mask (for example, see Figure 11.7).

Many people believe that a Trinitron tube provides a sharper, cleaner image than a conventional CRT. (They also tend to cost a bit more than conventional CRTs.) In most cases, Trinitron monitors are identified as such in advertisements and product literature. If you aren't sure, be sure to ask the manufacturer or dealer before you buy.

By the way: A Trinitron tube has a thin wire running across the width of the screen about three-quarters of the way down the screen. This stabilization wire is often visible. (It depends on what patterns/colors are displayed on the screen.) Although it is a necessary part of the monitor, some people find its presence distracting.

LCD Displays

Because they are light and thin and don't require much power, LCDs are the display of choice for portable computers. They are also used in panels that project the image from a Macintosh onto a wall or free-standing screen.

An LCD screen is a sandwich of materials (see Figure 11.8). In the center is a layer of semiliquid crystals with a rod-shaped molecular structure. When no current is applied, the crystals form a somewhat random, twisted lattice that lets light pass through without obstruction. These crystals are surrounded on one side by vertical electrodes and on the other by horizontal electrodes. The electrodes form a grid; each intersection of a vertical and horizontal electronic represents a pixel.

The sandwich also includes two polarizing filters. When the rods in the liquid crystal are not aligned with the filters, light passes through the filters and is reflected back by the mirror, producing a light-colored pixel. However, when current is applied to the electrode grid, any pixel receiving current causes the crystal rods in the vicinity to change their orientation (to untwist). At that point, light is blocked by the filters, producing a dark pixel. The amount of current applied to a given pixel affects how much the crystals untwist. Monochrome LCDs use the same amount of current for each pixel; grayscale LCDs vary the amount of current.

In the simplest type of LCD, the light source comes from the screen's surroundings. This type of screen, used in the original Macintosh portable, requires very little power but doesn't produce a very bright image. The brightness of the image can be enhanced by supplying a light source at the back of the screen. Back-lighting does use more power than relying on a natural light source; however, it is required to produce an acceptable image that can be viewed in many surroundings.

There are two major LCD technologies: *passive matrix* and *active matrix*. A passive-matrix LCD sends current through its electrode grid one pixel at a time. Because the crystals begin to return to their original state as soon as the current moves on to the next pixel, passive-matrix LCDs aren't very bright or clear. Their displays must also be refreshed, just as CRT displays must be refreshed.

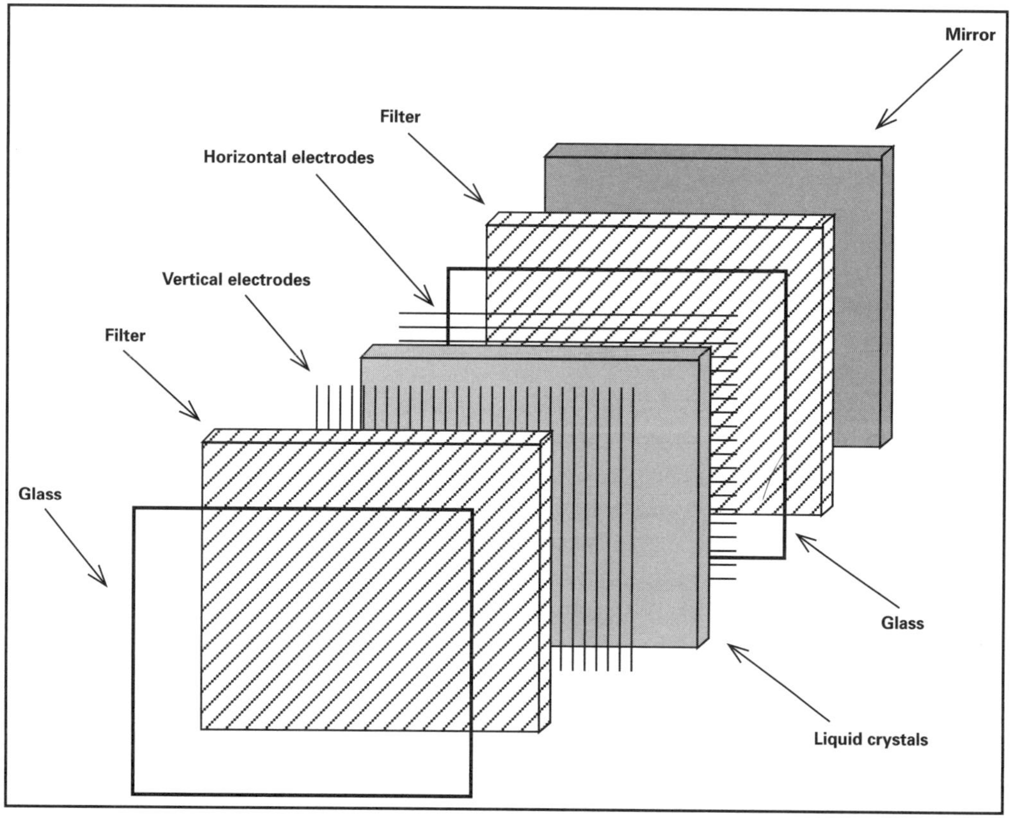

An active-matrix LCD has a transistor connected to each electrode. That means that current can be applied to all pixels at the same time. The current to an individual pixel can be turned on and left on as long as needed. Active-matrix LCDs are therefore brighter and sharper than passive-matrix LCDs. However, they consume more power, cutting down on the time a battery can power the computer before needing to be recharged.

A color LCD is considerably more complex than a monochrome or grayscale LCD. It has a film of colored stripes (red, green, and blue) placed between the front filter and glass. There is one set of three stripes for each pixel; there is also one vertical electrode for each stripe, tripling the number of vertical electrodes. To light a colored pixel, current is sent to the three stripes that form the pixel. The amount of current determines how much of each primary color is mixed into the final color of the pixel. This color mixing uses the same color subtraction principle as a color CRT; applying current blocks light, subtracting a percentage of a primary color from the color of the pixel.

Because color LCDs have more electrodes, they require more power than monochrome or grayscale LCDs. By the same token, a passive-matrix color LCD,

Figure 11.8 The composition of a monochrome or grayscale LCD screen

such as that used in the PowerBook 165c, uses less power than an active-matrix color LCD such as that used in the PowerBook 180c. However, the active-matrix LCD provides a sharper and brighter image.

Representing Colors and Shades of Gray

To manage its screen display, the Macintosh maintains a representation of every pixel on the screen in RAM. In earlier Macs, part of the regular RAM is used for the screen bit-map; in newer Macs, special video RAM is used. Video RAM means that you don't lose main memory space for video support. This has become particularly important as the number of colors and size of video displays has increased. The larger the video screen, the more pixels on the screen, and the more colors or shades of gray you use, the more memory is needed to represent the image. To understand why this is so, you need to know something about how colors are represented.

A monochrome monitor can use 1 bit to represent each pixel on the screen. A bit value of 0 represents a black pixel; a bit value of 1 represents a white pixel. The original 9-inch monochrome monitor, with its 72-dpi resolution, is 512 pixels across and 342 pixels down. It therefore takes 175,104 bits, or 21,888 bytes, to represent the entire screen image. Because it requires only 22K RAM, Macs with a 9-inch monochrome screen don't need video RAM; the 22K is a very small bite out of the machine's total storage.

Storage needs change dramatically when you introduce color or shades of gray; it's no longer possible to use 1 bit per pixel. Instead, the number of bits per pixel depends on how many colors or shades of gray your monitor is displaying. The Macintosh has a palette of several billion colors. When you set the number of colors from the monitors control panel, you determine how many of those colors can be seen at any one time. Depending on your video hardware, you may be able to display up to 256 shades of gray and/or 16.7 million colors. (Given the same number of colors and shades of gray, the screen image requires the same amount of memory regardless of whether you are working with color or grayscale.)

By the way: Setting the number of colors only affects how many can be seen at any one time. It doesn't indicate exactly which colors can be seen; that is usually under application program control.

To handle colors and shades of gray, the Macintosh numbers the colors or shades of gray it is using, beginning with 0. For example, if a monitor is currently displaying 16 colors, it numbers them from 0 to 15, using the binary number system. Because it takes 4 bits to represent the values 0 through 15, each pixel on the screen requires 4 bits in memory. A 13- or 14-inch color monitor with 640 pixels across and 480 pixels down has 307,200 pixels. At 4 bits per pixel, it takes 1,228,800 bits, or 153,600 bytes, to represent the screen image. However, a 21-inch monitor with 1,152 pixels across and 970 pixels down (1,117,440 total pixels) requires 4,469,760 bits, or 558,720 bytes.

When you go to 256 colors or shades of gray, the Macintosh needs 8 bits to hold a color number (*8-bit color*). (In binary, 8 bits hold the values 0 through 255.) That means that the 13- or 14-inch color monitor needs 307,200 bytes to represent its image; the 21-inch monitor needs 1,117,440 bytes.

The maximum number of colors supported by current video hardware is 16.7 million. It takes 24 bits per pixel to represent those colors (*24-bit color*). On a 13- or 14-inch monitor, the storage requirements are 921,600 bytes (almost 1Mb); the 21-inch monitor requires 3,352,320 bytes (more than 3Mb).

There are two generalizations you can draw from these numbers:

- The more colors or shades of gray displayed, the more storage needed to represent the image.

- The higher the number of pixels on a screen, the more storage needed to represent the image. (As you will remember, two monitors of the same size do not necessarily have the same number of total pixels.)

The high storage requirements of color and grayscale displays would take a considerable chunk out of RAM, especially in machines with 4Mb or less of main memory. The potential impact on main storage becomes even greater when you consider that most Macintoshes can accept more than one monitor. As a result, Macintoshes that support color and grayscale displays use special video RAM for storing screen bit-maps. If your Macintosh has video support on the motherboard, then that circuitry includes some video RAM and perhaps video RAM expansion slots. If your Macintosh has no video support on the motherboard, then video RAM is part of any video expansion boards you add.

How many colors/shades of gray do you need? Although 24-bit color is considered "true color," it isn't necessary for most applications. In fact, unless you are working with photographs, you probably don't need more than 8-bit color.

ADDING VIDEO RAM

If your Macintosh is one of those that has video circuitry on its motherboard, you can often increase the number of colors or shades of gray as well as the size of the monitor your computer can support by adding video RAM. Video RAM comes on a circuit board that looks much like a SIMM and usually can be purchased from any dealer that sells SIMMs.

Video RAM for the Color Classic

The Color Classic ships with 256K video RAM soldered to its motherboard. This supports up to 256 colors/shades of gray on its 10-inch screen. You can add another 256K (maximum of 512K) in an expansion slot to give you 32,768 colors. (Regardless of how much video RAM you have, you can't get more than 256 shades of gray.) As you can see in Figure 11.9, the video RAM slot is just behind the SIMM slots.

Video RAM for the LC, LC II, and Performa 400, 405, and 430

The LC, LCII, and Performa 400, 405, and 430 are shipped with a 256K video RAM card in their video RAM slot. This supports 256 colors or shades of gray on a 12-inch monitor but only 16 colors or shades of gray on a 13-inch monitor. This can be expanded to 512K (providing up to 32,767 colors on a 12-inch monitor and 256 colors or shades of gray on a 13-inch monitor) by replacing the 256K video RAM card with a 512K video RAM card. As in the Color Classic, the video RAM slot is just behind the SIMM slots (see Figure 11.10).

Video RAM for the LC III and Performa 450

The LC III and Performa 450 have 512K video RAM soldered on the motherboard, which supports 32,767 colors on a 12-inch display and 256 colors or shades of gray on 13-, 14-, and 16-inch monitors. A 256K video RAM board can be added to provide 32,767 colors on a 12-, 13-, or 14-inch monitor. It is placed in the LC III/Performa 450's single video RAM slot (see Figure 11.11).

Video RAM for the IIvi, IIvx, and Performa 600

The Macintosh IIvi, IIvx, and Performa 600 have 512K video RAM soldered to their motherboards, providing up to 256 colors/shades of gray on 12- or 13-inch monitors. The two video RAM slots can each be filled with a 256K video RAM board, bringing the total to 1Mb and providing for up to 32,767 colors on 12- and 13-inch displays. The two video RAM slots are located at the lower left of the motherboard (see Figure 11.12).

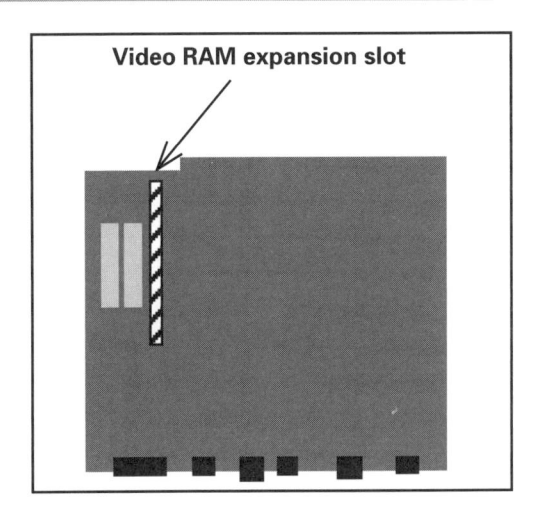

Figure 11.9 Location of video RAM slot in the Color Classic

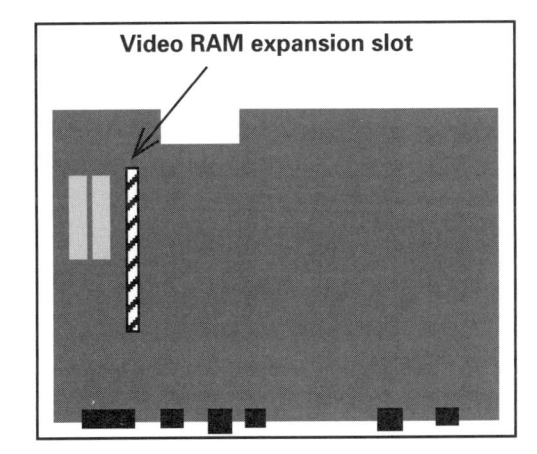

Figure 11.10 Location of video RAM slot in the LC, LC II, and Performa 400, 405, and 430

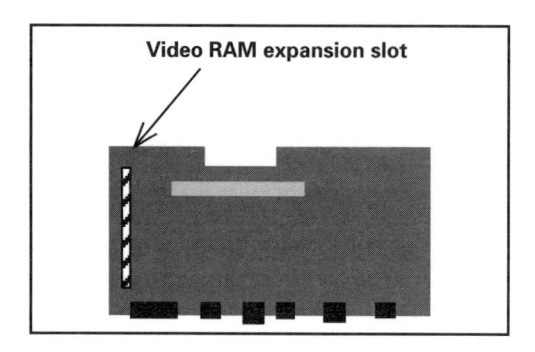

Figure 11.11 Location of video RAM slot in the LC III and Performa 450

Figure 11.12 Location of video RAM slots in the IIvi, IIvx, and Performa 600

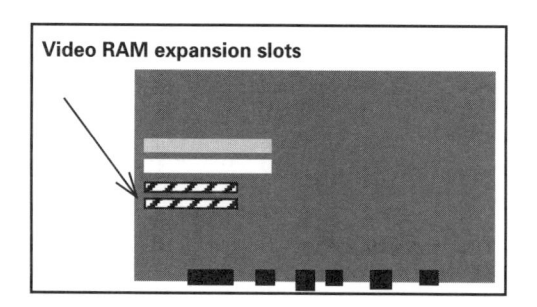

Figure 11.13 Location of video RAM slots in the Centris 610

Video RAM for the Centris 610

The Centris 610 ships with 512K video RAM soldered to its motherboard, supporting 32,768 colors on a 12-inch monitor, 256 colors/shades of gray on a 13- or 14-inch monitor, and 16 colors/shades of gray on a portrait display or 21-inch monitor. Placing a 256K video RAM board into each of the two video RAM expansion slots brings the total to 1Mb, providing 32,767 colors on monitors up with 16 inches and 256 colors/shades of gray on portrait displays and 21-inch monitors. The video RAM slots are located just below the SIMM slots (see Figure 11.13).

Video RAM and the Centris 660av

The Centris 660av has 1Mb of video RAM soldered to its motherboard. This provides 32,768 colors on a 12-inch monitor, 16,738 colors on monitors up to 16 inches, and 256 colors/shades of gray on monitors up to 21 inches. However, the Centris 660av has no video RAM expansion slots. You must therefore either live with the 1Mb of video RAM or use a NuBus slot to hold a third-party video board that provides more video RAM.

Video RAM for the Centris 650 and Quadra 800

The Centris 650 and Quadra 800 each have 512K video RAM soldered to their motherboards. Like the Centris 610, that base configuration supports 32,767 colors on a 12-inch monitor, 256 colors/shades of gray on a 13- or 14-inch monitor, and 16 colors/shades of gray on a portrait display or 21-inch monitor. Placing a 256K video RAM board in each of the two video RAM expansion slots provides a full 1Mb. After the upgrade, the computer can produce 32,767 colors on monitors up to 16 inches in size and 256 colors/shades of gray on a portrait display or 21-inch monitor. The video RAM slots are at the left of the motherboard, at a right angle to the SIMM slots (see Figure 11.14).

Video RAM for the Quadra 700

Like a Centris, the Quadra 700 has 512K video RAM soldered onto its motherboard. However, it has four (rather than two) video RAM expansion slots. The base configuration provides 32,767 colors on a 12-inch monitor, 256 colors/shades of gray on a 13- or 14-inch monitor, and 16 colors/shades of gray on a portrait display or 21-inch monitor. Adding four 256K video RAM boards brings the total to 2Mb and provides 32,767 colors on monitors up to 21 inches. (Note that you must add video RAM boards two at a time.) The video RAM slots are just below the SIMM slots (see Figure 11.15).

Video RAM for the Quadra 900 and 950

The Quadra 900 and 950 have 512K video RAM soldered on their motherboards, providing 32,767 colors on a 12-inch monitor, 256 colors/shades of gray on a 13- or 14-inch monitor, and 16 colors/shades of gray on a 21-inch monitor. Adding four 256K video RAM boards to the four slots brings the total to 2Mb, making it possible to display up to 32,767 colors on monitors up to 21 inches. (Note that you must add video RAM boards two at a time.). The video RAM slots can be found along the right edge of the motherboard (see Figure 11.16).

Video RAM for the Quadra 840av

Because of its position as a high-end multimedia machine, the Quadra 840av supports a maximum of 2Mb video RAM. It has 1Mb video RAM soldered to its motherboard and four video RAM expansion slots (must be filled two at a time). The base configuration supports 32,767 colors on a 12-inch monitor, 16,738 colors on a 13- or 14-inch monitor, and 256 colors/shades of gray on a portrait display or 21-inch monitor. The full 2Mb of video RAM provides 32,767 colors on all monitors up to 21 inches. Assuming the back edge of the motherboard (the side with the ports) is facing you, the video RAM slots can be found along that back edge (see Figure 11.17).

Video Accelerators

There is an inverse relationship between monitor capabilities and the speed with which the Macintosh can update the screen: The more colors you use, the higher the resolution of the monitor, and the larger the monitor, the slower the screen redraw. If you work with high-end graphics or simply want faster scrolling of graphics documents, then you should consider adding a video accelerator.

Video accelerators are expansion boards that provide support for 8-bit (256 colors) and/or 24-bit color (16.7 million colors) and at the same time speed up redrawing the screen. They have their own processors and usually their own on-board video RAM. Most are NuBus

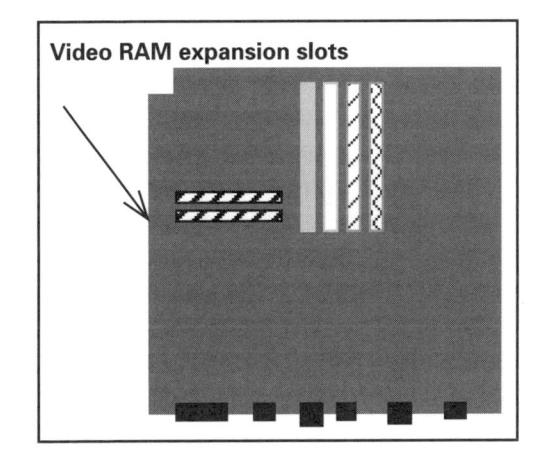

Figure 11.14 Location of video RAM slots in the Centris 650 and Quadra 800

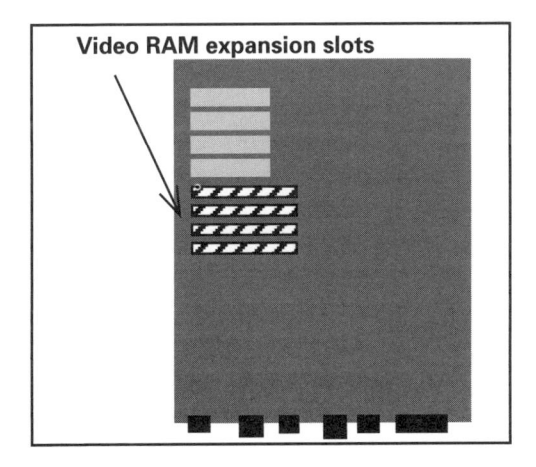

Figure 11.15 Location of video RAM slots in the Quadra 700

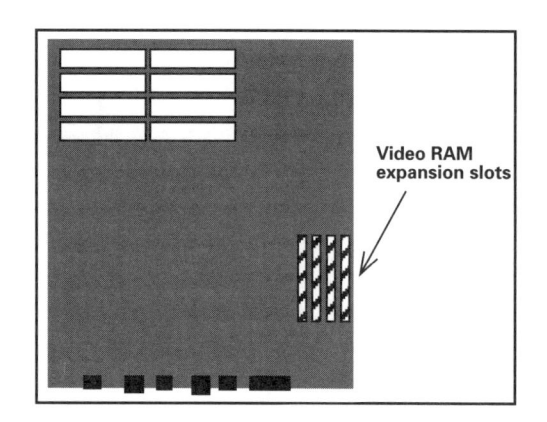

Figure 11.16 Location of video RAM slots in the Quadra 900 and 950

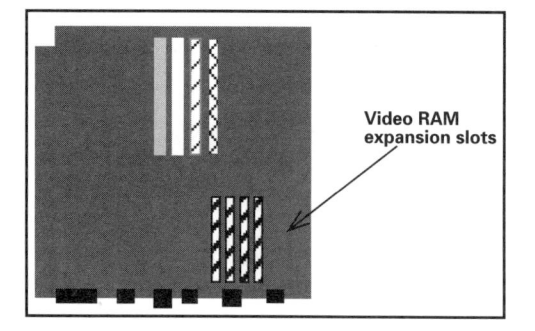

Figure 11.17 Location of video RAM slots in the Quadra 840av

boards, although a few are available for processor direct slots.

> **By the way:** Not all 24-bit video boards provide acceleration. If you are shopping for video accelerations, be sure that is exactly what you're buying.

There are three types of video accelerator boards. The first type accelerates *QuickDraw* operations. (QuickDraw is the group of programs in the Macintosh's ROM that draw, fill, size, and move objects.) The second accelerates specific operations in specific application programs. For example, many Adobe Photoshop operations don't use QuickDraw and therefore must be accelerated by special chips. The third type of accelerator combines both QuickDraw and application-specific acceleration.

Video boards (including video accelerators) do not necessarily work with every Macintosh monitor. In other words, there is a finite number of monitors that a given accelerator board can handle. When shopping for a video accelerator, make sure it works with your monitor or, if you are purchasing the monitor at the same time, that the board and monitor will work together.

A sampling of video accelerators can be found in Table 11.1. Most of these boards support multiple screen resolutions; some can switch resolution without rebooting the Macintosh. Notice that one board, the DayStar Charge, doesn't provide general QuickDraw acceleration. Instead, it is designed to accelerate specific applications such as PhotoShop. On the other hand, SuperMac's Thunder II and Thunder II light provide both QuickDraw and application-specific acceleration.

Chapter 11: Video

Table 11.1 Video Accelerators

Manufacturer	Model	Type of acceleration	Maximum Screen size 8-bit mode	Maximum Screen size 24-bit mode
DayStar	Charger*	Photoshop		
		Kodak Photo CD		
E-Machines	DoubleColor SX	QuickDraw	16-inch	
	Futura	QuickDraw		20-inch
Radius	UniversalColor24 0404	QuickDraw		16-inch
	UniversalColor24 0405	QuickDraw		20-inch
	PrecisionColor 24x	QuickDraw		21-inch
	PrecisionColor 24xk	QuickDraw		20-inch
	PrecisionColor 24xp	QuickDraw		17-inch
RasterOps	8XLi	QuickDraw	21-inch	
	24Sx Display Board	QuickDraw	13-inch	13-inch
	24Mx	QuickDraw		16-inch
	PaintBoard Li	QuickDraw	20-inch	20-inch
	24XLi	QuickDraw		21-inch
SuperMac	Spectrum/8 24 PDQ	QuickDraw	21-inch	13-inch
	ThunderLight	QuickDraw		21-inch
	Spectrum/24 Series IV	QuickDraw		20-inch
	Spectrum/24 PDQ Plus	QuickDraw	21-inch	21-inch
	Thunder II	QuickDraw		21-inch
		PhotoShop		
		Kodak Photo CD[†]		
	Thunder II Light	QuickDraw		21-inch
		Photoshop		
		Kodak Photo CD[†]		

*This board only accelerates specific applications; it does not provide QuickDraw acceleration.
[†]This board also accepts plug-in modules that accelerate other application programs.

Upgrading Older Macs

If you have an older Macintosh—the 128K, 512K, or 512Ke—your upgrade options are unfortunately very limited. All of today's upgrades require at least the 128K ROMs found in the Mac Plus. A 512Ke has those ROMs and an 800K disk drive. It therefore has some upgrade potential, although in most cases it won't be cost effective to upgrade. In fact, it probably isn't wise to sink any money into an older Mac at all; given the rate at which Macintosh technology is changing, even an upgraded older Mac still won't be able to deal with much of today's software. However, if you are determined to upgrade your older Mac rather than replace it, there are a few things you can do.

Dealing with a Macintosh 128K or 512K

Before you can even consider adding an accelerator board to a 128K or 512K Mac, you must add the 128K ROM/800K disk drive upgrade. Unfortunately, Apple no longer manufactures that upgrade. You therefore have the following alternatives:

- Use your Mac the way it is. If your Mac meets your needs, then this is the best option. However, current software is distributed on either 800K or 1.4Mb floppy disks. Without an external floppy drive that read 800K and/or 1.4Mb disks, you won't be able to add any software. The other major problem you will encounter with an unmodified 128K or 512K Mac is that current software generally requires more RAM than is installed in either of those machines.

- Look for a dealer in Macintosh parts that has the 128K ROMs and 800K disk drive available. Although possible, this option is very difficult. Most used parts dealers don't have ROMs that aren't already part of a motherboard. Keep in mind also that this doesn't give the computer any more RAM. The 128K and 512K Mac (and the 512Ke, for that matter) don't have SIMM slots. Memory expansion requires that a board be clipped or soldered onto the motherboard, but such memory expansion boards aren't being manufactured any more. The only feasible alternative is to add a CPU accelerator that provides room for SIMMs ($250 to $500 for the accelerator and $300 for 4Mb RAM). Adding the ROMs and disk drive also doesn't give you a SCSI port. SCSI ports cost around $115. Once you've added all these upgrades, your overall cost generally comes close to that of a new computer.

- Replace the motherboard with a Mac Plus motherboard (available for sellers of Macintosh parts). The Mac Plus motherboard costs about $250 and includes 128K ROMs, 1Mb RAM, a SCSI port, and the 800K disk drive. Keep in mind, however, that you can purchase a used Mac Plus for about $350. Dealers in used Macs will also take your 128K or 512K in trade, further reducing the cost of the Mac Plus. However, if you really need more computing power, then a Mac Plus isn't likely to meet your needs for very long. You can certainly add any upgrade that is available for the Plus, but when you add the cost of the Mac Plus to the cost of upgrades, you're spending as much as you would if you purchased a new computer. Replace the computer with either a Color Classic or an LC III. (The Classic II has little upgrade potential and therefore probably isn't a good investment at this point.)

To be brutally honest, an unmodified 128K or 512K has a lot of strikes against it. You can't load software directly from today's installation disks unless you have a higher-density external floppy drive. You can't run most current software or even System 6 because you don't have enough RAM. In addition, the power supplies in older Macs (including the 128K, 512K, 512Ke, and Plus) are notoriously bad. When a power supply fails, the most common remedy is to replace the entire board on which the power supply is located. The cost of a new power supply (about $150) plus all the other upgrades needed to make a 128K or 512K compatible with today's software will be more than the cost of a new computer.

DEALING WITH A MACINTOSH 512KE

Because the 512Ke has Mac Plus ROMs, it has several upgrade options. However, before you start adding things to the computer, consider the total cost carefully. In most cases, if you are adding more than one or two upgrades, it will cost less to purchase a new computer.

Macintosh 512Ke Accelerators

The 512Ke has no SIMM slots. Therefore the only way to increase its RAM is to add an accelerator board that includes SIMM slots. An accelerator board also provides the only opportunity to add a faster CPU, an FPU, and/or use virtual memory. Because it has a 24-bit address bus, the 512Ke can only address 16Mb of RAM. You will therefore be limited to a combined total of 16Mb real and virtual memory. In other words, if you place 4Mb RAM on an accelerator board, you can access another 12Mb of disk-based virtual memory. However, if you place 16Mb RAM on an accelerator board, there won't be any available virtual memory.

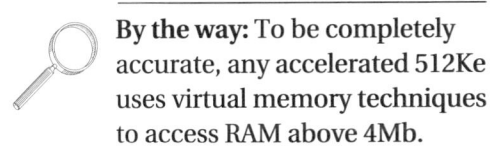

By the way: To be completely accurate, any accelerated 512Ke uses virtual memory techniques to access RAM above 4Mb. However, if more than 4Mb of physical RAM is installed on the accelerator board, access is faster than disk-based virtual memory because the virtual storage is actually physical RAM. Most CPU accelerators for the 512Ke are shipped with Virtual by Connectix, an INIT that provides virtual memory capabilities.

Most 512Ke-compatible accelerators include adapter circuits for an external monochrome monitor. The external monitor must be purchased separately. Sample accelerators for the 512Ke can be found in Table A.1. Although faster 68000 CPUs are available, they provide little advantage over the computer's original CPU other than providing a SCSI port and, in one case, video circuitry. If you do decide to upgrade rather then replace your 512Ke, choose a 68030 accelerator. Not only does a 68030 accelerator provide better performance, but it supports the maximum 16Mb RAM; a 68000 accelerator will only let you go to 4Mb.

Hard Disks for the Macintosh 512Ke

If a Macintosh 512Ke is upgraded with a SCSI port, then it can use any SCSI devices available for the Macintosh. However, without the SCSI port, there is only one hard drive option: the original HD 20, which connects to the external floppy drive connector. (An external floppy drive can be connected to the HD 20 so that you don't lose access to the second floppy drive.) As you might expect, the HD 20, which stores only 20Mb, hasn't been manufactured for years. However, it is an extremely reliable drive and can occasionally be found through used-Macintosh dealers.

Table A.1 Accelerators for the 512Ke

Manufacturer	Model	CPU	Speed	FPU	Features
NewLife	NewLife 1	68000	7.8MHz	Not available	RAM to 4Mb SCSI interface
NewLife	NewLife 2	68000	7.8MHz	Not available	RAM to 4Mb SCSI interface Video adapter circuits
NewLife	NewLife 25/33c	68030	25MHz	Included	RAM to 16Mb SCSI interface Video adapter circuits
Novy Systems	ImagePro	68030	16MHz	Optional	RAM to 16Mb Fan Power supply SCSI interface Video adapter circuits
Novy Systems	ImagePro	68030	25MHz	Optional	RAM to 16Mb Fan Power supply SCSI interface Video adapter circuits
Novy Systems	ImagePro	68030	33MHz	Optional	RAM to 16Mb Fan Power supply SCSI interface Video adapter circuits
Novy Systems	Quick30	68030	16MHz	Optional	RAM to 16Mb Installation retains access to 68000
Novy Systems	Quick30	68030	25MHz	Optional	RAM to 16Mb Installation retains access to 68000
Novy Systems	Quick30	68030	33MHz	Optional	RAM to 16Mb Installation retains access to 68000

Floppy Drives for the Macintosh 512Ke

Although most companies that manufacture Macintosh software are currently distributing their programs on 800K disks, that isn't likely to continue much longer. As you may have read in Chapter 10, in early 1994 Apple is planning to introduce several low-cost Macintoshes with floppy drives that aren't compatible with the traditional 400K and 800K Macintosh disks. (These will be single-speed drives that use the MFM encoding used in MS-DOS floppy disk drives.) Apple is therefore suggesting that all software vendors distribute their products on 1.4Mb disks, which can be read by both the SuperDrive and the new disk drives.

This disk drive switch means that even a 512Ke equipped with an accelerator board shortly won't be able to read the disks on which commercial software is distributed. (Although Apple suggests that software manufacturers provide a coupon that older Macintosh owners can mail in for 400K or 800K disks, such a solution certainly won't be convenient.) If you are upgrading and keeping your Macintosh 512Ke, you should seriously consider purchasing a SCSI floppy drive that handles 1.4Mb disks.

External Monitors for the Macintosh 512Ke

Assuming that you have installed an accelerator that includes video circuitry, the 512Ke can support a variety of external monochrome monitors. (Even with a 68030 CPU and software that runs in color or shades of gray, the 512Ke still can't produce a color or grayscale image because its ROMs don't support color.) Most of the accelerator board–based video circuitry will drive a full-page monitor. If you do a lot of word processing or page layout, then the full-page display can be very useful. Some accelerator boards, such as the ImagePro, also support 19-inch monitors, providing a view of nearly two full pages. (It takes a 21-inch monitor to display two entire pages side by side.)

The 512Ke Power Supply

The 512Ke suffers from the same power supply problems as the 128K, 512K, and Plus. Even if yours hasn't failed yet, it is likely to do so. If you are planning to upgrade your 512Ke, you should replace the power supply at the same time you add upgrades. Upgrades such as accelerator boards (especially those with video support) place a drain on the power supply that could trigger a failure. (Notice in Table A.1 that the accelerator boards from Novy Systems actually include a new power supply.)

Product/Vendor List

This appendix contains the names, addresses, and phone numbers of the manufacturers of the products mentionned in this book. It also includes listings for companies that buy, sell, and repair Macintoshes and Macintosh parts. The software listings are organized alphabetically by program name. Hardware listings are organized by vendor within general category.

Inclusion in this appendix does not constitute an endorsement of any product or vendor. Many product reviews can be found in *MacWorld*, *MacUser*, and *MacWEEK* magazines.

Software

Conflict Catcher
Casady & Greene, Inc.
22734 Portola Drive
Salinas, CA 93908-1119
Voice: (408) 484-9228

Crash Barrier
Casady & Greene, Inc.
22734 Portola Drive
Salinas, CA 93908-1119
Voice: (408) 484-9228

HDToolKit
FWB
2040 Polk St.
Ste. 215
San Francisco, CA 94109
Voice: (415) 474-8055

Help!
Teknosys, Inc.
3923 Coconut Palm Dr.
Ste. 111
Tampa, FL 33619
Voice: (800) 873-3494

MacEKG
Micromat Computer Systems
7075 Redwood Blvd.
Novato, CA 94945
Voice: (415) 898-6227
Fax: (415) 897-3901

Mode32
AppleComputer
20525 Mariani Ave.
Cupertino, CA 95014
Voice: (800) 776-2333

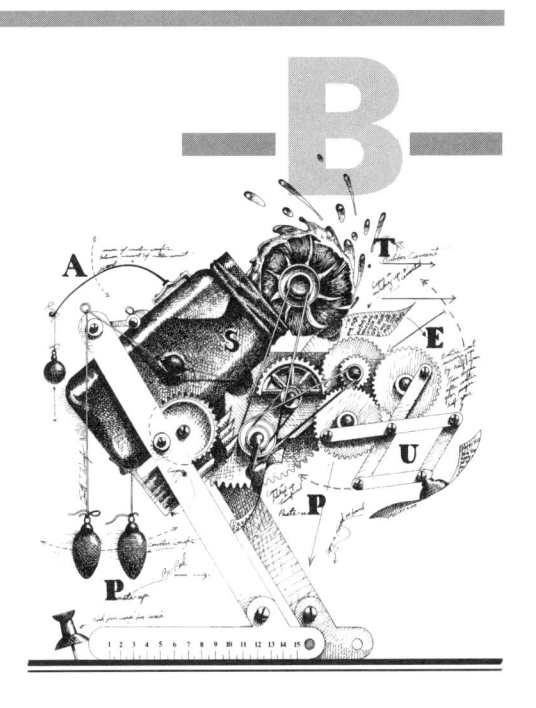

Norton Utilities
Symantec Corp.
10201 Torre Ave.
Cupertino, CA 95014
Voice: (800-441-7234)
Fax: (818) 543-1300

NOW Utilities
Now Software
319 S.W. Washington Street
Portland, OR 97204
Voice: (800) 237-3611

Peace of Mind
Polybus Systems
P.O. Box 7600
Nashua, NH 03060-7600
Voice: (506) 649-9600

Snooper
Maxa Corp.
116 Maryland Ave.
Suite 100
Glendale, CA 91206
Voice: (800) 788-6292

Virtual
Connectix Corp.
2655 Campus Dr.
San Mateo, CA 94403
Voice: (800) 950-5880

HARDWARE UPGRADES

The following vendors manufacture upgrade products for Macintoshes. Some have "FaxBack" facilities from which you can order product literature. If you have a fax machine, ask a sales representative whether FaxBack is available.

CPU Accelerators

Applied Engineering
3210 Betline
Dallas, TX 75234
Voice: (800) 554-MACS
Fax: (214) 484-1365

DayStar Digital
5556 Atlanta Hwy
Flowery Branch, GA 30542
Voice: (800) 962-2077
Fax: (404) 967-3018

Digital Eclipse Software Inc.
5515 Doyle Street
Suite No. 1
Emeryville, CA 94608
Voice: (510) 547-6101
Fax: (510) 547-6104

Extreme Systems
1050 Industry Drive
Tukwila, WA 98188
Voice: (206) 575-2524
Fax: (206) 575-3928

Fusion Data Systems
8920 Business Park Drive
Suite 350
Austin, TX 78759
Voice: (800) 285-8313
Fax: (512) 338-5326

Harris International, Ltd.
400 Commerce Court
Vadnais Heights, MN 55127
Voice: (800) 738-3726
Fax: (612) 482-0762

MacProducts USA
608 West 22nd St.
Austin, TX 78705-5116
Voice: (800) 622-3475
Fax: (512) 499-0888

Mobius Technologies, Inc.
5835 Doyle Street
Emeryville, CA 94608
Voice: (800) 523-7933
Fax: (510) 654-2834

NewLife Computer Corporation
603 March Road
Kanata, Ontario
Canada K2K 2M5
Voice: (800) 663-6395
Fax: (613) 592-9738

Novy Systems, Inc.
107 East Palm Way
Suite Number 14
Edgewater, FL 32132
Voice: (904) 427-2358
Fax: (904) 428-0765

Peripheral Outlet
327 East 14th
P.O. Box 2329
Ada, OK 74820
Voice: (800) 256-6581
Fax: (405) 436-2245

Radius, Inc.
1710 Fortune Drive
San Jose, CA 95131-1744
Voice: (800) 227-2795
Fax: (408) 434-0127

Cache Cards

Applied Engineering
3210 Betline
Dallas, TX 75234
Voice: (800) 554-MACS
Fax: (214) 484-1365

DayStar Digital
5556 Atlanta Hwy
Flowery Branch, GA 30542
Voice: (800) 962-2077
Fax: (404) 967-3018

Logica Research
Voice: (800) 880-0988

Expansion Chassis

DGR Technologies, Inc.
1219 West Sixth Street
Austin, TX 78703
Voice: (512) 476-9855
Fax: (512) 476-6399

Second Wave, Inc.
9430 Research Blvd.
Echelon II, Suite 260
Austin, TX 78759-6541
Voice: ((512) 434-9661
Fax: (512) 343-9663

Sonnet Technologies Inc.
18004 Sky Park Circle
Suite 260
Irvine, CA 92714-6428
Voice: (714) 261-2800
Fax: (714) 261-2461

FPUs and PMMUs

Diamond Computer Resources
13377 Pon Springs Rd.
Suite 105
Austin, TX 78729
Voice: (800) 541-7126
Fax: (512) 219-1132

Mac Upgrade Specialists
2177 Aliso Creed Rd
Suite 145
Alisa Viejo, CA 92656-3366
Voice: (800) 266-3622
Fax: (714) 362-5428

Memory Plus
22 Water Street
Westboro, MA 01581
Voice: (800) 388-7587
Fax: (508) 366-7344

Peripheral Outlet
327 East 14th.
P.O. Box 2329
Ada, OK 74820
Voice: (800) 256-6581
Fax: (405) 436-2245

Sonnet Technologies
18004 Sky Park Circle 260
Irvine, CA 92714
Voice: (800) 945-3668
Fax: (714) 261-2461

Power Supplies

800-WE-FIX-MACS
2306-k Walsh Ave.
Santa Clara, CA 95051
Voice: (800) 933-4962

Big Mac Computers
10837 Santa Monica Blvd.
Los Angeles, CA 90025
Voice: (310) 470-7099
Fax: (310) 470-8099

Maximum Fix Laboratories
2804 W. Washington Ave.
Yakima, WA 98903
Voice: (800) 927-6415

SIMMs and Video RAM

The Chip Merchant
9541 Ridgehaven Ct.
San Diego, CA 92123
Voice: (800) 426-6375

Mac Xtra
1075 Bellevue Way N.E., Suite 114
Bellevue, WA 98004
Voice: (800) 553-4230

Memory Direct
7911 Professional Circle
Huntington Beach, CA 92648
Voice: (800) 969-6348

Memory Plus
22 Water Street
Westboro, MA 01581
Voice: (800) 388-7587

Newer Technologies
7803 E. Osie
Suite 105
Wichita, KS 67207
Voice: (800) 678-3726
Fax: (316) 685-9368

Peripheral Outlet
327 East 14th
P.O. Box 2329
Ada, OK 74820
Voice: (800) 256-5681

TechWorks
4030 Braker Lane West, Suite 350
Austin, TX 78759
Voice: (800) 765-9864

SCSI Accelerators

ATTO
Baird Research Park
1576 Sweet Home Road
Amherst, NY 14228
Voice: (716) 688-4259
Fax: (716) 636-3630

Loviel
5599 W. 78th St.
Edina, MN 55439
Voice: (612) 835-3553

FWB
2040 Polk Street
Suite 214
San Francisco, CA 94109
Voice: (415) 474-8055
Fax: (415) 775-2125

MacProducts USA
608 W. 22nd St.
Austin, TX 87805
Voice: (800) 622-3475

Mass Microsystems
810 West Maude Ave.
Sunnyvale, CA 94098
Voice: (800) 522-7979
Fax: (408) 733-5499

MicroNet Technology
20 Mason
Irvine, CA 92718
Voice: (714) 837-6033

PLI
47421 Bayside Pkwy.
Fremont Park, CA 94538
Voice: (800) 288-8754

ProComm Technology
2181 Dupont Dr.
Irvine, CA 92715
Voice: (800) 800-8600

Storage Dimensions
1656 McCarthy Blvd.
Milpitas, CA 95035
Voice: (408) 954-0710

Video Accelerators

E-Machines
215 Moffett Park Drive
Sunny Vale, CA 94089-1374
Voice: (800) 334-3005
FaxBack: (800) 541-7680

Radius
1710 Fortune Drive
San Jose, CA 95131-1744
Voice: (800) 227-2795
Fax: (408) 434-0127

RasterOps
2500 Walsh Ave.
Santa Clara, CA 95051
Voice: (800) 729-2656
FaxBack: (800) SAY-COLOR

SuperMac
215 Moffett Park Drive
Sunny Vale, CA 94089-1374
Voice: (800) 334-3005
Faxback: (800) 541-7680

SCSI FLoppy Drives

Dayna Communications
50 S. Main St.
Salt Lake City, UT 84144
Voice: (801) 531-0600

PLI
47421 Bayside Pkwy.
Fremont Park, CA 94538
Voice: (800) 288-8754

Slot Expanders

DGR Technologies
1219 West Sixth St.
Suite 205
Autin, TX 78703-5208
Voice: (800) 235-9748

Second Wave
9430 Research Blvd.
Echelon II, Suite 260
Austin, TX 78759-6541
Voice: (512) 343-9661

Sonnet Technologies
18004 Sky Park Circle 260
Irvine, CA 92714
Voice: (800) 945-3668
Fax: (714) 261-2461

MISCELLANEOUS

PowerKey
Sophisticated Circuits
19017 120th Ave. N.E.
Suite 106
Bothell, WA 98011
Voice: (800) 827-4669

SIMM Extractor
Stratos Innovations
2025 First Ave.
Market Place Tower PH-B
Seattle, WA 98121
Voice: (206) 448-1388
Fax: (206) 448-7830

SALES, REPAIRS, AND PARTS

The vendors in this section repair damaged Macintoshes, sell replacement parts, and/or purchase and resell used Macintoshes.

Used Hardware Brokers

Boston Computer Exchange
55 Temple Place
Boston, MA 02111
Voice: (617) 542-4414

Used Macintosh Purchasers/Resellers

CRA Systems Inc.
300 South 13th St.
Waco, TX 76701
Voice: (800) 375-9000

Maya Computer
145 Palisade
Dobbs Ferry, NY 10522
Voice: (800) 541-2318

Pre-Owned Electronics
205 Burlington Road
Bedford, MA 01730
Voice: (800) 274-5343
Fax: (617) 275-4848

River Computer Inc.
Box 1239
Waitsfield, Vermont 05673
Voice: (800) 998-0098

Shreve Systems
1200 Marshall St.
Schreveport, LA 71101
Voice: (800) 227-3971

Macintosh Parts

Maximum Fix Laboratories, Inc.
2804 W. Washington Ave.
Yakima, WA 98903
Voice: (800) 927-6415

Pre-Owned Electronics
205 Burlington Road
Bedford, MA 01730
Voice: (800) 274-5343
Fax: (617) 275-4848

Shreve Systems
1200 Marshall St.
Schreveport, LA 71101
Voice: (800) 227-3971

Soft Solutions
907 River Road #98
Eugene, OR 97404
Voice: (503) 461-1136

Repairs

800-WE-FIX-MACS
2306-K Walsh Ave.
Santa Clara, CA 95051
Voice: (800) 933-4962

Hi-Tek Services Inc.
32950 Alvarado-Niles Road
Union City, CA 94587
Voice: (800) 285-3508

Soft Solutions
907 River Road #98
Eugene, OR 97404
Voice: (503) 461-1136

Glossary

Accelerator board: An expansion board that contains a CPU that replaces or augments the CPU shipped with a Macintosh.

Access arm: The rod to which disk drive read/write heads are attached.

Active matrix LCD: An LCD that has a separate electrode for each pixel and that can send current to individual pixels, producing a bright, crisp display.

Adapter circuit: A circuit that acts as an interface between a computer and an external device such as a disk drive, printer, or modem.

Address bus: The portion of the system bus that carries addresses from the CPU to other parts of the computer, including main memory and external devices.

Address space: The total range of memory that a computer can access.

Address: The location of a byte within a computer's address space.

Allocation block: The minimum amount of disk space that can be allocated to a file each time the file size is increased.

ALU: The abbreviation for *arithmetic logic unit*.

American Standard Code for Information Interchange: An 8-bit coding scheme used to represent characters (letters, numbers, punctuation marks, and so on).

Analog board: A circuit board found in compact Macs such as the Plus and SE that contains the power supply and video circuitry.

Aperture mask: A thin metal sheet punctured with hundreds of thousands of minute holes, placed inside the front of a CRT, that ensures that the CRT's electron gun lights each pixel precisely.

Apple Desktop Bus: A circuit that supports a daisy chain of input devices such as a keyboard, mouse, trackball, or graphics tablet.

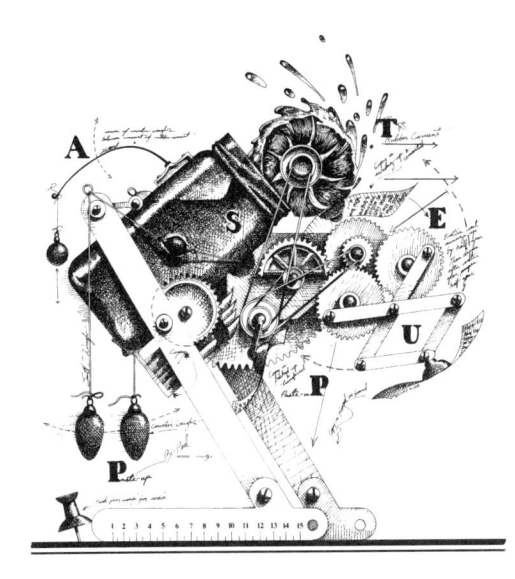

Apple Sound Chip: The circuit that generates Macintosh sound.

Arithmetic logic unit: The part of the CPU that performs arithmetic and logical operations on data.

ASC: The abbreviation for *Apple Sound Chip*.

ASCII: The abbreviation for *American Standard Code for Information Interchange*.

Assembler: A program that translates a program written in assembly language into machine language that a computer can execute.

Bank: A group of SIMM slots that must be completely filled with SIMMs of the same size and speed or completely empty.

Bernoulli drive: A disk drive that uses a high-density floppy disk on which to store data.

Binary point: The dividing point between the whole number portion and the fractional portion of a binary number.

Binary: A numbering system based on powers of 2.

Bit: One binary digit.

Bit-mapped: Using a pattern of bits to represent an image, either on a screen or on another output device.

Boom: A vertical post to which access arms are attached and which moves toward the center of a disk and away from it, moving the read/write heads on the access arms over the tracks on the disk.

Boot blocks: Blocks on a disk volume that contain information needed to boot a Macintosh.

Brownout: A dip in electrical voltage that, if severe enough, can interrupt the processing of a computer.

Bus master: An expansion board that can take control of the system bus to transfer data directly between an external device and main memory, without involving the CPU.

Bus: An electrical pathway that connects the parts of a computer.

Byte smearing: A technique of duplicating 8 or 16 bits of data into an entire 32-bit register so that a computer can read the data from any part of the register rather than a specific part.

Byte: Eight bits; the amount of data need to store one ASCII character; the unit with which computer memory and external storage are measured.

Cache hit: A successful search by a CPU of a data cache for a piece of data or an instruction cache for the next program instruction.

Cache miss: An unsuccessful search by a CPU of a data cache for a piece of data or an instruction cache for the next program instruction.

Catalog file: A disk directory file that keeps track of the hierarchical structure of files and folders.

Cathode Ray Tube: The evacuated tube that forms the basis of monitors used with desktop Macintoshes.

CISC: The abbreviation for *Complex Instruction Set Computer*.

Clump: The amount of space (one or more allocation blocks) added to a file by a program whenever the program needs to give the file more disk space.

Compiler: A program that translates an entire program written in a high-level language such as BASIC, C, Pascal, or COBOL into machine language before the program is executed.

Complex Instruction Set Computer: A computer in which the entire instruction set is part of the CPU.

Control signals: Signals sent by the CPU to parts of the computer to tell them what to do.

Control unit: The part of the CPU that sends control signals.

Convergence: Focusing the electron guns in a three-gun color monitor so that they are all concentrated on the same pixel.

Copy-back cache: A data cache that makes changes to data in the cache but not main memory whenever a write operation is performed.

CPU: The abbreviation for *Central Processing Unit*.

Cross-linked files: Two or more files that share the same physical space on disk as the result of a disk directory error.

CRT: The abbreviation for *Cathode Ray Tube*.

Cycles per second: In physics, the number of times a wave of energy (e.g., sound, light, or electricity) pulses per second; the unit of measurement for the speed of a CPU's internal clock, reflecting how often the clock sends a pulse down a control line in the system bus.

Cylinder: A part of a disk assembly made up of the same track on all the disk surfaces in the disk drive.

Data bus: The portion of the system bus that carries data from one part of the computer to another.

Data cache: High-speed static RAM used to hold the data that will be used in the near future by a running program.

Decode: The action performed by the CPU when it determines what an instruction code is telling it to do.

Device driver: Software that acts as a translator between the computer and an external device such as a disk drive or printer.

Device-independent I/O: Input and output performed in the same way by a program, regardless of what hardware is involved in the I/O.

DIP switch: The abbreviation for *dual in-line pin switch*.

Direct memory access: Input and output operations that take place between an I/O device and main memory without the intervention of the CPU.

Disk cache: A holding area in RAM for the data stored on a disk most likely to be used next by an executing program.

Disk interleave: The order in which sectors on a track are filled (1:1 interleave = adjacent sectors; 1:2 interleave = every other sector; 1:3 = every third sector).

Disk mirroring: Using a second disk volume to keep an on-line backup of disk volume.

Dot pitch: A ratio reflecting the smallest pixel and highest resolution a monitor can display.

Dots per inch: The number of pixels per inch on a monitor surface; the number of dots per inch printed by a printer.

dpi: The abbreviation for *dots per inch*.

DRAM: The abbreviation for *dynamic RAM*.

Dual in-line pin switch: A switch, often appearing in groups of 8 or 16, used to provide a single binary value to a piece of hardware.

Glossary

Dynamic RAM: The type of RAM used as main memory; relatively inexpensive RAM whose contents must be periodically refreshed so that the circuit retains its contents.

8-bit color: A color display that uses 8 bits to represent each color or shade or gray, providing 256 colors or shades of gray at the same time.

Even parity: An error-checking scheme in which a 1 is added to a byte if the number of 1s in the byte is even and a 0 is added to the byte if the number of 1s in the byte is odd.

Excess notation: The fixed quantity added to the exponent of a floating-point number so that the smallest exponent that the computer can store is equal to 0 and the largest exponent is equal to the maximum value that can be stored in the number of bits allocated to the exponent.

Execute: The action a CPU takes to perform whatever a program instruction tells it to do.

Expansion board: A circuit board that plugs into a computer's bus to provide added capabilities.

Exponent: The power to which the base (e.g., 2) of a floating-point number is raised.

Extent: A term used as a synonym for *allocation block*; the minimum amount of disk space that can be allocated to a file when it needs additional space.

Extents overflow file: A disk directory file used when the Catalog file is full to hold information about which disk blocks are allocated to specific disk files.

Fetch: The action taken by the CPU to retrieve a program instruction or data from main memory or a cache during program execution.

Fetch-decode-execute cycle: The process used by the CPU to execute each instruction in a program, involving fetching an instruction from main memory or a cache, decoding the instruction to determine what the CPU is to do, and actually performing the action.

Fixed hard disk: A hard disk sealed in a case.

Floating-point unit: A processor that handles floating-point arithmetic operations.

Floptical: A high-density floppy drive that uses lasers to achieve a storage capacity of around 21Mb.

Flyback transformer: A component on the analog board of early compact Macintoshes that steps up the power from the computer's power supply so that it supplies enough voltage to drive the CRT.

FPU: The abbreviation for *floating-point unit*.

Frame: The time it takes to move an electron gun from the bottom to top of a CRT monitor so that it can begin another raster scan.

Full-page display: A monitor that displays one full 8.5- x 11-inch page.

G: An abbreviation for *gigabyte*.

Gb: The most common abbreviation for *gigabyte*.

Gigabyte: A quantity a little over a billion bytes (exactly 2^{30}, or 1,073,741,824, bytes).

Gray market dealers: Vendors who are not authorized Apple dealers yet sell Apple hardware.

Grayscale: Multiple shades of gray (as opposed to just black and white) in an image.

Group-code recording: A method of encoding data for storage on a disk, used by Macintosh disk drives.

Gun: The source of electrons in a CRT monitor.

Head crash: The impact of read/write heads on a disk's surface, causing physical damage to the surface of the disk.

Hertz: Cycles per second.

Hz: The abbreviation for *Hertz*.

INIT: A program that is loaded into a Macintosh's RAM during the boot process and which remains there as long as the machine is in use.

Input device: A piece of hardware that takes data from the outside world and translates it into a format a computer can understand.

Instruction cache: High-speed static RAM used to hold the "next" instructions in a program to speed up program execution.

Instruction set: All the things a CPU knows how to do.

Integer: A whole number; a number without a fractional portion.

Integrated Wozniak Machine: A circuit in early Macintoshes used to control floppy drives.

Interleave: see *Disk interleave.*

Interpreter: A program that translates a program written in a language such as BASIC or Pascal into machine language at the time the program is run.

IOSB: The circuit used to handle most I/O operations in the Quadra 800, Centris 610, and Centris 650.

IWM: The abbreviation for *Integrated Wozniak Machine.*

K: The most commonly used abbreviation for *kilobyte.*

Kilobyte: Approximately 1,000 bytes (exactly 2^{10}, or 1,024 bytes)

LCD: The abbreviation for *liquid crystal display.*

Least significant digit: the rightmost digit in a number, regardless of the numbering system in which the digit is based.

Line conditioner: Power-protection hardware that not only provides surge protection but adjusts for low, and sometimes high, voltages to provide steady voltage to a computer.

Line: A single circuit in a bus used to carry either a high voltage or a low voltage (a 1 or a 0).

Liquid crystal display: A display that uses electric current to change the direction of semiliquid crystals that, when viewed through with a polarizing filter, either permit light to pass or block it, forming an image from a pattern of dots.

Logic board: The main circuit board in a Macintosh, containing at least the CPU, main memory, the system bus, and expansion slots.

Logical block: A unit of 512 bytes of disk storage; the smallest amount of storage that can be allocated on a disk; all or part of an allocation block.

M: A less common abbreviation for *megabyte*; a common abbreviation for megabit.

Magneto-optical drive: A disk drive that uses a laser to store and read a magnetic field placed on an optical disk.

Mantissa: The significant digits of a

floating-point number (e.g., in 2.88 x 10^{15}, 2.88 is the mantissa).

Master directory block: A disk block that contains housekeeping information about a disk volume, such as its name, the number of files and directories in the volume, and the location of the volume's Catalog file.

Math coprocessor: Another term for a *floating-point unit*; a processor that handles floating-point arithmetic operations.

Mb: The most common abbreviation for *megabyte*.

Mbyte: An abbreviation for *megabyte*.

MDB: The abbreviation for *master directory block*.

meg: An abbreviation for *megabyte*.

Megabyte: Approximately 1 million bytes (exactly 2^{20}, or 1,048,576, bytes).

Megahertz: One million hertz; 1 million cycles per second.

Memory management unit: A processor used to handle memory management activities.

Memory-mapped I/O: Input and output operations that are performed like reads from and writes to memory, regardless of the type of hardware device.

MFM: An abbreviation for *modified frequency modulation*.

Mhz: An abbreviation for *megahertz*.

MMU: An abbreviation for *memory management unit*.

Modified frequency modulation: A type of encoding used to store data on MS-DOS disks; a type of disk encoding that can be read by Macintosh SuperDrives.

Monochrome: Using only one color on a background color; black-and-white images and displays.

Most significant digit: The leftmost digit of a number.

Motherboard: The main circuit board in a Macintosh that contains circuits such as the CPU, main memory, the system bus, and I/O controllers; another term for a *logic board*.

Nanosecond: 10^{-9} seconds.

Non-return-to-zero, inverted: A type of encoding used to represent data on a Macintosh magnetic disk.

ns: The abbreviation for *nanosecond*.

NuBus: A type of expansion slot found in the Macintosh II, Centris, and Quadra line of computers; a type of expansion slot connected to the system bus through the NuBus controller.

Odd parity: An error-checking scheme in which a 1 is added to a byte if the number of 1s in the byte is odd and a 0 is added to the byte if the number of 1s is even.

Optical drive: A term commonly used to refer to a magneto-optical drive.

Output device: A piece of hardware that takes data from a computer and translates into a format that a user can understand.

Package: The casing in which a microchip is placed so that it can be connected to a computer.

Page frame: A block of physical RAM into which a page of virtual memory can be placed.

Page: The unit of memory that a virtual memory system swaps between virtual storage on disk and real storage in RAM.

Paged Memory Management Unit: A memory management unit designed to handle virtual memory.

Parallel: In general, anything that runs side by side; in data transfer, transferring an entire word of data at one time.

Parameter RAM: Battery-backed RAM that contains startup and configuration information for a Macintosh, including the current date and time and the startup disk.

Parity bit: An extra bit added to a byte to check the accuracy of the transmission of that byte from one part of the computer to another.

Parity: An error-checking scheme used to verify that a byte has been transmitted correctly from one part of the computer to another.

Park the heads: Move the heads of a hard disk away from portions of the disk that contain data to avoid the possibility of a head crash.

Partition: A logical section of a hard disk, viewed by the Macintosh operating system as a distinct disk volume.

Passive-matrix LCD: An LCD in which power is applied to one pixel at a time, requiring regular screen refresh.

Phosphor: A chemical used to coat the inside of a CRT screen; a chemical that emits light when struck by an electron beam.

Picture element: A single dot on a computer monitor screen.

Pipelining: A technique for speeding up the operation of a CPU by having more than one instruction in the decode phase of the fetch-decode-execute cycle at the same time.

Pixel: The commonly used contraction for *picture element*.

Platter: A single disk that is part of a hard disk assembly.

PMMU: The abbreviation for *paged memory management unit*.

Port: The connection between an external device (e.g., a disk drive or printer) and the adapter circuit that provides an interface between the device and the computer.

Portrait display: A monitor, usually with a 15-inch diagonal, that displays an entire 8.5 × 11-inch page.

Power surge: A sudden rise in electrical voltage that can damage electronic equipment such as computers.

PRAM: The abbreviation for *parameter RAM*.

Processor direct slot: An expansion slot that is connected directly to the Macintosh's system bus.

Program counter: A register in the CPU that keeps track of where the next program instruction to be executed is located in main memory.

QuickDraw: A set of programs in the Macintosh's ROM that manage graphics objects (drawing, filling, rotating, changing size, moving, and so on).

RAID: The abbreviation for r*edundant arrays of inexpensive disks*.

RAM: The abbreviation for *random access memory*.

Random access memory: Physical main memory that can be read from and written to; physical main memory that loses its contents when electrical power is removed.

Raster scanning: Drawing the image on a CRT by moving a beam of electrons across and down the back of the screen, lighting phosphors touched by the beam.

Read only memory: Physical main memory that can be read from but not written to; physical main memory that retains its contents when electrical power is removed.

Read/write head: Hardware that reads to and writes from a mass storage device such as a disk.

Real address space: The range of addresses available for physically installed main memory.

Reduced Instruction Set Computer: A type of computer with a very small instruction set that uses software to emulate the instructions it needs that aren't part of its instruction set.

Redundant arrays of inexpensive disks: A set of large hard disks managed together so that they appear to the computer as a single, very large hard disk.

Register: A small amount of RAM set aside for specific storage purposes; a storage area in a CPU or peripheral device adapter circuit.

Retrace: Moving the electron gun from one edge of a CRT to the other to begin another pass across the screen.

RGB monitor: A red-green-blue CRT; a CRT monitor with three electron guns and red, green, and blue phosphors.

RISC: The abbreviation for *reduced instruction set computer*.

Row: In a Macintosh Plus or SE, the term used to describe a bank of SIMM slots.

SCC: The abbreviation for *serial communications controller*.

Scientific notation: A format for base 10 floating-point numbers in which a mantissa is multiplied by 10 raised to some power (e.g., 2.1586×10^{-18}).

SCSI ("skuzzy"): The abbreviation for *Small Computer Systems Interface*.

Seek time: The time it takes to move an access arm in a disk drive to a track on which a read or write operation will be performed.

Seek: The action of moving an access arm in a disk drive to a track on which a read or write operation will be performed.

Serial communication controller: A circuit that handles transfers between a Macintosh's serial ports and the CPU.

Serial: In general, anything that runs one after the other; in data transmission, sending one bit after another, in a single-file line.

Shadow mask: Another term for an aperture mask; a thin metal sheet punctured with hundreds of thousands of minute holes, placed inside the front of a CRT, that ensures that the CRT's electron gun lights each pixel precisely.

Significand: Another term for *mantissa*; the significant digits of a floating-point number (e.g., in 2.88×10^{15}, 2.88 is the mantissa).

SIMM: The abbreviation for *single in-line memory module*.

Single in-line memory module: A small circuit board containing RAM chips that plugs into a Macintosh motherboard to provide additional RAM.

Slot: An opening in a computer's system bus into which expansion boards can be plugged to provided additional capabilities to the computer.

Small Computer Systems Interface: An adapter circuit for connecting peripheral devices (e.g., disk drives, tape drives, and scanners) to a computer; a parallel interface for transferring data between a daisy-chain of peripheral devices and a computer.

Sonora: A circuit used in the Macintosh LC III to control input and output operations.

Spice: A circuit used in the Macintosh Color Classic to control input and output operations.

Spindle: The cylindrical core over which the platters in a hard disk are placed; the motorized core of a hard disk.

Static RAM: High-speed RAM used in instruction and data caches; high-speed RAM that retains its contents after the signal that set the contents of the RAM is removed (electrical power must remain).

Super Woz Integrated Machine: In Macintoshes after the SE, the circuit used to control floppy disk drives.

Surge protector: A power-protection device that protects electronic equipment from sudden rises in electrical voltage.

SWIM: The abbreviation for *Super Woz Integrated Machine*.

SyQuest drive: A disk drive that uses removable hard disk platters.

System bus: The main electrical pathway that connects all the parts of a microcomputer.

System unit: The box in which the major circuits of a microcomputer are contained, including the CPU, FPU, system bus, main memory, and some adapter circuits.

32-bit clean: A program that has been written to run without problems using 32-bit addressing.

32-bit dirty: A program that uses the upper 8 bits of a 32-bit address for purposes other than addressing memory and therefore can't run without problems in a 32-bit addressing environment.

Two-page display: A monitor with a 19-, 20-, or 21-inch diagonal.

Tower case: A system unit designed to sit upright on the floor rather than lengthwise on a desktop.

24-bit color: A color display that uses 24 bits to represent each color, providing 32,767 colors at the same time.

Uninterruptible power supply: A power-protection device that provides backup power from a battery when normal electrical power is interrupted.

UPS: The abbreviation for *uninterruptible power supply*.

V8 gate array: A circuit used in the Macintosh LC and LC II to handle input and output operations.

Versatile Interface Adapter: A circuit used in many Macintoshes to handle input and output operations.

VIA: The abbreviation for *versatile interface adapter*.

Video RAM: RAM used to store the image displayed on a Macintosh screen.

Virtual address space: The total range of addresses available when using virtual memory.

Virtual memory: A way of extending the amount of physical RAM installed in a computer by using disk space to simulate additional RAM.

Virus: A malicious program that propagates itself into a computer system without the user's knowledge and destroys data or otherwise interferes with normal data processing.

Volume bit map: A disk directory file that indicates which blocks in a disk volume are in use and which blocks are available.

Volume information block: Another term for a master directory block.

VRAM: The abbreviation for *video RAM*.

Word: The amount of data a computer normally handles as a unit; in the Macintosh, 32 bits.

Write-back cache: Another term for a copy-back cache; a data cache that makes changes to data in the cache but not main memory whenever a write operation is performed.

Write-through cache: A data cache that makes changes to both data in the cache and data in main memory whenever a write operation is performed.

Photo Credits

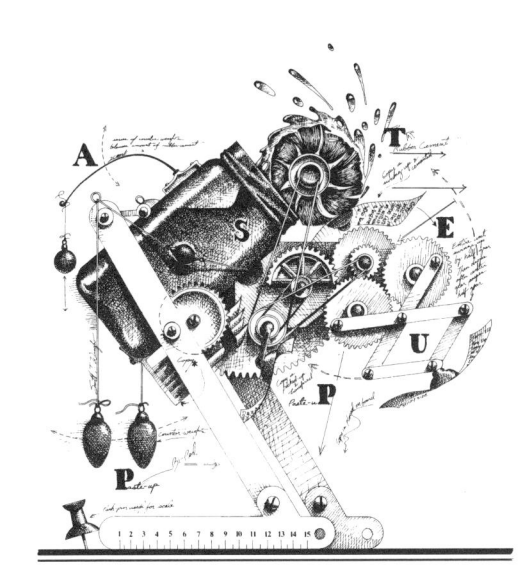

Figure 1.2: Courtesy of Black Gryphon Ltd. **Figure 1.7:** Courtesy of Apple Computer Inc.

Figure 2.1: Courtesy of Apple Computer Inc. **Figure 2.2:** Courtesy of Apple Computer Inc. John Greenleigh, Photographer. **Figure 2.3:** Courtesy of Apple Computer Inc. John Greenleigh, Photographer. **Figure 2.4:** Courtesy of Apple Computer Inc. John Greenleigh, Photographer. **Figure 2.5:** Courtesy of Apple Computer Inc. John Greenleigh, Photographer. **Figure 2.6:** Courtesy of Apple Computer Inc. John Greenleigh, Photographer. **Figure 2.7:** Courtesy of Apple Computer Inc. John Greenleigh, Photographer. **Figure 2.8:** Courtesy of Apple Computer Inc. **Figure 2.9:** Courtesy of Apple Computer Inc. John Greenleigh, Photographer.

Figure 3.2: Courtesy of Apple Computer Inc. **Figure 3.4:** Courtesy of Black Gryphon Ltd. **Figure 3.5:** Courtesy of DayStar Digital. **Figure 3.6:** Courtesy of DayStar Digital. **Figure 3.7:** Courtesy of DayStar Digital. **Figure 3.8:** Courtesy of DayStar Digital. **Figure 3.9:** Courtesy of DayStar Digital. **Figure 3.10:** Courtesy of DayStar Digital. **Figure 3.11:** Courtesy of DayStar Digital. **Figure 3.12:** Courtesy of DayStar Digital. **Figure 3.13:** Courtesy of DayStar Digital. **Figure 3.14:** Courtesy of DayStar Digital. **Figure 3.15:** Courtesy of DayStar Digital. **Figure 3.16:** Courtesy of DayStar Digital. **Figure 3.17:** Courtesy of Focus Enhancements. **Figure 3.18:** Courtesy of DayStar Digital. **Figure 3.19:** Courtesy of DayStar Digital. **Figure 3.20:** Courtesy of DayStar Digital. **Figure 3.21:** Courtesy of DayStar Digital. **Figure 3.22:** Courtesy of Black Gryphon Ltd. **Figure 3.23:** Courtesy of Black Gryphon Ltd. **Figure 3.24:** Courtesy of Black Gryphon Ltd. **Figure 3.25:** Courtesy of Black Gryphon Ltd.

Figure 4.23: Courtesy of MAXA Corporation. **Figure 4.24:** Courtesy of Apple Computer Inc.

Figure 5.6: Courtesy of TechWorks. **Figure 5.7:** Courtesy of Focus Enhancements. **Figure 5.8:** Courtesy of Black Gryphon Ltd. **Figure 5.9:** Courtesy of DayStar Digital. **Figure 5.10:** Courtesy of DayStar Digital. **Figure 5.11:** Courtesy of DayStar

Digital. **Figure 5.13:** Courtesy of DayStar Digital. **Figure 5.14:** Courtesy of Apple Computer Inc. **Figure 5.16:** Courtesy of DayStar Digital. **Figure 5.18:** Courtesy of DayStar Digital. **Figure 5.23:** Courtesy of DayStar Digital. **Figure 5.24:** Courtesy of DayStar Digital. **Figure 5.25:** Courtesy of DayStar Digital. **Figure 5.26:** Courtesy of Apple Computer Inc. **Figure 5.27:** Courtesy of Focus Enhancements.

Figure 6.2: Courtesy of DayStar Digital.

Figure 7.3: Courtesy of Black Gryphon Ltd.

Figure 10.9: Courtesy of APS. **Figure 10.10:** Courtesy of PLI. **Figure 10.11:** Courtesy of Pinnacle Micro.

Figure 11.1: Courtesy of Apple Computer Inc. **Figure 11.2:** Courtesy of Apple Computer Inc. **Figure 11.3:** Courtesy of Apple Computer Inc.

INDEX

A

Accelerator boards
   and SIMMs, 147
   definition, 41–42
   FPUs, 147
   hardware compatibility, 150
   installation, 148–149
   power requirements, 193
   software compatibility, 150
   sources of, 151
   speed, 147
   type of CPU, 146
   upgrading, 149–150
   video circuitry, 148
   warranties, 150–151
Accelerator boards *see also* names of specific Macintosh models
Access arm, 202
Active-matrix LCDs *see* Monitors, LCD
Adaptor circuits, 8–9
ADB
   definition, 9
   power requirements, 194–196
Addresses, 5, 104–108
Address space, 104, 105
Allocation blocks, 208

ALUs, 2
American Code for Information Interchange *see* ASCII
Aperture grill, 242
Aperture mask, 240
Apple Desktop Bus *see* ADB
Apple Sound Chip *see* ASC
AppleTalk, 9
Apple Workgroup Servers, 31–32
Arithmetic logic units *see* ALUs
ASC, 12
ASCII, 6

B

Bernoulli drives *see* Disk drives, Bernoulli
Binary system, 4–5
Bit-map
   definition, 3
Boom, 202
Boot blocks, 209–210
Brownouts, 196–199
Bus
   and RAM, 104–105
   definition, 7–8
   problems with, 188–189

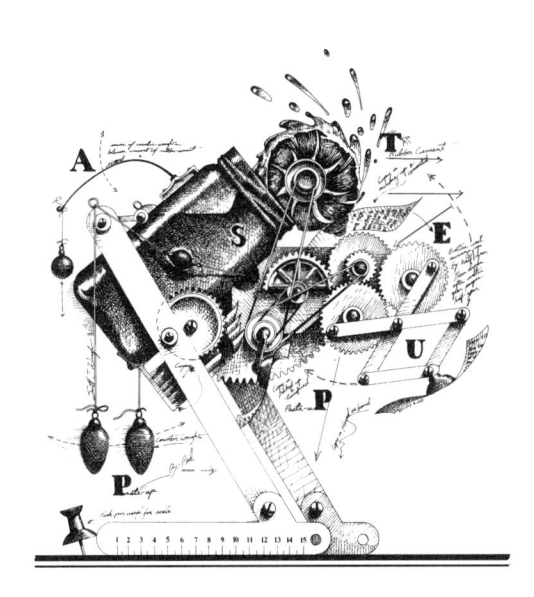

C

Cache, copy-back, 174–175
Cache, data, 144–145, 173–174
Cache, instruction
   definition, 42, 173–174
   function of, 144–145
   operation of, 174–175
Cache, write-back, 174–175
Cache, write-through, 174–175
Cartridge drives *see* Disk drives,
      cartridge
Catalog file, 211
Cathode ray tube displays *see* Monitors,
      CRT
CD-ROM *see* Disk drives, CD-ROM
Central processing units *see* CPUs
Centris 610
   logic board upgrade, 186
   opening the case of 70–72
   RAM allocation, 106–107
   RAM configurations, 131–132
   RAM installation, 134–135
   system bus, 104
   system configurations, 26–27
   upgrade options for, 63–64
   video RAM, 248
Centris 650
   opening the case of 70–72
   RAM allocation, 106–107
   RAM configurations, 133–134
   RAM installation, 134–135
   system bus, 104
   system configurations, 27–28
   upgrade options for, 63–64
   video RAM, 248
Centris 660av
   opening the case of 70–72
   RAM allocation, 106–107
   RAM configurations, 131–132
   RAM installation, 134–135
   system bus, 104
   system configurations, 27
   upgrade options for, 63–64
   video RAM, 248
CISC, 2
Clumps, 208
Cold solder problems, 187–188
Color monitors *see* Monitors, color
Complex instruction set computers *see*
      CISC
Component swapping, 84–86
Conflict Catcher, 82
Convergence, 241
Corrupted startup disk problems, 93–96
CPU accelerators *see* Accelerator boards
CPUs
   caches, 173–175
   definition, 1–3
   operation of, 142–146
   upgrade overview, 41–42
Crash Barrier, 77–78
Crashes, 77–82, 96–99
CRTs *see* Monitors, CRT
Cycles per second, 2
Cylinders, 204

D

DaynaFile, 212

Index

Deciding whether to upgrade, 44
Device drivers, 104–105
Diagnostic hardware, 99–102
Diagnostic software, 86–93, 223–230
Diagnostic techniques, 84–86, 93–102
Disinfectant, 79–80
Disk drives
    boot blocks, 209–210
    catalog file, 211
    clumps, 208
    cylinders, 204
    data encoding, 205–206
    extents overflow file, 211
    formatting, 206–207
    interleaving, 207–208
    master directory blocks, 210
    platters, 202
    read/write heads, 202–203
    rotation speeds, 204–205
    sectors, 203–204
    tracks, 203
    volume bit-map, 210–211
    volumes, 208–211
Disk drives, Bernoulli, 216
Disk drives, cartridge, 217–218
Disk drives, CD-ROM, 218
Disk drives, floppy
    circuits for, 12
    cleaning, 214–215
    dirt in, 214–215
    misalignment, 213–214
    overview, 6–7
    repair disk for troubleshooting, 94–96
    troubleshooting, 213–215
    upgrade overview, 42–43
    upgrading, 212–213
Disk drives, floppy *see also* SuperDrive
Disk drives, floptical, 201, 216
Disk drives, hard
    accelerator boards, 235–236
    allocation blocks, 208
    corrupted startup disk, 93–96
    deciding on disk capacity, 219–220
    diagnostic software, 223–230
    file damage, 220–221
    head crash, 203
    logical organization, 208–211
    logical blocks, 208
    mechanical problems, 223
    media damage, 221–223
    overview, 6–7
    partitioning, 208
    power requirements, 193
    RAID, 219
    repair software, 223-230
    SCSI chains, 230–235
    spin speeds, 202
    troubleshooting, 220–223
    upgrade options, 215–219
    upgrade overview, 42–43
Disk drives, optical, 216–217
Dot pitch, 241

E

Electrical power *see* Power supplies
Ethernet boards, 64
Expansion boards
    architecture of, 66–67

definition, 9
installing, 73–75
Extents overflow file, 211
External storage, 5–6

F

Fetch-decode-execute cycle, 142–146
Floating point numbers, 3, 178–181
Floating point units *see* FPUs
Floppy disk drives *see* Disk drives, floppy
Flopticals *see* Disk drives, floptical
Formatting, 206–207
Full-page display, 238
FPUs
   deciding whether to add, 181
   definition, 3
   on accelerator boards, 147
   types, 181
   upgrade overview, 42
Frame, 240

G

Gigabyte, 5
Graphics tablet, 7
Grayscale monitors *see* Monitors, grayscale

H

Hangs, 77–78
Hard disk drives *see* Disk drives, hard
Hard Disk ToolKit, 228–230
Head crash, 203

Help!, 82–83
Hexadecimal, 96–97

I

INIT conflicts, 80–83, 96
Input devices, 7
I/O
   device-independent, 105–106
   memory-mapped, 105
Installing SIMMs, 111
Instruction cache *see* Cache, instruction
Instruction execution, 142–146
Instruction set, 142
Integrated Wozniak Machine *see* IWM
Interleaving, 207–208
IWM, 12

K

Kilobyte, 5

L

LCDs *see* Monitors, LCD
Line conditionners, 197–199
Lines (in a bus), 104
Liquid crystal displays *see* Monitors, LCD
Logic boards
   circuits on, 10–12
   contents of, 183–184
   installation, 186
   troubleshooting, 186–190
   upgrade overview, 42
Logical blocks, 208

M

MacEKG, 86–87
Macintosh Centris *see* Centris
Macintosh Classic
    accelerator boards, 154, 156
    cache boards, 175–176
    logic board upgrade, 184
    opening the case of, 67–69
    RAM allocation, 106
    RAM configurations, 116–117
    RAM installation, 117–118
    system bus, 104–105
    system configurations, 15–16
    upgrade options for, 48–50
Macintosh Classic II
    accelerator boards, 160
    opening the case of, 67–69
    RAM allocation, 107–108
    RAM configurations, 118
    RAM installation, 119–120
    system bus, 104
    system configurations, 16
    upgrade options, 56–57
Macintosh Color Classic
    FPU, 182
    opening the case of, 69–70
    RAM allocation, 107–108
    RAM configurations, 118
    RAM installaion, 120–121
    system bus, 104
    system configurations, 17
    upgrade options for, 58
    video RAM, 247
Macintosh, disposing of, 64–66

Macintosh 512K
    opening the case of, 67–69
    RAM allocation, 106
    system bus, 104–105
    upgrade options, 253–254
Macintosh 512Ke
    accelerator boards, 255–256
    floppy disk drives, 256
    hard disk drives, 255
    monitors, 257
    opening the case of, 67–69
    power supplies, 257
    RAM allocation, 106
    system bus, 104–105
Macintosh LC
    accelerator boards, 157, 159–160
    cache boards, 175–176
    FPU, 182
    logic board upgrades, 184–185
    opening the case of, 70–71
    RAM allocation, 107–108
    RAM configurations, 118
    RAM installation, 119
    system bus, 104
    system configurations, 18–19
    upgrade options for, 51–52
    video RAM, 247
Macintosh LC II
    accelerator boards, 160–162
    cache boards, 175–176
    FPU, 182
    logic board upgrade, 185
    opening the case of, 70–71
    RAM allocation, 107–108

RAM configurations, 118
RAM installation, 119
system bus, 104
system configurations, 18–19
upgrade options for, 56–58
video RAM, 247
Macintosh LC III
   cache boards, 175–176
   FPU, 182
   opening the case of, 70–71
   RAM allocation, 106–107
   RAM configurations, 131–132
   RAM installation, 134–135
   system bus, 104
   system confiruations, 19–20
   upgrade options for, 58
   video RAM, 247
Macintosh 128K
   opening the case of, 67–69
   RAM allocation, 106
   system bus, 104–105
   upgrade options, 253–254
Macintosh, opening the case of, 67
Macintosh Performa *see* Performa
Macintosh Plus
   accelerator boards, 152–154
   adding a SuperDrive, 212–213
   opening the case of, 67–69
   power supply problems, 194
   RAM allocation, 106
   RAM configurations, 113–114
   RAM installation, 115–116
   system bus, 104–105
   system configurations, 13–14

   upgrade options for, 45–47
Macintosh Portable
   opening the case of, 72–74
   RAM allocation, 106
   RAM configurations, 135–136
   RAM installation, 136–137
   system bus, 104–105
   system configurations, 32–33
   upgrade options for, 50
Macintosh PowerBook *see* PowerBook
Macintosh Quadra *see* Quadra
Macintosh SE
   accelerator boards, 154–155
   adding a second floppy drive, 212
   adding a SuperDrive, 212–213
   cache boards, 175–176
   opening the case of, 67–69
   RAM allocation, 106
   RAM configurations, 114–115
   RAM installation, 115–116
   ROM upgrades, 213
   system bus, 104–105
   system configurations, 14
   upgrade options for, 47–48
Macintosh SE/30
   accelerator boards, 160–161
   cache boards, 175–176
   opening the case of, 67–69
   RAM allocation, 106–107
   RAM configurations, 124–125
   RAM installation, 125–126
   system bus, 104
   system configurations, 14–15
   upgrade options for, 55–56

Index

Macintosh, selling, 64–65
Macintosh II
   accelerator boards, 157–158
   adding a second floppy drive, 212
   adding a SuperDrive, 212–213
   cache boards, 175–176
   logic board upgrade, 185
   opening the case of, 70–72
   PMMU, 178
   RAM allocation, 106–107
   RAM configurations, 124–125, 126–127
   RAM installation, 128–129
   ROM upgrades, 213
   system bus, 104
   system configurations, 20–21
   upgrade options for, 53–55
Macintosh IIci
   accelerator boards, 166, 168
   cache boards, 175–176
   logic board upgrade, 185
   opening the case of, 70–72
   RAM allocation, 106–107
   RAM configurations, 124–125
   RAM installation, 129
   system bus, 104
   system configurations, 21–23
   upgrade options for, 59–61
Macintosh IIcx
   accelerator boards, 164–165
   cache boards, 175–176
   logic board upgrade, 185
   opening the case of, 70–72
   RAM allocation, 106–107
   RAM configurations, 124–125
   RAM installation, 129
   system bus, 104
   system configuration, 21–22
   upgrade options for, 59–61
Macintosh IIfx
   accelerator boards, 170–171
   adding a second floppy drive, 212
   opening the case of, 70–72
   RAM allocation, 106–107
   RAM configurations, 124–125, 127–128
   RAM installation, 128–129
   system bus, 104
   system configurations, 25–26
   upgrade options for, 59–60
Macintosh IIsi
   accelerator boards, 166–167
   cache boards, 175–176
   opening the case of 70–72
   RAM allocation, 106–107
   RAM configurations, 121
   RAM installation, 121
   system bus, 104
   system configurations, 23
   upgrade options for, 61–62
Macintosh IIvi
   accelerator boards, 169
   opening the case of, 70–72
   RAM allocation, 106–107
   RAM configuration, 121–122
   RAM installation, 122
   system bus, 104
   system configurations, 23–24

upgrade options for, 62
video RAM, 247
Macintosh IIvx
   accelerator boards, 169–170
   cache boards, 175–176
   logic board upgrade, 185
   opening the case of, 70–72
   RAM allocation, 106–107
   RAM configuration, 121–122
   RAM installation, 122
   system bus, 104
   system configurations, 23–25
   upgrade options for, 62
   video RAM, 247
Macintosh IIx
   accelerator boards, 163–164
   adding a second floppy drive, 212
   cache boards, 175–176
   logic board upgrade, 185
   opening the case of, 70–72
   RAM allocation, 106–107
   RAM configurations, 124–125, 127
   RAM installation, 128–129
   system bus, 104
   system configurations, 20–21
   upgrade options for, 58–59
MacTest Pro, 91–93
Magneto-optical drives *see* Disk drives, optical
Main memory, 3–6
Main memory *see also* RAM
Master directory blocks, 210
Math coprocessors *see* FPU
Megabyte, 5

Memory management unit *see* MMU
Memory-mapped I/O, 105
Misaligned floppy drives, 213–214
MMU, 12
Monitors
   convergence, 241
   phosphors, 239–243
   pixels, 238
   resolution, 238–239, 240–241
   size, 237–238
Monitors, color, 241–243, 244–245, 245–246
Monitors, CRT, 239–243
Monitors, grayscale, 7, 239–241, 245–246
Monitors, LCD, 243–245
Monitors, monochrome, 7, 239–241
Monitors, RGB, 241–242
Monitors, Trinitron, 242–243
Monitors *see also* Video
Monochrome monitors *see* Monitors, monocrhome
Motherboards *see* Logic boards
Motorola 68000, 1, 104–105
Motorola 68020, 1, 144–146, 178
Motorola 68030, 1, 141–142, 144–146, 178
Motorola 68040, 1, 83–84, 141, 144–146, 178
Mouse, 7

N

Network boards, 64
Norton Utilities, 223–227
NuBus, 8, 188–189

Index

O

Operating system conflicts, 82–83
Optical disks *see* Disk drives, optical
Output devices, 7

P

Paged memory management unit *see* PMMU
Parameter RAM *see* PRAM
Partitioning, 208
Passive-matrix LCDs *see* Monitors, LCD
PDS, 8, 188–189
Peace of Mind, 90–91
Performa 200
  accelerator boards, 160
  opening the case of, 67–69
  RAM allocation, 107–108
  RAM configurations, 118
  RAM installation, 119–120
  system bus, 104–105
  system configurations, 16
  upgrade options for, 56–57
Performa 400
  accelerator boards, 160–162
  opening the case of, 70–71
  RAM allocation, 107–108
  RAM configurations, 118
  RAM installation, 119
  system bus, 104
  system configurations, 18–19
  upgrade options for, 56–58
  video RAM, 247
Performa 405
  accelerator boards, 160–162
  opening the case of, 70–71
  RAM allocation, 107–108
  RAM configurations, 118
  RAM installation, 119
  system bus, 104
  system configurations, 18–19
  upgrade options for, 56–58
  video RAM, 247
Performa 430
  accelerator boards, 160–162
  opening the case of, 70–71
  RAM allocation, 107–108
  RAM configurations, 118
  RAM installation, 119
  system bus, 104
  system configurations, 18–19
  upgrade options for, 56–58
  video RAM, 247
Performa 450
  opening the case of, 70–71
  RAM allocation, 106–107
  RAM configurations, 131–132
  RAM installation, 134–135
  system bus, 104
  system configurations, 19–20
  upgrade options for, 58
  video RAM, 247
Performa 600
  accelerator boards, 169–170
  FPU, 182
  opening the case of, 70–72
  RAM allocation, 106–107
  RAM configuration, 121–122

RAM installation, 122
system bus, 104
system configurations, 23–25
upgrade options for, 62
video RAM, 247
Phosphors, 239–243
Picture element, 238
Pipelining, 144–146
Pixels, 238
Platter, 212
PMMU
    definition, 12
    operation of, 176–178
    upgrade overview, 42
Ports
    AppleTalk, 9
    definition, 8
    SCSI, 9
    serial, 9, 12
PowerBook Duo 210
    opening the case of, 73–75
    RAM allocation, 106–107
    RAM configurations, 138
    RAM installation, 138–139
    system bus, 104
    system configurations, 38–39
    upgrade options for, 62–63
PowerBook Duo 230
    opening the case of, 73–75
    RAM allocation, 106–107
    RAM configurations
    RAM installation, 138–139
    system bus, 104
    system configurations, 38–39

upgrade options for, 62–63
PowerBook 100
    opening the case of, 73–75
    RAM allocation, 106
    RAM configurations, 136–137
    RAM installation, 138–139
    system bus, 104–105
    system configurations, 34–35
    upgrade options for, 50–51
PowerBook 140
    accelerator boards, 171
    FPU, 182
    opening the case of, 73–75
    RAM allocation, 106–107
    RAM configurations, 136–137
    RAM installation, 138–139
    system bus, 104
    system configurations, 35
    upgrade options for, 62–63
PowerBook 145
    FPU, 182
    opening the case of, 73–75
    RAM allocation, 106–107
    RAM configurations, 136–137
    RAM installation, 138–139
    system bus, 104
    system configurations, 36
    upgrade options for, 62–63
PowerBook 145B
    opening the case of, 73–75
    RAM allocation, 106–107
    RAM configurations, 136–137
    RAM installation, 138–139
    system bus, 104

system configurations, 36
upgrade options for, 62–63
PowerBook 160
  accelerator boards, 171
  FPU, 182
  opening the case of, 73–75
  RAM allocation, 106–107
  RAM configurations, 137–138
  RAM installation, 138–139
  system bus, 104
  system configurations, 36–37
  upgrade options for, 62–63
PowerBook 165c
  FPU, 182
  opening the case of, 73–75
  RAM allocation, 106–107
  RAM configurations, 137–138
  RAM installation, 138–139
  system bus, 104
  system configurations, 37–38
  upgrade options for, 62–63
PowerBook 170
  opening the case of, 73–75
  RAM allocation, 106–107
  RAM configurations, 136–137
  RAM installation, 138–139
  system bus, 104
  system configurations, 35–36
  upgrade options for, 62–63
PowerBook 180
  opening the case of, 73–75
  RAM allocation, 106–107
  RAM configurations, 137–138
  RAM installation, 138–139
  system bus, 104
  system configurations, 36–37
  upgrade options for, 62–63
PowerBook 180c
  opening the case of, 73–75
  RAM allocation, 106–107
  RAM configurations, 137–138
  RAM installation, 138–139
  system bus, 104
  system configurations, 38
  upgrade options for, 62–63
Power outages, 196–199
Power requirements, 192–193
Power supplies
  problems with, 192, 194
  protecting, 196–199
  sizes of, 191–193
  upgrade overview, 42
Power surgers, 196–197
PRAM, 10
Processor direct slot *see* PDS
Program execution, 142–146

Q

Quadra 700
  cache boards, 175–176
  opening the case of, 70–72
  RAM allocation, 106–107
  RAM configurations, 122
  RAM installation, 122–123
  system bus, 104
  system configurations, 29
  upgrade options for, 63–64
  video RAM, 248–249

Quadra 800
   cache boards, 175–176
   logic board upgrade, 186
   opening the case of, 70–72
   RAM allocation, 106–107
   RAM configurations, 133–134
   RAM installation, 134–135
   system bus, 104
   system configurations, 30–31
   upgrade options for, 63–64
   video RAM, 248
Quadra 840av
   cache boards, 175–176
   opening the case of, 70–72
   RAM allocation, 106–107
   RAM configurations, 133–134
   RAM installation, 134–135
   system bus, 104
   system configurations, 31
   upgrade options for, 63–64
   video RAM, 249
Quadra 900
   cache boards, 175–176
   logic board upgrade, 185–186
   opening the case of, 70–72
   RAM allocation, 106–107
   RAM configurations, 129–131
   RAM installation, 131
   system bus, 104
   system configurations, 29
   upgrade options for, 63–64
   video RAM, 249
Quadra 950
   cache boards, 175–176
   opening the case of, 70–72
   RAM allocation, 106–107
   RAM configurations, 129–131
   RAM installation, 131
   system bus, 104
   system configurations, 29–30
   upgrade options for, 63–64
   video RAM, 249

R

RAID, 219
RAM
   allocation, 106–108
   amount supported in a Macintosh, 104–108
   deciding how much is needed, 103–104
   definition, 3
   installation problems, 112–113
   installation procedures, 111
   upgrade overview, 41
RAM *see also* names of specific Macintosh models
Random access memory *see* RAM
Raster scanning, 240
Read-only memory *see* ROM
Read/write heads, 202–203
Reduced instruction set computers *see* RISC
Redundant arrays of inexpensive disks *see* RAID
Registers, 2
Repair disk for troubleshooting, 94–96
Repair software, 223–230

Resolution, 238–239, 241
Retrace, 240
RGB monitors *see* Monitors, RGB
RISC, 2–3
ROM
    definition, 3–4
    32-bit clean, 105
    upgrading, 213

S

Sad Mac codes, 96–99
Scanner, 7
SCC, 12
SCSI
    accelerator boards, 64, 235–236
    cable length, 231
    circuits for, 12
    definition, 8–9
    effect of position in chain, 231
    IDs, 231–232
    termination, 232–235
    troubleshooting, 230–235
SCSI-2, 235–236
Sectors, 203–204
Seek, 202
Serial Communication Controller *see* SCC
Shadow mask, 240
Single in-line memory module *see* SIMMs
SIMMs
    and accelerator boards, 147
    banks, 109
    installation problems, 112–113
    installation procedures, 111
    slots, 110
    sources of, 110
    speeds, 109–110
    types of, 108–209
68000 *see* Motorola 68000
68020 *see* Motorola 68020
68030 *see* Motorola 68030
68040 *see* Motorola 68040
Slots
    definition, 8
    problems with, 104–105
Small Conputer Systems Interface *see* SCSI
Snooper, 87–89
Snooper NuBus board, 99–100
Startup Manager, 81–82
SuperDrive, 205–206, 212–213
SuperFloppy, 212
Surge protectors, 197–198
SyQuest drives *see* Disk drives, cartridge
System bus
    and RAM, 104–105
    definition, 7–8
    problems with, 188–189
System crashes, 77–82, 96–99
System hangs, 77–78
System unit, 1, 8

T

TechStep, 101–102
Termination, 232–235
32-bit clean, 105
Token-ring boards, 64

Trackball, 7
Tracks, 203
Trinitron monitors *see* Monitors, Trinitron
Two-page display, 238

U

Uninteruptable power supplies *see* UPSs
Upgrades
   deciding when to, 44
UPSs, 197–199

V

Versatile Interface Adaptor *see* VIA
VIA, 10–12
Video
   accelerator boards, 148, 249–251
   power requirements, 193
   upgrade overview, 43
Video RAM
   adding, 247–249
   definition, 3
   problems with, 189–190
   upgrade overview, 43
Video RAM *see also* names of specific Macintosh models
Viruses, 78–80
Virtual memory, 176–178
Volume bit-map, 210–210
Volume information blocks *see* Master directory blocks
Volumes, 208–211

W

Word, 6